Latin America

Latin America
Conflict and Creation

A HISTORICAL READER

Edited by

E. BRADFORD BURNS

University of California, Los Angeles

PRENTICE HALL Englewood Cliffs, New Jersey 07632

Library of Congress Cataloging-in-Publication Data

Latin America: conflict and creation : a historical reader / edited
  by E. Bradford Burns.

  1. Latin America—History. 2. College readers. I. Burns, E.
Bradford.
F1410.L387   1993
980—dc20   92-13345
ISBN 0-13-526260-7   CIP

Acquisitions editor: Stephen Dalphin
Editorial/production supervision and
   interior design: Barbara Reilly
Copy editor: James Tully
Cover design: Miriam Recio
Prepress buyer: Kelly Behr
Manufacturing buyer: Mary Ann Gloriande
Editorial assistant: Caffie Risher

© 1993 by Prentice-Hall, Inc.
Englewood Cliffs, New Jersey 07632

Printed in the United States of America
20 19 18 17 16

ISBN   0-13-526260-7

Prentice-Hall International (UK) Limited, *London*
Prentice-Hall of Australia Pty. Limited, *Sydney*
Prentice-Hall Canada Inc., *Toronto*
Prentice-Hall Hispanoamericana, S.A., *Mexico*
Prentice-Hall of India Private Limited, *New Delhi*
Prentice-Hall of Japan, Inc., *Tokyo*
Editora Prentice-Hall do Brasil, Ltda., *Rio de Janeiro*

Dedication

In memory of those Iowa artists and writers, my early predecessors, who helped to introduce into our country a better understanding of Latin America. In particular I salute:

The artist Lowell Houser (1902-1971), whose "The Development of Corn" mural (1937) adorns the Ames Post Office and whose glass "Indian Murals" (1939) illuminate the Bankers Life Building, Des Moines.

The historian Irving Berdine Richman (1861-1938) of Muscatine, author of *San Francisco Bay and California in 1776* (1911), *California under Spain and Mexico* (1911), and *The Spanish Conquerors* (1919).

E. Bradford Burns
Muscatine, Iowa

Contents

Preface

Two conflicting trends contribute to the powerful drama of the creation of nations and nationalities in Latin America: the imposition of first European and then United States institutions from the sixteenth century onward and the local efforts to alter them. Together, they molded the past, just as they shape the region's present reality. That lively drama of conflict and creation serves as the central theme of this text.

Within that theme, three goals emerge. First, the text reproduces documents selected to provide a better understanding of both the Latin American past and present, in particular the efforts to create viable nation-states. More than a political formality, such a creation also requires complementary social and economic institutions. Second, the text introduces a wide variety of documentation. Artwork, short stories, poetry, folk tales, and travel accounts provide insights into society past and present, just as valuable as the more conventional, recognized sources such as newspaper reports, letters, political essays, and histories. In their use, they require imagination, intellectual involvement, and interpretation. Those three qualities expand the ability of any documentation to enrich the understanding of past and present. Third, the text draws most heavily from Latin American and Iberian sources. These pages primarily reflect what the Latin Americans think about themselves and their geographical, social, cultural, political, and economic environments. Thus, the text emphasizes the views, insights, and perceptions of the very peoples whose societies we study. No voices can be more significant than those of the participants themselves in the creation of Latin America.

Within these goals and the broad drama of conflict and creation, this collection of documents introduces eight broad topics in a generally chronological fashion. It begins with the meeting of two peoples previously unknown to each other, the Europeans and the Indians of the Americas, an encounter fraught with momentary and recurrent drama. It then proceeds to examine the means by which Europeans acquired land and the labor to work it; concepts of political power and its exercise; characteristics of societies and cultures as they amalgamated Indian, African, and European contributions; and the more recent search for economic development as well as political changes. Finally, this reader concludes with a reminder that formidable challenges to the creation of viable nation-states and societies still remain. They in turn engender future challenges and further conflict. Thus the creative process continues.

This text emerges from my own approaches to the teaching of Latin American history as well as from the interests expressed by the students I have been privileged to teach. I express my thanks to Professor Marshall C. Eakin, Vanderbilt University; Professor Winthrop R. Wright, University of Maryland, College Park; and Professor Jan Knippers-Black, Monterey Institute of International Studies, for their careful reading of the manuscript and their thoughtful suggestions.

Latin America

1

The Encounter

The encounter of Europe and the Americas heralded an unexpected dimension to the formation of the modern world. It obviously provoked diverse reactions. Curiosity and wonder characterized the reactions of the Spaniards and Portuguese when they first viewed the Americas and their inhabitants. For their part, the peoples of the Western Hemisphere initially reacted with curiosity mixed with apprehension. Two quite diverse peoples met. One conquered and imposed, forcing the Americas to conform to European trade demands. The other was conquered, yet resisted. Those realities shaped the attitudes and institutions of the hemisphere. Their impact remains plainly visible after five centuries.

For the native peoples of the hemisphere, those centuries proved to be traumatic. The few who lived through the conquest, labor demands, and introduction of new diseases faced daunting changes. The Europeans introduced new values engendered by the rise of capitalism, perhaps most importantly the individual ownership of land with its use for profit. The Indians maintained a communal approach toward land use: the availability of land to anyone who wanted to work it; no claims to land that was not worked; and an emphasis on subsistence agriculture. An understanding of the contrasting concept of land use and value explains much of the dynamic of Latin American history for the past five hundred years. The burdens imposed by European conquest and settlement rested heavily on the Indians—and later on the imported African slave. Time has done little to lessen them.

An Abundant Nature
and Promises of Wealth

In summarizing his impressions of his first voyage, Christopher Columbus rhapsodized about the beauty and bounty of nature. He depicted a cornucopia of foodstuffs, spices, and precious metals. He mentioned more than once the one word certain to attract the attention of his royal patrons: gold. Nor did he neglect to remind the monarchs of the splendid opportunity to bring the heathen into the Catholic faith. The spiritual and material rewards promised to be plentiful. Still, a kind of innocence pervaded Columbus's report: the wonder at what the Spaniards had found and observed. Had they reached Asia or stumbled across an earthly paradise?

THIS SAID ISLAND of Juana [Cuba] is exceedingly fertile, as indeed are all the others; it is surrounded with many bays, spacious, very secure, and surpassing any that I have ever seen; numerous large and healthful rivers intersect it, and it also contains many very lofty mountains. All these islands are very beautiful, and distinguished by a diversity of scenery; they are filled with a great variety of trees of immense height, and which I believe to retain their foliage in all seasons; for when I saw them they were as verdant and luxuriant as they usually are in Spain in the month of May,—some of them were blossoming, some bearing fruit, and all flourishing in the greatest perfection, according to their respective stages of growth, and the nature and quality of each: yet the islands are not so thickly wooded as to be impassable. The nightingale and various birds were singing in countless numbers, and that in November, the month in which I arrived there. There are besides in the same island of Juana seven or eight kinds of palm trees, which, like all the other trees, herbs, and fruits, considerably surpass ours in height and beauty. The pines also are very handsome, and there are very extensive fields and meadows, a variety of birds, different kinds of honey, and many sorts of metals, but no iron. In that island also which I have before said we named Española [Hispaniola], there are mountains of very great size and beauty, vast plains, groves, and very fruitful fields, admirably adapted for tillage, pasture, and habitation. The convenience and excellence of the harbours in this island, and the abundance of the rivers, so indispensable to the health of man, surpass anything that would be believed by one who had not seen it. The trees, herbage, and fruits of Española are very different from those of Juana, and moreover it abounds in various kinds of spices, gold, and other metals. The inhabitants of both sexes in this island, and in all the others which I have seen, or of which I have received information, go always naked as they were born, with the exception of some of the women, who use the covering of a leaf, or small bough, or an apron of cotton which they prepare for that purpose. None of them,

Source: "First Voyage of Columbus. A Letter Addressed to the Noble Lord Rafael Sanchez . . . by Christopher Columbus," in R. H. Major (ed.), *Christopher Columbus: Four Voyages to the New World* (New York: Corinth Books, 1961), pp. 4–10, 13–15, 17.

as I have already said, are possessed of any iron, neither have they weapons, being unacquainted with, and indeed incompetent to use them, not from any deformity of body (for they are well-formed), but because they are timid and full of fear. They carry however in lieu of arms, canes dried in the sun, on the ends of which they fix heads of dried wood sharpened to a point, and even these they dare not use habitually; for it has often occurred when I have sent two or three of my men to any of the villages to speak with the natives, that they have come out in a disorderly troop, and have fled in such haste at the approach of our men, that the fathers forsook their children and the children their fathers. This timidity did not arise from any loss or injury that they had received from us; for, on the contrary, I gave to all I approached whatever articles I had about me, such as cloth and many other things, taking nothing of theirs in return: but they are naturally timid and fearful. As soon however as they see that they are safe, and have laid aside all fear, they are very simple and honest, and exceedingly liberal with all they have; none of them refusing any thing he may possess when he is asked for it, but on the contrary inviting us to ask them. They exhibit great love towards all others in preference to themselves: they also give objects of great value for trifles, and content themselves with very little or nothing in return. I however forbad that these trifles and articles of no value (such as pieces of dishes, plates, and glass, keys, and leather straps) should be given to them, although if they could obtain them, they imagined themselves to be possessed of the most beautiful trinkets in the world. It even happened that a sailor received for a leather strap as much gold as was worth three golden nobles, and for things of more trifling value offered by our men, especially newly coined blancas, or any gold coins, the Indians would give whatever the seller required; as, for instance, an ounce and a half or two ounces of gold, or thirty or forty pounds of cotton, with which commodity they were already acquainted. Thus they bartered, like idiots, cotton and gold for fragments of bows, glasses, bottles, and jars; which I forbad as being unjust, and myself gave them many beautiful and acceptable articles which I had brought with me, taking nothing from them in return; I did this in order that I might the more easily conciliate them, that they might be led to become Christians, and be inclined to entertain a regard for the King and Queen, our Princes and all Spaniards, and that I might induce them to take an interest in seeking out, and collecting, and delivering to us such things as they possessed in abundance, but which we greatly needed. They practise no kind of idolatry, but have a firm belief that all strength and power, and indeed all good things, are in heaven, and that I had descended from thence with these ships and sailors, and under this impression was I received after they had thrown aside their fears. . . . In all these islands there is no difference of physiognomy, of manners, or of language, but they all clearly understand each other, a circumstance very propitious for the realization of what I conceive to be the principal wish of our most serene King, namely, the conversion of these people to the holy faith of Christ, to which indeed, as far as I can judge, they are very favourable and well-disposed. . . .

As far as I have learned, every man throughout these islands is united to but one wife, with the exception of the kings and princes, who are allowed to have twenty: the women seem to work more than the men. I could not clearly understand whether the people possess any private property, for I observed that one man had the charge of distributing various things to the rest, but especially meat and provisions and the like. I did not find, as some of us had expected, any cannibals amongst them, but on the contrary men of great deference and kindness. Neither are they black, like the Ethiopians: their hair is smooth and straight: for they do not dwell where the rays of the sun strike most vividly. . . .

They assure me that there is another island larger than Española, whose inhabitants have no hair, and which abounds in gold more than any of the rest. I bring with me individuals of this island and of the others that I have seen, who are proofs of the facts which I state. Finally, to compress into few words the entire summary of my voyage and speedy return, and of the advantages derivable therefrom, I promise, that with a little assistance afforded me by our most invincible sovereigns, I will procure them as much gold as they need, as great a quantity of spices, of cotton, and of mastic (which is only found in Chios), and as many men for the service of the navy as their Majesties may require. I promise also rhubarb and other sorts of drugs. . . . □

Beautiful Lands and Innocent Natives

Under the command of the Portuguese navigator Pedro Alvares Cabral, a small fleet of ships sailed from Portugal in early 1500 to follow up Vasco da Gama's discovery of the first all-water route to India. Veering westward from their course, the Portuguese sighted land on April 22. Cabral at once claimed it for his king and explored the coast. A government official, Pero Vaz de Caminha, wrote the monarch a glowing report of the beautiful lands and the innocent natives. The initial reaction bespoke the discovery of a kind of Eden. Dated May 1, 1500, this letter is the first chronicle from Brazil, a name derived from its early important export, brazilwood.

THIS SAME DAY, at the hour of vespers, we sighted land, that is to say, first a very high rounded mountain, then other lower ranges of hills to the south of it, and a plain covered with large trees. The admiral named the mountain Easter Mount and the country the Land of the True Cross. . . .

We caught sight of men walking on the beaches. The small ships which arrived first said that they had seen some seven or eight of them. We let down the longboats and the skiffs. The captains of the other ships came straight to this flagship, where they had speech with the admiral. He sent Nicolau Coelho on shore to examine the river. As soon as the latter began to approach it, men came out on to the beach in groups of twos and threes, so that, when the longboat reached the river mouth, there were eighteen or twenty waiting.

Source: "The Letter of Pero Vaz de Caminha" in E. Bradford Burns (ed.), *A Documentary History of Brazil* (New York: Knopf, 1966), pp. 20–29.

They were dark brown and naked, and had no covering for their private parts, and they carried bows and arrows in their hands. They all came determinedly towards the boat. . . .

They are of a dark brown, rather reddish colour. They have good well-made faces and noses. They go naked, with no sort of covering. They attach no more importance to covering up their private parts or leaving them uncovered than they do to showing their faces. They are very ingenuous in that matter. They both had holes in their lower lips and a bone in them as broad as the knuckles of a hand and as thick as a cotton spindle and sharp at one end like a bodkin. They put these bones in from inside the lip and the part which is placed between the lip and the teeth is made like a rook in chess. They fit them in in such a way that they do not hurt them nor hinder them talking or eating or drinking.

Their hair is straight. They shear their hair, but leave it a certain length, not cutting it to the roots, though they shave it above the ears. One of them had on a kind of wig covered with yellow feathers which ran round from behind the cavity of the skull, from temple to temple, and so to the back of the head; it must have been about a hand's breadth wide, was very close-set and thick, and covered his occiput and his ears. It was fastened, feather by feather, to his hair with a white paste like wax (but it was not wax), so that the wig was very round and full and regular, and did not need to be specially cleaned when the head was washed, only lifted up.

When they came, the admiral was seated on a chair, with a carpet at his feet instead of a dais. He was finely dressed, with a very big golden collar round his neck. Sancho de Toar, Simão de Miranda, Nicolau Coelho, Aires Correia, and the rest of us who were in the ship with him were seated on this carpet. Torches were lit. They entered. However, they made no gesture of courtesy or sign of a wish to speak to the admiral or any one else.

For all that, one of them gazed at the admiral's collar and began to point towards the land and then at the collar as if he wished to tell us that there was gold in the country. And he also looked at a silver candlestick and pointed at the land in the same way, and at the candlestick, as if there was silver there, too. We showed them a grey parrot the admiral had brought with him. They took it in their hands at once and pointed to the land, as if there were others there. We showed them a ram, but they took no notice of it. We showed them a hen, and they were almost afraid of it and did not want to take it in their hands; finally they did, but as if alarmed by it. . . .

One of them saw the white beads of a rosary. He made a sign to be given them and was very pleased with them, and put them round his neck. Then he took them off and put them round his arm, pointing to the land, and again at the beads and at the captain's collar, as if he meant they would give gold for them.

We took it in this sense, because we preferred to. If, however, he was trying to tell us that he would take the beads and the collar as well, we did not choose to understand him, because we were not going to give it to him. Then he returned the beads to the man who had given them to him. . . .

They [three Portuguese] went a good league and a half to a hamlet of nine or ten houses. They said those houses were each as big as this flagship. They were made of wooden planks sideways on, had roofs of straw, and were fairly high. Each enclosed a single space with no partitions, but a number of posts. High up from post to post ran nets, in which they slept. Down below they lit fires to warm themselves. Each house had two little doors, one at one end and one at the other. Our men said that thirty or forty people were lodged in each house, and they saw them there. They gave our men such food as they had, consisting of plenty of *inhame* [manioc], and other seeds there are in the country which they eat. It was getting late, however, and they soon made all our men turn back, for they would not let any of them stay. They even wanted to come with them, our men said. Our men exchanged some varvels and other small things of little value which they had brought with them for some very large and beautiful red parrots and two small green ones, some caps of green feathers, and a cloth of many colours, also of feathers, a rather beautiful kind of material, as Your Majesty will see when you receive all these things, for the admiral says he is sending them to you. We returned to our ships. . . .

The admiral had said when we had left the boat that it would be best if we went straight to the cross which was leaning against a tree near the river ready to be set up on the next day, Friday; we ought then all to kneel and kiss it so that they could see the respect we had for it. We did so and signed to the ten or twelve who were there to do the same, and they at once all went and kissed it.

They seem to be such innocent people that, if we could understand their speech and they ours, they would immediately become Christians, seeing that, by all appearances, they do not understand about any faith. Therefore if the exiles who are to remain here learn their speech and understand them, I do not doubt but that they will follow that blessed path Your Majesty is desirous they should and become Christians and believe in our holy religion. May it please God to bring them to a knowledge of it, for truly these people are good and have a fine simplicity. Any stamp we wish may be easily printed on them, for the Lord has given them good bodies and good faces, like good men. I believe it was not without cause that He brought us here. Therefore Your Majesty who so greatly wishes to spread the Holy Catholic faith may look for their salvation. Pray God it may be accomplished with few difficulties.

They do not plough or breed cattle. There are no oxen here, nor goats, sheep, fowls, nor any other animal accustomed to live with man. They only eat this *inhame,* which is very plentiful here, and those seeds and fruits that the earth and the trees give of themselves. Nevertheless, they are of a finer, sturdier, and sleeker condition than we are for all the wheat and vegetables we eat.

While they were there that day they danced and footed it continuously with our people to the sound of one of our tambourines, as if they were more our friends than we theirs. . . .

. . . All the coastal country from one point to the other is very flat and very beautiful. As to the jungle, it seemed very large to us seen from the sea; for, look as we would, we could see nothing but land and woods, and the land seemed very extensive. Till now we have been unable to learn if there is gold or silver or any other kind of metal or iron there; we have seen none. . . . □

The Marvels of the Aztec Capital

In his classic account, *The True History of the Conquest of New Spain,* Bernal Díaz del Castillo recalled his first impressions of Tenochtitlán, the Aztec capital, in 1519. It equalled in size and splendor anything the Spaniards had ever seen. The Aztec ruler resided in Tenochtitlán, and Bernal Díaz provided an evocative view of the European perception of how the Aztec court functioned. The awe conveyed in this text pervades many of the early Spanish chronicles of Mexico and Peru. The early writers marvelled at the societies they encountered.

A S SOON AS THE messengers had been despatched, we set out for Mexico, and as the people of Huexotzingo and Chalco had told us that Montezuma had held consultations with his Idols and priests whether he should allow us to enter Mexico, or whether he should attack us, and all the priests had answered that his Huichilobos had said he was to allow us to enter and that then he could kill us, as I have already related in the chapter that deals with the subject, and as we are but human and feared death, we never ceased thinking about it. As that country is very thickly peopled we made short marches, and commended ourselves to God and to Our Lady his blessed Mother, and talked about how and by what means we could enter [the City], and it put courage into our hearts to think that as our Lord Jesus Christ had vouchsafed us protection through past dangers, he would likewise guard us from the power of the Mexicans.

We went to sleep at a town called Iztapalatengo where half the houses are in the water and the other half on dry land, where there is a small mountain (and now there is an Inn there) and there they gave us a good supper. . . .

The next day, in the morning, we arrived at a broad Causeway, and continued our march towards Iztapalapa, and when we saw so many cities and villages built in the water and other great towns on dry land and that straight and level causeway going towards Mexico, we were amazed and said that it was like the enchantments they tell of in the legend of Amadis, on account of the great towers and cues and buildings rising from the water, and all built of masonry. And some of our soldiers even asked whether the things that we saw were not a dream? It is not to be wondered at that I here write it down in this manner, for there is so much to think over that I do not know how to describe it, seeing things as we did that had never been heard of or seen before, not even dreamed about.

Thus, we arrived near Iztapalapa, to behold the splendour of the other Caciques who came out to meet us, who were the Lord of the town named Cuitlahuac, and the Lord of Culuacan, both of them near relations of Montezuma. And then when we entered that city of Iztapalapa, the appearance of the palaces in which they lodged us! How spacious and well built they were, of beautiful stone work and cedar wood, and the wood of other sweet scented trees, with great rooms and courts, wonderful to behold, covered with awnings of cotton cloth.

Source: Bernal Díaz del Castillo *The True History of the Conquest of New Spain* (London: The Hakluyt Society, 1908), Vol. 1, pp. 118–121; Vol. 2, pp. 34–63 passim.

When we had looked well at all of this, we went to the orchard and garden, which was such a wonderful thing to see and walk in, that I was never tired of looking at the diversity of the trees, and noting the scent which each one had, and the paths full of roses and flowers, and the many fruit trees and native roses, and the pond of fresh water. There was another thing to observe, that great canoes were able to pass into the garden from the lake through an opening that had been made so that there was no need for their occupants to land. And all was cemented and very splendid with many kinds of stone [monuments] with pictures on them, which gave much to think about. Then the birds of many kinds and breeds which came into the pond. I say again that I stood looking at it and thought that never in the world would there be discovered other lands such as these, for at that time there was no Peru, nor any thought of it. [Of all these wonders that I then beheld] today all is overthrown and lost, nothing left standing. . . .

Early next day we left Iztapalapa with a large escort of those great Caciques whom I have already mentioned. We proceeded along the Causeway which is here eight paces in width and runs so straight to the City of Mexico that it does not seem to me to turn either much or little, but, broad as it is, it was so crowded with people that there was hardly room for them all, some of them going to and others returning from Mexico, besides those who had come out to see us, so that we were hardly able to pass by the crowds of them that came; and the towers and cues were full of people as well as the canoes from all parts of the lake. It was not to be wondered at, for they had never before seen horses or men such as we are.

Gazing on such wonderful sights, we did not know what to say, or whether what appeared before us was real, for on one side, on the land, there were great cities, and in the lake ever so many more, and the lake itself was crowded with canoes, and in the Causeway were many bridges at intervals, and in front of us stood the great City of Mexico, and we,—we did not even number four hundred soldiers! and we well remembered the words and warnings given us by the people of Huexotzingo and Tlaxcala and Tlamanalco, and the many other warnings that had been given that we should beware of entering Mexico, where they would kill us, as soon as they had us inside.

Let the curious readers consider whether there is not much to ponder over in this that I am writing. What men have there been in the world who have shown such daring? But let us get on, and march along the Causeway. When we arrived where another small causeway branches off (leading to Coyoacan, which is another city) where there were some buildings like towers, which are their oratories, many more chieftains and Caciques approached clad in very rich mantles, the brilliant liveries of one chieftain differing from those of another, and the causeways were crowded with them. The Great Montezuma had sent these great Caciques in advance to receive us, and when they came before Cortés they bade us welcome in their language, and as a sign of peace, they touched their hands against the ground, and kissed the ground with the hand. . . .

The Great Montezuma was about forty years old, of good height and well proportioned, slender, and spare of flesh, not very swarthy, but of the natural colour and shade of an Indian. He did not wear his hair long, but so as just to cover his ears, his scanty black beard was well shaped and thin. His face was somewhat long, but cheerful, and he had good eyes and showed in his appearance and manner both tenderness and, when necessary, gravity. He was very neat and clean and bathed once every day in the afternoon. He had many women as mistresses, daughters of Chieftains, and he had two great Cacicas as his legitimate wives, and when he had intercourse with them it was so secretly that no one knew anything about it, except some of his servants. He was free from unnatural offences. The clothes that he wore one day, he did not put on again until four days later. He had over two hundred chieftains in his guard, in other rooms close to his own, not that all were meant to converse with him, but only one or another, and when they went to speak to him they were obliged to take off their rich mantles and put on others of little worth, but they had to be clean, and they had to enter barefoot with their eyes lowered to the ground, and not to look up in his face. And they made him three obeisances, and said: "Lord, my Lord, my Great Lord," before they came up to him, and then they made their report and with a few words he dismissed them, and on taking leave they did not turn their backs, but kept their faces toward him with their eyes to the ground, and they did not turn their backs until they left the room. I noticed another thing, that when other great chiefs came from distant lands about disputes or business, when they reached the apartments of the Great Montezuma, they had to come barefoot and with poor mantles, and they might not enter directly into the Palace, but had to loiter about a little on one side of the Palace door, for to enter hurriedly was considered to be disrespectful.

For each meal, over thirty different dishes were prepared by his cooks according to their ways and usage, and they placed small pottery brasiers beneath the dishes so that they should not get cold. They prepared more than three hundred plates of the food that Montezuma was going to eat, and more than a thousand for the guard. When he was going to eat, Montezuma would sometimes go out with his chiefs and stewards, and they would point out to him which dish was best, and of what birds and other things it was composed, and as they advised him, so he would eat, but it was not often that he would go out to see the food, and then merely as a pastime.

I have heard it said that they were wont to cook for him the flesh of young boys, but as he had such a variety of dishes, made of so many things, we could not succeed in seeing if they were of human flesh or of other things, for they daily cooked fowls, turkeys, pheasants, native partridges, quail, tame and wild ducks, venison, wild boar, reed birds, pigeons, hares and rabbits, and many sorts of birds and other things which are bred in this country, and they are so numerous that I cannot finish naming them in a hurry; so we had no insight into it, but I know for certain that after our Captain censured the sacrifice of human beings, and the eating of their flesh, he ordered that such food should not be prepared for him thenceforth.

Let us cease speaking of this and return to the way things were served to him at meal times. It was in this way: if it was cold they made up a large fire of live coals of a firewood made from the bark of trees which did not give off any smoke, and the scent of the bark from which the fire was made was very fragrant, and so that it should not give off more heat than he required, they placed in front of it a sort of screen adorned with figures of idols worked in gold. He was seated on a low stool, soft and richly worked, and the table, which was also low, was made in the same style as the seats, and on it they placed the table cloths of white cloth and some rather long napkins of the same material. Four very beautiful cleanly women brought water for his hands in a sort of deep basin which they called "xicales," and they held others like plates below to catch the water, and they brought him towels. And two other women brought him tortilla bread, and as soon as he began to eat they placed before him a sort of wooden screen painted over with gold, so that no one should watch him eating. Then the four women stood aside, and four great chieftains who were old men came and stood beside them, and with these Montezuma now and then conversed, and asked them questions, and as a great favour he would give to each of these elders a dish of what to him tasted best. They say that these elders were his near relations, and were his counsellors and judges of law suits, and the dishes and food which Montezuma gave them they ate standing up with much reverence and without looking at his face. He was served on Cholula earthenware either red or black. While he was at his meal the men of his guard who were in the rooms near to that of Montezuma, never dreamed of making any noise or speaking aloud. They brought him fruit of all the different kinds that the land produced, but he ate very little of it. From time to time they brought him, in cup-shaped vessels of pure gold, a certain drink made from cacao which they said he took when he was going to visit his wives, and at the time he took no heed of it, but what I did see was that they brought over fifty great jugs of good cacao frothed up, and he drank of that, and the women served this drink to him with great reverence.

Sometimes at meal-times there were present some very ugly humpbacks, very small of stature and their bodies almost broken in half, who are their jesters, and other Indians, who must have been buffoons, who told him witty sayings, and others who sang and danced, for Montezuma was fond of pleasure and song, and to these he ordered to be given what was left of the food and jugs of cacao. Then the same four women removed the table cloths, and with much ceremony they brought water for his hands. And Montezuma talked with those four old chieftains about things that interested him, and they took leave of him with the great reverence in which they held him, and he remained to repose. . . . □

Visual Depiction of the Indians

Words alone were not enough to satisfy European curiosity about the native peoples. Engravings, drawings, paintings, and even forced visits of Indians themselves followed. Wood engravings of those Tupinambá Indians encountered by the Europeans along the Brazilian coast accompanied Jean de Léry's informative account published in 1578, *Narrative of a Voyage Made to the Land of Brazil.*

Visual depictions of the Indians varied erratically from one-eyed giants to idealized copies of Europeans. There is much one can learn from these depictions by questioning the motives of the artists. The classic example that follows is from de Léry's *Narrative*, which portrayed the Tupinambá as remarkably similar in appearance to Europeans. Perhaps more informatively, the engraving included plants, fruits (the pineapple appears in the lower left), the bow and arrow, and the hammock. Indeed, the hammock intrigued Europeans, who quickly adopted it. As one Portuguese enthusiastically testified, "Would you believe that a man could sleep suspended in a net in the air like a bunch of hanging grapes? Here this practice is common. I tried it, and I will never again be able to sleep in a bed, so comfortable is the rest one gets in a net." Cultural transfer had begun, and the direction was by no means one-way.

A wood engraving of Tupinambá Indians published in Jean de Léry, *Narrative of a Voyage Made to the Land of Brazil (1578).*

A Negative Impact of Conquest on Indian Society

In the decades following Spain's major conquests in the New World, a few thoughtful observers revealed doubts about the benefits they might have conferred on the native populations. In 1589, one of the conquerors of Peru, Mancio Sierra de Leguízamo, testified that Spain had corrupted and ruined a worthy Incan civilization. On his deathbed, he repented of the wrongs he had done. He questioned whether the conquest and subsequent colonization had improved or disturbed a once well-ordered life. Enshrined by time, such doubts later became a major theme in both Indianist and nationalist literature throughout Latin America.

BEFORE BEGINNING MY WILL, I declare that for many years I have wished for the opportunity to advise his Catholic Majesty, King Philip, our Lord—seeing how Catholic and very Christian he is and how zealous in the service of our Lord God—of what is necessary for the relief of my soul because of the large part I played in the discovery, conquest, and settlement of these Kingdoms when we took them away from those who were Lords Inca and possessed and ruled them as their own, putting them under the royal crown. His Catholic Majesty should understand that the said Incas had these kingdoms governed in such a manner that in all of them there was not a single thief, nor man of vice, nor idle man, nor any adulterous or bad woman; nor were people of loose morals permitted among them. Men had honorable and useful occupations; uncultivated lands, mines, pastures, hunting grounds, woods, and all kinds of employments were so managed and distributed that each person knew and held his own estate, and no one else took possession of it or deprived him of it; nor was there any litigation over it. Military enterprises, although they were frequent, did not obstruct commercial matters, and the latter did not impede farming nor anything else; in everything, from the most important to the most trifling, there was order and methodical arrangement. The Incas, as well as their governors and captains, were respected and feared by their subjects as persons of great capacity and leadership; and since we found that they were the ones who had the strength and authority to offer resistance, we had to deprive them of their power and goods by force of arms in order to subdue and oppress them for the service of our Lord God and in order to take away their land and put it under the royal crown. Our Lord God having permitted it, it was possible for us to subjugate this kingdom with such a multitude of people and riches, and those who had been lords we made servants, as is well known.

    . . . His Majesty should understand that my motive in making this declaration is to unburden my conscience of guilt for having destroyed by our bad example people of such good conduct as were these natives, both men and women,

Source: "The Testament of Mancio Sierra de Leguízamo" in Lewis Hanke (ed.), *History of Latin American Civilization: Sources and Interpretations: Vol. 1. The Colonial Experience* (Boston: Little, Brown, 1967), pp. 78–79. With permission of Lewis Hanke.

and so little given to crime or excess. An Indian who had 100,000 pesos in gold and silver in his house would leave it open and put a broom or small stick across the doorway as a sign that the owner was not there; with this, according to their custom, no one could go inside nor take anything from within. When they saw that we had doors and keys in our houses, they thought that this was due to fear that they would kill us, but they did not believe that anyone would take or steal the property of another; and thus when they saw that among us there were thieves and men who incited their wives and daughters to sin, they regarded us with disdain. These natives have become so dissolute with their offenses against God because of the bad example we have given them in everything that their former extreme of doing no evil has been transformed, so that today they do little or no good. . . . In addition, those who were kings and lords, wealthy and obeyed, have come to such a low estate that they and their descendants are the poorest men in the kingdom. Moreover, we Spaniards even want to force them to serve as bearers, to clean and sweep our houses, to carry refuse to the dung-heaps, and to perform even lowlier tasks. And to avoid such tasks, these Inca Lords have started to learn shoe-making and similar trades, taking advantage of an ordinance of the Viceroy, D. Francisco de Toledo, that natives who served the public did not have to perform personal service, for Toledo's ordinance has greater influence than their being free men. Many things of this nature are permitted, which His Majesty would do well to realize and correct for the relief of his conscience and those of us who were discoverers and settlers and caused these ills. I can do no more than to inform his Catholic Majesty of these conditions, and with this I beg God to absolve me of my guilt, which I myself confess. I am moved to speak because I am the last survivor of all the discoverers and conquerors since, as is well known, there is no other left in this kingdom or outside of it. □

Indian Lamentations

Aztec poetry recorded the trauma of the European conquest. The three selections below, composed in the mid-1520s by Aztec poets, speak directly of the disaster of the conquest. Pain replaced joy. The depth and frankness of these laments convey the intense emotions of the Indians as they confronted their new reality.

The Fall of Tenochtitlán

OUR CRIES of grief rise up
and our tears rain down,
for Tlatelolco is lost.

Source: Lewis Hanke (ed.), *Latin America: A Historical Reader* (Boston: Little, Brown, 1974), pp. 63–65. With permission of Lewis Hanke.

The Aztecs are fleeing across the lake;
they are running away like women.

How can we save our homes, my people?
The Aztecs are deserting the city:
the city is in flames, and all
is darkness and destruction.

Motelchiuhtzin the Huiznahuacatl,
Tlacotzin the Tlailotlacatl,
Oquitzin the Tlacatecuhtli
are greeted with tears.

Weep, my people:
know that with these disasters
we have lost the Mexican nation.
The water has turned bitter,
our food is bitter!
These are the acts of the Giver of Life. . . . □

The Imprisonment of Cuauhtémoc

THE AZTECS are besieged in the city;
the Tlatelolcas are besieged in the city!

The walls are black,
the air is black with smoke,
the guns flash in the darkness.
They have captured Cuauhtémoc;
they have captured the princes of Mexico.

The Aztecs are besieged in the city;
the Tlatelolcas are besieged in the city!

After nine days, they were taken to Coyoacan:
Cuauhtémoc, Coanacoch, Tetlepanquetzaltzin.
The kings are prisoners now.

Tlacotzin consoled them:
"Oh my nephews, take heart!
The kings are prisoners now;
they are bound with chains."

The king Cuauhtémoc replied:
"Oh my nephew, you are a prisoner;
they have bound you in irons.

"But who is that at the side of the Captain-General?
Ah, it is Doña Isabel, my little niece!
Ah, it is true: the kings are prisoners now!

"You will be a slave and belong to another:
the collar will be fashioned in Coyoacan,
where the quetzal feathers will be woven.

"Who is that at the side of the Captain-General?
Ah, it is Doña Isabel, my little niece!
Ah, it is true: the kings are prisoners now!" □

Flowers and Songs of Sorrow

NOTHING BUT flowers and songs of sorrow
are left in Mexico and Tlatelolco,
where once we saw warriors and wise men.

We know it is true
that we must perish,
for we are mortal men.
You, the Giver of Life,
you have ordained it.

We wander here and there
in our desolate poverty.
We are mortal men.
We have seen bloodshed and pain
where once we saw beauty and valor.

We are crushed to the ground;
we lie in ruins.
There is nothing but grief and suffering
in Mexico and Tlatelolco,
where once we saw beauty and valor.

Have you grown weary of your servants?
Are you angry with your servants,
O Giver of Life? □

Murals Depicting Cuauhtémoc

In 1951, David Alfaro Siqueiros (1896–1974), one of Mexico's leading artists, painted two murals that focused on the last Aztec emperor, Cuauhtémoc. The murals were titled "Torture" and "Resurrection." They constitute part of a vast artistic effort to glorify the Aztec ruler and his lengthy struggle against the Spanish invader Hernán Cortés. Siqueiros depicted the burning of the emperor's feet by the faceless Spaniards in order to force him to reveal the location of the royal treasury. Through that torture, the Spanish tormented all Indians. The second mural showed Cuauhtémoc triumphant. He slew the Spanish centaur of oppres-

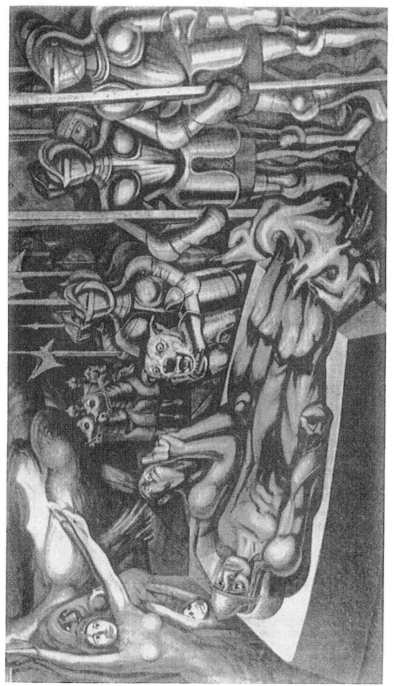

"Torture of Cuauhtémoc," mural, Mexico, 1951 (David Alfaro Sigueiros, 1896–1974).

"Resurrection of Cuauhtémoc," mural, 1951 (David Alfaro Siqueiros, 1896–1974).

sion. To do so, he adopted the European armament of the period, a concept fraught with controversial symbolism. Side by side, the murals speak of historical realities: the torture and the quest for vindication. The murals, located in the Palace of Fine Arts in Mexico City, serve as perceptual documents of reality and hope.

The King and the Indian

The Indians of the Western Hemisphere expressed their ideas through a rich oral literature. Those spoken stories, repeated and reshaped across time, also serve as a useful insight into people's attitudes. The following story from Nicaragua exemplifies that literature. While its origin remains lost in time, the story still circulated widely during the nineteenth century. Variations of it can be found elsewhere in Latin America. The story, titled "The King and the Indian," centers on a favorite theme: the ability of the Indians to "outsmart" the "whites" in general but the authorities in particular. It reveals, among other things, a confidence in themselves and, by inference, their attitude toward the encounter with Europeans.

ONE DAY AN INDIAN was leaving his village when the Spanish mayor called to him, "Where are you going, Indian?"

"I'm off to the city on some errands."

"What are you going to do, steal chickens?" said the mayor with a laugh.

The remark offended the Indian but he didn't let his face show it. He thought to himself, "The mayor is always putting us down. Well, I think I'll teach him a good lesson."

"Well, Mr. Mayor," the Indian replied, "I'm going to visit my friend the King. I'm going to have lunch with him."

"What the devil! You're not going to talk with the King, much less have lunch with him."

The Indian answered, "I bet my mule against your horse that I am going to have lunch with the King." The mayor owned a handsome horse, a Peruvian steed worth more than five thousand pesos, while the Indian had an old, broken-down mule that wouldn't even serve as a meal for a buzzard. The mayor responded, "With great pleasure, I accept that bet. I'm going to accompany you to see if you have lunch with the King."

The two set out together and upon arriving at the palace one of the soldiers stopped them and asked, "What do you want, Indian?"

Very humbly the Indian replied, "Well, I only wanted to visit the King in order to ask him a little question."

The guard answered brusquely, "The King has no time to talk with the likes of you. Ask me the question."

Source: Pablo Antonio Cuadra and Francisco Pérez Estrada, *Muestrario del Folklore Nicaragüense* (Managua: El Fondo de Promoción Cultural Banco de América, 1978), pp. 105–108. With the permission of Pablo Antonio Cuadra.

The Indian said, "I only wanted to ask the King if a piece of gold about the size of my fist would have much value."

His eyes wide, the guard said, "OK, hold on just a second." He ran to get the captain of the guard.

The captain asked, "What do you want, Indian?"

With great humility he replied again, "Well, I only wanted to visit the King in order to ask him a little question. I only wanted to ask him if a piece of gold about the size of my fist would have much value." At that point the Indian raised a well-callused fist scarred by cuts and bruises.

The captain said, "Hang on just a second, Indian." He entered the palace. Immediately he returned on the run and said, "Look, Indian, by pure chance the King isn't busy right now and he can talk with you. Enter."

Accompanied by the mayor, the Indian entered the palace and the King embraced him warmly, saying, "How are you, my little Indian? How is your wife? And how is the corn crop? Are the kids well?"

The King began chatting with him amiably. After a short time, the King said, "Look, my friend, it is time for lunch. Stay here with me and have lunch."

The Indian said, "Oh, Your Majesty, I am very sorry, but I have many errands to run while I am here in the city."

The King, somewhat impatiently, said, "No, my dear man, stay here with me. I insist. You can't refuse the invitation of your King!" To which the Indian responded, "Well, if Your Majesty insists, then I can't refuse." And he and the mayor sat down at the King's table.

Needless to say, the mayor was downcast and sad. In his mind he bid farewell to his handsome Peruvian steed and said to himself, "Hmmmm, I want to see how the Indian gets out of this mess. I'm certain he hasn't a grain of gold. He's got himself into trouble now."

The servants brought them an exquisite banquet with three kinds of meats, four kinds of fruit, three varieties of wine, and they all ate joyfully except the mayor who was so downcast that he couldn't swallow a bite. After the banquet, the King offered the Indian a glass of cognac and one of those fat cigars the King enjoyed smoking. Afterwards, the King said to the Indian, "Well, my friend, they told me that you wanted to ask me something. What is your question?"

The Indian said, "I only wanted to ask Your Majesty what a piece of gold the size of my fist would be worth?"

The King said, "That is difficult to answer because much depends on the quality of the gold. But, tell me, my friend, where did you find this piece of gold the size of your fist?"

The Indian answered, "Well, in reality I haven't found it yet. But just in case I might find such a piece, I wanted to know how much it might be worth."

The King became furious and shouted to the mayor, "Why have you brought this country bumpkin here to waste my time?" The King added to an official at this side, "Throw this mayor in jail. I'm going to teach him a lesson that he can't fool with me."

And the Indian left to return to his quiet little village. □

An Indian Assessment of Europe

In 1844, fourteen Ioway Indians visited Europe to perform their dances, songs, and ceremonies. They also wanted to learn something of the origin of white people, earn money for their tribe—already being pushed westward from the Mississippi to the Missouri River and suffering a sharp population decline—and to educate Europeans about the Indians and the plights imposed upon them by relentless white encroachments. George Catlin (1796–1872), a U.S. artist who lived many years among the Indians and bequeathed a magnificent legacy of portraits of them, traveled with the Ioways. They considered him a "great friend." He kept a thoughtful, compelling record of their tour from which the following spoken Indian observations are extracted. Although brief, they convey the dismay of the Indians at some consequences of European behavior and institutions and the apprehensions of their baleful influence on the natives of the Americas.

THE GREAT SPIRIT has made our skins red and the forests for us to live in. He has also given us our religion, which has taken our fathers to "the beautiful hunting grounds," where we wish to meet them. We don't believe that the Great Spirit made us to live with pale faces in this world, and we think He has intended we should live separate in the world to come.

My friends, we know that when white men come into our country we are unhappy. The Indians all die or are driven away before the white men. Our hope is to enjoy our hunting grounds in the world to come, which white men cannot take from us. We know that our fathers and our mothers have gone there, and we don't know why we should not go there too.

My friends, you have told us that the Son of the Great Spirit was on earth, and that he was killed by white men, and that the Great Spirit sent him here to get killed; now we cannot understand all this. This may be necessary for white people, but the red men, we think, have not yet got to be so wicked as to require that. If it was necessary that the Son of the Great Spirit should be killed for white people, it may be necessary to them to believe all this; but for us, we cannot understand it.

My friends, you speak of the "good book," that you have in your hand. We have many of these in our village. We are told that "all your words about the Son of the Great Spirit are printed in that book, and if we learn to read it, it would make good people of us." I would not ask why it doesn't make good people of the pale faces living all around us? That they can all read the good book, and they can understand all that the black coats [clergymen] say, and still we find they are not so honest and so good a people as ours. This we are sure of. Such is the case in the country about us, but here we have no doubt [that] the white people who have so many to preach and so many books to read are all honest and good. In our country the white people have two faces, and their

Source: Excerpts from Indian speeches in George Catlin, *Adventures of the Ojibbeway and Ioway Indians in England, France, and Belgium* (London: Printed by the Author at His Indian Collection, No. 6, Waterloo Place, 1852), II, 40, 41–42, 61, 143, 176.

tongues branch in different ways. We know that this displeases the Great Spirit, and we do not wish to teach it to our children.

We believe the Great Spirit requires us to pray to Him, which we do, and to thank Him for everything we have that is good. We know that He requires us to speak the truth, to feed the poor, and to love our friends. We don't know of anything more that he demands; he may demand more of white people, but we don't know that.

My friends, we don't know that we have ever resisted the word of the Great Spirit. If the Great Spirit sent the small pox into our country to destroy us, we believe it was to punish us for listening to the false promises of white men. It is white man's disease, and no doubt it was sent amongst white people to punish them for their sins. It never came amongst the Indians until we began to listen to the promises of white men, and to follow their ways; it then came amongst us, and we are not sure but the Great Spirit sent it to punish us for our foolishness. There is another disease sent by the Great Spirit to punish white men [syphilis], and it punishes them in the right place, the place that offends. We know that disease has been sent to punish them; that disease was never amongst the Indians until white men came. They brought it, and we believe we shall never drive it out of our country.

My friends, I hope my talk does not offend you. We are children, and you will forgive us for our ignorance. The Great Spirit expects us to feed the poor; our wives and children at home are very poor. Wicked white men kill so many of our hunters and warriors with *fire-water* that they bring among us, and leave so many children among us for us to feed when they go away that it makes us very poor. Before they leave our country they destroy all the game also, and do not teach us to raise bread, and our nation is now in that way and very poor; and we think that the way we can please the Great Spirit first is to get our wives and children something to eat and clothes to wear. . . .

We believe that the Great Spirit has made our religion good and sufficient for us if we do not in any way offend him. We see the religion of the white people dividing into many paths [the diversity of faiths and interpretations of the Bible], and we cannot believe that it is pleasing to the Great Spirit. The Indians have but one road to their religion, and they all travel in that, and the Great Spirit has never told them that it was not right.

My friends, our ears have been open since we came here, and the words we have heard are friendly and good; but we see so many kinds of religion, and so many people drunk and begging when we ride in the streets, that we are a little more afraid of white man's religion than we were before we came here.

My friends, the Indians occupied all the fine hunting grounds long before the white men came to them, but the white men own them nearly all now, and the Indians' hunting grounds are mostly all gone. The Indians never urge white men to take up their religion; they are satisfied to have them take a different road, for the Indians wish to enjoy their hunting grounds to themselves in the world to come. . . .

My friends, you have advised us to be charitable to the poor, and we have this day handed you 360 dollars to help the poor in your hospitals. We have not time to see those poor people, but we know you will make good use of the money for them; and we shall be happy if, by our coming this way,'we shall have made the poor comfortable.

My friends, we Indians are poor, and we cannot do much charity. The Great Spirit has been kind to us though since we came to this country [Great Britain], and we have given altogether more than 200 dollars to the poor people in the streets of London before we came here [Birmingham]; and I need not tell you that this is not the first day that we have given to the poor in this city.

My friends, if we were rich, like many white men in this country, the poor people we see around the streets in this cold weather, with their little children barefooted and begging, would soon get enough to eat and clothes to keep them warm.

My friends, it has made us unhappy to see the poor people begging for something to eat since we came to this country. In our country we are all poor, but the poor all have enough to eat and clothes to keep them warm. We have seen your poorhouses and been in them, and we think them very good; but we think there should be more of them and that the rich men should pay for them.

My friends, we admit that before we left home we all were fond of *fire-water,* but in this country we have not drunk it. Your words are good, and we know it is a great sin to drink it. Your words to us on that subject can do but little good for we are but a few; but if you tell them to the white people who make the *fire-water* and bring it into our country to sell and can tell them also to the thousands whom we see drunk with it in this country, then we think you may do a great deal of good; and we believe the Great Spirit will reward you for it.

My friends, it makes us unhappy in a country where there is so much wealth to see so many poor and hungry and so many as we see drunk. We know you are good people and kind to the poor and we give you our hands in parting, praying that the Great Spirit will assist you in taking care of the poor and making people sober . . .

My friends, I am willing to talk with you if it can do any good to the hundreds and thousands of poor and hungry people that we see in your streets every day when we ride out. We see hundreds of little children with their naked feet in the snow, and we pity them, for we know they are hungry, and we give them money every time we pass by them. In four days we have given twenty dollars to hungry children. We give our money only to children. We are told that the fathers of these children are in the houses where they sell *fire-water,* and are drunk, and in their words they every moment abuse and insult the Great Spirit. You talk about sending *black-coats* among the Indians. Now, we have no such poor children among us; we have no such drunkards or people who abuse the Great Spirit. Indians dare not do so. They pray to the Great Spirit, and he is kind to them. Now we think it would be better for your teachers all to stay at home and go to work right here in your own streets where all your good work is wanted. This is my advice. I would rather not say any more.□

"To Columbus"

Marking the four-hundredth anniversary of the arrival of Christopher Columbus in the Caribbean, Rubén Darío penned a poem in 1892 addressed to the "Admiral of the Ocean Sea." The Nicaraguan poet had electrified the Spanish-speaking world in 1888 with his innovative verses published under the title *Azul.* That book elevated him to the rank of the foremost poet in the Spanish language. Not surprisingly, then, "To Columbus" attracted much attention and circulated widely. In the many festivities commemorating the European arrival (or Encounter), Darío's words struck a somber note, a reminder of negative reactions to the event and the subsequent history of colonization. In the broadest sense, Columbus symbolized European domination, the dependency of the Americas, and the failure of Latin America to develop economically and politically. In that sense, Darío used the anniversary to voice rising nationalist sentiments.

UNFORTUNATE ADMIRAL! Your poor America,
your beautiful, hot-blooded, virgin Indian love,
the pearl of your dreams, is now hysterical,
her nerves convulsing and her forehead pale.

A most disastrous spirit rules your land:
where once the tribesmen raised their clubs together,
now there is endless warfare between brothers,
the selfsame races wound and destroy each other.

The stone idol is gone, and in its place
a living idol sits upon a throne,
while every day the pallid dawn reveals
the blood and ashes in the fields of neighbors.

Disdaining kings, we give ourselves our laws
to the sound of cannons and of bugle-calls,
and now, on the sinister behalf of black kings,
each Judas is a friend of every Cain.

We love to drink the festive wines of France;
day after day we sing the *Marseillaise*
in our indigenous, semi-Spanish voices,
but end by roaring out the *Carmagnole.*

The treacheries of ambition never cease,
the dream of freedom lies in broken bits.
This crime was never committed by our chiefs,
by those to whom the mountains gave their arrows.

Source: From *Selected Poems of Rubén Darío,* Lysander Kemp, translator. © 1965. By permission of the University of Texas Press.

They were majestic, loyal, and great-hearted;
their heads were decorated with rare feathers.
Oh if the white men who came had only been
like the Atahualpas and the Moctezumas!

When once the seed of the iron race from Spain
was planted in the womb of the Americas,
the heroic strength of great Castile was mixed
with the strength of our own Indians of the mountains.

Would to God that these waters, once untouched,
had never mirrored the white of Spanish sails,
and that the astonished stars had never seen
those caravels arriving at our shores!

The mountains saw how the natives, who were free
as eagles, came and went in the wild forest,
hunting the deer, the puma, and the bison
with the sure arrows they carried in their quivers.

A chief, though rough and bizarre, is worth far more
than a soldier who roots his glory in the mud,
who has caused the brave to groan beneath his car
or the frozen mummies of Incan lords to tremble.

The cross you brought to us is now decayed,
and after the revolution of the rabble,
the rabble writing today defiles the language
written by great Cervantes and Calderón.

A gaunt and feeble Christ walks through the streets,
Barabbas can boast of slaves and epaulets,
and the lands of Chibcha, Cuzco, and Palenque
have seen wild beasts acclaimed and decorated.

Evil mischance has placed afflictions, horrors,
wars, and unending fevers in our way:
O Christopher Columbus, unfortunate admiral,
pray to God for the world that you discovered! □

In the Ancient Land of the Aztecs, the Hurrah for Columbus Is Muted

As the Latin Americans contemplated their history five-hundred years after the arrival of Columbus, their frustrations with persistent poverty, minimal economic development, foreign interventions, and political unrest mounted. The celebratory programs planned for 1992 provoked lively discussions of ethnicity and national heritage, themes particularly significant in nations whose populations boast of mixed racial heritages. Writing from Mexico City, Louis Uchitelle linked the anniversary of the Encounter with Mexico's continuing efforts to define its own past and heritage, thorny but vital questions in cultural history and for national identity.

NOWHERE IN THE Western hemisphere is the celebration of the 500th Columbus Day, in 1992, bringing on more of a debate about the nation's true heritage than in Mexico.

The issue—a hot one among academics who air their views in newspaper articles—is whether Mexicans should see themselves as more European than Indian, or vice versa, or a balance of the two strains, plus one or two others. And the most likely outcome of all the discussion is that nothing will be resolved and that Mexico will go through 1992 more quietly than the rest of the hemisphere.

"The anniversary will be an intellectual one; we have not planned concrete celebrations," said José Muria, a historian and a founder of the Government-sponsored anniversary planning commission. "There will be small things: seminars, meetings, museum exhibits and the publication of a new history of Mexico."

Mexico is unusual among the nations that emerged in the New World. Far more than the others, it became a melting pot of Europeans and Indians, so that today nearly 90 percent of Mexico's 81 million people are mestizos, descended from both groups. Even people whose features make them appear to be mostly of European descent acknowledge—sometimes with pride, sometimes reluctantly—that they have at least some Indian blood.

A Troublesome Holiday

"There was much talk, in the 16th century, of separate republics, one Indian and one Spanish, and of co-existence," said Silvio Zavala, a historian. "But trying to perpetuate such a black and white difference denies the mestizaje that actually took place."

This mestizo sense of themselves makes the quincentennial of Christopher Columbus's landfall, on Oct. 12, 1492, a particularly troublesome holiday in Mexico. It is one that requires, in Mr. Muria's view, an exploration not only of the Indian and Spanish contributions, but also of the African influence. Tens of thousands of slaves, brought mostly to the Gulf coast, also intermingled with Indians and Spanish, so much so that Mexico today does not have a separate black minority.

Elsewhere in the Western Hemisphere, where intermarriage was not as commonplace, the anniversary celebrations are shaping up to be mostly splashy odes to Columbus and the world he opened to European culture. Replicas of his ships, the *Niña,* the *Pinta* and the *Santa María,* for example, will visit more than 40 ports in the United States in 1992. And even in Peru, with its huge Indian popula-

Source: Louis Uchitelle, "In the Ancient Land of the Aztecs, the Hurrah for Columbus Is Muted," *The New York Times,* September 6, 1990, p. A12. Copyright © 1990 by *The New York Times* Company. Reprinted by permission.

tion, the emphasis is not on mourning the destruction of the Inca empire, but on celebrating the Spanish discovery.

Peru is less troubled about its Spanish heritage then Mexico, perhaps because mestizaje never took hold and Peru's small, powerful upper middle class still traces its bloodlines back to the original Spanish families. A bronze statue of the conquistador Francisco Pizarro, who decimated the Incas, occupies a prominent spot in Lima's central plaza, while in Mexico City, Pizarro's counterpart, Hernán Cortés, conqueror of the Aztecs, is hidden from view.

In all the city, only one Cortés statue is on display, a bust placed in a passageway of the Hospital de Jesús, which Cortés founded in 1524. The Paseo de la Reforma, a broad, historic central avenue, on the other hand, is punctuated every few blocks with statues of Aztec chieftains and Mexican heroes. Only a single statue of Columbus, near one end of the avenue, acknowledges the debt to Spanish culture, and that statue has become a staging area for periodic anti-Spanish protests.

The protagonists of these protests are representatives of Mexico's most important minority: seven million Indians whose ancestors failed to be included in the mestizaje. Although Mexicans honor their Aztec heritage, the big Indian minority lives in poverty in rural communities and Oct. 12, 1992, is essentially an opportunity for Indians to protest their hardship. It is to be a day of "dignity and resistance" to the colonial murderers of 60 million Indians, an Indian rights group declared in a recent newspaper advertisement.

But the Indians represent an enduring minority view in a nation that every few generations shifts its appraisal of its heritage and identity. In 1892, the 400th anniversary, for instance, the emphasis was on Mexico's Spanish roots, which seemed a proper antidote to the 19th-century incursions of France and the United States.

After the Mexican Revolution of 1910, the Aztec heritage became the ideal, although the Indian minority remained in poverty. And today, as the 500th anniversary approaches and Mexico becomes more industrialized, a new appraisal is under way.

Edmundo O'Gorman, a historian at the University of Mexico, represents one extreme, arguing that the New World was not discovered, but was invented by the Spanish to fulfill their various expansionist and utopian needs. In this view, the native Indians become secondary to the Spanish creation.

Mr. O'Gorman's opposite is Miguel León Portilla, another University of Mexico historian, who argues that, absent the European intrusion, the Indians would have developed along their own rich path and that their contributions to the Mexican heritage have to be listed alongside those of the Spanish.

Homer Aridjis, a poet and novelist, offers such a listing in support of his argument that 1992 should be thought of not as the anniversary of Spain's discovery of a New World or its conquest of that world, but as the Spanish and the Indians "mutually discovering each other."

His list of comparative contributions includes, on the Spanish side, the Spanish language, printing (in 1539), horses, dogs, wheat, candles and measles. From the Indians came an enrichment of the language with numerous new words and expressions, along with corn, tobacco, tomatoes and dozens of other foods, and the introduction into Europe of various new diseases, the most famous being syphilis. ☐

Cultural Symbiosis

Latin American literature boasts of a rich treasure of short stories, those fictional narratives dedicated to packing a maximum literary punch with a minimum number of words. They often provide a useful insight into local society. When they do, they offer a valuable means—another type of document—to better understand Latin America.

The Peruvian novelist Ciro Alegría (1909–1967) combines two significant themes, the powerful landscape and cultural symbiosis, in his story "The Stone and the Cross." Whether it was the Andes, the Amazon, the Atacama Desert, or the tropical rain forests, the Europeans encountered the raw power of a formidable nature, for which the Indians traditionally expressed the greatest reverence. This encounter with nature pervades Latin American literature, as reflected in Alegría's short story. He also highlights the cultural interplay between Indian and European, a symbiosis that still shapes Latin America and gives it varied and distinctive characteristics. The dynamics of groups of people well integrated into their physical environment forced to mingle with other groups of peoples new to and challenged by that environment contribute to the drama and shaping of the Americas after 1492. Alegría's tightly woven story summarizes complex relationships.

The Stone and the Cross

THE TREES BECAME SMALLER as the grade got steeper. The trail heaved, tracing violent curves between scrawny cacti, squat bushes, and angular rocks. The two horses were panting, and their riders had stopped talking. If a stone rolled off the path, it continued to bounce downhill sometimes dislodging others in its fall, and all were as grains of sand sliding down the grandeur of the Andes.

Suddenly, there were not even bushes or cacti. The rocks increased in size, expanding into slabs, grey and red, pointing toward the summit, standing vertically in dark boulders like immense stairs-steps, or wrought into proud peaks that pierced the taut sky. Large rocks were scattered like huts in the distance, or stacked wall-like, forming a gigantic circle around the infinite. Where there was some earth, wild grass known as *ichu* grew tenaciously. The sun's brilliance formed pools in the yellow-grey grass.

The horses' and riders' breath began to freeze into fleeting, whitish puffs. The men felt the cold in their goose-pimpled skin, in spite of their thick woolen

Source: Ciro Alegría, "The Stone and the Cross," in Arturo Torres-Rioseco (ed.), *Short Stories of Latin America* (New York: Las Americas Publishing Co., 1963), pp. 111–120.

clothes and compact vicuna ponchos. The one in the lead turned his head as he halted his horse, and said:

"Won't you feel *soroche* [altitude sickness], child?"

The boy he addressed answered, "I don't think so. I have climbed as high as the Manancancho with my father."

Then the one who had asked the question eyed the road that struggled upward, and spurred on. He was an old Indian, with an expressionless face. Beneath the rush hat whose shade somewhat concealed the coarseness of his face, his eyes sparkled like two black diamonds buried in stone. The boy following him was a white child about ten years old, still new to long trips in the bramble thickets of the craggy Andes, for which reason his father had assigned the Indian to him as a guide. The road to the village where the school was crossed a country whose reaches grew ever lonelier and higher.

That the child was white could be easily seen, although the child knew very well through his mother's veins coursed a few drops of Indian blood. However, the child was considered white because of his color and also because he belonged to the landed class which had dominated the Indian village for more than four centuries.

The boy traveled behind the old man without any consideration for the fact that the latter was doing him a service. He was completely accustomed to having the Indians serve him. At that moment, the boy was thinking about his home and some of the events of his short life. It was certainly true that he had climbed with his father as far as Manancancho, the mountain on their hacienda that had attracted his attention because occasionally it was covered with snow. But the mountains he was climbing now were higher, and perhaps the *soroche,* the sickness of the high passes of the Andes, would attack him when he reached its frozen summit. And where might that famous cross be anyway?

On rounding the slope of the mountain, the riders ran into some men leading a string of tired mules that could hardly be seen under their immense loads. The packs smelled of coca and were covered by blankets that the muleteers would use at the inn. The vivid colors of the blankets were jubilant brushstrokes against the uniformly grey rocks and grass fields.

The guide and the child, with some difficulty, got through the slow-moving mules. On top of the two packs on one of the mules there was a large, beautifully blue, almost lustrous stone.

"The devotional stone," the guide remarked.

The two riders, going as fast as the steep trail allowed, still climbing, left the muleteers in the distance. From time to time, they would hear some fragment of the drivers' shouts: "Uuuuuuuuu!". . . "Aaaaaaaaaa!" These would be multiplied by the echoes. It seemed as if several parties were driving mules among the rocks. But the immensity of the range soon became silent. Every now and then, the wind would whistle through the grass. When it ceased, the silence of the stones seemed to grow, its grandeur, born in darkened depths, rising impetuously toward the sky.

Below, the muleteers and their drove grew smaller, until they seemed a string of busy ants, carrying their burdens on their backs. The shadow of a cloud passed slowly over the slope of the mountain, tinting the grass fields a deeper hue. When it moved across the rushes, the shadow folded into airy waves.

The riders took the road that cut obliquely across a cliff. The rock had been worked with dynamite and pick. The eyes of the alert beasts were bright, and their breath more audible. The white child would not have known how to calculate the time it took them to get across the cliff riding over bare rock, at the edge of the precipice. Perhaps twenty minutes, or maybe an hour. The crossing ended when the trail, after curving and opening up like a door, led onto the plain. The old man mumbled:

"The very *jalca* itself!"

It was the Andean plateau. The wild grass grew short in the cold desolation of the plain. Behind the plain, another range of mountains rose. The wind was blowing tenaciously, running freely across the plain, ruffling the blades, howling. The route was marked through the *ichu* by a number of paths, ruts dug into the clay-earth by travelers. Large bluish and reddish stones jutted up on either side like gigantic warts on the plain.

Medium-sized stones were scarce, and there were even fewer small enough to be carried. The Indian dismounted suddenly, and walked straight to a stone he had spotted.

"Shall I get one for you, child?" he asked.

"No," was the boy's reply.

Even so, the old man looked for another, and returned with two. They filled both his large hands. Parsimoniously, looking at the white child out of the corner of his eye, he put them in the saddlebags behind the packsaddle, one on each side. He rode on then, and he said:

"One must carry the stones all the way from here. There are none farther on. . . ."

The boy pointed with his finger, and said disdainfully:

"That muleteer carrying a stone is really more than silly. Imagine carrying it so far!"

"Perhaps he made some promise, child. Look at the cross. . . ."

The old man pointed with his index finger to the top of the ridge. The boy did not see the cross in spite of his good eyesight, but he knew that the Indian, although he was very old, probably had better eyesight. The cross must be there.

The devout old man was referring to the great Cross on High (Cruz del Alto), known throughout that whole area to be miraculous and revered. It was situated at the spot where the trail crossed the top of the highest range. It was customary for all travelers who passed that way to leave a stone near its pedestal.

The boy also carried something concerning the cross, but he carried it inside himself, between his chest and back. On leaving home, his father had said to him:

"Don't place a stone at the cross. That's what Indians and cholos do . . . that's for ignorant people."

He remembered his exact words.

The boy knew that his father was not a believer but a rationalist, something he did not understand. But his mother was indeed a believer, and wore a small gold cross on her breast, and lit votive lamps before a niche in which she kept an image of the Virgin of Sorrows. The boy thought that maybe if he had had time to ask his mother, she would have told him to place a stone before the cross. He was pondering all this when the Indian's voice sounded, daring to warn him:

"The stone is a form of devotion, little master. Everyone who goes by must place a stone."

"Even the masters?"

"The masters too. It is a devotion."

"I don't believe you. What about my father? . . ."

"Frankly, I never went with him past the Cross on High, but I swear to you that he must have done it. . . ."

"That's not true. My father says that stuff is for ignorant people."

"May the Holy Cross forgive the master."

"A stone is a stone."

"Don't say that, little master. Remember that I saw Doctor Rivas, the judge in the village, man of letters that he is, man of much learning, place his stone. Why, he even shed a few tears. . . ."

The wind increased preventing them from talking. It raised their ponchos, and struck them in the face. The boy, in spite of being an Andean, began to feel really cold. Some pools of frozen water reflected the buffeted figures of the horses and riders. The fringes of their ponchos seemed like banners in the wind. When the wind subsided a little, the old man said once more:

"Place your stone, little master. Those who don't, run into evil. . . . And I don't want anything evil to befall you, little master."

The boy did not answer him. He knew the old Indian very well as he had lived near the big house in a hut as old as himself. The old man called the boy "child" by habit, thus achieving his proper rank of old man, but when the Indian wanted the boy to do him a favor, he began calling him "little master" without thinking. "Little master, your father promised to get me a machete, and he has forgotten. Please remind him, little master." And now once more, the Indian tried the old refrain of "little master." He made still another attempt:

"Listen to me, little master. Years and years ago, a Christian by the name of Montuja, or something like that, came up from the coast. Yes; that was his name. Well, this Montuja didn't want to place a stone at the Cross; he just laughed. He laughed. And who could have foreseen then that as the man crossed these pampas, on this side of these very same lagoons, so the story goes, he was struck by lightning, and killed right where he was standing. . . ."

"Aha!"

"It's true, little master. And it was clear that the bolt was meant for him. The man was riding with three others, who had placed their stones, and only Montuja was killed."

"It must have been a coincidence. Nothing has ever happened to my father, so you see."

The old man thought for a while and then said:

"May the Holy Cross forgive the master, but you, little master. . . ."

The white child, feeling he should not go on arguing with an Indian, interrupted the old man to say, "Shut up."

The Indian hushed.

Violent or calm, the wind did not stop blowing. Its persistence made it feel like an ice-cold bath. The boy's hands were stiff, and he felt that his legs were going to sleep. This might also be due to fatigue, and the altitude. Perhaps his blood was not circulating well. A slight humming had begun to sound in the depths of his ears. Making a swift decision, the boy dismounted, saying to his guide: "Pull my horse. . . . Go on!"

Without another word they began to walk, the guide and the two horses in front. The boy slung his poncho over his back. He felt the tips of his toes stiff and cold, and his legs obeyed him badly. He could hardly breathe, as if he needed much more rarified air, and his heart was pounding. After walking along for ten minutes, he became very tired, but in spite of everything, he stubbornly continued to walk. He had heard his father say that in the Andes, one must sometimes travel at altitudes of ten, twelve, fourteen thousand feet, and even higher. He did not know at what altitude he found himself at that moment, but undoubtedly, it must be very high. His father had also talked to him about how one should behave at these high altitudes, and that was what he was now doing. Only, it was difficult even to walk. To cross a flat area was fatiguing. The altitude robbed him of breath. The blowing wind had lashed his face as if it were a horsewhip. When he touched it, it burned. A salty taste grew stronger in his mouth. His lips were split and bleeding. The blood stained his fingers. He thought how his mother would have nursed him, and a deep anguish knotted his throat. His nostalgia for his mother made obstinate tears fill his eyes. He dried them rapidly, so as not to be seen crying by that Indian who stupidly was carrying two stones. Fortunately, his feet were beginning to warm up, and his legs felt less stiff.

Actually, the Indian had not stopped watching the boy in his own way, that is, on the sly. The Indian felt a certain admiration for the young white boy who was adequately facing his first taste of high altitude, observing him from the security of his own knowledge of the region and his Indian's traditional physical fortitude. Still, the Indian felt a certain uneasiness, even fear, at the boy's irreverence, in which he thought he saw something typical of all whites, that is, evil. No Indian would dare to talk like that. But he lacked the right words to make the boy understand, and after all, he had been ordered to keep quiet.

The boy, who was feeling better since even his hands had grown warm, shouted: "Hey! I'm going to mount."

The old man brought the horse closer, but said: "Wait a little while yet."

The Indian dismounted, took out of one of the saddle bags a package wrapped in ochre-colored paper. It contained grease used to cure leather. He smeared the boy's face with it, saying as he did so:

"It is good for puna burns. . . . You have to cure yourself as I do, child. . . . These high Andean plateaus will yet make you part Indian. . . ."

The grease smelled bad, and the boy was being treated like leather, yet, without abandoning his arrogance, he smiled, although with a certain caution, because his split lips hurt when he stretched them.

Trotting on, the boy caught sight of the cross standing high in a hollow of the ridge. Atop a promontory, the cross extended its arms into space, under the immense sky.

A short distance away, they came to the ridge. The stones that formed it were grey-brown and blue, and not even grass was growing among them. The trail climbed, cutting zig-zag paths among the rocks. The trail as well as the surrounding ground, was practically clean of any stone of carrying size.

The child, returning to their conversation, said:

"And when did the devotion of placing stones begin?"

"There is no memory of it. My old father used to tell of it, and his old father before him."

"It is right to place votive lamps and to light candles before images of saints and crosses. . . . But stones!"

"It is all the same, little master. And note that a stone is not to be disdained. What would the world be without stone? It would sink. Rocks uphold the earth."

"That is something else. My father says that the Indians are so ignorant, that they even worship stones. There are mounds of stones which they hold to be gods, and they take offerings of *coca* and *chicha* to them. One of them is the Huara, isn't it?"

"That's true, little master. . . . It is a pile of stones. But why aren't you going to place a stone at the cross? The cross is the cross. . . ."

Both were silent. Neither the old man nor the boy knew anything of the innumerable mythical stones in their ancestral history, yet, in some way, the discussion had disturbed them both. Beyond the reasons they had given each other, there were still others which they were unable to bring to the surface of their minds with words. The old man felt a confused sorrow for the boy, and thought of him as a mutilated being who shrank from a profound alliance with the earth and stones, the dark fountains of life. The child seemed to be outside existence, like a rootless tree, or as absurd as a tree with its roots in the air. To be white, after all, and up to a certain point, turned out to be a very sad thing.

The boy, on his part, would have liked to shake the old man's faith, but he found that the word ignorance meant very little; that in the last analysis, it lacked any meaning at all in the face of faith. It was evident that the old man had his own explanation of things, or, if he did not, it made no difference to him. Unable to go beyond these considerations, he accepted them as facts which might be explained later.

The road plunged into a gulley, and coming out of it, in the deepest part of the curve circling the peaks, the riders found the revered Cross on High.

It stood about fifty feet from the road, to one side, its timber blackened by time. The quadrangular pedestal on which it stood was completely covered with stones piled there by the devout. The stones surrounding the cross covered a large area, perhaps two hundred meters around.

The Indian dismounted; and the white child did so too in order to have a better view of what was going on. The old man took the two stones out of the saddlebags placing one on the ground, in full view, right on top of the saddlebags themselves. Holding the other in his hand, he walked over to the edge of the pile, and with his eyes chose an appropriate place. He removed his hat, and bowing low, in the attitude of prayer, he placed his own stone on top of the others. Then he looked at the cross. He did not move his lips, but he seemed to be praying.

There was a quiet fervor in his eyes. Under his disheveled white hair, his wrinkled, citron-colored face reflected the nobility his untroubled faith gave him. There was something profoundly moving and at the same time dignified, about his whole attitude.

Not wishing to disturb him, the boy stepped a short distance away, and climbing up a small hill about halfway up the ridge, was able to see the widest panorama of peaks his eyes had ever seen.

At the horizon, the mountains were etched, blue and black, their sharp edges somewhat flattened, against the clouds that formed a white frame. Nearer to the boy, the hills took on different colors: purple, reddish, black, pale-yellow, according to their contours, their height, and their distance, sometimes surging up from the banks of rivers that meandered like grey serpents. Tinted by trees and huts at their base, the mountains in their heights grew cleaner of earth, until their peaks, if not crowned by shimmering snow, ended in dramatic crescendos of bare rock. The rock sang its epic clamor of abyss, peak, ocean promontory, ridge, and all other types of sharp mountain-top and ruffled summit, lofty rock-heap, and angry peak, in an endless series whose grandeur was magnified by their air of eternity. Symbolically, perhaps, that whole world of stone was there at the foot of the cross, in the offerings of thousands of songs, of votive stones carried there throughout time, throughout countless years, by the people of that world of stone.

Silently, the white child walked up to the saddlebags, took the stone, and stepped forward to make his offering. □

2

Patterns for Wealth

To the monarchs of Spain and Portugal, the Americas offered several splendid opportunities. They could carry the Roman Catholic faith to new areas and to new peoples, a divine mission they took very seriously. At the same time, they viewed the newly discovered continents as vast storehouses of wealth and, consequently, power. One Portuguese king openly referred to Brazil as his "great milk cow." For their part, the individual Spaniards and Portuguese who ventured to the American colonies hoped to enrich themselves.

Although the extraction of gold and silver represented one highly coveted source of wealth, agriculture over the long run proved to be more lucrative. From the beginning, the Iberians generously appropriated land for themselves, and in accordance with rising capitalist trends held it through individual titles. Reflecting both the vastness of the land and the scanty number of Spaniards and Portuguese, the new European-owned estates in the Americas dwarfed in size their counterparts on the Iberian peninsula. Land, however, was worthless without laborers. The Iberians spent centuries ingeniously devising ways to coax or coerce others to turn their lands into profits. In the process they established land ownership and labor recruitment patterns particularly beneficial for themselves and their heirs, but increasingly detrimental for the Indians and their offspring, and disastrous for the Africans and their descendants. The following documents illustrate those patterns and suggest some of the consequences of them. What are the consequences of these patterns for Latin America?

An Example of a Colonial Land Grant

Conquerors and colonists alike coveted land. Land offered prestige, security, and the opportunity for wealth. The Iberians often seized the land, but also through petition to Crown officials they requested title to it. The 1706 land grant, which is described below and which was given by the captain-general in Rio de Janeiro to Balthazar Fernandes Leme, a Portuguese settler in southern Brazil, is typical. By any measurement generous, the grant conferred on the colonist no less than twelve square miles.

FERNANDO MARTÍNS MASCARENHAS, etc. Be it known to all who see this land grant that in response to a petition, sent to me by Balthazar Fernandes Leme—married inhabitant of the town of Curitiba, who, for his sustenance and that of his family, needs a share of land to farm and to raise livestock, both of which will benefit His Majesty in the taxes to be paid—for the land beginning at the holdings of Bazílio da Silva Salgado and running in a direction from east to west five leagues along the big river below on the left side and into the hinterlands another five leagues from north to south, in which he asked me in the end and at the conclusion to have the kindness to give these above-mentioned lands as a grant for the above-mentioned farm and livestock raising, since no other person has already received or been given those lands according to the Purveyor of the Royal Treasury and the Attorney of the Crown, I do grant to Balthazar Fernandes Leme in the name of His Majesty, may God guard him, the land three leagues in length and one in width beginning at the boundary of Bazílio da Silva Salgado and running in a direction from east to west along the big river below on the left side because these lands are vacant and do not involve any third party. No one may make claim to these lands after this land grant becomes effective provided that within two years the grantee inhabits and cultivates these lands. Should the grantee fail to do this or sell them to someone who will cultivate them he is deprived of any claim to the land and the land will be judged vacant and available for anyone who can cultivate it and will be granted to the other according to the orders of His Majesty dated October 22, 1698. I command all the military and judicial officers of this captaincy and of his district to take note of the land grant which confers title of the above-mentioned lands on the said Balthazar Fernandes Leme in accordance with the above-mentioned declaration and to fulfill and carry out the provisions of this land grant. To achieve this, I order placed on this document my signature and my seal with my coat of arms accordingly as it is registered in the books of the secretariat of this government. Enacted in the city of S. Sebastian of Rio de Janeiro on the 12th day of the month of April of the year 1706. □

Source: "Land Grant Given to Balthazar Fernandes Leme, written by Secretary Bertholomeu Sigueira Cordovil, and signed by D. Fernando Martins M. de Lancastro, April 12, 1706" in E. Bradford Burns, *A Documentary History of Brazil* (New York: Knopf, 1967), pp. 93–94.

Establishing the Basis
for the Encomienda System

Barely a decade after Columbus's first voyage, Queen Isabel of Spain had to make a momentous decision concerning Indian labor recruitment. Colonists in the Caribbean decried the unwillingness of the Indians to work on their estates, and they petitioned the monarch for permission to force them to labor. Many churchmen opposed the idea. Caught between the cross and the sword, the queen acquiesced to the landowners' demand, decreeing an arrangement of required labor for which the Indians would receive payment, protection, and instruction in the Christian faith. In short, the Indians were "entrusted" to the landlords, an arrangement known as the *encomienda*, derived from the verb "to entrust." To soothe her troubled conscience, Isabel insisted in her decree that the Indians were a "free people."

MEDINA DEL CAMPO, Dec. 20, 1503. Isabella, by the Grace of God, Queen of Castile, etc. In as much as the King, my Lord, and I, in the instruction we commanded given to Don Fray Nicholas de Ovando, Comendador mayor of Alcantara, at the time when he went to the islands and mainland of the Ocean Sea, decreed that the Indian inhabitants and residents of the island of Española, are free and not subject . . . and as now we are informed that because of the excessive liberty enjoyed by the said Indians they avoid contact and community with the Spaniards to such an extent that they will not even work for wages, but wander about idle, and cannot be had by the Christians to convert to the Holy Catholic Faith; and in order that the Christians of the said island . . . may not lack people to work their holdings for their maintenance, and may be able to take out what gold there is on the island . . . and because we desire that the said Indians be converted to our Holy Catholic Faith and taught in its doctrines; and because this can better be done by having the Indians living in community with the Christians of the island, and by having them go among them and associate with them, by which means they will help each other to cultivate and settle and increase the fruits of the island and take the gold which may be there and bring profit to my kingdom and subjects:

I have commanded this my letter to be issued on the matter, in which I command you, our said Governor, that beginning from the day you receive my letter you will compel and force the said Indians to associate with the Christians of the island and to work on their buildings, and to gather and mine the gold and other metals, and to till the fields and produce food for the Christian inhabitants and dwellers of the said island; and you are to have each one paid on the day he works the wage and maintenance which you think he should have . . . and you are to order each cacique to take charge of a certain number of the said

Source: Lesley Byrd Simpson, *The Encomienda in New Spain. The Beginning of Spanish Mexico*, 3rd ed. (Berkeley: University of California Press, 1956), pp. 30–31. Copyright © 1950, 1966 Lesley Byrd Simpson.

Indians so that you may make them work wherever necessary, and so that on feast days and such days as you think proper they may be gathered together to hear and be taught in matters of the Faith. . . . This the Indians shall perform as free people, which they are, and not as slaves. And see to it that the said Indians are well treated, those who become Christians better than the others, and do not consent or allow that any person do them any harm or oppress them.

I, THE QUEEN□

A Grant of Encomienda

For long and loyal services to the Spanish Crown, Julián Gutiérrez Altamirano received in southern Chile a generous encomienda in 1566. It stated the obligations of the encomendero (person receiving an encomienda) to both king and Indians. It also guaranteed him access to tribute and labor, possible portals to prosperity.

R ODRIGO DE QUIROGA, governor and captain-general of these provinces of Chile from Nueva Extremadura to the Straits of Magellan, on behalf of His Majesty, etc. I have been informed by you, Licentiate Julián Gutiérrez Altamirano, that twenty-three years ago you came from the kingdoms of Spain to serve His Majesty in this part of the Indies; that you went to the kingdom of Tierra Firme as an officer of the viceroy Blasco Núñez de Vela in the campaign against Gonzalo Pizarro; that afterwards you went to the kingdom of Peru and served his Majesty with the licentiate Pedro Gasca against the said Pizarro until he was captured and killed; that after peace and tranquility had been restored to Peru, you came to this government fifteen years ago to further serve His Majesty and that you took part in the discovery, conquest, and settlement of all the cities that have been colonized from Santiago to the Straits; that in many of them you have been a lieutenant and captain and have had many expenses while supporting yourself in the service of His Majesty and that you have been a captain and officer of all these provinces and have served with your arms, horses, servants, and slaves at great expense but with great glory in many important ventures, risking your person, as is the custom among noble gentlemen of your quality and profession, for as such you are esteemed; and that as a result you are very poor and deeply in debt. For these and many other reasons, which I will not set forth here but which are just and redound to your credit, and in order to give you partial compensation for your many services, labors, and expenditures, in the name of His Majesty I hereby commend to you, the said licentiate Julián Gutiérrez Altamirano, the tributary group known as Millapoa with the cacique called

Source: Lewis Hanke (ed.), *History of Latin American Civilization: Sources and Interpretations: Vol. 1. The Colonial Experience* (Boston: Little, Brown, 1967), pp. 152–154. With permission of Lewis Hanke.

Reuqueando and with the other Indian nobles and subjects of said group, together with its division and water-hole, as well as the nobles called Quiloioya and Taroande with their nobles and subjects, all of whom have their land and residence in the district of the city of Concepción on both sides of the Bío-Bío River.

I grant this encomienda to you by virtue of its relinquishment by the licentiate Hernando de Castro, resident of the city of Concepción, to whom the said Indians were commended in the name of His Majesty by my predecessor, the governor Pedro de Villagra, and on the same terms in which they were held by him and by Francisco de Castañeda, also resident in Concepción, who received them from the governor Pedro de Valdivia, so that you may make use of them in accordance with the royal commands and ordinances and with the condition that you treat them well, seek their preservation and increase, and instruct them in matters pertaining to our holy Catholic faith, the natural law, and orderly conduct; if you are in any way negligent, let the burden fall upon your conscience, not upon mine nor that of His Majesty. I commend the said Indians to you with the further condition that in collecting their tributes and benefits you abide by the regulations and assessments that have been or may be fixed, that you keep arms and a horse in order to serve His Majesty in time of war, that you repair the bridges and royal road within the borders of your encomienda, and that you do everything else which may be commanded by His Majesty's magistrates in Concepción. After the magistrates have seen this document, they are to give you possession of the said caciques and Indians and see to it that you are not deprived of them without due process of law under the penalty of a payment of 2,000 gold pesos each to His Majesty.

Done at Cañete de la Frontera on the third of June, 1566. Rodrigo de Quiroga. By command of the lord governor. Diego Ruiz de Olivier. □

A Petition to the King to Grant Permanent Encomiendas

In this undated petition to the Spanish monarch, several lawyers in Mexico requested that the grants of encomienda be made permanent. The petition reiterated the vital importance of the control over labor that the landowners recognized as the true source of wealth. While the labor supply dwindled during the sixteenth century, landowners persistently tried to control it.

The monarch, on the other hand, concluded that through the encomienda he had weakened his authority over the Indians, thereby strengthening the position of the landowners. That situation countered the growth of royal absolutism. The king denied such petitions for permanent encomiendas. Increasingly, the *repartimiento*, a temporary allotment of Indians to landowners by a royal judge for specific tasks, reasserted royal control over the native populations in an effort to check the power of the landowners. The struggle to control Indian labor was long and complex. The landowners demonstrated endless ingenuity in the search for and control of workers for their plantations and estates.

W E, THE PROCURADORES of New Spain, affirm that it is necessary, as clearly demonstrated by evidence, opinions, and petitions which we have submitted, for the better service to God and to Your Majesty, for the good of the natives themselves, and for the good of the Spaniards resident in these lands, that the Indians be entrusted permanently [in encomienda] to landowners. Only thus will these lands bear fruit and bring profit. . . .

We beg that Your Majesty order an examination of the arguments which we have put forth. Others can also be cogently made that these lands will not fructify unless the landowners can count on a permanent Indian labor force, one granted in perpetuity by Your Majesty. Otherwise, there will be no one to cultivate the land, to work on the estates, and to engage in crafts. In short, there will be no profits. Spaniards themselves will not devote their time and energy to the tasks at hand unless they are assured of a permanent labor force. Wealth does not derive from the Indians. Left alone, they will not produce wealth for Your Majesty. Wealth, in fact, comes from the Spaniards who have and direct an Indian labor force to produce it. The wealth Spain receives comes not from the Indians but from those Spaniards who have Indians working for them. . . .

Nothing is asked of nor taken from the Indians beyond which they are able to give. Those who pay tribute of any kind do so only when they have surplus. Lacking such surplus, they render personal services, which are not harmful either to body or to soul. In fact, the light work given them liberates them from idleness. They benefit from contact with the Spaniards from whom they learn good customs and habits. Furthermore, it has always been the practice in these parts for the Indians to render personal service.

Reason limits the possibility of exploitation. At any rate, the Indians are too intelligent to consent to exploitation. They resist it as successfully as Spaniards do. The institution of permanent labor will assure the Indians better care and treatment than the vassals of Castile receive because what we seek is the well-being of the natives. The encomienda in perpetuity which we seek will enhance Your Kingdom and Your Majesty. . . .

Alonzo de Villanueva. Gonzalo López.□

Slave Labor on a Brazilian Plantation

With the death or disappearance of the Indians in the Caribbean and along the Brazilian coast, the Spaniards and the Portuguese began to import Africans as slaves in the early sixteenth century. Slavery spread throughout Latin America as one other means to resolve labor shortages. That nefarious institution remained rooted in the hemisphere for more than three and one-half centuries. The Portuguese introduced slavery into Brazil in the early sixteenth century, and the Brazilians did not abolish the institution until 1888.

Source: This text was adapted freely from Charles W. Hackett (ed.), *Historical Documents Relating to New Mexico, Nueva Vizcaya, and Approaches Thereto, to 1773* (Washington, D.C.: Carnegie Institution, 1923), pp. 147, 149, 151. With permission of the publisher.

In 1865, recalling memories of his youth in the northern province of Maranhão, the Brazilian F. A. Brandão, Jr., described the work routine for the plantation slaves. Besides the human destruction, the Brazilian noted the ecological damage, an early reference to that effect of the plantation system.

O N THE PLANTATIONS there is no law but the absolute will of the master, which is rudely delegated to the overseer, usually a trusted slave. And since there is no better wedge than a chunk of the wood itself, the overseer surpasses his master's intentions when enforcing his orders, making extraordinary demands upon the workers in the tedious service in the fields.

At six o'clock in the morning the overseer forces the poor slave, still exhausted from the evening's labors, to rise from his rude bed and proceed to his work. The first assignment of the season is the chopping down of the forests for the next year's planting, using a scythe to hack down the smaller trees. This work normally goes on for two months, depending upon the type of jungle being cut and the stamina of the slaves.

The next step is destruction of the large trees, and this, like the previous work, continues for twelve hours each day. At night the slaves return home, where evening work of two or more hours awaits them, depending upon the character of the master. They set fire to the devastated jungle, and then they cut and stack the branches and smaller tree trunks which have escaped the fire and which, occupying the surface of the earth, could hinder development of the crop.

These mounds of branches are again burned, and the result is a sad and devastating scene! Centuries-old tree trunks which two months before had produced a cool, crisp atmosphere over a broad stretch of land, lie on the surface of a field ravaged by fire and covered with ashes, where the slaves are compelled to spend twelve hours under the hot sun of the equator, without a single tree to give them shelter.

This destruction of the forests has exhausted the soil, which in many places now produces nothing but grasses suitable for grazing cattle. The temperature has intensified, and the seasons have become irregular. The rains at times damage the crops, and at other times there is no rain at all. The streams and certain shallow rivers, such as the Itapucurú, have dried up or have become almost unnavigable, and lumber for building has become very rare, or is only found at a great distance from the settlements.

When it finally rains toward the end of December or early January, the slaves begin to seed the devastated fields, and the only tool they use in planting cotton is a small hoe, and for the rice and millet they use nothing but a stick with an iron point to hollow out the ground.

After this comes the weeding. This is painful labor for the slaves, who, with nothing to work with but a weeding-hook, are forced to stand in a stooped position during the entire day, cutting the shoots or other native plants, and enduring a temperature in the sun of 40° Celsius. This work, which is the most arduous, continues as long as it takes for the plants to fully establish themselves.

The next step is the rice cutting in May or June, which each slave accomplishes with a small knife, cutting the stems one by one, and at night beating them with a branch to loosen the grains. During this phase of their labor the overseers demand a certain number of *alqueires* of rice from each slave, and if the unfortunate person does not produce what is demanded of him, the tragedy is brought to an end with *the daily bread of the slave,* that is, the lash.

There is still another kind of work no less exacting, in which the masters make even greater demands. This is the picking of the cotton crop. To accomplish this the slaves disperse themselves over a certain part of the field, collecting the pods and depositing them in a basket or sack which each slave carries for this purpose attached to his waist.

Under a brutally hot sun, the atmosphere bathed in exhausting light, the slave unsteadily forces himself to pick the nearest pod, responding only to the terrible system of injustice which condemns him, with no appeal to clemency; with no hope of reward except respite from daily labor. . . . From time to time he interrupts the silence of these deserts with his melancholy song, inspired by his slave condition, whose rhythm itself is often set to the crack of a whip!□

Forced Labor Recruitment

Historically, the perennial need to recruit an adequate number of workers challenged the landowners. Labor was too scarce and, hence, too valuable a commodity for them to leave recruitment to mere chance. They sometimes used the services of labor contractors. Such contractors, often a euphemism for greedy thugs who earned a reward for each body they produced, were not above force, threat, or coercion. Often, awakening from drunken stupors, unsuspecting victims found that the contractor had tricked them while intoxicated into affixing an X to a labor contract they could neither read nor understand. Such practices frequently led to debt peonage, or debt servitude, and many other abuses.

In the following print, the master Mexican engraver José Guadalupe Posada (1852–1913) depicted and condemned forced labor recruitment. This engraving appeared during the last years of the long rule of Mexican President Porfirio Díaz (in office 1876–1911). The lettering on the building reads "Bureau of Labor Recruitment," while the finer print below announces "Voluntary Contracts." All indications in the engraving suggest the recruitment was anything but voluntary. Toughs drag or carry "volunteers." Meanwhile, those who signed the "voluntary contracts" stand behind bars. In the upper left-hand corner, the sun frowns on the scene below. Posada's cogent graphic commentary on such recruitment in the early twentieth century in reality denounced nearly four centuries of similar practices.

The fact that this illustration appeared on a broadside (large sheet of paper) means it enjoyed wide circulation, art for popular consumption rather than for the gallery. It helped to arouse public protest against the harsh historical reality of forced labor.

"Forced Labor Recruitment," engraving, Mexico, c. 1900 (José Guadalupe Posada, 1852–1913).

A Comfortable Life

Andrés Chacón, an encomendero of Trujillo, Peru, while by no means the richest man in his region, lived a comfortable life. He raised sheep, goats, pigs, cows, mules, and horses; he possessed orchards; he cultivated wheat and his mill ground flour. He collected a variety of tributes from "his" Indians. Both black slaves and Indians worked for him. Mindful of the importance of Indian labor for his diverse rural enterprises, Chacón sought to treat his workers benevolently, the better to keep them attached to him. The following excerpt from his letter to his brother in 1570 suggests how one Spaniard established a pattern of wealth for himself based on land ownership and ready access to laborers. Andrés Chacón adapted to his geographical and cultural environments, just as he adapted Spanish colonial institutions to his needs.

I AM HERE IN THIS PLACE much of the year because it is so luxuriant. To be able to stay, I have sheep, goats and pigs here, and I did have cows, but recently I sold them because they damaged the Indians' crops. I have a constant supply of milk, cream, and curds. This valley, or rather the Indians and my property, are close to the sea, where the Indians catch a thousand kinds of fish, and have many nets they fish with. And as they like me well, when they have good luck they bring fish to me. I have maize from tributes, and a mill where wheat is ground. And certainly we have very good fare, with the capons they give me as tribute, and the very fat kids and muttons; all is from the harvest and tribute, and praise to God, the excess here could feed all of those boys. I have four pounds of fish and two chickens in tribute daily. In the previous assessment they were obliged to give me 600 bushels of wheat and 500 of maize, but in this assessment that was just made the amounts were reduced by half, because I requested it of the inspector, since if I die, I want them relieved; I have more than enough with the wheat and the maize they give me now.

I have here next to the mill four or five hundred fig trees that yield a harvest of fifty hundredweight, and there are orange trees and some vines that yield grapes to eat. The Indians here suffer because the river of the valley is so variable, full of water in the winter and empty in the spring, and some years they have scarcity, but since they are fishermen, they get everything they need from the neighboring people in exchange for fish.

I have a farm in Trujillo where I grow wheat to maintain my household, and I have a mill in the middle of it to grind the wheat that is harvested and other wheat that is grown by surrounding neighbors. I have there a dozen Indian couples and two blacks, one of whom watches a flock of goats and sheep to supply the house. But since there are many livestock around the town, the animals are thin, and the milk is less abundant than here. And besides I have in Trujillo two black women who make bread and cook for everyone, and a mulatto woman who serves Ana López, embroidering and sewing and serving at table along with

Source: James Lockhart and Enrique Otte (eds.), *Letters and People of the Spanish Indies: The Sixteenth Century* (London and New York: Cambridge University Press, 1976), pp. 69–70. With permission of the publisher.

the Indian women and girls. There are five or six other Indian women who are laundresses and help the black women make bread, so that there are twenty or twenty-five people eating there, including the Indian women and boys and blacks serving at the house. I have said this so you will see whether or not I have much to maintain and support. □

Sugar Plantations in Brazil at the End of the Colonial Period

In contrast to the more languid rural estates of Andrés Chacón, the sugar plantations of northeastern Brazil bustled to export to the European markets. Sugar plantations located near the Atlantic coast tended to be intensively exploited. Refining the cane into marketable sugar required investment and technology. The growth, harvesting, and processing of the cane demanded a large labor force. African slaves, an impressive capital investment for the owners, met that demand.

Residing in Pernambuco from 1816 to 1818, the French cotton merchant L. F. de Tollenare described the economy and rural customs of a region that had lucratively produced sugar for three centuries. He discussed four significant groups: the large sugar planters, the medium-sized tenant farmers, the small cultivators, and the African slaves. The large plantations, combining both feudal and capitalist characteristics, set the tone for rural and urban life. Propelling an export economy across three centuries, the plantations were vital to the colonial mission of Brazil and the well-being of Portugal.

I WILL DIVIDE THE inhabitants of these regions into three classes (I am not speaking of the slaves, who are nothing but cattle). These three classes are:

1.   The owners of sugar mills [*senhores de engenho*], the great landowners.
2.   The *lavradores,* a type of tenant farmer.
3.   The *moradores,* squatters or small cultivators.

The sugar-mill owners are those who early received land grants from the Crown, by donation or transfer. These subdivided grants constitute considerable properties even today, as can be seen from the expanses of 7,000 and 10,000 acres of which I spoke earlier; the Crown does not have more lands to grant; foreigners should be made aware of this.

There are some sugar-mill owners who interest themselves in the theoretical aspects of agriculture and who make some effort to improve the methods of cultivation and production. I was conscious of their existence, at least, because of the derision of which they were the object. I visited six mills and encountered few notable men.

Source: "The Masters and the Slaves: A Frenchman's Account of Society in Rural Pernambuco Early in the Nineteenth Century" in Robert Edgar Conrad (ed.), *Children of God's Fire: A Documentary History of Black Slavery in Brazil* (Princeton, N.J.: Princeton University Press, 1983), pp. 63–71. Copyright © 1983 by Princeton University Press. Reprinted by permission of Princeton University Press.

With bare legs, clad in a shirt and drawers or a dressing gown of printed calico, the sugar-mill owner, armed with a whip and visiting the dependencies of his estate, is a king who has only animals about him: his blacks; his squatters or *moradores,* slaves whom he mistreats; and some hostile vassals who are his tenants or *lavradores.*

The great distances and lack of security on the roads do not encourage contacts with neighbors. Not even in the church are there opportunities to meet, because each mill either has its own chapel, or, what is more frequently the case, there isn't any church and no religious worship is carried on at all. The Portuguese government, which requires that a chaplain sail aboard merchant ships, would perhaps promote the progress of civilization by ordering that a priest be maintained at mills which have a certain number of blacks.

When a sugar-mill owner visits another one, the ladies do not make their appearance. I spent two days in the house of one of them, a very charming man who overwhelmed me with kindness, and I did not see his family either in the living room or at the dinner table. On a different occasion I arrived unexpectedly after supper at the house of another of them, the splendor of which promised better taste; I noticed on the floor a piece of embroidery which seemed to have been tossed there suddenly. I asked for a glass of water in order to have a chance to go into the next room, but they made me wait for a long time. The lady of the house prepared a choice meal, but I did not see her. Furthermore, the same thing happened to me in a country house near Recife that belonged to a native of Lisbon.

In these houses, where the owners reside for the whole year, one does not observe anything fashioned to make them comfortable; one does not even find the avenue which among [the French] adorn both the simple property and the sumptuous chateau, neither parks, nor gardens, nor walks, nor pavillions. Living in the midst of forests, the inhabitants seem to fear shadows; or, more precisely stated, up to the edge of the forest around the mill everything is denuded and scorched to a distance of a quarter of a league. I witnessed at Salgado [a sugar plantation near the town of Cabo] the cutting down for firewood of orange groves which the previous owner had planted near the house, either for his pleasure or his profit.

Generally the residences are elevated on pillars; the cellar serves as a stable or as a dwelling place for the blacks; a long stairway provides access to the main floor, and it is on this level, or terrace, where one can enjoy the cool air. The rooms do not have ceilings; instead the timberwork of the roof is exposed and, between its extremities and the walls that hold it up, there is a free space of five inches to increase the air currents. The interior divisions are made with simple lath partitions measuring nine to ten feet in height, so that all the rooms have the roof as a common ceiling.

Luxury consists of a great variety of silverware. When a foreigner is entertained, in order to wash himself he is given splendid vessels made of this metal, of which also the coffee trays used at table, the bridles and stirrups for the horses, and knife hilts are made. Some sugar-mill owners showed me luxurious and expensive English firearms, and I also saw porcelain tea sets from England of the most beautiful type.

I ought to say a few words about meals. Supper consists of an abundant and thick soup, in which garlic abounds, or some other plant of a very pronounced and disagreeable taste which I did not recognize. The first plate is boiled meat which is not very succulent, the tastelessness of which they try to conceal with bacon, which is always a little rancid, and with manioc flour, which each serves himself with his fingers. For a second plate they serve a chicken ragout and rice with pepper. Bread is not seen, although it is much appreciated; they could manufacture it from foreign flour, which Recife is well supplied with, but it is not the custom. The black men or mulatto women (I saw many of the latter serving at table) fill the glasses with wine as soon as they are emptied, but people do not persist in drinking; liqueurs are not served with dessert. . . .

The sugar-mill owners are the only landholders. The only exceptions I know of are some chapels erected 100 or 150 years ago by the piety of the Portuguese and endowed with 50 to 60 uncultivated acres. . . . The extension of the lands owned by the mills is therefore immense, and the capital invested in them is much less considerable than it was in the French [Caribbean] islands. Only the most important establishments have 140 to 150 blacks. One could estimate the importance of the mills by the number of slaves, if it were not for the existence of the *lavradores*.

The *lavradores* are tenants without leases. They plant cane, but do not own mills. They send the harvested cane to the mill that they are dependent upon, where it is transformed into sugar. Half of it belongs to the *lavrador* and half to the sugar-mill owner. The latter keeps the molasses, but furnishes the cases for the sugar. Each one pays his tithe separately. The *lavradores* normally possess from six to ten blacks and themselves wield the hoe. They are Brazilians of European descent, little mixed with mulattoes. I counted from two to three *lavradores* per mill.

This class is truly worthy of interest since it possesses some capital and performs some labor. Nevertheless, the law protects it less than it does the mill owners. Since they do not make contracts, once a piece of land becomes productive, the mill owner has the right to expel them without paying compensation. It should be recognized that leases of only a year are not very favorable to agriculture. The *lavrador* builds only a miserable hut, does not try to improve the soil, and makes only temporary fences, because from one year to the next he can be expelled, and then all his labor is lost. He invests his capital in slaves and cattle, which he can always take with him. . . .

If I estimate an average of eight blacks for each *lavrador,* and sugar production at fifty *arrobas* per slave, which is not too much considering the vigilance and labor of the master himself, I can calculate the annual income of each *lavrador* at four hundred *arrobas* of sugar [about 12,800 pounds], which six or seven years ago was sold for about 3,000 francs. Now, this income is clear, since the *lavrador* does not buy anything at all to feed his blacks, and he lives very frugally from the manioc he plants.

Therefore, this class of capitalists, if favored by the government, is destined some day to exercise a major role in the political economy of Brazil. Consider the influence that they would have if the government would guarantee leases for nine years, and especially if an agrarian law were adopted that would obligate the present owners to make concessions, at stipulated prices, of certain parts of their uncultivated lands to anyone who might wish to buy them. Yet today everything remains exactly the opposite. I was witness to a rich mill owner's expulsion from his property of *all* the *lavradores* and squatters whom his less wealthy predecessors had allowed to establish themselves there. The number of exiles reached almost 600 persons, the property measuring two square leagues in size [about thirty square miles]. . . .

The *lavradores* are quite proud to receive on a basis of equality the foreigner who comes to visit them. Under the pretext of seeking shelter, I entered the houses of several to speak with them. The women disappeared as in the homes of ladies, though I was always offered sweets. I never managed to get them to accept the little presents of cheap jewelry which I had supplied myself with for the trip. This noble pride caused me to respect the hard-working *lavradores,* a class intermediate between the haughty mill owner and the lazy, subservient, and humble squatter. The *lavrador* has a miserable house, for the reasons I have already mentioned. However, when he abandons the hoe to go to Serinhaem [a nearby town] or to church, he dresses himself up like a city man, rides a good horse, and has stirrups and spurs made of silver.

The *moradores* or squatters are small settlers to whom the sugar-mill owners grant permission to erect a hut in the middle of the forest and to farm a small piece of land. The rent they pay is very small, worth at the most a tenth part of their gross product, without an obligation to pay the royal tithe. Like the *lavradores,* they do not have a contract, and the master can send them away whenever he wishes. As a general rule they are mixtures of mulattoes, free blacks, and Indians, but Indians and pure blacks are rarely encountered among them. This free class comprises the true Brazilian population, an impoverished people because they perform little labor. It would seem logical that from this class a number of salaried workers would emerge, but this does not happen. The squatter refuses work, he plants a little manioc, and lives in idleness. His wife has a small income because, if the manioc crop is good, she can sell a bit of it and buy some clothing. This comprises their entire expense, because their furniture consists of only a few mats and clay pots. Not even a manioc scraper is found in all their houses.

The squatters live isolated, far from civil and religious authority, without comprehending, so to speak, the value of property. They replaced the Brazilian savages but have less value, since the latter at least had some political and national affiliation. The squatters know only their surroundings, and look upon all outsiders practically as enemies. The sugar-mill owners court their women for their pleasure; they flatter them greatly, but from these seductions acts of vengeance as well as stabbings result. Generally speaking, this class is hated and feared. Because they pay them little or badly and often rob them, the sugar-mill owners who have the right to dismiss the squatters fear taking this dangerous step in a country that lacks police. Assassinations are common, but do not result in any pursuit whatsoever. I knew a certain mill owner who did not travel alone a quarter of a league from his house, because of the hostility and treachery of his squatters. He had incurred their wrath, and I had similar reasons to fear them when I entered their huts. . . .

I promised to make a quick survey of the black population. I am not in possession, however, of enough information about the laws that govern them to be able to deal with the matter adequately. Here is what I can say at the moment in respect to them.

The Salgrado mill contains about 130 to 140 slaves, including those of all ages, but there is no written list of them. Deducting the children, the sick, and the people employed in domestic service and in the infirmary, there remain only about a hundred people who are fit for agricultural labor. During the four or five months that the sugar harvest lasts, the toil of the mill blacks is most violent; they alternate so as to be able to stay on their feet for eighteen hours. I said earlier that they received for food a pound of manioc flour and seven ounces of meat. Here it is distributed already cooked. There are few properties on which slaves are allowed to plant something for themselves. Passing through the forests I sometimes came upon small clearings where the blacks had come secretly to plant a little manioc. These were certainly not the lazy ones. Nevertheless, Gonçalo [a slave] told me not to speak about it to their master, because this could expose them to punishment.

Upon arrival from Africa, the blacks who have not been baptized in Angola, Mozambique, or another place where there are Portuguese governors, receive baptism upon disembarking; this is nothing but a pointless formality, because they are not given any instruction whatsoever. At certain mills I saw the blacks being married by the priest, but in others they are united only by their whims or inclinations. In either case the master may sell separately the husband and the wife and the children to another buyer, regardless of how young they may be. A black baby is worth 200 francs at birth. Some masters make their slaves hear mass, but others save the cost of a chaplain, claiming that the sacrifice of the mass is a matter too grand for such people. Finally, there are mill owners who are more or less formalistic in matters of religion, and more or less able to appreciate its influence upon the conduct and habits of their slaves. It seems to me that it is in the interest of the masters to maintain family ties.

At the Salgado mill I saw only good slave quarters; everywhere, for that matter, they are of stone and lime and well roofed. Those of Salgado are ten feet wide and fifteen feet in depth, with a small interior division forming almost two rooms. It has a door which can be locked with a key, and a round opening toward the field to provide ventilation. The brick floor is two feet above the level of the adjacent ground, which makes such houses much more healthful than those of many French peasants. Each black is supposed to have his own private room, but love and friendship generally prevent them from living alone.

A mat, a clay cup or a gourd, sometimes a few clay pots, and some tatters and rags make up the furnishings of the home of a black couple. All have permission to light a fire in their rooms and they take advantage of it. Their food is furnished to them already prepared, so that they have no need to cook. However, the fire is a distraction for them and serves for preparing fish or other food which they manage to acquire, lawfully or not. I observed that they were very careful to lock their doors and that when they were barred inside their houses they opened them with great reluctance. Although I was rather friendly with them in Salgado, I had some difficulty in satisfying my curiosity regarding the interior of their huts. I also saw some of the latter that were made of mud and covered with cocoa leaves. . . .

The black women generally have a flexible and elegant figure, the shoulders and arms very well formed. Many are seen who could qualify as pretty women if their necks were longer, giving more freedom to their heads. Their breasts are firm and fleshy, and they seem to understand their value, proving themselves very wise by concealing them, since this, in fact, is the way they commit terrible sins. It is unusual to see a black woman, even seventeen or eighteen years of age, whose neck has retained the shape which we prize so much and which European art imitates more or less badly. Nevertheless, they are not without a certain ability to hide its flaccidness [goiter?] with a piece of blue or red cloth. They tie these under their armpits, arrange the draping nicely over their waists and thighs, and make a large knot over the bosom, which hides the deformity I have just mentioned. The shoulders remain naked and the knees nearly uncovered, the scantiness of the cloth, which is made even tinier because of the part reserved for creating the knot, betraying all the body's movements, and I must say that they are all attractive and very graceful. . . . Their legs are normal, but their feet are damaged by hard work and the lack of footwear. They habitually have their heads uncovered, though some are given round hats which are not very becoming to them. They are happy when they can adorn themselves with a necklace or some bits of jewelry. Many of them, lacking such ornaments, attach a feather or a small round stick of wood to their ears. A tobacco pipe a foot long is usually thrust through the knotted cloth over the breast, and there it figures majestically like the dagger belonging to a leading lady of the theater.

This is the portrait of the black women who fix themselves up a bit. One sees others in a state of abandonment which is much less picturesque, dressed in a tattered shirt and an old petticoat which leaves the part beneath the breasts uncovered. Always, however, when they wrap their bodies or heads with a piece of cloth, the result is quite agreeable. . . .

The men have a better appearance when they are naked than the women, because of the flabbiness of the breasts that disfigures the latter. They are less robust than our porters, but the habit of going about without clothing makes their movements less wooden. What they possess that is better are their arched chests and their sinewy thighs. It is rare to see gray and wrinkled persons among them. Their black, shiny-smooth skin, destitute of hair, allows one to observe the entire play of their very active muscles. The arms and especially the legs are usually weak, but I saw some blacks with Apollo-like physiques.

Those coming from Africa have their shoulders, arms, and chests covered with symmetrical marks, which seem to be made with a hot iron, and the women also display these marks. For clothing the men are given a shirt and some breeches, but these garments evidently make them uncomfortable, and few preserve them, particularly the shirts. Most of the time they are satisfied with tying a rope around their loins from which hangs, both in front and behind, a small piece of cloth with which they try to hide that which modesty does not permit them to display.

The children also get clothing, but they make quick work of it so that they can go about naked. When they reach fourteen or fifteen years of age they are beaten with switches to make them more careful. At that time some are seen wearing their shirts hung over one shoulder in the fashion of Roman patricians, and, seen thus, they are reminiscent of Greek statues.

The blacks employed in domestic service, or close to their masters, dress with less elegance and more in the European manner. They take care of their breeches and shirts and sometimes even possess a waistcoat. Gonçalo had an embroidered shirt, and when he wore his lace hat and small trinkets which I had given him his pride was greater than that of any dandy; but when we went out hunting, his greatest pleasure was to leave at home both his necessary and unnecessary items of clothing. □

3

Patterns for Power

Between 1804 and 1824, most of Latin America achieved independence from France, Spain, or Portugal. The search for effective governance then challenged the newly independent Latin Americans. A dilemma beset them: whether to adhere to the genetic principles of inherent authority characteristic of both the father of the family and the monarch, namely social and political patriarchy, or to adopt the theories of contractual governance persuasively advocated by the philosophers of the European Enlightenment. Latin Americans vacillated between the familiar and the novel. Such indecision encouraged the very political disorder they desperately hoped to avoid. While the Latin Americans wrote constitutions with numbing regularity, those documents served more as exercises in political theory than as practical guides for governance. From independence onward, theory favored contractual governance while practice drew from patriarchal experience. Within the contradictions, strong, highly personalistic leaders, the *caudillos,* appeared to impose order and to govern arbitrarily, mocking rather than eliminating the idealistic constitutions to which they paid verbal homage.

Governance by *caudillos* characterized the political life of Latin America during its first century of independence. Indeed, it never totally disappeared. The concept of the "strong leader" remains deeply imbedded in the office of the presidency throughout Latin America.

From independence to the present, the search for viable political structures remains a constant theme of the national histories of Latin America. Of course, that search is by no means unique to Latin America in either the nineteenth or the twentieth century. Globally, most peoples duplicated it as they attempted to move from "traditional" and/or "colonized" to "modern" societies.

Bolívar's Political Prescriptions

From Venezuela to Bolivia, Simón Bolívar (1783–1830) liberated much of Spanish South America. On various occasions, the grateful citizens called upon him to govern them. No stranger to the growing avocation of writing constitutions, he frequently dispensed political advice. Both genetic and contractual principles guided his political thought, and he combined them in a variety of ways in the constitutions he proposed. In the excerpts below, Bolívar puts forth his political ideas, first before the Congress of Angostura, Venezuela, in 1819, and then in defending the constitution he wrote for Bolivia in 1826.

The fear of anarchy increasingly persuaded Bolívar of the need for a strong executive. In proposing his ideas at Angostura, he drew on the English monarchy for guidance. Reflecting the hierarchical and patriarchal experience of the Venezuelan elite, Bolívar attempted a compromise between past genetic experience and contemporary contractual theories of government. Although he favored political liberties and extolled the virtues of a constitution—the contract—he also advocated a strong executive and an hereditary senate.

Increasing political turmoil strengthened Bolívar's patriarchal proclivities. The constitution he proposed for Bolivia in 1826 not only authorized a Chamber of Censors, a third legislative body to provide further balance and authority, but called for a patriarchal president-for-life who would appoint his own successor. Experience tipped Bolivar's political preferences to favor a type of "genetic governance," more complimentary to the social and political experiences of the past.

The significance of these two documents lies in the ambiguities characteristic of the mind of one of Latin America's foremost political thinkers of the independence period. Idealism clashed with practicality; hope struggled with doubt; borrowed theories subverted local experience. Those patterns not only reflected the contradictions inherent in political change during the independence period but they still remain to bedevil the political process in Latin America.

The Congress of Angostura, 1819

L ET US REVIEW THE PAST to discover the base upon which the Republic of Venezuela is founded.

America, in separating from the Spanish monarchy, found herself in a situation similar to that of the Roman Empire when its enormous framework fell to pieces in the midst of the ancient world. Each Roman division then formed an independent nation in keeping with its location or interests; but this situation differed from America's in that those members proceeded to reëstablish their former associations. We, on the contrary, do not even retain the vestiges of our original being. We are not Europeans; we are not Indians; we are but a mixed

Source: Vicente Lecuna, Harold A. Bierck, Jr., and Lewis Betrand (eds.), *Selected Writings of Bolivar* (New York: The Colonial Press, 1951), Vol. 1, pp. 175–191; Vol. 2, pp. 596–602.

species of aborigines and Spaniards. Americans by birth and Europeans by law, we find ourselves engaged in a dual conflict: we are disputing with the natives for titles of ownership, and at the same time we are struggling to maintain ourselves in the country that gave us birth against the opposition of the invaders. Thus our position is most extraordinary and complicated. But there is more. As our rôle has always been strictly passive and our political existence nil, we find that our quest for liberty is now even more difficult of accomplishment; for we, having been placed in a state lower than slavery, had been robbed not only of our freedom but also of the right to exercise an active domestic tyranny. Permit me to explain this paradox. . . .

America . . . received everything from Spain, who, in effect, deprived her of the experience that she would have gained from the exercise of an active tyranny by not allowing her to take part in her own domestic affairs and administration. This exclusion made it impossible for us to acquaint ourselves with the management of public affairs; nor did we enjoy that personal consideration, of such great value in major revolutions, that the brilliance of power inspires in the eyes of the multitude. In brief, Gentlemen, we were deliberately kept in ignorance and cut off from the world in all matters relating to the science of government.

Subject to the threefold yoke of ignorance, tyranny, and vice, the American people have been unable to acquire knowledge, power, or [civic] virtue. The lessons we received and the models we studied, as pupils of such pernicious teachers, were most destructive. We have been ruled more by deceit than by force, and we have been degraded more by vice than by superstition. Slavery is the daughter of Darkness: an ignorant people is a blind instrument of its own destruction. . . .

Does not *L'Esprit des lois* state that laws should be suited to the people for whom they are made; that it would be a major coincidence if those of one nation could be adapted to another; that laws must take into account the physical conditions of the country, climate, character of the land, location, size, and mode of living of the people; that they should be in keeping with the degree of liberty that the Constitution can sanction respecting the religion of the inhabitants, their inclinations, resources, number, commerce, habits, and customs? This is the code we must consult. . . .

Venezuela had, has, and should have a republican government. Its principles should be the sovereignty of the people, division of powers, civil liberty, proscription of slavery, and the abolition of monarchy and privileges. We need equality to recast, so to speak, into a unified nation, the classes of men, political opinions, and public customs. . . .

Nothing in our fundamental laws would have to be altered were we to adopt a legislative power similar to that held by the British Parliament. Like the North Americans, we have divided national representation into two chambers: that of Representatives and the Senate. The first is very wisely constituted. It enjoys all its proper functions, and it requires no essential revision, because the Constitution, in creating it, gave it the form and powers which the people deemed necessary in order that they might be legally and properly represented. If the Senate were hereditary rather than elective, it would, in my opinion, be the basis, the tie, the very soul of our republic. In political storms this body would arrest the thunderbolts of the government and would repel any violent popular reaction. Devoted to the government because of a natural interest in its own preservation, a hereditary senate would always oppose any attempt on the part of the people to infringe upon the jurisdiction and authority of their magistrates. It must be confessed that most men are unaware of their best interests and that they constantly endeavor to assail them in the hands of their custodians—the individual clashes with the mass, and the mass with authority. It is necessary, therefore, that in all governments there be a neutral body to protect the injured and disarm the offender. To be neutral, this body must not owe its origin to appointment by the government or to election by the people, if it is to enjoy a full measure of independence which neither fears nor expects anything from these two sources of authority. The hereditary senate, as a part of the people, shares its interests, its sentiments, and its spirit. For this reason it should not be presumed that a hereditary senate would ignore the interests of the people or forget its legislative duties. The senators in Rome and in the House of Lords in London have been the strongest pillars upon which the edifice of political and civil liberty has rested. . . .

The creation of a hereditary senate would in no way be a violation of political equality. I do not solicit the establishment of a nobility, for, as a celebrated republican has said, that would simultaneously destroy equality and liberty. What I propose is an office for which the candidates must prepare themselves, an office that demands great knowledge and the ability to acquire such knowledge. All should not be left to chance and the outcome of elections. The people are more easily deceived than is Nature perfected by art; and, although these senators, it is true, would not be bred in an environment that is all virtue, it is equally true that they would be raised in an atmosphere of enlightened education. Furthermore, the liberators of Venezuela are entitled to occupy forever a high rank in the Republic that they have brought into existence. I believe that posterity would view with regret the effacement of the illustrious names of its first benefactors. I say, moreover, that it is a matter of public interest and national honor, of gratitude on Venezuela's part, to honor gloriously, until the end of time, a race of virtuous, prudent, and persevering men who, overcoming every obstacle, have founded the Republic at the price of the most heroic sacrifices. And if the people of Venezuela do not applaud the elevation of their benefactors, then they are unworthy to be free, and they will never be free.

A hereditary senate, I repeat, will be the fundamental basis of the legislative power, and therefore the foundation of the entire government. It will also serve as a counterweight to both government and people; and as a neutral power it will weaken the mutual attacks of these two eternally rival powers. In all conflicts the calm reasoning of a third party will serve as the means of reconciliation. Thus the Venezuelan senate will give strength to this delicate political structure, so sensitive to violent repercussions; it will be the mediator that will lull the storms and it will maintain harmony between the head and the other parts of this political body. . . .

. . . No matter how closely we study the composition of the English executive power, we can find nothing to prevent its being judged as the most perfect model for a kingdom, for an aristocracy, or for a democracy. Give Venezuela such an executive power in the person of a president chosen by the people or their representatives, and you will have taken a great step toward national happiness.

No matter what citizen occupies this office, he will be aided by the Constitution, and therein being authorized to do good, he can do no harm, because his ministers will coöperate with him only insofar as he abides by the law. If he attempts to infringe upon the law, his own ministers will desert him, thereby isolating him from the Republic, and they will even bring charges against him in the Senate. The ministers, being responsible for any transgressions committed, will actually govern, since they must account for their actions. The obligation which this system places upon the officials closest to the executive power, that is, to take a most interested and active part in governmental deliberations and to regard this department as their own, is not the smallest advantage of the system. Should the president be a man of no great talent or virtue, yet, notwithstanding his lack of these essential qualities, he will be able to discharge his duties satisfactorily, for in such a case the ministry, managing everything by itself, will carry the burdens of the state.

Although the authority of the executive power in England may appear to be extreme, it would, perhaps, not be excessive in the Republic of Venezuela. Here the Congress has tied the hands and even the heads of its men of state. This deliberative assembly has assumed a part of the executive functions, contrary to the maxim of Montesquieu, to wit: A representative assembly should exercise no active function. It should only make laws and determine whether or not those laws are enforced. Nothing is as disturbing to harmony among the powers of government as their intermixture. Nothing is more dangerous with respect to the people than a weak executive; and if a kingdom has deemed it necessary to grant the executive so many powers, then in a republic these powers are infinitely more indispensable.

If we examine this difference, we will find that the balance of power between the branches of government must be distributed in two ways. In republics the executive should be the stronger, for everything conspires against it; while in monarchies the legislative power should be superior, as everything works in the monarch's favor. The people's veneration of royal power results in a self-fascination that tends greatly to increase the superstitious respect paid to such authority. . . .

A republican magistrate is an individual set apart from society, charged with checking the impulse of the people toward license and the propensity of judges and administrators toward abuse of the laws. He is directly subject to the legislative body, the senate, and the people: he is the one man who resists the combined pressure of the opinions, interests, and passions of the social state and who, as Carnot states, does little more than struggle constantly with the urge to dominate and the desire to escape domination. He is, in brief, an athlete pitted against a multitude of athletes. . . .

Abstract theories create the pernicious idea of unlimited freedom. Let us see to it that the strength of the public is kept within the limits prescribed by reason and interest; that the national will is confined within the bonds set by a just power; that the judiciary is rigorously controlled by civil and criminal laws, analogous to those in our present Constitution—then an equilibrium between the powers of government will exist, the conflicts that hamper the progress of the state will disappear, and those complications which tend to hinder rather than unite society will be eliminated. □

The Constitution for Bolivia, 1826

M Y DRAFT OF A constitution for Bolivia provides for four branches of government, an additional one having been devised without affecting the time-honored powers of any of the others. The electoral [legislative] branch has been accorded powers not granted it in other reputedly very liberal governments. These powers resemble, in great part, those of the federal system. I have thought it expedient and desirable, and also feasible, to accord to the most direct representatives of the people privileges that the citizens of every department, province, and canton probably desire most. Nothing is more important to a citizen than the right to elect his legislators, governors, judges, and pastors. The electoral college of each province represents its needs and interests and serves as a forum from which to denounce any infractions of the laws or abuses of the magistrates. I might, with some truth, describe this as a form of representation providing the rights enjoyed by individual governments in federal systems. In this manner, additional weight has been placed in the balance to check the executive; the government will acquire greater guarantes, a more popular character, and a greater claim to be numbered among the most democratic of governments. . . .

The legislative body is so composed that its parts will necessarily be in harmony. It will not find itself divided for lack of an arbiter, as is the case where there are only two chambers. Since this legislature has three parts, disagreement between two can be settled by the third. The issue is thus examined by two contending parties and decided by an impartial third party. In this way no useful law is without effect; at least it shall have been reviewed once, twice, and a third time before being discarded. In all matters between two contending parties, a third party is named to render the decision. Would it not be absurd, therefore, if, in matters of the deepest concern to the nation, this expedient, dictated by practical necessity, were scorned? The chambers will thus observe toward each other the consideration which is indispensable in preserving the unity of the Congress, which must deliberate without passion and with the calm of wisdom. Our modern congresses, I shall be told, consist of only two houses. This is because England, which has provided the model, was forced to have the nobility and the people represented in two chambers; and, while the same pattern was followed in North America where there is no nobility, it may be presumed that the habits acquired under British rule inspired this imitation. The fact is that two deliberating bodies are always found to be in conflict. It was for this reason that Sieyès insisted on only one—a classic error.

The first body [I propose] is the Chamber of Tribunes. It has the right to initiate laws pertaining to finance, peace, and war. It exercises the immediate supervision of the departments administered by the executive branch with a minimum of interference by the legislative branch.

The Senators enact the codes of law and the ecclesiastical regulations and supervise the courts and public worship. The Senate shall appoint the prefects, district judges, governors, *corregidores,* and all the lesser officials in the department of justice. It shall submit to the Chamber of Censors nominations for members of the Supreme Court, archbishops, bishops, prebendaries, and canons. Everything relating to religion and the laws comes within the province of the Senate.

The Censors exercise a political and moral power not unlike that of the Areopagus of Athens and the censors of Rome. They are the prosecuting attorneys [*fiscales*] against the government in defense of the Constitution and popular rights, to see that these are strictly observed. Under their aegis has been placed the power of national judgment, which is to decide whether or not the administration of the executive is satisfactory.

The Censors are to safeguard morality, the sciences, the arts, education, and the press. The Censors exercise the most fearful yet the most august authority. They can condemn to eternal opprobrium arch criminals and usurpers of the sovereign authority. They can bestow public honors upon citizens who have distinguished themselves by their probity and public service. The sceptre of glory has been placed in their hands, for which reason the Censors must possess integrity and a conduct above reproach. For any trespass on their part, however slight, they shall be prosecuted. To these high priests of the laws I have entrusted the preservation of our sacred tablets, as it is for them to denounce the violators of these laws.

The President of the Republic, in our Constitution, becomes the sun which, fixed in its orbit, imparts life to the universe. This supreme authority must be perpetual, for in non-hierarchical systems, more than in others, a fixed point is needed about which leaders and citizens, men and affairs can revolve. "Give me a point where I may stand," said an ancient sage, "and I will move the earth." For Bolivia this point is the life-term President [*presidente vitalicio*]. Upon him rests our entire order, notwithstanding his lack of powers. Not only has he been rendered headless in order that none may fear his intentions, but his hands have been tied so that he can do no harm.

The President of Bolivia enjoys many of the powers of the [North] American chief executive but with limitations that favor the people. His term of office is that enjoyed by the President of Haiti. For Bolivia, I have borrowed the executive system of the most democratic republic in the world.

The island of Haiti, if you will permit the digression, was in a state of perpetual insurrection. Having experimented with an empire, a kingdom, and a republic, in fact every known type of government and more besides, the people were compelled to call upon the illustrious Pétion to save them. After they had put their trust in him, Haiti's destinies pursued a steady course. Pétion was made President for life, with the right to choose his successor. Thus, neither the death of that great man nor the advent of a new president imperiled that state in the slightest. Under the worthy Boyer, everything has proceeded as tranquilly as in a legitimate monarchy. There you have conclusive proof that *a life-term president, with the power to choose his successor,* is the most sublime inspiration amongst republican regimes.

The President of Bolivia will be less dangerous than the President of Haiti, as the succession is provided for in a manner that better secures the interests of the state. Moreover, the President of Bolivia is deprived of all patronage. He can appoint neither governors, nor judges, nor ecclesiastic dignitaries of any kind. This limitation of powers has never before been imposed in any constituted government. One check after another has thus been placed upon the authority of the head of the government, who will in every way find that the people are ruled directly by those who exercise the significant functions of the commonwealth. The priests will rule in matters of conscience, the judges in matters involving property, honor, and life, and the magistrates or men of state in all major public acts. As they owe their position, their distinction, and their fortune to the people alone, the President cannot hope to entangle them in his personal ambitions. If to this is added the natural growth of opposition which a democratic government experiences throughout the course of its administration, there is reason to believe that, under this form of government, usurpation of the popular sovereignty is less likely to occur than under any other. . . .

The constitutional limitations upon the President of Bolivia are the narrowest ever known. He can appoint only the officials of the Ministries of the Treasury, Peace, and War; and he is Commander in Chief of the army. These are his only powers.

Administration is the province of the Cabinet, which is responsible to the Censors and subject to the close vigilance of every legislator, governor, judge, and citizen. The revenue officers and soldiers, who are agents of the Cabinet alone, are hardly the persons calculated to make it the object of public affection, and therefore its influence will be next to nothing.

Of all the higher officials, the Vice President is the one with the most limited power. He must obey both the legislative and the executive branches of a republican government. From the former, he receives the laws, and from the latter his instructions, and he must proceed between these two branches, following the narrowest of paths, with precipices on either side. Despite these disadvantages, this form of government is better than an absolute government. Constitutional limitations increase political consciousness, thereby giving hope of ultimately finding a beacon light which will act as a guide through the ever-present shoals and reefs. These limitations serve as dikes against the violence of our passions, which are prompted by selfish interests. . . .

The President of the Republic will appoint the Vice President, who will administer the affairs of the state and succeed the President in office. By means of this device we shall avoid elections, which result in that great scourge of republics— anarchy, which is the handmaiden of tyranny, the most imminent and terrible peril of popular government. Compare the tremendous crises in republics when a change of rulers takes place with the equivalent situation in legitimate monarchies. . . .

If hereditary succession perpetuates the monarchical system and is all but universal, is not the plan which I have just proposed, wherein the Vice President succeeds to the presidency, much more expedient? What if hereditary princes were chosen for merit and not by fate? What if, instead of wallowing in idleness and ignorance, they were put in charge of government administration? They would unquestionably be more enlightened monarchs, and they would contribute to the happiness of their peoples. Indeed, Legislators, monarchy, which rules the world, has won its claim for approval by means of the hereditary principle, which renders it stable, and by *unity,* which makes it strong. Hence, although a ruling prince is a spoiled child, cloistered in his palace, reared on adulation, and swayed by every passion, this other prince, whom I might venture to call the impossible man, is a ruler of men, for, by virtue of power firmly and constantly applied, he maintains order and willing subordination among the citizens. Do not forget, Gentlemen, that these great advantages are combined in a life-term presidential and vice presidential tenure and a vice presidential succession. . . . □

Political Advice from a Father
to His Son

Between 1821 and 1858, anarchy shook Nicaragua with unusual violence even within a politically unstable Latin America. No caudillo emerged to stem civil wars and chaos. In the early 1840s, a local newspaper, the *Mentor Nicaragüense,* offered some political advice for governance framed as a letter from a father to his son. The concept of the father personally educating his son characterized classic patriarchy.

The letter highlighted the paternal relationship of the chief executive with his people: "Love your subjects as your children." It urged him to act like the compassionate father. Not surprisingly during a period of protracted turmoil, the letter emphasized the restoration and preservation of order. Significantly, it made no mention of relations with the legislature and limited its remarks on the judiciary to the recommendation of constant vigilance over the courts.

While extolling a constitution, the letter also expressed disillusion with contractual governance. In fact, the very appearance of the letter, with advice typifying the patriarchal mentality, testified to the strength of the genetic approach to politics. Thus, as Latin America moved from its second to third political generation after independence, patterns for the exercise of paternal political power were being reaffirmed. With the political contract reduced to a formality, the patriarchal proclivity continued to shape political behavior.

U PON LEARNING THAT HIS SON had just been elected to the presidency of one of the nations of Latin America, the father wrote to him with the following advice:

I do not rejoice; rather, I cry bitterly, my son, over the news that you sent me of your election as head of the nation. When I think of you in such a lofty position, my heart trembles because I feel that it is dangerous. . . . I fear more

Source: *Mentor Nicaragüense* (Granada), January 15, January 22, February 5, and April 16, 1842.

than anything else that the temptations and forces that surround you might erode the virtue, integrity, and honor that I taught you; they will counter the principles of natural, public, and human law upon which both people's happiness and political stability depend; they will lead to political dishonesty and trickery whose consequences are shame, misery, and destruction.

But since events have conspired to put you at such risk and to cause me such misgivings, since you now find yourself endangered and unable to retreat, it is essential to keep your good sense and to press forward with that same hope held by the farmer who tills the rocky soil or the navigator who guides his ship into the harbor during a storm. I want to offer you some advice, my son, drawn from the experience and love of a father and a citizen.

In the first place, you have to understand that the destiny which seems to have raised you above other men making you freer than they are really has reduced you to their slave and servant. You have given up all your freedom; you no longer belong to yourself nor to me. Your entire being belongs to the nation; everything is for the fatherland; everything belongs to the fatherland. You are a total slave to the laws. You are the passive and vigilant servant of the people. It is true that your duties to law and to the people are honorable but they are no less servitude and slavery. There is no place for pride, arrogance, and haughtiness. It is better to cultivate temperance, humility, and moderation. You should be gentle and kind in your treatment of all persons without making distinctions. You should hear, listen, and serve all with attention and patience; you must not look down on anyone, much less offend him because he might be humble or ignorant. The unfortunate, the downtrodden, the widow, and the orphan look to you, if not for the remedy to their ills, at least for some alleviation from them through your humane and compassionate treatment. You must give them friendly and loving advice or, if need be, a convincing and gentle denial. Such behavior will earn for you the respect and love of the people, the love and respect that so much and powerfully influence public administration. It is quite different qualitatively from hatred and disgust heaped upon governments that treat the people with brutality, dishonesty, and harshness.

Keep in mind, my son, what the learned Fénelon advised monarchs, which is applicable to all who govern: "Those who think only in making themselves feared and who employ oppression to obtain obedience are the scourge of mankind. They may well succeed in earning the fear they desire but they are also hated and detested. They have much more to fear from their subjects than their subjects do from them. Love your subjects as your own children; take pleasure in being loved by them. When they enjoy the precious gifts of peace and happiness they attribute them to the good monarch under whom they live. The monarch will exercise greater authority over his subjects when affection rather than fear exists. In such a situation, they not only obey but find satisfaction in obedience." You must be more than simply pleasant to everyone; you must also be willing to hear and to listen to them. Erect no obstacle that would keep the people from you. Take care that your subordinates and your servants do not prevent them from approaching you. Treat all people equally. Never barricade your door. Even when you are busiest and most preoccupied, be prepared to honor the old adage, "The door to the king is never closed."

Constantly bear in mind the solemn pact you entered into with the people. That sublime pact is sacred, worthy of the respect of gods and men alike. Any violation of that sacred contract constitutes a horrible and sacrilegious crime. You have sworn to uphold the contract. It is the majestic instrument of union putting forth the relations between the governed and the governor. It outlines for all their mutual duties and responsibilities. That agreement is the base, the solid foundation of the political edifice. It also is the machine, of which you are the principal cog, that drives and runs everything else. That contract is and ought to be the subject of your respect and veneration, just as the Ark of the Covenant was for the Israelites. It is the oracle you must always consult. You should occupy yourself day and night reading and contemplating it. You must observe it religiously. You must make certain it is rigorously followed and permit no one to violate it.

I repeat to you what you have already read in a wise author's advice and should be written on the front of all governmental buildings: "The Constitution of the State and its laws are the basis of political and social tranquility, the firmest support of political authority, and the guarantee of the liberty of all citizens."

The constitution is worthless and the best laws useless if they are not religiously observed. It is your duty to keep tireless watch over the nation, making certain that both officials and citizens obey the law. To subvert the constitution and to violate its laws are capital crimes against society. If persons invested with authority commit such crimes, they compound them with the treacherous abuse of the power others confided in them. Then, the nation must punish them with all the vigor at its command. Respect of and adherence to the constitution must be constant. No motive is sufficient to suspend or frustrate that constancy, not even appeals to special circumstances, reasons of State, and public welfare. Such old and trite appeals, repeatedly invoked by governments, serve only as an attempt to disguise abuse. Even in the most trying times, the laws must be observed. There can be no excuse to infringe upon or to suspend the constitution. . . .

If all government is an evil, albeit a necessary one, it is desirable, my son, that whoever governs does so as intelligently and sensibly as possible in order to make government bearable. You must not abuse power or tolerate its abuse by other officials or bureaucrats; nor can you acquiesce in the faults and excesses committed by others. If the goal of government is, as by its very nature it should be, the happiness and well-being of all, then he who exercises the high and sacred executive office has to be a virtual Argus whose hundred eyes continually watch every branch of public administration, scrutinizing the conduct of every official and employee to make certain that they correctly carry out their responsibilities.

In naming public functionaries, it is necessary to be extremely careful to select men who will serve you and the State well and to avoid those who lack honesty or otherwise are not qualified. Remember that no one is subjected to trickery or misrepresentation more than the chief executive. . . . In particular, beware of those men motivated by "a mania for government employment." They are ambitious. Always near at hand importuning for an appointment of some kind, they form a kind of "court," a "herd" of flattering followers. They flatter to deceive you. . . . Select your subordinates with the greatest care. . . . Search out the talented, honorable, and enlightened with the single goal in mind that they are able to serve society well. Otherwise, you discredit yourself and invite just and severe criticism. Good men will resent such unworthy appointees. Then, public morale slumps, depressing public spirit; the inevitable result is indifference and paralysis. . . .

Above all else, you must make certain that the police act correctly, efficiently, and in accordance with the laws because they ensure order and stability. The principal objective of government is the presentation of public order and tranquility. You well know, thanks to long, sad, and painful experience, that a major vice inherent in democracy is chaos, which perpetuates backwardness and eventually brings about the ruin of the State. Generally, chaos originates not among honest men, nor among virtuous fathers of families, nor among the property owners but rather arises from the immorality of ambitious idlers and vagabonds who, because they do not want to work, have nothing to lose and no other way to satisfy their many vices. They promote disorder so that they can indulge their unlimited depravation. This grave and contagious evil needs to be eradicated at its origin by making absolutely certain the government, the courts, and the police with full use of all legal methods tenaciously pursue all who foment disorder in any way and subject them to the rigors of the penal code. Show no mercy because impunity multiplies, encouraging all delinquents to take advantage of any leniency or tolerance. These disturbers of public peace, sworn and mortal enemies of society, prejudice and erode society and the order upon which it must rest. They are a festering sore. Thus, as the surgeon finds it necessary to cut out the infected part of the body in order to save his patient's life, so should those charged with police duties separate with the knife of law the infectious members of society from the others in order to prevent the disease from spreading to the entire political and social body. I charge you to exercise scrupulous vigilance in the application of these police laws because they alone—not violent and unconstitutional methods—are sufficient to preserve the desired order without which villages, towns, and cities become places of horror, assault, and fear, a thousand times more dangerous than the forests inhabited by tigers, lions, and panthers.

All aspects of the public treasury require the constant attention of the chief executive in order to avoid deceit, evasion, and abuse. These funds are sacred both because of their sources and their destinations. You, my son, are the Supreme Treasurer. You are responsible for the honest collection, safekeeping, and wise spending of state revenues. You bear the responsibility of preventing fraud and misappropriation and of scrupulously applying the law to anyone guilty of those high crimes. Your care and vigilance in those matters must be of the same intensity as the temptation money exerts. The temptations to defraud are endless. History demonstrates that governments seldom spend money wisely, thereby causing great harm to the public. The public watches the treasury and is acutely aware of fraud, misappropriation, and dishonesty. All public officials are watchful of what happens with revenues because their salaries come from the treasury and it might happen that in their concern for payment they claim to see things that do not happen. Often they themselves speak and complain against the government that employs them, thereby wrongly discrediting it. Constantly watch over the spending of public funds to prevent those abuses, which can abound both in the management of the funds and in the spending of them. Take scrupulous care that all handling of funds follows the letter of the law.

Be certain that all public employees receive their pay punctually. Those who are not paid promptly will not serve with that dedication, eagerness, and constancy which are required. It is difficult to reprimand or discipline an unpaid employee. Never pay some employees and not pay others. No other action creates a greater feeling of injustice and inequity, which, in turn, creates sentiments of hate and malice toward the government.

My son, I wanted to speak with you about everything pertaining to government, but it is impossible. My letter already is too long. I conclude with one last piece of useful advice for you and for the State. If after exhausting all your efforts to maintain peace, if after investing all your strength and talent for the good of the State, you find that affairs are not satisfactory, that the legislature from which you expect support remains indifferent or even hostile, do not hesitate one moment in firmly but humbly tending your resignation. Never remain in a position in which you can do no good and in which your own future as well as that of the State are exposed to a disaster. Likewise, never for a single moment entertain the idea of retaining power against the will of the people and based only on force. Certain disaster results from such an arbitrary course. No, in truth, I do not expect such behavior from you. Constantly evoke the guidance and protection of Heaven in your undertakings. I likewise will do the same. Your loving father.□

The Caudillo in Spanish America

Despite the best intentions of constitutions infused with the ideals of the Enlightenment, *caudillaje*, governance by the caudillo, became a well-established institution throughout Latin America. Attempts to define, explain, rationalize, or criticize that major political phenomenon abound. In the early 1950s, the Argentine sociologist Fernando N. A. Cuevillas defined caudillaje and caudillo as follows: "I would use 'caudillaje' to apply to that regime which consists of the personification or incarnation of authority, where he who governs acts with an extraordinary charismatic moral ascendancy over his people: advising them, guiding them, leading them paternally. The power of the caudillos is inspired authority before it is juridical authority. Caudillaje appears as a social institution full of ethical content (political and military control, the authentic totality of power, the psychic leadership of the governed, the moral magnetism of the leader's personality), which makes it most suitable for those States whose political life is determined by the integration of individual and collective traditional values." Although vague, the definition still provides much understanding of a fundamental Latin American political reality. While closely associated with the nineteenth century, caudillos also populated the twentieth.

In an interpretive study of nineteenth-century Spanish-speaking Latin America, the Peruvian historian Francisco García Calderón (1883–1953) emphasized the dominance of the caudillo. Even during the later decades as the nation-building process gained greater complexity and sophistication, caudillaje persisted, contributing to, integrating with, and, perhaps, being strengthened by the new political order and economic prosperity. Echoing intellectual trends very common among late nineteenth and early twentieth-century writers, García Calderón paid attention in this essay written in 1912 to race and geography as determining factors in the formation of societies and consequently of history. He also shared the positivistic conclusion that political and social evolution was taking place to the benefit of the Latin American nations and their populations. His views in this essay sum up many conclusions of the elites of the period. The reader garners both their perspective on the nineteenth century and an insight into the historical vision of the governing class of the early twentieth century.

I N THE BEGINNING, military and ecclesiastical authorities determined ritual, customs, dogma, and laws. A kind of consensus ruled; individuals accepted without discussion or doubts the basic rules of social life. Thereafter, history records a struggle between authority and liberty, a progressive affirmation of individual wills, an assertion of destructive and critical individualism.

Throughout the Americas, political development followed this same course. Invariably we find the sequence of two periods, the first military and the second civilian. The independence movements gave rise to the period of militarism. Then, at varying times, depending on the circumstances of the individual nations, the military is pushed from power or renounces it without violence, and economic interests reigned supreme. Civilians took control of the governments. The military regimes were not theocracies, as in some monarchies; the president did not combine civil and religious functions. Nevertheless, the period of civilian rule often involved a strong reaction against the Church, initiating a period of anticlericalism or radicalism. Oligarchies were in charge after independence triumphed. Later, the military gave way to plutocracy.

After the death of Alexander the Great, his generals disputed control over the provinces in Europe, Asia, and Africa. The empire disintegrated into decadence. The same thing happened among the lieutenants of Simón Bolívar. They dominated much of South America during the succeeding half century. Juan José Flores in Ecuador, José Antonio Páez in Venezuela, Andrés Santa Cruz in Bolivia, and Francisco Paula de Santander in Colombia governed as the heirs of the Liberator [Bolívar]. As long as the shadow of that magnificent warrior covered the destinies of South America, the caudillos triumphed, consecrated by their link to Bolívar. That reality infused a kind of monarchical principle into a political unconscious humanity. The Liberator left South America in the hands of a dynasty.

The wars were civil conflicts, the quarrels of generals ambitious for power. United during the colonial period, remaining united during the struggle for independence, vast areas that once were viceroyalties splintered into new nations, linking their fortunes to the generals. Upon the field of battle the various national consciences were roughly shaped. The generals imposed arbitrary limits upon the peoples; they were the creators of the history of the Americas; they impressed the crowds with pomp and pageantry, by military displays as brilliant and gaudy as the processions of the Roman Catholic Church, by uniforms, medals, and military order. They labeled themselves Regenerators, Restorers, Protectors.

Although tumultuous, the first period boasted of color, energy, and vio-

Source: The text is adapted freely from Francisco García Calderón, *Latin America: Its Rise and Progress* (New York: Charles Scribner's Sons, 1913), pp. 86–96.

lence. The individual acquired an extraordinary prestige, as in the time of the Tuscan Renaissance, the French Terror, or the English Revolution. The rude and bloodstained hand of the caudillo forced the amorphous masses into durable molds. Ignorant soldiers ruled; the evolution of the republics was uncertain. There was no history properly called because there was no continuity. There was a perpetual repetition caused by successive rebellions. The same men appeared with the same promises and the same methods. The political comedy repeated itself periodically: rebellion, a dictator, a program of national restoration. Anarchy and militarism universally characterized political behavior.

As in Europe, anarchy led to dictatorship, which, in turn, provoked an immediate rebellion. From spontaneous disorder we passed to formidable tutelage. The example of France was repeated on a new stage: The anarchy of democratic experimentation foretold the rise of the caudillo. The dictators, like the kings of modern states, must defeat local challenges, in the case of the Americas, the provincial generals. Men like Porfírio Díaz, Gabriel García Moreno, and Antonio Guzmán Blanco triumphed. Rebellion followed rebellion until the emergence of a tyrant who dominated the life of the nation for twenty or thirty years.

As the governments of Díaz, Guzmán Blanco, Diego Portales, and Juan Manuel de Rosas demonstrate, material progress was the work of the autocracy. The great caudillos wanted nothing to do with abstractions. Their pragmatic minds urged them to encourage commerce, industry, immigration, and agriculture. The long periods of peace they imposed promoted the appearance of significant economic forces.

In political and economic matters, the dictators professed their Americanism. They represented the new mixed races, traditions, and agriculture. They were hostile to the influences of the Roman Catholic Church, European capitalism, and foreign incursions. Their essential function, like the modern kings after feudalism, was to unite classes and/or castes into one political society. In one sense, then, these tyrants created a kind of democracy; they often depended on the support of the people, those of mixed races, the Indians, and Afro-Americans, against the oligarchies. They dominated the former colonial elites, favored the mixture of the races, and liberated the slaves.

Anarchy was spontaneous. . . . The times seemed hostile to order and to civilization. Thus José Gervasio Artigas at one time fought against the King of Spain, the Argentines, and the Portuguese. A patriot to the death, he rejected all subjugation. Martín Güemes fought against both Spaniards and Argentines.

The general ideas of the period were simple. There was faith in political constitutions; men aspired to ideological perfection. They believed in congresses but distrusted government. Constitutions separated the powers, thereby weakening the executive. The liberalism embodied in the constitutions was notable. In accordance with the ideas of Montesquieu, the constitutions usually established three branches of government in an effort to ensure political equilibrium. They recognized all the liberties, the press and assembly as well as the rights of property and economic freedoms. They accepted trial by jury, popular petition, and universal male suffrage—in short, the whole republican ideal. They also endorsed a State religion, Roman Catholicism, thus paving the way for religious strife and all the "Red and Black" revolts and conspiracies in the history of the Americas.

In some republics, elections were direct; in others, indirect, by means of electoral colleges, which selected the president and legislators. In general, the constitutions bestowed political rights with a generous hand. The judiciary was independent, the judges sometimes being elected, other times being named by congress. However, justice and law were ineffective. Usually the president could not be re-elected.

These constitutions imitated those of France and the United States; they were charters of a generous and hybrid species. In reality they created presidential regimes with impotent legislatures. The military chiefs exerted powerful pressures. The theory of the social and political contract served only as heady rhetoric for public speeches.

Motives for rebellion and civil war varied. In Ecuador men fought for the caudillos; in Colombia, for ideas; in Chile, for or against the oligarchy. The fighting involved most of the population. Rebellion was the common heritage of these nations. Warrior races, Indian and Spaniard, peopled the Americas, and their bellicose spirit explained the disorder of the republics. Castes and traditions were inimical. The psychological instability characteristic of primitive peoples subverted discipline and authority.

Two social classes, the military and the intellectuals, opposed each other since the advent of the republics. They disputed power, although sometimes the intellectuals allied with the generals. Using reasoning of a refined Byzantine nature, the "doctors" [intellectuals] justified the dictatorships as well as independence.

The generals distrusted the lawyers, who represented the intellectual traditions of the colonies: Páez hated the lawyers the same way Napoleon hated the ideologues. Vanquished by military power, the "doctors" then became the docile secretaries of the generals and caudillos; they drafted laws and constitutions; they expressed in polished prose the rude statements of their chiefs. Still, they subtly opposed the violence; they used their university knowledge against the ignorance of the despots.

Racial conflicts took place in addition to class struggles. The mixed races opposed the oligarchies. The new American race was hostile to the aristocrats of the capitals. The Indians lived isolated in the interior in conditions little changed from the colonial past. The metropolis, whether it was Buenos Aires, Lima, or Caracas, displayed a European facade increasingly alien to the masses. Along the South American coast, with its closer contact with Europe, new ideas took hold, exotic customs were introduced, while the interior of the continent remained more American, slow to accept the unrest and novelty characteristic of the capitals. Thus, a triple movement came into being: the common classes against the heirs of the colonial aristocracy; the provinces against the capitals; and the interior against the coast.

The provinces desired autonomy; the capitals, monopoly of power and national unity. The metropolitan centers were liberal; the provinces were conservative. Leaders disguised their real ambitions under a cloak of general ideas: They supported unity or federation, a military or a civilian regime, Catholicism or radicalism. In Argentina, the provinces fought the capital; in Venezuela, an emerging middle sector composed of mixed races opposed the "white" oligarchy; in Chile the liberals opposed the conservatives, the landowners; in Mexico, the federalists fought the centralists; in Ecuador the radicals opposed the conservatives; in Peru, the conflict pitted those favoring civilian rule against the military caudillos. The diversity of those quarrels revealed one common principle: Two classes were in conflict, the landowners against the landless, the descendant of the Spaniards against the people of mixed races, or the oligarchy against the generals representing a barbarous democracy.

Each republic manifested some distinctive characteristics of the universal warfare. In Argentina during the colonial period, the provinces enjoyed a partial autonomy, the remote antecedents of federalism. Unity seemed an imposition on the part of Buenos Aires, which controlled the treasury and custom houses and monopolized national credit and revenue. Chile, the long, narrow country with the mighty Andes serving as a granite wall to contain it, opted for a unitary republic. Any debates between federalism and centralism were brief. Unity was possible in Peru, the center of a highly effective viceroyalty with its well-established and powerful authority. Some aspects of the struggles remain obscure and contradictory. In Ecuador, Peru, Venezuela, and Mexico, there was enmity between the coastal and highland regions. Lima and Caracas were capitals near the coast; Mexico City and Quito were capitals in the mountains, far removed from the coast. Yet, in Peru the struggle was civil and military; in Ecuador, conservative and liberal; and in Mexico, federal and central. Why do we not find in Argentina and Bolivia the religious struggles that lasted for such a long time in Colombia? To understand fully this diversity, we must study the psychology of the different *conquistadors*—Castellan, Biscayan, Andalusian—and the different Indian groups subjugated—Quechuas, Araucanians, Chibchas, Aztecs—and the degree to which the two mixed. Further, the effects of the various geographies themselves on the racial mixtures would vary.

Confusion reigned supreme over the vast regions. The elites were not always conservative, just as the ordinary people of mixed races were not always liberal. Reactionary autocracies, like that of Portales in Chile, and liberal autocracies, like that of Guzmán Blanco in Venezuela, existed. While the federalists were usually democrats and liberals, on occasion they could be conservative and autocratic. The democrats of Peru were reactionary in matters of religion; those of Chile were radical. The civil regime was conservative in Bolivia under Mariano Baptista and in Ecuador under García Moreno, but liberal in Mexico under Benito Juárez and in Chile under Domingo Santa María and José Manuel Balmaceda. Militarism was radical under José Hilario López in Colombia but conservative under General Ramón Castilla in Peru. When political evolution followed its logical development, federalism, liberalism, and democracy formed a trilogy, while the oligarchy remained conservative and unitarian.

Rebellions with programs that opposed a caste system and favored the rights of the mixed races prepared the way for a new period in the history of the Spanish-speaking republics. But in societies dominated by a small and well-established aristocracy it was not easy to introduce democracy. Slavery continued after independence, even though liberals made notable gains both in manumission and in reforming the institution of slavery. Manumission increased rapidly after mid-century. The military class, accessible to all, replaced the old nobility. The mixing of the races accelerated. New economic interests appeared. Society became more complex. Rebellions, dictatorships, and anarchy were necessary contributors to the dissolution of the old society.

The age of generals gave way to a period of economic growth and prosperity in which wealth increased, industrialization got underway, the laboring class became more varied, and incorporation became a characteristic of commerce and even agriculture. Cooperation, organization, and solidarity, all practically unknown during the age of anarchy, characterized the new economic growth. The new economic interests sought peace and order for their expansion.

Political squabbles diminished, giving way to a new political order that seemed to adhere, at least formally, to the constitutions. Plutocracies arose and exerted their influence in politics, always against internal rebellions and external wars. Immigration increased, changing both racial composition and class structures. Economic progress took place despite the governments. The energetic individuals of the military period were followed by more anonymous, collective, and hard-working groups. The caudillo receded into the background, replaced by the captains of industry, the merchants, and the bankers. Wealth replaced courage as primary virtue by which individuals and peoples were judged. Values changed. Education, foresight, and common sense determined success in an industrial democracy. Those who succeeded in industry and commerce began to replace members of the old patrician class, and as that happened class rigidities and religious issues faded. Slowly, conflicts diminished and modernity emerged.

It is impossible to point to an exact time or event that marked the end of the military period and the beginning of the economic revival. The twilight of the caudillos has been a long one. Even the economic changes and growth can be the work of those caudillos who were also pacifiers: General José Manuel Panda in Bolivia, General Julio Roca in Argentina, Nicolás de Piérola in Peru, and José Batlle y Ordóñez of Uruguay, not to forget the greatest of them all, Porfírio Díaz of Mexico.

Economically speaking, this period of economic growth was superior to the first period of sterile rebellion. It was also superior from the political point of view because institutions have been perfected and constitutional behavior better defined. The municipalities and the legislatures have acquired a relative autonomy. To that degree, they have achieved a victory over the executive office, which was omnipotent during the military period. That period has ended and with it a certain excitement and heroic audacity. The republics in their new period of order and progress provide less drama. □

The Brazilian Constitution of 1824: Contractual, Genetic, and Patriarchal

Prince Pedro, heir to the Portuguese throne, declared Brazil's independence in 1822. He and then his son, Pedro II, ruled the Empire of Brazil until 1889. During the period of the monarchy, Brazil enjoyed an impressive degree of political order and stability, a sharp contrast to its Spanish-speaking neighbors. Further, unlike the Spanish viceroyalties, Brazil maintained its unity after independence.

Emperor Pedro I promulgated the Constitution of 1824, a contract he devised between the Crown and its subjects. It was genetic, providing for a monarchy, and patriarchal, placing nearly all power in the hands of a strong emperor, the omnipotent father, who served as the chief executive and also wielded the "Moderating Power." It also ranks as Brazil's, and one of Latin America's, longest-lived—and seemingly most successful—constitutions. That longevity and success speaks cogently to questions of legitimacy and public perception of power.

TITLE III—*Of the Powers and National Representation.*

Art. 9. The division and harmony of the Political Powers are the principal safeguard of the Rights of the Citizens and the most secure means of making effective the guarantees which the Constitution offers.

Art. 10. The Political Powers recognized by the Constitution of the Empire of Brazil are four: the Legislative Power, the Moderating Power, the Executive Power, and the Judiciary Power.

Art. 11. The representatives of the Brazilian Nation are the Emperor and the General Assembly.

Art. 12. All these Powers, in the Empire of Brazil, are delegations of the Nation.

TITLE IV—*Of the Legislative Power.*

Chapter I—*Of the Branches of the Legislative Power and Its Powers.*

Art. 13. The Legislative Power is delegated to the General Assembly with the sanction of the Emperor.

Art. 14. The General Assembly is composed of two branches: the Chamber of Deputies and the Chamber of Senators or Senate.

Chapter II—*Of the Chamber of Deputies.*

Art. 35. The Chamber of Deputies is elective and temporary.

Art. 36. It is the prerogative of the Chamber of Deputies to have the initiative on

1. Taxes.
2. Recruitment.
3. The designation of a new dynasty in event the reigning house becomes extinct.

Art. 37. Also to have initiation in the Chamber of Deputies are

1. An examination of the past administration and the reform of its abuses.
2. The discussion of proposals made by the Executive Power.

Source: E. Bradford Burns (ed.), *A Documentary History of Brazil* (New York: Knopf, 1966), pp. 212–218.

Art. 38. It is the prerogative of the same Chamber to initiate an indictment of the Ministers of State and Counselors of State.

Chapter III—*Of the Senate.*

Art. 40. The Senate is composed of members chosen for life and it will be organized by provincial elections.

Art. 41. Each Province will have as Senators half its number of Deputies; in the case that its number of Deputies be uneven, the number will be half of the lowest even number so that if a Province has eleven Deputies it will have five Senators.

Art. 42. The Province which has only one Deputy will elect one Senator also despite the aforesaid rule.

Art. 43. The Elections will be held in the same manner as for the Deputies but in triple lists so that the Emperor can select one-third of the total list.

Art. 44. Vacancies in the Senate will be filled in the same manner as for the first election in each respective province.

Art. 45. To be a Senator it is required

1. To be a Brazilian citizen and to have possession of his political rights.
2. To be forty years of age or older.
3. To be a person of knowledge, capacity, and virtues with preference given to those who have given service to the Nation.
4. To have an annual income from property, industry, commerce, or employment exceeding eight hundred thousand *réis*.

Art. 46. Princes of the Imperial House are Senators by right and will take their place in the Senate upon reaching the age of twenty-five.

TITLE V—*Of the Emperor.*

Chapter I—*Of the Moderating Power.*

Art. 98. The Moderating Power is the key to the entire political organization and it is delegated exclusively to the Emperor as the Supreme Chief of the Nation and its First Representative so that he constantly can watch over the maintenance of the independence, equilibrium, and harmony of the other Political Powers.

Art. 99. The Person of the Emperor is inviolable and sacred. He is not subject to any responsibility.

Art. 100. His titles are "Constitutional Emperor and Perpetual Defender of Brazil" and he should be addressed as Imperial Majesty.

Art 101. The Emperor exercises the Moderating Power.

1. By naming Senators in conformity with Article 43.
2. By convoking the General Assembly extraordinarily between sessions when the good of the Empire demands it.
3. By sanctioning the Decrees and Resolutions of the General Assembly so that they will have the force of law: Article 62.

4. By approving and suspending entirely the Resolutions of the Provincial Councils: Articles 86 and 87.

5. By postponing or adjourning the General Assembly and by dissolving the Chamber of Deputies in those cases in which the well-being of the State requires it; by convoking immediately another to substitute for it.

6. By naming and freely dismissing the Ministers of State.

7. By suspending the Magistrates in the cases provided in Article 154.

8. By paroling and by moderating the penalties imposed on criminals condemned by sentence.

9. By conceding amnesty in urgent cases or when counseled by humanity and the good of the State.

Chapter II—*Of the Executive Power.*

Art. 102. The Emperor is the Chief Executive Power and he exercises his office through the Ministers of State.

His principal prerogatives are:

1. To convoke the new ordinary General Assembly on the 3rd of June of the third year of the existing Legislature.

2. To name Bishops and to furnish Ecclesiastical Benefices.

3. To name Magistrates.

4. To supply the rest of the civil and political employees.

5. To name the Commandants of the Force of Land and Sea and to remove them when the service of the Nation demands it.

6. To name Ambassadors and other Diplomatic and Commercial Agents.

7. To direct Political Negotiations with Foreign Nations.

8. To make treaties of offensive and defensive Alliance, of Subsidy and Commerce, afterwards carrying them out, with the knowledge of the General Assembly when the interests and security of the State permit it. If the Treaties concluded in time of peace involve cession or exchange of Territory of the Empire or of Possessions to which the Empire has a right, they will not be ratified until they have been approved by the General Assembly.

9. To declare war and to make peace, sharing with the Assembly the communications compatible with the interests and security of the State.

10. To grant letters of naturalization in the form of Law.

11. To grant Titles, Honors, Military Orders, and Distinctions in recognition for services given to the State, the pecuniary grants depending on the approval of the Assembly when they are not designated and evaluated by Law.

12. To expedite the decrees, instructions, and regulations adequate for the proper execution of the Laws.

13. To decree the application of the funds approved by the Assembly to the various branches of public administration.

14. To concede, or to deny, sanction to the Decrees in Council and Apostolic Letters and any other Ecclesiastical Constitutions which are not contrary to the Constitution; and by preceding the approval of the Assembly they become the general will.

15. To provide all that might be necessary for the internal and external security of the State in accordance with the Constitution.

Chapter V—*Of the Ministry.*

Art. 131. There will be various Secretaries of State. The Law will designate the duties of each and their number, joining them together or separating them as best suits the situation.

Art. 132. The Ministers of State will sign all the Acts of the Executive Power without which they cannot be executed.

Chapter VI—*Of the Council of State.*

Art. 137. There will be a Council of State composed of life-term Councilors named by the Emperor.

Art. 138. Their number will not exceed ten.

Art. 140. To be a Councilor of State it is necessary to possess the same qualities as a Senator.

Art. 142. The Councilors are heard in all business of a grave nature and general measures of Public Administration, principally on the declaration of war, the arrangements for peace, negotiations with foreign nations as well as on all occasions when the Emperor proposes to exercise any of the prerogatives of the Moderating Power indicated in Article 101 with the exception of No. 6.

TITLE VI—*Of the Judiciary Power.*

Only Chapter—*Of the Judges and Tribunals of Justice.*

Art. 151. The Judiciary Power is independent and will be composed of Judges and Jurors which take part in Civil and Criminal Cases in the manner determined by the Codes.

Art. 152. The Jurors will pronounce on the facts; the judges will apply the law.

Art. 153. Judges of law are permanent which is not understood to mean that they cannot be moved from one place to another in the time and manner determined by the law. □

The Brazilian Emperor's Perception of His Own Role

Ascending the Brazilian throne in 1840, Emperor Pedro II ruled until 1889, when the military replaced the monarchy with a republic. Most judge his long rule as liberal, benevolent, and beneficial. The somewhat somber, frock-coated emperor took his duties seriously. One of the best insights into his own perception of his patriarchal role emerges from a poem he wrote in 1852. The emperor believed he ruled in accordance with the dictates of "national opinion." He took little or no note of "public opinion." He advised his daughter, Princess Isabel, of the difference between national opinion and public opinion as a way to prepare her to serve as regent during his visits abroad. That advice reveals one important way Emperor Pedro II formed his judgments.

Poem: *"If I Am Pious, Clement, Just . . ."*

IF I AM PIOUS, CLEMENT, JUST,
　　I'm only what I ought to be:
The sceptre is a weighty trust,
　　A great responsibility;
And he who rules with faithful hand,
　　With depth of thought and breadth of range,
The sacred laws should understand,
　　But must not, at his pleasure, change.

The chair of justice is the throne:
　　Who takes it bows to higher laws;
The public good, and not his own,
　　Demands his care in every cause.
Neglect of duty,—always wrong,—
　　Detestable in young or old,—
By him whose place is high and strong,
　　Is magnified a thousandfold.

When in the east the glorious sun
　　Spreads o'er the earth the light of day,
All know the course that he will run,
　　Nor wonder at his light or way:
But if perchance the light that blazed
　　Is dimm'd by shadows lying near,
The startled world looks on amazed,
　　And each one watches it with fear.

I likewise, if I always give
　　To vice and virtue their rewards,
But do my duty thus to live;
　　No one his thanks to me accords.

But should I fail to act my part,
　　Or wrongly do, or leave undone,
Surprised, the people then would start
　　With fear, as at the shadow'd sun.□

Sources: The poem by Emperor Pedro II comes from D.P. Kidder and J. C. Fletcher, *Brazil and the Brazilians* (Philadelphia: Childs & Peterson, 1857), p. 595. The advice to Princess Isabel can be found in D. Pedro II, *Conselhos à Regente* (Rio de Janeiro: Livraria São José, 1958), pp. 27–28.

Advice to My Daughter and Heir

YOUR OWN INTELLIGENT sense of duty is your best guide. However, the advice of your experienced father may help you.

The political system of Brazil is based on national opinion, which many times is not the same as what is called public opinion. It is the duty of the emperor to study constantly national opinion and to obey it. The study is difficult, and the way elections are held make it no less so. They do not necessarily reveal national opinion. In order to achieve an understanding of that, I urge you to pay close attention to the following advice: In order to understand the complexities of contemporary issues, it is absolutely indispensable that the emperor remain free of all political party prejudices. At the same time, it is wise to know what the natural and just goals of the parties are. It is necessary to listen, although with discreet reserve, to political opinion, particularly to the expressions of the most honest and intelligent men of each party. The emperor must inform himself dispassionately of everything the Brazilian press as well as members of the national and provincial legislatures have to say. While it is prudent to listen attentively, everything must be accepted cautiously in the constant search for national opinion. □

The Brazilian Monarchy and the Empowerment of Youth and a Woman

Both social and political patriarchy evoke images of domination by aged males. While that image is all too often correct, Brazil under the monarchy provided some notable exceptions. It excluded neither youth nor a woman from the exercise of supreme power. Prince Pedro was twenty-four when he declared Brazil's independence and received the crown as emperor in 1822. In 1831 he abdicated in favor of his son, who assumed the throne as Pedro II at age fourteen. During his long reign (1840–1889), Emperor Pedro II temporarily turned over the scepter three times to his daughter, Princess Isabel, to rule as regent. She was twenty-four years old on the first occasion. Princess Isabel distinguished herself as the first female to serve as chief of state in the Western Hemisphere. She promoted and signed many laws, none more important than the "Golden Law" of 1888, which ended slavery in Brazil.

Pedro I (1798–1834) ascended the throne as Emperor of Brazil in 1822. He abdicated in 1831. This painting depicts him at approximately the time of his coronation.

Pedro II (1825–1891) ruled as Emperor of Brazil from 1840 until the military deposed him in 1889, substituting a republic for the monarchy. This painting portrays the adolescent emperor.

Isabel (1846–1921). Married to the French nobleman Count d'Eu in 1864, she ruled as regent on three occasions, 1871, 1876, and 1888, each coinciding with critical events in Brazilian politics.

4

Modernity Vies with Tradition

Although independence formally liberated most of Latin America from colonial rule, the social and economic institutions continued to bear a strong resemblance to those forged during more than three centuries of colonial status. The institutional structures at mid-century augured poorly for the creation of viable nation-states.

Commentators on life in nineteenth-century Latin America often discussed the interplay of its "medieval" and "modern" characteristics. Embracing the "progress" transforming the industrialized nations of the North Atlantic as their goal, some elites hoped to eradicate the medieval in favor of the modern. To finance that transformation, they exported ever larger amounts of agrarian and mineral products. Increasingly dependent on those exports, the new nations subordinated themselves to a role as junior partners in international trade, a pattern well established during the long colonial period and strengthened during the nineteenth century. The pursuit of a Europeanized progress financed by exports often dispossessed ordinary people of their lands and cultures while providing them with limited access to new opportunities—the education a modern society required, for example—or the dignity and security their own folk communities once offered. Loss of land was the major threat to folk society and folk culture. To the degree the communal past withered, capitalism triumphed. A provocative question asks whether ordinary people enjoyed a better quality of life under the communal structures of the past or the new capitalist ones.

Latin American Society in the Mid-Nineteenth Century

The City and the Countryside: Civilization versus Barbarism

In a series of popular essays in 1845, the Argentine intellectual—and later president—Domingo Faustino Sarmiento (1811–1888) lamented that much of the population, particularly the rural folks, lived in the twelfth century. He characterized them as barbaric. Further, he reasoned that the objective of any government should be to lead the nation from that barbarity into the nineteenth century, into the civilization exemplified by Europe. That new civilization would enter Latin America through the cities. He posed the dynamic dichotomy of the struggle between the civilized city and the barbaric countryside as a major theme of nineteenth-century Latin American history.

Sarmiento selected the merchant, lawyer, and political figure Bernardino Rivadavia as the essence of progress in the formative period between 1810 and 1827. Sarmiento praised his efforts to Europeanize the emerging Argentina and contrasted him with Juan Manual de Rosas, who dominated Argentina between 1829 and 1852. With links to the countryside, the *gaucho,* and the folk, Rosas represented, at least in the judgment of Sarmiento, the very barbarism that must be eradicated so that Argentina could progress.

To the Latin American elites, Sarmiento eloquently phrased the plan to Europeanize—that is, to modernize—the newly independent American countries. To re-create Europe in the New World cost money. The elites planned to use investments, loans, and, most importantly, the income from the sale of exports to finance the changes they envisioned. They hoped that education would prepare the Indians, the Afro-Americans, and mestizos for European progress. If not, they planned to replace the American barbarians with European immigrants.

THE PEOPLE WHO inhabit these extensive districts belong to two different races, the Spanish and the native; the combinations of which form a series of imperceptible gradations. The pure Spanish race predominates in the rural districts of Cordova and San Luis, where it is common to meet young shepherdesses fair and rosy, and as beautiful as the belles of a capital could wish to be. In Santiago del Estero, the bulk of the rural population still speaks the Quichua dialect, which plainly shows its Indian origin. The country people of Corrientes use a very pretty Spanish dialect. . . . The Andalusian soldier may still be recognized in the rural districts of Buenos Ayres; and in the city foreign surnames are the most numerous. The negro race, by this time nearly extinct (except in Buenos Ayres), has left, in its zambos and mulattoes, a link which connects civilized man with the denizen of the woods. This race mostly inhabiting cities, has a tendency to become civilized, and possesses talent and the finest instincts of progress.

Source: Domingo F. Sarmiento, *Life in the Argentine Republic in the Days of the Tyrants: Or, Civilization and Barbarism* (New York: Hafner, n.d.), pp. 10–15, 54–55, 126–127, 246–247. With permission of the publisher.

With these reservations, a homogeneous whole has resulted from the fusion of the three above-named families. It is characterized by love of idleness and incapacity for industry, except when education and the exigencies of a social position succeed in spurring it out of its customary pace. To a great extent, this unfortunate result is owing to the incorporation of the native tribes, effected by the process of colonization. The American aborigines live in idleness, and show themselves incapable, even under compulsion, of hard and protracted labor. This suggested the idea of introducing negroes into America, which has produced such fatal results. But the Spanish race has not shown itself more energetic than the aborigines, when it has been left to its own instincts in the wilds of America. Pity and shame are excited by the comparison of one of the German or Scotch colonies in the southern part of Buenos Ayres and some towns of the interior of the Argentine Republic; in the former the cottages are painted, the front-yards always neatly kept and adorned with flowers and pretty shrubs; the furniture simple but complete; copper or tin utensils always bright and clean; nicely curtained beds; and the occupants of the dwelling are always industriously at work. Some such families have retired to enjoy the conveniences of city life, with great fortunes gained by their previous labors in milking their cows, and making butter and cheese. The town inhabited by natives of the country presents a picture entirely the reverse. There, dirty and ragged children live, with a menagerie of dogs; there, men lie about in utter idleness; neglect and poverty prevail everywhere; a table and some baskets are the only furniture of wretched huts remarkable for their general aspect of barbarism and carelessness. . . .

Upon the boundless expanse above described stand scattered here and there fourteen cities, each the capital of a province. The obvious method of arranging their names would be to classify them according to their geographical position. . . . But this manner of enumerating the Argentine towns has no connection with any of the social results which I have in view. A classification adapted to my purpose must originate in the ways of life pursued by the country people, for it is this which determines their character and spirit. I have stated above that the proximity of the rivers makes no difference in this respect, because the extent to which they are navigated is so trifling as to be without influence upon the people.

All the Argentine provinces, except San Juan and Mendoza, depend on the products of pastoral life; Tucuman avails itself of agriculture also, and Buenos Ayres, besides raising millions of cattle and sheep, devotes itself to the numerous and diversified occupations of civilized life.

The Argentine cities, like almost all the cities of South America, have an appearance of regularity. Their streets are laid out at right angles, and their population scattered over a wide surface, except in Cordova, which occupies a narrow and confined position, and presents all the appearance of a European city, the resemblance being increased by the multitude of towers and domes attached to its numerous and magnificent churches. All civilization, whether native, Spanish, or European, centres in the cities, where are to be found the manufactories, the shops, the schools and colleges, and other characteristics of civilized nations. Elegance of style, articles of luxury, dress-coats, and frock-coats, with other European garments, occupy their appropriate place in these towns. I mention these small matters designedly. It is sometimes the case that the only city of a pastoral province is its capital, and occasionally the land is uncultivated up to its very streets. The encircling desert besets such cities at a greater or less distance, and bears heavily upon them, and they are thus small oases of civilization surrounded by an untilled plain, hundreds of square miles in extent, the surface of which is but rarely interrupted by any settlement of consequence.

The cities of Buenos Ayres and Cordova have succeeded better than the others in establishing about them subordinate towns to serve as new foci of civilization and municipal interests; a fact which deserves notice. The inhabitants of the city wear the European dress, live in a civilized manner, and possess laws, ideas of progress, means of instruction, some municipal organization, regular forms of government, etc. Beyond the precincts of the city everything assumes a new aspect; the country people wear a different dress, which I will call South American, as it is common to all districts; their habits of life are different, their wants peculiar and limited. The people composing these two distinct forms of society do not seem to belong to the same nation. Moreover, the countryman, far from attempting to imitate the customs of the city, rejects with disdain its luxury and refinement; and it is unsafe for the costume of the city people, their coats, their cloaks, their saddles, or anything European, to show themselves in the country. Everything civilized which the city contains is blockaded there, proscribed beyond its limits; and any one who should dare to appear in the rural districts in a frock-coat, for example, or mounted on an English saddle, would bring ridicule and brutal assaults upon himself.

The whole remaining population inhabit the open country, which, whether wooded or destitute of the larger plants, is generally level, and almost everywhere occupied by pastures, in some places of such abundance and excellence, that the grass of an artificial meadow would not surpass them. Mendoza and especially San Juan are exceptions to this general absence of tilled fields, the people here depending chiefly on the products of agriculture. Everywhere else, pasturage being plenty, the means of subsistence of the inhabitants—for we cannot call it their occupation—is stock-raising. Pastoral life reminds us of the Asiatic plains, which imagination covers with Kalmuck, Cossack, or Arab tents. The primitive life of nations—a life essentially barbarous and unprogressive—the life of Abraham, which is that of the Bedouin of to-day, prevails in the Argentine plains, although modified in a peculiar manner by civilization. The Arab tribe which wanders through the wilds of Asia, is united under the rule of one of its elders or of a warrior chief; society exists, although not fixed in any determined locality. Its religious opinions, immemorial traditions, unchanging customs, and its sentiment of respect for the aged, make altogether a code of laws and a form of government which preserves morality, as it is there understood, as well as order and the association of the tribe. But progress is impossible, because there can be no progress without permanent possession of the soil, or without cities, which are the means of developing the capacity of man for the processes of industry, and which enable him to extend his acquisitions. . . .

Before 1810, two distinct, rival, and incompatible forms of society, two differing kinds of civilization existed in the Argentine Republic: one being Spanish, European, and cultivated, the other barbarous, American, and almost wholly of native growth. The revolution [1810] which occurred in the cities acted only as the cause, the impulse, which set these two distinct forms of national existence face to face, and gave occasion for a contest between them, to be ended, after lasting many years, by the absorption of one into the other.

I have pointed out the normal form of association, or want of association, of the country people, a form worse, a thousand times, than that of the nomad tribe. I have described the artificial associations formed in idleness, and the sources of fame among the gauchos—bravery, daring, violence, and opposition to regular law, to the civil law, that is, of the city. These phenomena of social organization existed in 1810, and still exist, modified in many points, slowly changing in others, and yet untouched in several more. These foci, about which were gathered the brave, ignorant, free, and unemployed peasantry, were found by thousands through the country. The revolution of 1810 carried everywhere commotion and the sound of arms. Public life, previously wanting in this Arabico-Roman society, made its appearance in all the taverns, and the revolutionary movement finally brought about provincial, warlike associations, called *montoneras,* legitimate offspring of the tavern and the field, hostile to the city and to the army of revolutionary patriots. As events succeed each other, we shall see the provincial montoneras headed by their chiefs; the final triumph, in Facundo Quiroga, of the country over the cities throughout the land; and by their subjugation in spirit, government, and civilization, the final formation of the central consolidated despotic government of the landed proprietor, Don Juan Manuel Rosas, who applied the knife of the gaucho to the culture of Buenos Ayres, and destroyed the work of centuries—of civilization, law, and liberty. . . .

Thus elevated, and hitherto flattered by fortune, Buenos Ayres set about making a constitution for itself and the Republic, just as it had undertaken to liberate itself and all South America: that is, eagerly, uncompromisingly, and without regard to obstacles. Rivadavia was the personification of this poetical, utopian spirit which prevailed. He therefore continued the work of Las Heras upon the large scale necessary for a great American State—a republic. He brought over from Europe men of learning for the press and for the professor's chair, colonies for the deserts, ships for the rivers, freedom for all creeds, credit and the national bank to encourage trade, and all the great social theories of the day for the formation of his government. In a word, he brought a second Europe, which was to be established in America, and to accomplish in ten years what elsewhere had required centuries. Nor was this project altogether chimerical; all his administrative creations still exist, except those which the barbarism of Rosas found in its way. Freedom of conscience, advocated by the chief clergy of Buenos Ayres, has not been repressed; the European population is scattered on farms throughout the country, and takes arms of its own accord to resist the only obstacle in the way of the wealth offered by the soil. The rivers only need to be freed from governmental restrictions to become navigable, and the national bank, then firmly established, has saved the people from the poverty to which the tyrant would have brought them. And, above all, however fanciful and impracticable that great system of government may have been, it was at least easy and endurable for the people; and, notwithstanding the assertions of misinformed men, Rivadavia never shed a drop of blood, nor destroyed the property of any one; but voluntarily descended from the Presidency to poverty and exile. Rosas, by whom he was so calumniated, might easily have been drowned in the blood of his own victims; and the forty millions of dollars from the national treasury, with the fifty millions from private fortunes which were consumed in ten years of the long war provoked by his brutalities, would have been employed by the "*fool— the dreamer*—Rivadavia," in building canals, cities, and useful public buildings. Then let this man, who died for his country, have the glory of representing the highest aspirations of European civilization, and leave to his adversaries that of displaying South American barbarism in its most odious light. For Rosas and Rivadavia are the two extremes of the Argentine Republic, connecting it with savages through the pampas, and with Europe through the River La Plata. . . .

Ah! when will an impartial history of the Argentine Republic be written? And when will its people be able, without fear of a tyrant, to read the terrible drama of the revolution,—the well-intentioned and brilliant, but chimerical government of Rivadavia; the power and brutal deeds of Facundo Quiroga; and the administration of Rosas, the great tyrant of the nineteenth century, who unconsciously revived the spirit of the Middle Ages, and the doctrine of equality armed with the knife of Danton and Robespierre. . . . If we lack an intelligent population, let the people of Europe once feel that there is permanent peace and freedom in our country, and multitudes of emigrants would find their way to a land where success is sure. No, we are not lowest among Americans. Something is to result from this chaos; either something surpassing the government of the United States of North America, or something a thousand times worse than that of Russia,—the Dark Ages returned, or political institutions superior to any yet known.☐

Social Life in Brazil in the Middle of the Nineteenth Century

The twentieth-century Brazilian social historian Gilberto Freyre (1900–1987) looked back nostalgically at the mid-nineteenth century. He viewed his compatriots through the eyes of both the sugar plantation and urban elites, and he has been widely criticized for depicting Brazilian slavery benignly. Brazil may have been languishing in the "Middle Ages," but Freyre was unable to condemn it with any of the fervor of Sarmiento. In fact, he seemed to relish the distinctive flavor of Brazil before it modernized. He found around the "big house"—rural or urban—the nucleus of a distinctly Brazilian civilization or, as he frequently phrased it, "the new world in the tropics." A patriarchal voice echoes throughout this selection.

I N THEIR MATERIAL environment and, to a certain extent, in their social life, the majority of Brazilians of the fifties were in the Middle Ages: the élite only was living in the eighteenth century. Only a few men, such as the emperor him-

Source: Gilberto Freyre, "Social Life in Brazil in the Middle of the Nineteenth Century," *Hispanic American Historical Review,* 5 (1922), pp. 599–622.

self, and a few women, such as Nisia Floresta, were conscious of the Europe of John Stuart Mill, hoop-skirts, Sir Charles Lyell, George Sand, four-wheeled English carriages, and Pius IX. Politically the English type of government was the model after which a sensible, and even sophisticated, oligarchy, in whose power the stern emperor often intruded like a big moral policeman, governed the country. Among some of those oligarchs such subtleties and nuances of political theory as "what is the nature and what are the limits of the moderating power in a parliamentary monarchy?" were often discussed. But more practical subjects occupied their attention: the better administration of civil justice, the building of railways, the relations with the boisterous republics to the south, the slave trade. They were studious and took their responsibilities seriously. The imperial senate was, during the fifties and early sixties, an assembly of brilliant minds. . . .

In an examination of the economic structure of Brazilian society in the middle of the nineteenth century we find on one side a class of landowners and slaveholders; on the other, the mass of slaves, and between the two a few "petits bourgeois" and small farmers, not counting the bureaucracy and leaving out the mercantile interests—the bulk of which was foreign. A sort of medieval landlordism prevailed. Land was owned by coffee planters in the south, cattle-proprietors in the inland provinces and Rio Grande do Sul, by *senhores de engenho* (sugar planters) in the Northeast, especially in Pernambuco. Along the coast and in scattered points of the interior were extensive monastic estates. The class of small farmers were the "*roceiros,*" not a few of whom were colored freedmen. Most of the *petit bourgeoisie* was composed of *marinheiros,* or newly arrived Portuguese. Some of these were able to rise, by their perseverance, from being keepers of kiosks or small grocershops, and *mascates,* or peddlers, to the comfortable merchant class—the fathers of future statesmen, diplomats, and judges. The liberalism of the empire, so eager to recognize individual merit, was favorable to newcomers.

By the middle of the nineteenth century the population of Brazil was, roughly speaking, seven millions. . . . Of these he [F. Nunes de Souza] classed 2,120,000 as whites: 1,100,000 as free colored, 3,120,000 as negro slaves, 180,000 as free native African, and 800,000 as Indians. Miscegenation was going on freely. As early as 1818 or 1819 the French naturalist Auguste de Saint-Hilaire found such a mixture of races in São Paulo that he described it as an "étrange bigarrure d'où resultent des complications également embarrassantes pour l'administration et dangereuses pour la morale publique" [strange mixture from which arises complications equally embarrassing for the administration and dangerous for public morale]. Alfred R. Wallace found in Para "a most varied and interesting mixture of races."

"There is" he writes, "the fresh-colored Englishman, who seems to thrive as well here as in the cooler climates of his country, the sallow American, the swarthy Portuguese, the more corpulent Brazilian, the merry Negro and the apathetic but finely formed Indian; and between these a hundred shades and mixtures which it requires an experienced eye to detect." The American, C. S. Stewart, U.S.N., who visited Brazil in the early fifties, was surprised at "the fearfully mongrel aspect of the population. . . ."

It was in the fifties that the first railways were built in Brazil but only in the seventies did they become a serious factor in the economic and social life of the country. . . . Steam navigation made notable progress in Brazil during the fifties. It was followed by improvements in the towns it touched. Para, for instance, gained much from the line of regular steamers on the Amazon, inaugurated in 1854. Such luxuries as camphene lights and macadam generally followed steam-navigation. Hence the progress noted by foreign observers in coast and riverside towns. The others were hardly affected by any touch of progress until railways penetrated the country. They remained truly medieval—no public lighting, no street cleaning, no macadam. And medieval they were in their customs and in their relations to the great landowners around whose estates the towns and villages were scattered.

The power of the great planters was indeed feudalistic, their patriarchalism being hardly restricted by civil laws. Fletcher, who traveled through the interior of Brazil, wrote: "The proprietor of a sugar or cattle estate is, practically, an absolute lord." And he adds: "The community that lives in the shadow of so great a man is his feudal retinue: and, by the conspiracy of a few such men, who are thus able to bring scores of lieges and partisans into the field, the quiet of the province was formerly more than disturbed by revolts which gave the government much trouble." Oliveira Lima says that those communities living in the shadow of the great planters were very heterogeneous: he compares them to the army of lieges that the Portuguese nobles of the eighteenth century kept in their states: *bravi* or rascals, bull fighters, friars, guitarrists, etc. The large Brazilian estate was a self-sustaining unit—economically and socially—depending little on the world outside its large wood gates. It had its cane-fields or its coffee-plantations, and plantations of mandioc, black beans, and other produce, for its own consumption. Its population included, besides the owner and his family, *feitores,* or overseers, *vaqueiros,* or shepherds, sometimes a chaplain and a tutor, carpenters, smiths, masons, and a multitude of slaves. Fletcher visited a coffee estate in Minas Geraes which contained an area of sixty-four square miles. Besides the rows of coffee trees he noticed large tracts of mandioc, cotton and sugar, an abundance of cattle, and one hundred and fifty hives with bees. . . .

The work people of the plantations were well-fed, and attended to by their master and mistress as a "large family of children." They had three meals a day and a little rum (*caxaca*) in the morning. Their breakfast consisted of farina or *pirão,* with fruits and rum; at midday they were given a very substantial meal of meat or fish; in the evening, black beans, rice, and vegetables. On holidays it was customary on certain estates to have an ox killed for the slaves and a quantity of rum was given to make them merry. Then they would dance the sensuous measures of the *batuque* or other African dances or sing or play the *marimba.*

As a rule the slaves were not overworked in the households either in the plantations or in the city. It is true that much was being said in the fifties, of cruel treatment of slaves in Brazil, by the British anti-slavery propaganda. Later on the British dark account of conditions was to be repeated in Brazil by Brazilian anti-slavery orators such as the young Nabuco and Sr. Ruy Barbosa—men inflamed by the bourgeois idealism of Wilberforce as well as by a very human desire for personal glory—and they did it in so emphatic a language that the average Brazilian believes today that slavery was really cruel in his country. The powerful fancy won over reality. For, as a matter of fact, slavery in Brazil was anything but cruel. The Brazilian slave lived the life of a cherub if we contrast his lot with that of the English and other European factory-workers in the middle of the last century. Alfred R. Wallace—an abolitionist—found the slaves in a sugar plantation he visited in North Brazil "as happy as children. . . ." But it is an English clergyman—the Reverend Hamlet Clark, M.A., who strikes the most radical note: "Nay indeed, we need not go far to find in free England the absolute counterpart of slavery: Manighew's London Labour, and London Poor, Dicken's Oliver Twist, Hood's Song of the Shirt and many other revelations tell of a grinding, flinty-hearted despotism that Brazilian slaveowners never can approach." As Professor Hayes points out, in England, "audiences wept at hearing how cruel masters licked their cowering slaves in Jamaica: but in their own England little Englishmen and Englishwomen ten years old were being whipped to their work," sometimes "in the factories of some of the anti-slavery orators."

At sunset the whistle of the sugar-mill closed the day's work on the Brazilian plantation. The workpeople came then for their last meal, after which they went to bed. But first they came to ask their master's and mistress' blessing: "Benção, nhonho! Benção Nhanha!" holding out their right hand. Then the master and the mistress would say: "Deus te abençoe" (God bless you), making at the same time the sign of the cross.

In a typical Brazilian city-home of the higher class—say, the home of a custom-house officer—slaves numbered on the average fifteen or twenty. Since slaves were plentiful, certain necessities, and even luxuries, were produced at home, under the careful oversight of the mistress; cloth was cut and made into dresses, towels and undergarments; wine was distilled; lace and crivo (a sort of embroidery) were manufactured. Besides this the housewife superintended the cooking, the preserving, the baking of cakes, the care of the sick; taught her children and their black playmates the Lord's Prayer, the Apostles' Creed, and the Ave Maria. . . .

Slaves were plentiful. The staff of a large city-house included cooks, those trained to serve in the dining room, wet-nurses, water carriers, footmen, chambermaids—the latter sleeping in their mistresses' rooms and assisting them in the minutest details of their toilette, such as picking lice, for instance. Sometimes there were too many slaves. A lady told Doctor Fletcher that she "had nine lazy servants at home for whom there was no employment" and another one that she could not find enough work to keep her slaves out of idleness and mischief. It is easy to imagine how some housewives became pampered idlers, spending their days languidly in gossiping, or at the balcony, or reading some new novel of Macedo or Alencar. . . .

It is true that the Brazilian lady of the fifties did not go out for her shopping. She was a house prisoner. Moorish prejudices kept her from those pretty shops of fancy goods, bonnets, jewelry, *bijouterie,* which travelers admired so much in Rio de Janeiro, the Italian naval officer Eugenio Rodriguez describing them as "elegantissimi magazini." But at home she did not stay in her hammock.

In a typical home works of all kinds went on during the day. Linen, silk, milli-nery, fancy goods, were bought from samples and pattern-books, after much running of negro boys from shop to the house: or, in many cases, from the ped-dler who came once or twice a week, making a noise with his yardstick. It was not necessary to go to the market to buy vegetables, fruit, or eggs since vendors of these rural products, as well as of milk, meat, and fish, came to the home. There were itinerant coppersmiths who announced themselves by hitting some old stewpan with a hammer. Even novels were sold at the door. Paulo Barreto tells that Alencar and Macedo—"the best sellers" of the period—had negroes go from house to house, selling their novels in baskets. Therefore, the fact that the Brazilian woman did not go to the shops does not mean that she was too lazy to do her own shopping. She did it. And after the shopping was done in the morning it was she who superintended the various kinds of work going on in the house-hold. . . . Fletcher who, though a Protestant clergyman, enjoyed the intimacy of many a home in Brazil, thought that the Brazilian housewife answered to the description of the "good woman" in the last chapter of Proverbs: "she looketh well to the ways of her household and eateth not the bread of idleness." Carlos de Laet—the last brilliant mind of a departed order—tells us that "to accuse a lady of not knowing how to manage her household was then the most unpleasant offence to her." Oliveira Lima characterizes the Brazilian housewife of this pe-riod as possessing "ability to manage" (*capacidade administrativa*), without which it was impossible to keep such large households going. Others might be quoted to show that in this matter the weighing of evidences reveals an active, rather than an idle woman, as the typical Brazilian housewife in slavery days.

The double standard of morality prevailed in the fifties: the lily-like woman was idolized while incontinence in the man was slightly regarded. It is true that the Emperor Dom Pedro II. made the standards of sexual morality stricter for those who were around him or who aspired to political eminence. He was a sort of Queen Victoria in breeches—only more powerful—and watched the statesmen like a moral detective. It is commonplace that he refused to appoint men to emi-nent positions on account of irregularities in their private life—a tradition which the Republican leaders found too foolish to maintain. But the emperor's influ-ence was only felt in the high spheres of officialdom. In the large country estates irregularities went on freely, the colored girls constituting a disguised harem where either the master or his sons satisfied their exotic sexual tastes. . . .

In his attitude towards his wife the Brazilian of the fifties was a true patri-arch of the Roman type. She was given authority in the household, but not out-side. Outside she was to be, legally and socially, the shadow of her husband. "A promenade below, with the chance of a flirtation, is denied her," the American C. S. Stewart remarks in his book. Pointing out the virtues of the Brazilian ma-tron in the *ancient régime,* of which he is the most eminent survivor, the Count Carlos de Laet says that "she knew how to obey her husband." Monsieur Expilly, a French feminist who visited Brazil in the fifties, was indignant at what he calls "le despotisme paternel" and "la politique conjugale. . . ."

While the woman spent most of her time indoors, the man—the city man—

spent most of his, out—in the street, in the plaza, at the door of some French hotel or in his office or warehouse. The condition was much like that in ancient Greece where people thought, with the wise old Xenophon, that "it is not so good for a woman to be out-of-doors as in, and it is more dishonourable for a man to stay in than to attend to his affairs outside." Brazilian men, like the Greeks, enjoyed the easy fellowship of the street and the plaza—and in the street and the plaza they discussed politics, Donizetti, the Aberdeen Bill, and transacted business. We are told by Sampaio Ferraz, in his excellent work "O Molhe de Olinda," that in Pernambuco, during the last half of the nineteenth century, the most important business was transacted outdoors, under the trees of Lingoeta. Lithogravures of the period, which I examined in Oliveira Lima's collection, show the streets—Rua Direita and Largo da Alfandega in Rio, Lingoeta in Pernambuco, and so on—full of groups of men, talking, smoking, taking snuff, while coffee or sugar carriers run with their cargoes, their half-naked bodies shining with oily sweat. The sentiment of home was not strong among the Brazilian men when the patriarchal family was in its full vigor. Nor did they have mundane clubs—unless if we accept as such the Masonic lodges. The street was their club.

This may serve as an explanation of the fact that the city Brazilians of the fifties did not seem to have attractive homes. Twenty years before a French traveler, Louis De Freycinet, had observed that the Brazilians spent most of their time sleeping, or outdoors, or, sometimes, receiving their friends: therefore they only needed—the Frenchman thought—a reception room and the bedrooms. . . .

At eight or nine the girl was sent to a religious boarding school and kept there until she was thirteen or fourteen. There her training, begun at home, was continued. She was trained in that fine art—the art of being a woman. Music, dancing, embroidery, prayers, French, and sometimes English, a thin layer of literature—such were the elements of a girl's education in the boarding school. She came back a very romantic, and sometimes bewitching, little creature, reading Sue, Dumas, and George Sand, besides the gossiping *pacotilhas* such as *A Marmota* and Alencar's saccharine, but often erotic, *folhetins*. And how she could pray! And how she could dance! The dances of the period were the quadrille, the lanciers, and the polka; to dance them well, to be light as a feather and tiny as a piece of lace, was the highest ideal of a girl—I was told by a lady who took dancing lessons from the same teacher as Princess Isabel.

Ladies bloomed early. The years of giddy childhood were short. At fourteen or fifteen the girl dressed like a lady. Docility, and even timidity, was considered a grace. The girl was trained to be timid or, at least, to look timid before people—as timid as a little boy before the circus elephant. The Brazilian girl of the fifties was everything that the so-called "very modern" girl is not. "Perhaps they were too timid"—Carlos de Laet writes of the girls of that period—"but they were adorable in the timidity." Those very timid girls were playful and talkative when given a chance. Max Radiquet tells of the custom of the Brazilian society girls going to the imperial chapel in Rio de Janeiro, where an excellent orchestra assisted by a choir of Italian soprani played every Friday evening. There "pendant toute la durée de ce concert religieux les femmes accroupées sur leur caire de tapisserie prenaient sans scruple des sorbets et des glaces avec les jeunes gens qui venaient converser avec elles dans le lieu saint.'' When such merry rendezvous, in the shadow of the church, were not possible—and the custom was discontinued just as dances in the churches were discontinued—love-making had to be even more platonic. There was, for instance, love-making by means of a fan—that is, girls could make their fans speak a particular language of love which all lovers were supposed to understand. "It all depended on how the fan was held," an old lady explained to me while her tapering, white fingers handled a delicate fan in a thousand and one ways.

But as a rule marriage did not result from romantic lovemaking. The man whom the girl married in her early teens was seldom her own choice. He was her parents', or her father's, choice. An English traveler describes how betrothals were made: "Some day the father walks into the drawing room, accompanied by a strange gentleman, elderly or otherwise. 'Minha Filha,' he remarks, 'this is your future husband.'" Sometimes the "future husband" was a pleasant surprise—a pale youth of twenty-three or twenty-five, a ruby or an emerald sparkling from his forefinger, his moustaches perfumed, his hair smooth, oily . . . a hero who had escaped from some bright German oleogravure or from the pages of a novel. And romantic love developed between the contracting parties. But other times the "future husband" was some fat, solid, newly-rich Portuguese, middle-aged, his neck short and his hands coarse. Perhaps a very fine person—inside; but what a death-blow for a sentimental girl of the fifties. And yet she often accepted him—the potbellied one—such a marriage being nothing more than a business partnership. Unfortunate marriages of the latter type became a favorite theme with Brazilian writers of fiction in the sixties and seventies, Guimaraes' *Historia de Uma Moça Rica* being typical of that literature. But one should be discriminating in the matter: some marriages arranged by the girl's parents were as happy as marriages ordinarily are.

Early marriages meant early procreation. At fifteen a girl was generally a mother. Sometimes she was a mother at fourteen and even thirteen. The Reverend Walter Colton wrote in his diary: "A Brazilian lady was pointed out to me to-day who is but twelve years of age, and who has two children, who were frolicking around her steps. . . ." And he adds ". . . ladies here marry extremely young. They have hardly done with their fictitious babies, when they have the smiles and tears of real ones." As a consequence, girls faded early, having tasted in a hurry the joy of careless youth.

The boy, too, was born middle-aged. Dom Pedro's prematurity may be taken as typical. He was made an emperor at fifteen, and he was then very thoughtful and serious; at twenty he was an old man. Youth flew from him in a gallop. Brazilian education favored then, more than in a later day, the prematurity of the boy. Very early he was sent to the *collegio*, where he lived and boarded. Though his home might be a street or two off, very seldom—usually once a month—was he allowed to go there. He often got from home boxes of cakes and bon-bons, but no such things as toys. Toys were for little boys; he was nine or ten, nearly a man. As a rule he studied hard his Latin grammar, his rhetoric, his French classics, his sacred history, his geography. When that big occasion—the final examinations—came, he shone, answering well all that Padre So-and-So asked about Horace, Noah, Rebecca, rules of punctuation, the verb *amare;* and all that some other teacher asked about Racine, Vesuvius, and what not.

At fifteen or sixteen the boy finished his studies in the *collegio*. It was time to go to the professional school. Here, as in the girls' betrothal, it was the father's or family's choice that generally prevailed. The tendency was to scatter the boys in different schools, so that the family would be represented in different professions. One was picked to go to Pernambuco or São Paulo to study law or diplomacy; another to enter the medical school; a third to be a cadet in the military school; a fourth to go to the seminary. Among the most pious families it was considered a social, as well as a moral, failure not have a son studying for the priesthood. Sometimes the youngest son, though of no churchly turn of mind, was the scapegoat. The family simply had to have a *padre*. As to the stupid son, who could not make good anywhere, the sensible parents sent him to business, which was looked down upon by gentlemen.

The flower of the family was picked for the law school—the law school being the training-ground, not for magistracy only, but for the parliament and the cabinet also, and for diplomacy. There were two law schools—that of Olinda, in Pernambuco, and that of São Paulo. Writing from São Paulo in 1855 Doctor Kidder said of its law school: "It is here and at the Pernambuco Law School (which contains three hundred students in the regular course) that the statesmen of Brazil receive that education which so much better fits them for the Imperial Parliament and the various legislative assemblies of their land than any preparatories that exist in the Spanish-American countries."

The "regular course," to which Doctor Kidder refers, came after a sort of pre-law course which included Latin, geometry, rational and moral philosophy, and other subjects. The "regular course" extended over a period of five years, the following subjects being studied: philosophy of law, public law, analysis of the imperial constitution, Roman law, diplomacy, ecclesiastical law, civil law, mercantile and maritime law, political economy, and theory and practice of general law. . . .

It is amazing how the Brazilians of the fifties managed to live in such miserable conditions of dirt and bad smell as they did. There was practically no public hygiene to speak of. It is in a semi-official outline of the history of public health services in Brazil that the following description appears, of Rio de Janeiro in the middle of the nineteenth century: "A filthy city, in which, it may be said, there was no air, no light, no sewers, no street cleaning; a city built upon bogs where mosquitoes freely multiplied." Mme. Ida Pfeiffer saw, as she walked through the streets of Rio, carcasses of dogs, cats, and even a mule, rotting. She also refers to "le manque complet d'égouts"—the complete lack of sewers. This condition was common to the other cities of the empire—even to Pernambuco, where the Dutch had left a touch of their cleanliness. Charles Darwin, who was there in the thirties, writes of its filthy streets and offensive smells, comparing it to oriental towns. In all the towns of the empire the removal of garbage, ashes, decaying matter, and vegetables, and human excrements was made in the crudest and also the most picturesque way. Those wastes were put in pipes or barrels, nicknamed *tigres,* and carried on the heads of slaves who dumped them into rivers, the sea-shore, and alleys. Sometimes as a witness referred to a later-day Brazilian hygien-ist, "the bottom of the barrel would cast off, the contents soiling both the carrier and the streets." The decaying material was left near the bridges or on the sea-shores, flocks of carrion crows being depended upon to do the work of scaveng-ers. The removal of the garbage and human waste was generally made after the church bells rang "ten o'clock." In Pernambuco the *tigres* were emptied from the bridges into the rivers Capibaribe and Beberibe: in Rio they were taken on the heads of slaves to be emptied "into certain parts of the bay every night, so that walking in the streets after 10 o'clock is neither safe nor pleasant." This quotation is from Ewbanks who adds: "In this matter Rio is what Lisbon is and what Edinburg used to be."

As there were no sewers to carry off the drainage there was no plumbing in the houses. The system of water supply was that of the *chafariz,* or public fountain. There was a constant dashing to and fro of big negro water carriers, taking water for the houses, sometimes to the third or fourth floor, where the kitchen was located. Those water carriers worked harder, perhaps, than any other class of slaves; for Brazilians made free use of water, thus making up in personal cleanliness what was lacking so painfully in public hygiene. Next to his hot coffee and his snuff, a Brazilian loved a hot bath best of all. Everywhere—in cities and in the great as well as the humble houses of the interior—water, soap, and a large clean towel welcomed a guest. On examining statistics of the period, I found that more than one third of the seventy-two factories then existing in the empire were soap factories.

Though there was no plumbing in the houses and bathtubs were unknown, rich and poor took a sheer joy in bathing. Poor people bathed in rivers, under the public eye. Landing in Para, the American, John Esaias Warren, was attracted to the freedom with which people bathed and swam in the river. "The first spectacle which arrested our attention," he writes, "was that of a number of persons of both sexes and all ages, bathing indiscriminately together in the waters of the river, in a state of entire nudity." And his comment is: "The natives of Para are very cleanly and indulge in daily ablutions; nor do they confine their baths to the dusky hours of the evening but may be seen swimming about the public wharfs at all hours of the day." While the well-to-do in the cities used "gamellas" or large wooden bowls for their ablutions, those in country states—gentlemen and ladies alike—went to the nearest stream where they could also enjoy a good swim. The suburban *chacaras* in Pernambuco, along the Capibaribe river, had crude bathhouses made of coconut palms. There the ladies undressed and then dipt into the water in free, white, nakedness, like happy mermaids.

It was customary to wash one's hands before and after a meal, the slaves bringing bowls with beautifully embroidered towels. Doctor Fletcher noticed this in Rio as well as in the interior of Minas, where he traveled in an oxcart. Not many years before Saint-Hilaire had been delighted at the apostolic simplicity with which the small farmers in Minas Geraes came themselves with a basin and a towel to wash their guest's feet before he went to bed. Children had their feet washed by their mothers or negro nurses before going to bed. On this occasion their feet were also examined, so that *bichos de pe* might be extracted with a pin, if found. . . . □

The Export Economy

A Sugar Plantation in Cuba

The first viable agrarian export from the Western Hemisphere to Europe, sugar shipments began in the early sixteenth century and continue five centuries later. Traditionally the Caribbean and Brazil have been the primary exporters, but nearly every region has grown some sugar at some time. Sugar production requires technology and impressive financial investment. To succeed over the centuries, it acquired the characteristics of a capitalist enterprise, shedding many of the neo-feudal traits observed in other plantation and estate enterprises.

In 1859, Richard Henry Dana, Jr., a U.S. citizen, visited Cuba and wrote this perceptive account of a successful sugar plantation on an island whose history has been and remains closely intertwined with its export.

SUGAR-MAKING BRINGS with it steam, fire, smoke, and a drive of labor, and admits of and requires the application of science. Managed with skill and energy, it is extremely productive. Indifferently managed, it may be a loss. The sugar estate is not valuable, like the coffee estate, for what the land will produce, aided by ordinary and quiet manual labor only. Its value is in the skill, and the character of the labor. The land is there, and the Negroes are there; but the result is loss or gain, according to the amount of labor that can be obtained, and the skill with which the manual labor and the mechanical powers are applied. It is said that at the present time, in the present state of the market, a well-managed sugar estate yields from fifteen to twenty-five per cent on the investment. This is true, I am inclined to think, if by the investment be meant only the land, the machinery, and the slaves. But the land is not a large element in the investment. The machinery is costly, yet its value depends on the science applied to its construction and operation. The chief item in the investment is the slave labor. . . .

The sugar plantation is no grove, or garden, or orchard. It is not the home of the pride and affections of the planter's family. It is not a coveted, indeed, hardly a desirable residence. Such families as would like to remain on these plantations are driven off for want of neighboring society. Thus the estates, largely abandoned by the families of the planters, suffer the evils of absenteeism, while the owners live in the suburbs of Havana and Matanzas, and in the Fifth Avenue of New York. The slave system loses its patriarchal character. The master is not the head of a great family, its judge, its governor, its physician, its priest and its father, as the fond dream of the advocates of slavery, and sometimes, doubtless, the reality, made him. Middlemen, in the shape of administradores, stand be-

Source: Richard Henry Dana, Jr., *To Cuba and Back* (Carbondale: Southern Illinois University Press, 1966), pp. 54–65. With permission of the publisher.

tween the owner and the slaves. The slave is little else than an item of labor raised or bought. The sympathies of common home, common childhood, long and intimate relations and many kinds offices, common attachments to house, to land, to dogs, to cattle, to trees, to birds—the knowledge of births, sicknesses, and deaths, and the duties and sympathies of a common religion—all those things that may ameliorate the legal relations of the master and slave, and often give to the face of servitude itself precarious but interesting features of beauty and strength—these they must not look to have. This change has had some effect already, and will produce much more, on the social system of Cuba.

There are still plantations on which the families of the wealthy and educated planters reside. And in some cases the administrador is a younger member or a relative of the family, holding the same social position; and the permanent administrador will have his family with him. Yet, it is enough to say that the same causes which render the ingenio no longer a desirable residence for the owner make it probable that the administrador will be either a dependent or an adventurer; a person from whom the owner will expect a great deal, and the slaves but little, and from whom none will get all they expect, and perhaps none all they are entitled to.

In the afternoon we went to the sugar-house, and I was initiated into the mysteries of the work. There are four agents: steam, fire, cane juice, and Negroes. The results are sugar and molasses. At this ingenio, they make only the Muscovado, or brown sugar. The processes are easily described, but it is difficult to give an idea of the scene. It is one of condensed and determined labor.

To begin at the beginning, the cane is cut from the fields by companies of men and women, working together, who use an instrument called a machete, which is something between a sword and a cleaver. Two blows with this slash off the long leaves, and a third blow cuts off the stalk, near to the ground. At this work, the laborers move like reapers, in even lines, at stated distances. . . .

Ox-carts pass over the field, and are loaded with the cane, which they carry to the mill. . . . At the mill, the cane is tipped from the carts into large piles, by the side of the platform. From these piles, it is placed carefully, by hand, lengthwise, in a long trough. This trough is made of slats, and moved by the power of the endless chain, connected with the engine. In this trough, it is carried between heavy, horizontal, cylindrical rollers, where it is crushed, its juice falling into receivers below, and the crushed cane passing off and falling into a pile on the other side. . . .

Thus, on one side of the rollers is the ceaseless current of fresh, full, juicy cane-stalks, just cut from the open field; and on the other side, is the crushed, mangled, juiceless mass, drifting out at the draught, and fit only to be cast into the oven and burned. . . .

From the rollers, the juice falls below into a large receiver, from which it flows into great, open vats, called defecators. These defecators are heated by the exhaust steam of the engine, led through them in pipes. All the steam condensed forms water, which is returned warm into the boiler of the engine. In the defecators, as their name denotes, the scum of the juice is purged off, so far as heat alone will do it. From the last defecator, the juice is passed through a trough into the first caldron. Of the caldrons, there is a series, or, as they call it, a train, through all which the juice must go. Each caldron is a large, deep, copper vat, heated very hot, in which the juice seethes and boils. At each, stands a strong Negro, with long, heavy skimmer in hand, stirring the juice and skimming off the surface. This scum is collected and given to the hogs, or thrown upon the muck heap, and is said to be very fructifying. The juice is ladled from one caldron to the next, as fast as the office of each is finished. From the last caldron, where its complete crystallization is effected, it is transferred to coolers, which are large, shallow pans. When fully cooled, it looks like brown sugar and molasses mixed. It is then shovelled from the coolers into hogsheads. These hogsheads have holes bored in their bottoms; and, to facilitate the drainage, strips of cane are placed in the hogshead, with their ends in these holes, and the hogshead is filled. The hogsheads are set on open frames, under which are copper receivers, on an inclined plane, to catch and carry off the drippings from the hogsheads. These drippings are the molasses, which is collected and put into tight casks.

I believe I have given the entire process. When it is remembered that all this, in every stage, is going on at once, within the limits of the mill, it may well be supposed to present a busy scene. The smell of juice and of sugar-vapor, in all its stages, is intense. . . .

On many plantations—on most, I suspect, from all I can learn—the Negroes, during the sugar season, are allowed but four hours sleep in the twenty-four, with one for dinner, and a half hour for breakfast, the night being divided into three watches, of four hours each, the laborers taking their turns. On this plantation, the laborers are in two watches, and divide the night equally between them, which gives them six hours for sleep. In the day, they have half an hour for breakfast and one hour for dinner. Here, too, the very young and the very old are excused from the sugar-house, and the nursing mothers have lighter duties and frequent intervals of rest. The women worked at cutting the cane, feeding the mill, carrying the bagazo in baskets, spreading and drying it, and filling the wagons; but not in the sugarhouse itself, or at the furnace doors. I saw that no boys or girls were in the mill—none but full-grown persons. The very small children do absolutely nothing all day, and the older children tend the cattle and run errands. And the engineer tells me that in the long run this liberal system of treatment, as to hours and duties, yields a better return than a more stringent rule.

He thinks the crop this year, which has been a favorable one, will yield, in well-managed plantations a net interest of from fifteen to twenty-five per cent on the investment; making no allowance, of course, for the time and skill of the master. This will be a clear return to planters like Mr. Chartrand, who do not eat up their profits by interest on advances, and have no mortgages, and require no advances from the merchants.

But the risks of the investment are great. The canefields are liable to fires, and these spread with great rapidity, and are difficult to extinguish. Last year Mr. Chartrand lost $7,000 in a few hours by fire. In the cholera season he lost $12,000 in a few days by deaths among the Negroes.

According to the usual mode of calculation, I suppose the value of the investment of Mr. Chartrand to be between $125,000 and $150,000. On well-managed estates of this size, the expenses should not exceed $10,000. The gross receipts, in sugar and molasses, at a fair rate of the markets, cannot average less than between $35,000 and $40,000. This should leave a profit of between eighteen and twenty-two per cent. Still, the worth of an estimate depends on the principle on which the capital is appraised. The number of acres laid down to cane, on this plantation, is about three hundred. The whole number of Negroes is one hundred, and of these not more than half, at any time, are capable of efficient labor; and there are twenty-two children below the age of five years, out of a total of one hundred Negroes.

Beside the engineer, some large plantations have one or more white assistants; but here an intelligent Negro has been taught enough to take charge of the engine when the engineer is off duty. This is the highest post a Negro can reach in the mill, and this Negro was mightily pleased when I addressed him as maquinista. There are, also, two or three white men employed, during the season, as sugar masters. Their post is beside the caldrons and defecators, where they are to watch the work in all its stages, regulate the heat and the time for each removal, and oversee the men. These, with the engineer, make the force of white men who are employed for the season.

The regular and permanent officers of a plantation are the mayoral and mayordomo. The mayoral is, under the master or his administrador, the chief mate or first lieutenant of the ship. He has the general oversight of the Negroes, at their work or in their houses, and has the duty of exacting labor and enforcing discipline. Much depends on his character, as to the comfort of master and slaves. . . .

With all the corps of hired white labor, the master must still be the real power, and on his character the comfort and success of the plantation depend. If he has skill as a chemist, a geologist, or a machinist, it is not lost; but, except as to the engineer, who may usually be relied upon, the master must be capable of overseeing the whole economy of the plantation, or all will go wrong. His chief duty is to oversee the overseers, to watch his officers, the mayoral, the mayordomo, the boyero, and the sugar masters. These are mere hirelings, and of a low sort, such as a slave system reduces them to; and if they are lazy, the work slackens; and if they are ill-natured, somebody suffers. The mere personal presence of the master operates as a stimulus to the work. This afternoon young Mr. Chartrand and I took horses and rode out to the canefield, where the people were cutting. They had been at work a half hour. He stopped his horse where they were when we came to them, and the next half hour, without a word from him, they had made double the distance of the first. It seems to me that the work of a plantation is what a clock would be that always required a man's hand pressing on the main spring. . . .

At six o'clock, the large bell tolls the knell of parting day and the call to the Oración. . . . On the plantations, it is treated only as the signal for leaving off work. The distribution of provisions is made at the storehouse, by the mayordomo, my host superintending it in person. The people take according to the number in their families; and so well acquainted are all with the apportionment, that in only one or two instances were inquiries necessary. The kitchen fires are lighted in the quarters, and the evening meal is prepared. I went into the quarters before they were closed. A high wall surrounds an open square, in which are the houses of the Negroes. This has one gate, which is locked at dark; and to leave the quarters after that time is a serious offence. The huts were plain, but reasonably neat, and comfortable in their construction and arrangement. In some were fires, round which, even in this hot weather, the Negroes like to gather.□

Rising Coffee Exports and Falling Food Surpluses in Brazil, 1850–1860

Export agriculture earned higher profits than did subsistence agriculture. Consequently, capital, labor, technology, and the best land tended to concentrate in the export sector of the economy to the detriment of the production of food for local consumption, an economic reality notable during the past half-millennium. As populations grew and urbanization increased at hitherto unprecedented rates in the nineteenth century, that reality adversely affected the diet of a majority of Latin Americans. Where once there was plenty, hunger and malnutrition appeared.

An early Brazilian economist, Sebastião Ferreira Soares, observed in 1860 that the rush to plant coffee trees in the province of Rio de Janeiro caused a decline in food production. Shortages of food required importation. The negative trend Ferreira Soares criticized not only continued but accelerated. It came to characterize ever-larger regions of Latin America, creating major economic crises by the mid-twentieth century. Latin Americans spent the hard currencies they earned from exports not on purchasing capital goods needed to induce economic development but rather on buying food they were perfectly capable of growing themselves. Ferreira Soares pointed to one significant cause for Latin America's economic underdevelopment.

E VER SINCE BRAZILIAN coffee began to find bigger European markets and to become our major export, its price, in accordance with the law of supply and demand, rose, encouraging our producers to expand their cultivation of the crop. The handsome profits from the coffee harvests caused the large planters to concentrate exclusively on its production. To a large degree, they abandoned the cultivation of food necessary to feed their workers. Without any thought of future consequences, they concentrated on the immediate profits they could earn. They did not seem to care that declining food production and increased demands for food in the very marketplaces where they once sold their surpluses would cause food prices to rise. Rising food prices eroded coffee profits. The smaller producers followed the example set by the large planters. The result is an economic crisis that affects the country. . . .

In general, the principal coffee planters seeing certain and immediate profits from coffee exports invested all their efforts in coffee production. They

Source: Sebastião Ferreira Soares, *Notas Estatísticas sobre a Produção Agrícola e Carestia dos Generos Alimentícios no Império do Brasil* (Rio de Janeiro: IPEA/INPES, 1977), pp. 19–20, 133–134, 279–280.

abandoned the food production, corn, manioc, and beans, which fed people. They made this false rationalization: With the profits earned from coffee, we can purchase the necessary food for our families and workers and come out ahead financially because manioc, corn, and beans cost very little and it is not profitable to employ workers to produce crops of little value when they can produce others of greater value.

At first glance, that argument seems to be logical and economically sensible. However, under further scrutiny, the logic diminishes, even disappears. In fact, the rationalization defies good economic sense because it refers only to the present with no thought of the future.

For that rationalization to be logical it would be necessary and indispensable that the foodstuffs no longer produced be imported from abroad at low prices and that increased purchases not alter the price substantially. This situation did not occur because the manioc, corn, and beans we once consumed were grown within our own country. Indeed, we even grew a surplus which we exported. Then, the principal coffee planters stopped growing food crops, which, at the same time the number of consumers increased. Hence, consumption rose, while production fell. We became customers in the same marketplace in which, until then, we sold our annual surpluses. The result of such erroneous rationalization and the chain of economic events which followed was the rise in food prices. . . .

Studying the statistics available until 1849–1850, it is possible to conclude that until that date our country exported many kinds of foodstuffs which today we must import, if only in very small amounts. Foodstuffs are not lacking in the markets, although before the warehouses groaned with surpluses that kept prices lower.

Statistics for the decade 1839–1840 to 1849–1850 reveal the following annual averages of our exports of these crops:

Rice	225,000	*alqueires*
Manioc flour	89,671	
Beans	9,010	
Tapioca	21,707	
Corn	19,271	
Bacon	5,902	*arrobas*
Cheese	1,756	

The statistics for 1853–1854 and thereafter reveal practically no exports of these items, except for manioc flour, which continued to be exported in the same quantity, most of it passing through the ports of Santa Catarina, and rice whose current export figures are around 50,000 *alqueires,* most of which Maranhão and Pará export.

The statistics that reveal falling exports of foodstuffs serve to prove the conclusion that I already made: the abandonment of their production in some provinces in order to produce exclusively coffee and other items for export. The food produced within the country tends to be sold in the coffee region, also the center of population concentration, but food prices have not declined. . . . The warehouses maintain food supplies. However, a large part of the population is impoverished and for them the food shortage is serious. □

Ordinary People
Face Economic Challenges

The Dispossessed in Rural Mexico

Obtaining an understanding of how the ordinary people lived in the middle of the nineteenth century is not easy. Illiterate, these people left few records. Much of the information about them comes from documents written by the elites. At the constitutional convention of 1856–1857, the Mexican reformer Ponciano Arriaga denounced the poverty of the dispossessed. He proposed a reform of truly revolutionary proportions. It would put unused land in the hands of the landless. Needless to say, the deputies ignored the proposal.

WHILE A FEW INDIVIDUALS possess immense idle lands that could support millions of people, the great majority of our citizens live in the most abject poverty, denied property, homes, and work.

A hundred constitutions and thousands of laws may proclaim abstract rights and beautiful though impractical theories, but our people cannot be free, republican, or happy under the absurd economic system that exists in Mexico.

There are Mexican landowners who occupy (if one can apply the word "occupation" to a purely imaginary thing) a greater extent of land than one of our sovereign States, greater even than one or more European countries.

Over this vast expanse of land, much of which lies idle, awaiting the fructifying touch of labor, live scattered four to five million Mexicans who have no other means of subsistence than agriculture yet are forbidden the use of the land. Since they cannot emigrate with the hope of making an honest living, they must become robbers or vagabonds or submit to the yoke of the landed monopolist who forces them to accept intolerable conditions of employment.

What reasonable hope can these unhappy men have of finding a legal escape from their condition of abject serfdom? How can anyone believe that the magic words of a written law will transform them into free citizens who know and defend the dignity and importance of their rights?

We proclaim *ideas* and forget *things*. We launch on discussions of rights and ignore the concrete facts. The constitution should be the law of the *land,* but we do nothing about the state of the *land.*

While our statesmen are busy organizing chambers, dividing powers, assigning powers and attributes, defining and limiting sovereignties, the rich landowners laugh at them, for they know that they are the true masters of society,

Source: Benjamin Keen (ed.), *Americans All: The Story of Our Latin American Neighbors* (New York: Dell, 1968), pp. 135–138. With permission of Benjamin Keen.

that true power is in their hands, that they exercise actual sovereignty. Our people justly complain that constitutions come and go, that governments rise and fall, that the law codes grow ever more mountainous and complex, that proclamations and "plans" follow swiftly on each other's heels. But after all these changes and upheavals, after so much disorder and sacrifice, nothing beneficial emerges for the people, for the classes that provide the soldiers who shed their blood in our civil wars, who fill the prisons and toil on the public works, who suffer all the evils of society and none of its blessings.

The unhappy farm laborers, especially those of the Indian race, are sold and lose their freedom for life. Their masters fix the wages they receive, provide them with such food and clothing as they please and charge them what they please. Imprisonment, torture, and infamy are the lot of the peon who should object to the landowner's decrees and orders.

With some very honorable exceptions, the rich Mexican landowner (who rarely knows his land foot-by-foot), or the majordomo who represents him, may be compared to a feudal lord of the Middle Ages. On his domain, with more or less formalities, he makes laws and executes them, administers justice and exercises civil powers, imposes taxes and fines, has jails, chains, and jailors, inflicts punishments and tortures, monopolizes trade and forbids any other business than that of his estate to be carried on without his consent. As a rule the judges and other public officials on these estates are the landowner's servants or tenants; they are henchmen incapable of acting freely, impartially, or justly, or of enforcing any law other than the absolute will of the master.

The landowners employ an infinite and complex variety of devices to exploit their peons, servants, or tenants. They force them to work without pay even on the days set aside for rest. They compel them to accept rotten seeds or sick animals which are charged to their trifling wages. They burden them with large dues and with parochial fees and taxes in excess of the scale agreed upon beforehand between the parish priest and the landowner or his majordomo. They force them to buy all their needs on the estate, paying them with vouchers or paper money which do not circulate in any other market. At certain periods of the year they supply them with shoddy goods whose price is fixed by the landowner or his majordomo, thus burdening them with debts from which they can never free themselves. They forbid them to use pastures and woods, fuel and water, or even the wild fruit of the fields, without the express permission of the master. In short, the landowner has over his tenants an unlimited and completely irresponsible power. □

The Indians Lose Their Land

Following the independence of Mexico, the elites purchased land from the State, the Church, and the Indians. The already large estates grew both in size and number.

The Indians often held their lands through their communities rather than through individual title. It was nearly impossible to purchase land from those communities, although the individual Indian was vulnerable to pressures to sell privately held land. Aware of that characteristic, the elites sought first to break up the community holdings into individual titles and then to induce the individual to sell. That movement was underway by mid-century and quickly divested many of the Indians of their lands.

The Mexican Constitution of 1857

The Liberals imposed a constitution on Mexico in 1857 that prohibited "corporations" from owning land. The *ejido,* the Indian community, was legally a corporation. Thus, Article 27 of that constitution abolished the ejido, which in effect subjected the Indians to a variety of pressures to sell their individual plots of land. The Mexican Indians' days of landholding were numbered.

ARTICLE 27. Private property shall not be taken without the consent of the owner, except for reasons of public utility and by prior indemnification. The law shall determine which authority shall make the expropriation and the provisions by which it shall be carried out.

No civil or ecclesiastical corporation of whatever character, designation, or object, shall have the legal capacity to acquire ownership to, or administer in its own behalf, landed property, except for buildings immediately and directly related to the services or purposes of said corporations.☐

Legal Protection Ends for the Lands
of the Indians of Colombia

While visiting the Orinoco Valley of Colombia in the 1850s, Isaac F. Holton, a U.S. citizen, observed that the legal protection afforded the lands of Indian communities was coming to an end. As elsewhere in Latin America, that legal change meant the eventual loss of the Indian lands to the large landowners.

I PROCEEDED SOUTH TO Choachí. This is a tolerable village, standing on a level spot on the sidehill, but a mile or more from the roaring stream that flowed along the base. Both sides of this river are thickly settled with Indians. I have not seen so much cultivation in all this country, and the scene delighted me inexpressibly. The district of Choachí contains 4691 inhabitants; Ubaque, a little farther on, 3399; while on the other side of the stream, the district of Fómeque contains 6645. The amount of white blood in all this multitude is quite small.

The land here has been kept in the hands of the Indians by a benevolent provision of the law, restraining them from selling except according to certain provisions; but, with the advancing ideas of liberty, it is seen that it is undemocratic to restrain thus a man's liberty. The matter is now with the provincial legislatures, and in some provinces these reserves—resguardas—can be sold only at auction, and in others, any man that can persuade one of these thoughtless

Source: Article 27 of the Mexican Constitution of 1857.

Source: Isaac F. Holton, *New Granada: Twenty Months in the Andes* (Carbondale: Southern Illinois University Press, 1967), pp. 108–109.

aborigines to sell to him can buy at any price, however small. It grieves me to hear that large numbers have sold. Among the most diligent buyers of resguardas is the cura of Choachí, who is now the owner of land that once was occupied by a score of families. □

Land Monopoly in Pernambuco, Brazil

In underpopulated Brazil, a few people claimed the land, although they worked only a tiny portion of it. The poor found it nearly impossible to gain access to the unused land. Lack of access doomed them to continued poverty. In 1856, a newspaper in Recife, capital of Pernambuco, pointed out that the large land-holdings created a barrier to both the economic growth and development of the nation.

WHAT FUTURE HAS THE continuously growing population of the interior? Will the new additions devote themselves to agriculture? No. The more enlightened part will come here to Recife to seek its fortune, to solicit some ridiculous job. The rest will go to the towns and other centers of population and there spend a miserable life because among us there is no industry that offers the free worker security and regular pay. . . .

And why do the youths of these unfortunate families, instead of entering into such precarious careers in public service, not take up farming? And for what reason, instead of learning the skills of a tailor, bricklayer, or carpenter, etc., do the sons of the less favored families not go back into the interior, why don't they become farmers? Why don't the inhabitants of the interior cultivate the soil? Why do those young people hunt out the towns? For all these questions there is but one answer and unfortunately it is convincing!

In the social state in which we live, the means of subsistence of the father of the family do not increase in proportion to the number of children, the general consequence of which is that the sons are poorer than their fathers and they possess less capital. Now, agriculture is closed by an insurmountable barrier to the less favored man, to anyone who does not have a certain amount of money. Agriculture is the chief source of production, the chief hope of our country. But since agriculture is closed by a barrier, it is necessary that that barrier fall, cost whatever it may.

And what is that barrier? Large landholdings. It is the terrible curse which has ruined and depopulated many other nations.

This region which extends along the entire coast of our province and inland for ten, twelve, or, at times, fifteen and eighteen leagues is divided into sugar plantations and properties whose dimensions vary from a quarter of a league square to two and three and even four and five leagues square.

Here, as the growing of sugarcane demands, a certain amount of land, which cannot be found everywhere, is devoted to the cultivation of the cane. Other parts of the plantation are dedicated to the woods that are necessary for

Source: *Diario de Pernambuco* (Recife), March 24, 1856.

sugar production, the pastures for the care of the oxen, and the gardens for the planting of manioc, indispensable for the feeding of the slaves. But still a major part of the plantations possesses vast extensions of uncultivated land that would be especially well suited for the small farmer and which, if cultivated, would be sufficient to furnish abundantly flour, corn, beans, etc., to all the population of the province and of the neighboring provinces with some produce left over for exportation.

The proprietors refuse to sell these lands or even to rent them. If you own thirty or forty *contos de réis* you can buy a sugar plantation, but if you are poor and want to buy or rent a small patch of land, you won't find any.

This is what makes the unproductive population of the cities, increases regularly the number of solicitors of public employment, and raises daily the crimes against property; and the country becomes poorer day by day in consequence of the increase of the number of consumers while the number of producers remains stationary or at best increases at a much slower rate.

But the large landowners say that they are far from refusing the poor people the land they need to cultivate. They say that when these landless poor ask for it they give them at a small rental or at times gratuitously not only land to plant but wood to build homes. That does happen but only at the pleasure of the large landowner.

Anytime he wants to, for any caprice or because they refuse to vote for his candidates or for any reason, he can order them off the land, and they have no recourse. How can you ask these people to plant when they have no certainty of harvesting? What incentive exists to induce them to improve the land from which they can be evicted at any moment?

On the land of the large property holders they do not enjoy any public right because they do not have any freedom; for them, the large landowners are the police, the courts, the administration, in short, everything. The lot of these unhappy people differs in nothing from the serfs of the Middle Ages. □

The Standard of Living of Workers in Northeastern Brazil

As Brazil's coastal towns and cities grew, a new class timidly appeared, a group neither slave nor slaveowner. It consisted of small merchants, young professionals and civil servants, new military officers, the workers, and the artisans. Crushed as they were in the economic vise between the large mass of slaves below and the powerful slaveowners above, their economic lot was not an easy one. One of the newspapers of Pernambuco commented in 1849 on the lowly and difficult position of the free workers, providing a glimpse, however inconclusive, of their standard of living.

THE AVERAGE DAILY WAGE of a man is 640 réis. Socially considered the man is the unification of three persons: husband, wife, and son. He must bear the maximum load of work, the work which will supply the other two.

Source: Gilberto Freyre, *Nordeste* (Rio de Janeiro: José Olympio, 1937), p. 237.

Supposing that each one eats a pound of meat per day . . . he will spend 300 réis on meat; if we add 80 réis for flour and 20 for firewood, we will have the man spend 400 réis per day on food or about 12$000 milreis per month; and as he must spend on housing about a third, more or less, of what he spends for food, this comes to another 4$000 milreis per month for a total of 16$000. He has left about four thousand milreis to spend on holy days, during sickness, for clothing, etc., which is impossible for a man who wants to live hygienically and honorably. But as it is well known that the poor live also with honor, it is interesting to learn how this is done. Dry meat, salted and dry—and many times spoiled—fish, flour without manioc, bad food, a hard bed, an uncomfortable house, ragged clothing are the products which the poor use. Even these come in limited amounts in order not to exceed the budget.

Under such conditions the family can only suffer. It will not have complete physical growth; its quantity of work will be less; its offspring will be deficient. From such a malnourished family comes the weak and cowardly soldier, the sensitive and powerless sailor. . . . □

A Description of the Indians of Andean Colombia

At the middle of the nineteenth century, the Indians still predominated in those countries from Mexico southward through Central America and the west coat of South America into Bolivia and Paraguay. The elite generally considered them a burden, a barrier to progress. Thus, their descriptions of the indigenous populations tend to be negative. Around 1860, the Colombian scholar José María Samper wrote the following essay on the Indians in his country. Although his views might be considered moderate, perhaps even enlightened, comparatively speaking, the essay reveals prejudices and a lack of understanding. In the final analysis, it probably says more about the elites than the Indians.

THE CHARACTER OF THE MASS of the Andine population (purely indigenous) is notable for patient labour, religious sentiment carried to the point of idolatry and the grossest superstition, lack of every truly artistic sentiment, love of a sedentary life, of immobility and routine, a humility full of timidity, dissimulated malice which somewhat tempers the relative stupidity of the *muisca,* a certain impassibility which makes him indifferent to all strong emotions, a great curiosity respecting purely material or exterior things, spirit of hospitality but slightly developed, and a patent incapacity to obey the impulse of Progress. . . . The Indian of the plateaux is wanting in enthusiasm and passion, but loves marriage and is faithful to his hearth and wife. Moreover, he loves his little bit of soil to servility and likes *chicha* to an excess which frequently leads him to drunkenness. He adores processions and mummeries and displays much credulity for the marvellous. Weak in hand-to-hand struggle because his strength resides only in his neck, back, and legs, and without any dash in combat, he displays nevertheless

Source: "Description of the Llanura and the Llanero of Colombia" in A. Curtis Wilgus (ed.), *Readings in Latin American Civilization* (New York: Barnes & Noble, 1946), pp. 249–250.

an astounding endurance in carrying enormous weights and exhibits the stupid valour of passive obedience. He can neither run nor ride a horse, but walks days without feeling any fatigue, provided he is given *chicha,* and he travels horrible roads and paths laden with some huge case of stupendous volume and weighing 150 kilograms or more, supporting himself on a heavy cane, bowed double with the load but never exhausted nor weakening. As poor a hunter as he is a fighter, because he lacks initiative, daring, and agility, he nevertheless makes an excellent soldier of the line. True, he rarely advances, but he never retreats, and ever knows how to die at his post, to which he seems nailed alike in victory as in defeat.

For the Indian of the Andine countryside, the ties of society are perilous, the schoolmaster is an incomprehensible myth, the *alcalde* a useless personage, the parish priest a demi-god, and the tax-collector little less than the pest or thunderbolt. His life is concentrated upon his primitive hut and half acre of farm, and his great festival day that upon which he goes to the marketplace, principally Bogotá, to sell his fruit and vegetables, his chickens and eggs, carried in reed cages laden on his back and strapped to his forehead. The *muisca* Indian is neither quarrelsome nor communicative, neither revengeful nor obsequious. Selfish, timid, and distrustful, he avoids written agreements, hides himself on recruiting days and elections and when a census is being taken, and does everything possible to evade taxes. In short, the descendant of the *muiscas* is a passive being, a kind of deaf-mute in the presence of European civilization, incapable of either good or bad, thanks to the sad state in which he has lived since the Conquest and to the inelasticity of his intellectual and moral faculties.

While the men are generally cold, suspicious, and hypocritical, the women on the contrary often show themselves frank, kind, unselfish, accessible to kind treatment, grateful, and good mothers. The women have no less endurance relatively than the men for long journeys and carrying heavy weights. Both sexes are fond of money for money's sake: they haggle impertinently and look with suspicion at all coin tendered them. It is but justice to recognize that all their defects are rather the consequence of vicious prior institutions and of the exploitation more or less crafty or violent to which these poor natives have been subjected by the priests, the large landed proprietors, and influential men of their small localities. These defects are also due to the absolute lack of elementary education in many rural districts. . . . □

The Limits of Education

Education could play a multitude of useful roles. Obviously, it could prepare people to participate more fully in a modern society. It could infuse a national feeling, a sense of unity of purpose and goals in all inhabitants. In short, education could serve as a major instrument for nation building. However, in nineteenth-century Latin America, education failed to realize its potential. Feeble educational institutions served primarily the elites. Probably less than 10 percent of the population was literate. The Brazilian social historian Fernando de Azevedo suggests the elitist contours of education in imperial Brazil. His remarks also apply to the rest of Latin America. Instead of unifying a nation, education further separated the privileged few from the impoverished many.

THIS EDUCATION OF AN ARISTOCRATIC TYPE, destined rather for the preparation of an élite than for the education of the people, was developed under the Empire, following without noticeable deviation the lines of its evolution, strongly marked by the intellectual traditions of the country, by the regime of patriarchal economy, and by the corresponding ideal of the man and citizen. The type of culture which it proposed to serve is not explained only by the colonial tradition, fundamentally European, which in a certain way led up to it, but is closely bound up with the forms and framework of the social structure which persisted throughout the Empire. In fact, with the change of the political state from colony to nation, and with the foundation in 1822 of the Constitutional monarchy, no modification in the structure of society took place, for it continued as in the colony to be organized on an agricultural, patriarchal economy with a slave base from the sugar mills of the north to the coffee plantations of the south, which were, by the middle of the nineteenth century, fully developed. In this regime of education at home and school, a regime calculated to create an anti-democratic culture of privileged classes and social distance between adults and children, rigor of authority, absence of collaboration on the part of women, the great difference in the education of the two sexes and the almost absolute domination of purely intellectual activities over those basically manual and mechanical, showed to what an extent a civilization based on slavery influenced the evolution of our education. The boy, treated on the whole either "like a demon once he was past the phase of being considered an angel, which was up to five or six" (in the words of Gilberto Freyre), when he did not wear a gown in the schools, put on a black coat, or "with all the severity of grown-up people except only in dimensions," would take his vengeance when he was a big boy, in the absence of discipline of the higher school, on the regime of authority in which fathers and teachers had asphyxiated his natural childish vivacity.

It is this sad and bleak aspect with which boys and girls appeared, all with the airs of adults, and it is this precocious, external maturity in clothes and manners which led a foreign traveler to call Brazil at this time "a country without children." As for the woman, generally treated with superiority by man who was almost a lord in relation to his own wife (and she frequently called him so), cloistered in the big houses, and suffocated in her personality, she devoted herself to household tasks, the care of her children, in general having no more than a domestic education, surrounded by slaves for all services, and occupied by her home, her piano and her needle "she was content with the mediocre life which was reserved for her, not seeking to enlarge her horizon nor improve her condition."[1] The slavery which cast dishonor upon work in its rude forms, ennobled leisure and stimulated parasitism, contributed to emphasize among us the repulsion for manual and mechanical activities and to make us consider arts and crafts

Source: Reprinted with permission of Macmillan Publishing Company from *Brazilian Culture: An Introduction to the Study of Culture in Brazil* by Fernando de Azevedo, translated from the Portuguese by William Rex Crawford. Copyright 1950, renewed 1978 by Macmillan Publishing Company, pp. 381–382; 374–375.

as vile occupations. According to the common opinion "to work, to submit one-self to any rule was the occupation of slaves." In this society, with its economy based upon the plantation and slavery, and which had therefore no interest in popular education, it was to the secondary and higher schools that the boys of the town flocked if they had any opportunity to study. Public activities, adminis-trative and political, which achieved a notable place on account of the life of the court and the parliamentary regime, and the titles given by the Emperor, contrib-uted still more to give an exaggerated value to the man of letters, to the bachelor of laws and the doctor, and the government along with the liberal professions became the principal consumer of the intellectual élite who were formed in the higher schools of the country. This contrast between the almost total absence of popular education and the development of a training for the élite, was necessarily to establish, as it did, an enormous lack of equality between the culture of the governed class with its extremely low level and that of the governing class, rising above a great mass of the illiterate,—"the human nebula separated out from the mass of the colonists"—, a little élite in which there figured men of a very refined culture and which, as Max Leclerc observed in 1890, would not be out of place among the elite of the most cultivated European societies. . . .

After Independence was proclaimed and the Empire of Brazil was founded in 1822, the victory of the liberals over the conservatives and the debates which went on in the Constituent Assembly of 1823 announced a new orientation for educational policy, under the influence of the ideals of the French Revolution, with which the liberals were imbued, and through the development of the na-tional spirit which obliged people to face the great problems of the country from a new point of view. Ideas, as usually happens, in crises of political change, took another direction and for the first time the concern for popular education,—as the basis for the system of universal suffrage, came to occupy the minds of the cultural élite made up of priests, bachelors of law and literati. But out of this political movement in favor of popular education, which was manifested in the debates and in the petitions presented to the Constituent Assembly dissolved in 1823, there came nothing but the law of October 20, 1823, which abolished the privileges of the State to give instruction, laying down the principle of liberty of teaching without restriction, Article 179, No. XXXII of the Constitution given by the Crown on December 11, 1823, which guarantees "free primary schooling for all citizens," and finally the law of October 15, 1827,—the only one which was promulgated in more than a century on the subject for the whole country and which ordered the creation of primary schools in all cities, towns and places (Article I) and in Article XI, "grade schools in the cities and towns which were the most populous." The results of this law, however, never corresponded to the intent of the legislator, for it failed on account of various causes, economic, technical and political. The government proved incapable of organizing popular education in the country. Few were the schools which it created, especially those for girls, which did not amount to more than twenty in the whole land in 1832, according to the testimony of Lino Coutinho; and in the illusory hope of solving the problem by the spread of the Lancaster method of teaching by the students, which practically dispensed with the professor, fifteen years passed (1823–1838) before all illusions were lost.

With regard to higher education, the debates in the Constituent Assembly seemed to mark a regression in the policy of Dom João VI. Instead of projects on the subject of special schools, there arose motions and proposals on university education and, among them, that of Fernandes Pinheiro, Viscount of São Leopoldo, who in the session of June 14 proposed that "there should be created immediately at least one university, for the seat of which it would seem that the city of São Paulo should be preferred on account of its natural advantages and reasons of general convenience." The project of the Constitution presented in the session of September 1, 1823, and signed by José Bonifácio, Antônio Carlos, Araújo Lima and others, adopted a measure calling in Article 250 for the creation of "primary schools in every township, secondary schools in every county, and universities in the most appropriate centers." The idea of unity and of the universality of teaching which appeared to prevail over that of special training, did not however succeed in leading to the slightest change in a form of policy, whose spirit of continuity was not broken for more than a century. During this century, higher learning remained almost entirely dominated by the professional and utilitarian spirit. No real effort was made to create a university; no institution of general culture and training appeared. To the schools of professional training instituted by Dom João VI, the first Empire added the two courses of juridical and social sciences, which, created by the law of August 11, 1827, were located, that of the city of São Paulo on March 1, in the Convent of São Francisco and that of Olinda on May 15, 1828, in the Monastery of São Bento. With the two faculties of law which were founded, one in the north and the other in the south and whose role was so important in the life of the country, the picture of schools destined for the preparation of the liberal professions was completed. Made up at the beginning, in the first half of the nineteenth century, of the two schools of medicine, into which in 1832 the Academies of Medicine and Surgery in Bahia and Rio were transformed, and of the Royal Military Academy, from which in 1833 the Naval School was separated and which took the name of Military School in 1839; and of those two new institutions,—a vigorous graft on the branch of higher professional training—, this group of schools, in which a whole élite of doctors, engineers and bachelors of law was prepared, was for a long time the most important center of professional and intellectual life in the nation.□

[1] . . . Max LeClerc, *Lettres du Brésil.* Chapter XI. L'esprit public. L'état social les moeurs et les institutions. (Paris: Plon, 1890), pp. 203–236.

5

Latin Americans Define Themselves

Nationalism is a force with tremendous potential to reshape Latin America. From the sixteenth century onward, the Latin Americans struggled to identify, define, and interpret themselves, most often in terms of their relationships with the peoples and nations of the North Atlantic. Nation building in the nineteenth century accelerated and diversified those struggles. Domingo F. Sarmiento urged Latin Americans to Europeanize, to re-create Europe in the New World. Geography, racial diversity, and historical experience challenged his prescription. They ordained uniqueness. As Latin Americans gained confidence and better understood themselves and their own best interests, they celebrated that uniqueness. They more closely identified with their fledgling nations, equating national well-being with their own. Nationalism intensified.

The efforts of Latin Americans to define themselves and their cultures provide useful insights into the motivation and psychology of the peoples of the region. Such insights partially explain causation, the perplexing "Why?" in history. An awareness of these Latin American self-perceptions and the nationalism they both fortify and draw from contributes to a better understanding of a complex region.

An Early Effort to Define Latin America

In 1856, the Chilean intellectual Francisco Bilbao (1823–1865) issued a strong— and early—statement about Latin America's uniqueness. The aggression of the United States in Mexico, the Caribbean, and Central America (the U.S. filibusters under the leadership of William Walker occupied Nicaragua at that moment) prompted Bilbao to urge South American unity in response to Yankee expansion. Fears of foreign aggression always excite the most basic political nationalism, the conflict pitting "us against them." The situation requires a clearer definition of "us" in order to differentiate "them." Like many Latin Americans, Bilbao found much to admire in the North Americans. At the same time, he believed that his compatriots must emphasize their own distinct characteristics. While referring to racial harmony, he highlighted the spiritual qualities of the Latin Americans. Attention to that harmony and spirituality evolved into dominant themes among these Latin Americans who sought to define their societies and in the process to distinguish themselves from the ever more powerful northern metropolis.

FIRST IT WAS TEXAS, then it was Northern Mexico and the Pacific that hailed a new master.

Today the skirmishers of the North are awakening the Isthmus with their shots, and we see Panama, that future Constantinople of America, doubtfully suspended over the abyss and asking itself: Shall I belong to the South or to the North?

There is the danger. Whoever fails to see it, renounces the future. Is there so little self-awareness among us, so little confidence in the intelligence of the Latin-American race, that we must wait for an alien will and an alien intellect to organize us and decide our fate? Are we so poorly endowed with the gifts of personality that we must surrender our own initiative and believe only in the foreign, hostile, and even overbearing initiative of individualism?

I do not believe it, but the hour for action has arrived.

This is the historic moment of South American unity; the second campaign, that will add the association of our peoples to the winning of independence, has begun. Its motive is the danger to our independence and the threat of the disappearance of the initiative of our race. . . .

The United States of South America has sighted the smoke of the campfires of the United States. Already we hear the tread of the young colossus that with its diplomacy, with that swarm of adventurers that it casts about like seed, with its growing power and influence that hypnotize its neighbors, with its intrigues among our peoples, with its treaties, mediations, and protectorates, with its industry, its merchant marine, its enterprises—quick to note our weaknesses and our weariness, quick to take advantage of the divisions among our republics, ever more impetuous and audacious, having the same faith in its imperial destiny as

Source: Benjamin Keen, *Readings in Latin American Civilization: 1492 to the Present* (Boston: Houghton Mifflin, 1967), pp. 512–515. With permission of Benjamin Keen.

did Rome, infatuated with its unbroken string of successes—that youthful colossus advances like a rising tide that rears up its waters to fall like a cataract upon the South.

The name of the United States—our contemporary, but one that has left us so far behind—already resounds throughout the world. The sons of Penn and Washington opened a new historical epoch when, assembled in Congress, they proclaimed the greatest and most beautiful of all existing Constitutions, even before the French Revolution.

Then they caused rejoicing on the part of sorrowing humanity, which from its torture-bed hailed the Atlantic Republic as an augury of Europe's regeneration. Free thought, self-government, moral freedom, and land open to the immigrant, were the causes of its growth and its glory. It was the refuge of those who sought an end to their misery, of all who fled the theocratic and feudal slavery of Europe; it provided a field for utopias, for all experiments; in short, it was a temple for all who sought free lands for free souls.

That was the heroic moment of its annals. All grew: wealth, population, power, and liberty. They leveled the forests, peopled the deserts, sailed all the seas. Scorning tradition and systems, and creating a spirit that devours space and time, they formed a nation, a particular genius. And turning upon themselves and beholding themselves so great, they fell into the temptation of the Titans. They believed they were the arbiters of the earth, and even rivals of Olympus.

Personality infatuated with itself degenerates into individualism; exaggeration of personality turns into egotism; and from there to injustice and callousness is but a step. They would concentrate the universe in themselves. The Yankee replaces the American; Roman patriotism, philosophy; industry, charity; wealth, morality; and self-interest, justice. They have not abolished slavery in their States; they have not preserved the heroic Indian races—nor have they made themselves champions of the universal cause, but only of the American interest, of Saxon individualism. They hurl themselves upon the South, and the nation that should have been our star, our model, our strength, daily becomes a greater threat to the independence of South America.

Here is a providential fact that spurs us to enter upon the stage of history, and this we cannot do if we are not united.

What shall be our arms, our tactics? We who seek unity shall incorporate in our education the vital elements contained in the civilization of the North. Let us strive to form as complete a human entity as possible, developing all the qualities that constitute the beauty or strength of other peoples. They are different but not antagonistic manifestations of human activity. To unite them, associate them, to give them unity, is our obligation.

Science and industry, art and politics, philosophy and Nature should march in a common front, just as all the elements that compose sovereignty should live inseparable and indivisible in a people: labor, association, obedience, and sovereignty.

For that reason let us not scorn, let us rather incorporate in ourselves all that shines in the genius and life of North America. Let us not despise under the pretext of individualism all that forms the strength of the race.

When the Romans wished to form a navy, they took a Carthaginian ship for their model; they replaced their sword with that of Spain; they made their own the science, the philosophy, and the art of the Greeks without surrendering their own genius; they raised a temple to the gods of the very peoples that they fought, as if in order to assimilate the genius of all races and the power of all ideas. In the same way should we grasp the Yankee axe in order to clear the earth; we should curb our anarchy with liberty, the only Hercules capable of overcoming that hydra; we should destroy despotism with liberty, the only Brutus capable of extinguishing all tyrants. And the North possesses all this because it is free, because it governs itself, because above all sects and religions there is a single common and dominant principle: freedom of thought and the government of the people.

Among them there is no State religion because the religion of the State is the State: the sovereignty of the people. That spirit, those elements, we should add to our own characteristics. . . .

Let us not fear movement. Let us breathe in the powerful aura that emanates from the resplendent star-spangled banner, let us feel our blood seething with the germination of new enterprises; let us hear our silent regions resounding with the din of rising cities, of immigrants attracted by liberty; and in the squares and woods, the schools and congresses, let the cry be repeated with all the force of hope: forward, forward! . . .

We know the glories and even the superiority of the North, but we too have something to place in the scales of justice.

We can say to the North:

Everything has favored you. You are the sons of the first men of modern Europe, of those heroes of the Reformation who crossed the great waters, bringing the Old Testament, to raise an altar to the God of conscience. A knightly though savage race received you with primitive hospitality. A fruitful nature and an infinite expanse of virgin lands multiplied your efforts. You were born and reared in the wooded fields, fired with the enthusiasm of a new faith, enlightened through the press, through freedom of speech—and your efforts were rewarded with abundance.

You received a matchless education in the theory and practice of sovereignty, far from kings, being yourselves all kings, far from the sickly castes of Europe, from their habits of servility and their domesticated manners; you grew with all the vigor of a new creation. You were free; you wished to be independent and you made yourselves independent. Albion fell back before the Plutarchian heroes that made of you the greatest federation in history. It was not so with us.

Isolated from the universe, without other light than that which the cemetery of the Escorial permitted, without other human voice than that of blind obedience, pronounced by the militia of the Pope, the friars, and by the militia of kings, the soldiers—thus were we educated. We grew in silence, and regarded each other with terror.

A gravestone was placed over the continent, and upon it they laid the weight of eighteen centuries of slavery and decadence. And withal there was word, there was light in those gloomy depths; and we shattered the sepulchral stone, and cast those centuries into the grave that had been destined for us. Such was the power of the impulse, the inspiration or revelation, of the Republic.

With such antecedents, this result merits being placed in the balance with North America.

We immediately had to organize everything. We have had to consecrate the sovereignty of the people in the bosom of theocratic education.

We have had to struggle against the sterile sword that, infatuated with its triumphs, believed that its tangent of steel gave it a claim to the title of legislator. We have had to awaken the masses, at the risk of being suffocated by their blind weight, in order to initiate them in a new life by giving them the sovereignty of the suffrage.

We who are poor have abolished slavery in all the republics of the South, while you who are rich and fortunate have not done so; we have incorporated and are incorporating the primitive races, which in Peru form almost the totality of the nation, because we regard them as our flesh and blood, while you hypocritically exterminate them.

In our lands there survives something of that ancient and divine hospitality, in our breasts there is room for the love of mankind. We have not lost the tradition of the spiritual destiny of man. We believe and love all that unites; we prefer the social to the individual, beauty to wealth, justice to power, art to commerce, poetry to industry, philosophy to textbooks, pure spirit to calculation, duty to self-interest. We side with those who see in art, in enthusiasm for the beautiful (independently of its results), and in philosophy, the splendors of the highest good. We do not see in the earth, or in the pleasures of the earth, the definitive end of man; the Negro, the Indian, the disinherited, the unhappy, the weak, find among us the respect that is due to the name and dignity of man!

That is what the republicans of South America dare to place in the balance opposite the pride, the wealth, and the power of North America.

But our superiority is latent. We must develop it. □

Salvation Through Originality

The Cuban patriot José Martí (1853–1895) understood the strengths and weaknesses of Latin America. In his brilliant essay "Our America," published in 1891, he admonished his peers for their blind allegiance to foreign ideas. In their haste to copy others, they refused to acknowledge Latin American realities. Martí insisted that Latin Americans must know themselves and their lands first so that they then could develop them in accordance with their own needs and potentials. He sounded the nationalists' call for originality.

TO GOVERN WELL REQUIRES AN understanding and appreciation of local realities. Anyone who would govern well in the Americas does not need to know how the Germans or the French govern themselves but rather needs to possess a

Source: Text adapted from "Nuestra America," *El Partido Liberal* (Mexico City), January 30, 1891, p. 4.

basic knowledge of his own country, its resources, advantages, and problems and how to utilize them for the benefit of the nation, and needs to know local customs and institutions. The goal is to reach that happy state in which everyone can enjoy the abundance Nature has bestowed so generously on the Americas. Each must work for that enjoyment and be prepared to defend that abundance with his life. Good government arises from the conditions and needs of each nation. The very spirit infusing government must reflect local realities. Good government is nothing more and nothing less than a balance of local needs and resources.

The person who knows his own environment is far superior to anyone dependent on imported books for knowledge. Such a natural person has more to contribute to society than someone versed in artificial knowledge. The native of mixed ancestry is superior to the white person born here but attracted to foreign ideas. No struggle exists between civilization and barbarism but rather between false erudition and natural knowledge. Natural people are good; they respect and reward wisdom as long as it is not used to degrade, humiliate, or belittle them. They are ready to defend themselves and to demand respect from anyone wounding their pride or threatening their well-being. Tyrants have risen to power by conforming to these natural elements; they also have fallen by betraying them. Our republics have paid through tyranny for their inability to understand the true national reality, to derive from it the best form of government, and to govern accordingly. In a new nation, to govern is to create.

In nations inhabited by both the educated and the uneducated, the uneducated will govern because it is their nature to confront and resolve problems with their hands, while the educated dither over which formula to import, a futile means to resolve local problems. The uneducated people are lazy and timid in matters related to intelligence and seek to be governed well, but if they perceive the government to be injurious to their interests they will overthrow it to govern themselves. How can our universities prepare men to govern when not one of them teaches anything either about the art of government or the local conditions? The young emerge from our universities indoctrinated with Yankee or French ideas, aspiring to govern a people they do not understand. Those without a rudimentary knowledge of political reality should be barred from a public career. Prizes should be awarded not for the best poetry but for the best essays on national reality. Journalists, professors, and academicians ought to be promoting the study of national reality. Who are we, where have we been, which direction should we go? It is essential to ask such basic questions in our search for truth. To fail to ask the right questions or to fail to answer them truthfully dooms us. We must know the problems in order to respond to them, and we must know our potentials in order to realistically frame our responses. Strong and indignant natural people resent the imposition of foreign solutions, the insidious result of sterile book learning, because they have little or nothing to do with local conditions and realities. To know those realities is to possess the potential to resolve problems. To know our countries and to govern them in accordance with that knowledge is the only way to liberate ourselves from tyranny. Europeanized education here must give way to American education. The history of the Americas, from the Incas to the present, must be taught in detail even if we forego the courses on ancient Greece. Our own Greece is much more preferable to the Greece which is not ours. It is more important and meaningful to us. Statesmen with a nationalist view must replace politicians whose heads are in Europe even though their feet remain in the Americas. Graft the world onto our nations if you will, but the trunk itself must be us. Silence the pedant who thrives on foreign inspiration.

There are no lands in which a person can take greater pride than in our own long-suffering American republics. The Americas began to suffer, and still suffer, from the effort of trying to reconcile the discordant and hostile elements which they inherited from a despotic and greedy colonizer. Imported ideas and institutions with scant relationship to local realities have retarded the development of logical and useful governments. Our continent, disoriented for three centuries by governance that denied people the right to exercise reason, began its independence by ignoring the humble who had contributed so much in the effort to redeem it. At least in theory, reason was to reign in all things and for everyone, not just scholastic reason at the expense of the simpler reason of the majority. But the problem with our independence is that we changed political formulas without altering our colonial spirit.

The privileged made common cause with the oppressed to terminate a system which they found opposed to their own best interests. . . . The colonies continue to survive in the guise of republics. Our America struggles to save itself from the monstrous errors of the past—its haughty capital cities, the blind triumph over the disdained masses, the excessive reliance on foreign ideas, and unjust, impolitic hatred of the native races—and relies on innate virtues and sacrifices to replace our colonial mentality with that of free peoples.

With our chest of an athlete, our hands of a gentleman, and our brain of a child, we presented quite a sight. We masqueraded in English breeches, a French vest, a Yankee jacket, and a Spanish hat. The silent Indians hovered near us but took their children into the mountains to orient them. The Afro-Americans, isolated in this continent, gave expression to thought and sorrow through song. The peasants, the real creators, viewed with indignation the haughty cities. And we the intellectuals wore our fancy caps and gowns in countries where the population dressed in headbands and sandals. Our genius will be in the ability to combine headband and cap, to amalgamate the cultures of the European, Indian, and Afro-American, and to ensure that all who fought for liberty enjoy it. Our colonial past left us with judges, generals, scholars, and bureaucrats. The idealistic young have been frustrated in efforts to bring change. The people have been unable to translate triumph into benefits. The European and Yankee books hold no answers for our problems and our future. Our problems grow. Frustrations mount. Exhausted by these problems and frustrations, by the struggles between the intellectual and military, between reason and superstition, between the city and countryside, and by the contentious urban politicians who abuse the natural nation, tempestuous or inert by turns, we turn now to a new compassion and understanding.

The new nations look about, acknowledging each other. They ask, "Who and what are we?" We suggest tentative answers. When a local problem arises, we are less likely to seek the answer in London or Paris. Our styles may all still originate in France but our thought is becoming more American. The new generation rolls up its sleeves, gets its hands dirty, and sweats. It is getting results. Our youth now understands that we are too prone to imitate and that our salvation lies in creativity. "Creativity" is the password of this new generation. The wine is from the plantain, and even if it is bitter it is our wine! They understand that the form a government takes in a given country must reflect the realities of that country. Fixed ideas must become relative in order for them to work. Freedom to experiment must be honest and complete. If these republics do not include all their populations and benefit all of them, then they will fail.

The new American peoples have arisen; they look about; they greet each other. A new leadership emerges which understands local realities. New leaders read and study in order to apply their new knowledge, to adapt it to local realities, not to imitate. Economists study problems within an historical context. Orators eschew flamboyance for sober reality. Playwrights people the stages with local characters. Academicians eschew scholastic theories to discuss pressing problems. Poets eschew marble temples and Gothic cathedrals in favor of local scenes. Prose offers ideas and solutions. In those nations with large Indian populations, the presidents are learning to speak Indian languages.

The greatest need of Our America is to unite in spirit. The scorn of our strong neighbor the United States is the greatest present danger to Our America. The United States now pays greater attention to us. It is imperative that this formidable neighbor get to know us in order to dissipate its scorn. Through ignorance, it might even invade and occupy us. Greater knowledge of us will increase our neighbor's understanding and diminish that threat.

A new generation reshapes our continent. This new generation re-creates Our America. It sows the seeds of a New America from the Rio Grande to the Straits of Magellan. The hopes of Our America lie in the originality of the new generation. □

Ariel: The Spiritual Nature of the Latin Americans

The quick victory of the United States over Spain in 1898 followed by the occupation of Cuba and Puerto Rico alarmed the Latin Americans, giving further impulse to nationalist feelings. The political stability, economic prowess, military power, and technological advances of the United States contrasted with Latin America's dependency and underdevelopment. The obvious differences cast a pall of despondency over Latin America, intensifying the sense of insecurity.

In 1900, José Enrique Rodó (1871–1917) published his brief book *Ariel.* It contributed to defining modern Latin American nationalism. While the Uruguayan scholar conceded the technological, material, and democratic achievements of the United States, he emphasized the spiritual superiority of the Latin Americans, their attraction to beauty and their lofty nobleness. Latin America played Ariel to the Caliban of the United States, the spiritual versus the material. Actually, Rodó only amplified the ideas of Bilbao and other intellectuals, but he made his observations at a propitious moment, the cresting of a new wave of U.S. expansion. *Ariel* appeared everywhere in Latin America. Students, in particular, hailed the conclusions of "the great teacher." This ubiquitous book still stands as a cornerstone of twentieth-century Latin American nationalism.

THAT EVENING THE WISE OLD TEACHER, whom we used to call Prospero after the sage in Shakespeare's *Tempest,* was bidding farewell to his students. They met with him for the last time after a long year of diligent study. They gathered in a large lecture hall whose dignity and austerity honored the shelves groaning under the weight of books of knowledge, the faithful companions of Prospero. However, the dominating feature in that hall was an exquisitely sculptured bronze representing Ariel from the *Tempest.* The teacher sat close to the statue. For that reason, the students called him Prospero, the name of the magician in the play loved and served by the spiritual Ariel. In all fairness, though, his manner of teaching and his very character were better reasons for the nickname.

Ariel, genius of the spirit, represents nobility in the symbolism of Shakespeare. Ariel embodies the nobleness of reason over base impulse. Lofty in motive, he represents the selflessness in action, the spiritual nature of civilization, and the grace of intelligence. In short, Ariel is the ideal toward which humanity aspires. He is the antithesis of Caliban, symbol of the mediocre and mundane.

The statue, a fine piece of art, perfectly reproduced the spirit at that very moment when, freed by the magic of Prospero, it is ready to take wing, to vanish into the air. With wings spread, dressed in a loose, floating cloak, his broad forehead uplifted, a tranquil smile dancing on his lips, the statue of Ariel recaptured that moment just before flight. It represented an ideal.

Prospero, lost in thought, caressed the head of the small statue. The teacher gathered his students around him. With affectionate attention, they listened to him lecture. . . .

Practicality and equality were the characteristics Europeans ascribed to the spirit of Americanism. Both of those characteristics immediately brought to mind the impressive and fruitful democracy of the United States of America with its power and prosperity. The United States stands as the extraordinary example of practicality, equality, and democracy. If the English gave birth to the concept of practicality, the United States serves as its incarnation. The citizens of the North preach the virtues of the triumph of practicality with all its material miracles. The United States has set out on a kind of moral conquest. Admiration for this power and achievement grows rapidly in the minds of our governing classes and, even more, perhaps, among the masses, easily impressed with victory or success. From admiration it is but one step to imitation. Common sense demonstrates the ease of that step. Human beings tend to imitate others whose superiority or prestige they admire. Thus, without physical conquest or compulsion, Latin Americans are willing to renounce their inheritance in an effort to regenerate themselves as North Americans. They dream of such a transformation. Most reforms or innovations copy the North American

Source: José Enrique Rodó, *Ariel* (Montevideo: Imprenta de Dornaleche y Reyes, 1900), pp. 5–7, 83–87, 89–90, 127–131, 134–141.

model. They display a virtual mania for the United States. Both reason and sentiment dictate that there should be limits to this mania.

Limit does not mean absolute rejection. I know that enlightenment, inspiration, and instruction lie in the example of the strong and successful. I understand that careful attention to material achievements and practicality can be useful to people in the process of development. New realities require flexibility. Still, I oppose denuding our people of their own characteristics and genius in order to clothe them with foreign identities. Thus, they sacrifice their originality, their genius. Once lost, they can never be recovered. Thoughtless efforts to transplant what is natural and spontaneous in one society into the soil of another where it has no roots, historically or naturally, will not work.

In societies, as in literature or in art, blind imitation produces an inferior copy of the original. Respect for one's own independence, judgment, and personality is a matter of pride. Cicero teaches us our duty to preserve our own personality. . . . We Latin Americans have our own inheritance, a great ethnic tradition to maintain, a sacred bond uniting us to the past, linking us to our history. Our honor bounds us to preserve this tradition for the future. Any external influence which we accept must not preclude our own fidelity to the past. We must apply our own genius to the process of fusing and molding the future.

More than once it has been pointed out that the great periods of history, the fertile periods, are the result of distinct but coexisting civilizations which while in opposition give impetus to the creativity of both. The two extremes of Athens and Sparta, for example, gave rise to the genius of both. So, the Americas need to maintain their original duality. This difference in genius neither excludes honorable emulation nor discourages solidarity. If there is to be some form of greater alliance in the future, it will result not from a one-sided imitation by one group of the other but rather from a reciprocity of influences, the skillful harmonizing of those attributes which constitute the peculiar glories of both. . . .

All devoted to propagating and preserving the ideal of the spirit in the Americas— whether it be in art, science, ethics, religious belief, or politics—must prepare for the future. The past belonged to the mighty arm wielding the sword; the present belongs to the calloused hand tilling the soil, constructing, and manufacturing; the future demands the preparation of the human spirit, that is the intellect.

Picture the Americas of the future! It will be hospitable to the intellect; it will give flight to the spirit; it will cradle the soul. It will be thoughtful without sacrificing action; it will be serene and strong without abjuring enthusiasm; it will radiate charm while engendering thought. Your future history depends on your attention to this vision of the Americas. You may not be its creators, but you can be its forerunners. To create the new human being, the new society, there must always be the pioneers, the forefathers, the prophets. The individuals give rise to the majority. The majority rules.

It is too much to expect all of this intellectual and spiritual change to occur within your single generation. While there will not be an entire transformation, one can expect progress. While the first fruits of the soil you cultivate may not be yours, they might be if you work diligently and audaciously. The best work results from patience and care; more is achieved by placing the goal high. Applause is not your reward but rather the satisfaction of achievement. . . .

I ask you to give of your spirit and soul for this labor for the future. For that reason I seek inspiration in the gentle and lovely image of Ariel here by my side. This bountiful Spirit selected by the genius of Shakespeare serves as our symbol. The sculptor rendered the statue appropriately spiritual. Ariel is beacon and the higher truth. Ariel is that sublime sentiment of the perfectibility of the human being. Ariel, the spirit, is the crowning glory of evolution. Ariel triumphant signifies the ideal and order in life, noble inspiration in thought, unselfishness in conduct, refined taste in art, heroism in action, delicacy and refinement of manners. Ariel is the hero, the epitome, the immortal. He possesses the invincible power to uplift human life. Though overcome a thousand and one times by the constant rebellions of Caliban, Ariel rises again renewed in youth and beauty. Ariel runs nimbly as if called by Prospero to all who really care for him and seek to find him. His kindly power reaches out even to those who would deny him. . . . I ask you not to remember my words but this little figure of Ariel. I hope that this image of bronze will be impressed forever on your own innermost spirit. . . .

May this bronze statue, graven in your hearts, help you to fulfill your lives. During the dark hours of discouragement, may it rekindle in your conscience the warmth of the ideal, may it return to your hearts the glow of a perishing hope. Ariel is your ally. This bright spirit will smile upon you in future times even though your own lies shadowed. I have faith in your will and in your strength. I have even greater faith in those you will teach and guide. I dream of that day when our majestic Andes Mountains will serve as the pedestal for this statue of Ariel. Mounted on such a lofty height he will serve as the beacon for the cult of the spirit. This is the genius of our people. . . .

Thus spoke Prospero. The youths departed after shaking the master's hand. His inspiring words echoed in each young mind. It was the final hour of dusk. A ray of the setting sun fell through the shadowy lecture hall. It touched the bronze statue, almost animating the face of the figure. The ray lingered as if to liberate the genius imprisoned in the bronze. The restive spark of liberated genius was thus transmitted to the departing students. For a long time they walked in silence, each absorbed in meditation. . . .

After a prolonged silence, the youngest of the group spoke, contrasting the idle movement of the human herd with the radiant beauty of the sky, "Observe that while the crowd walks along no one looks up to the heavens, while they look down upon this listless crowd. The stars vibrate. They remind me of the arms of the farmer sowing seed." ☐

The African Contribution
to Brazilian Civilization

A rich racial diversity characterized most of Latin America. The elite and the intellectuals, victims of the specious racial doctrines emanating from the North Atlantic, at first showed embarrassment with the diversity of races and racial mixture. Hence, their nineteenth-century efforts to define Latin America leaned heavily upon the European experience, neglecting the African roots.

No country owed a greater debt to Africa than Brazil. Yet, typical of tendencies throughout the hemisphere, historians focused scant attention on the contributions of the Afro-Brazilian to national history. Manuel R. Querino (1851–1923), son of humble but free Afro-Brazilian parents, challenged that proclivity. In the early twentieth century, he turned his attention to the study of history in order to combat racism and traditional historiography. He hoped to redress the historical concentration on the European experience in Brazil by showing the greater depth and diversity of the past. In a significant essay in 1916, "The African Contribution to Brazilian Civilization," Querino reminded Brazilians of the many contributions Africa made to national formation. The first Afro-Brazilian historian added a new voice and a much needed perspective to the efforts to define Brazil and, by extension, all of Latin America. Nationalism, if it was to be effective, had to embrace and exalt racial diversity.

The Arrival of the African in Brazil

THE BLACK COLONIST on arriving in America already was prepared for the work awaiting him here as a hunter, sailor, herdsman, extractor of salt, iron-worker, shepherd, farmer, tradesman, etc. At the time of the slave traffic, the African already knew how to seek out and extract minerals because gold, silver, lead, diamonds, and iron abounded in his homeland.

For a long time before he entered captivity the Negro [African] possessed skills and techniques which would be exploited in the New World. European explorers of the Dark Continent often made reference to them in their chronicles, noting with admiration their process for the manufacture of steel. [Henry Morton] Stanley reported that he had seen a native forge at which about a dozen men worked. The very pure iron the Africans produced was used to make lances, knives, and cutlasses. The blacksmith's art was much appreciated in the interior, where, because of isolation, the villages had to be self-sufficient. Each generation learned the traditional processes, which were numerous, and showed that even the people of the remote regions were progressive and perfectable. . . .

When the Portuguese left a temperate zone to settle in a torrid one quite different from home, they could not meet the demands of the tropics—taming the forests and tilling the soil—without the aid of allies adapted to the struggle in such regions. They were not satisfied with the enslavement of the American Indians, entire tribes of which had been eradicated first in Maranhão and Pará and then, in the eighteenth century, in Guairá. Indian slaves proved to be very unreliable and the subject of constant debates and conflicts between the colonizers and the authorities. So the settlers turned their covetous eyes toward Africa and from that continent took the rich prize which the American forests failed to supply them. The Portuguese, desirous of enriching themselves as much as possible with a minimum of effort, found it easy to justify their resort to the Negro settlers acquired in Africa. Without the Africans, the Europeans would have found it difficult, if not impossible, to colonize Brazil, particularly when one considers who composed the ranks of the first Portuguese settlers. Outside of royal servants occupying high administrative posts, they were criminals, men of shady reputation, and common soldiers.

From the beginning, then, it was necessary to import Africans, and within a short time the slave ships were depositing along the coast of Portuguese America hundreds upon hundreds of Africans destined to till the soil and perform every other type of labor. The *bandeirante* expeditions included the Negro because

Source: Manuel R. Querino, *A Raça Africana* (Salvador: Livraria Progresso Editora, 1955), pp. 123–152.

wherever the Negro could serve he was pressed into service. A black bandeirante discovered the first trace of gold along the banks of the Funil River in Ouro Prêto; another found the fabulous "Southern Star" diamond. Although the black worked hard, he did not escape the cruel punishments inflicted by the sting of the master's lash. The Negro slave bore his lot with real stoicism.

With the discovery of gold and the subsequent exploitation of the mines, the Africa slave traffic intensified. The numbers of black colonists entering the country increased rapidly. Greed also grew. Parasitism took on the aspect of a social institution and brought in its wake all kinds of vices and evils. As in the Spanish domains, the common man, impoverished in his native land where he sought in theft and begging some relief from the tortures of hunger while at the same time considering work beneath his dignity, assumed in the New World arrogant attitudes of the upper class and nobility. The idea of easy wealth banished from the thoughts of the famished adventurers any love for work which they considered degrading. Such attitudes, however, favored the men of color in the mechanical and artisan trades. The Portuguese considered apprenticeship in those occupations to be some sort of punishment inflicted on the humble, as though those occupations were degrading. Only the blacks worked. Manoel de Oliveira Lima has noted that the European depended heavily on the ever increasing number of blacks to clear and cultivate the vast territory conquered in South America. Robust, obedient, dedicated to his work, the African became the invaluable collaborator of the Portuguese in the sugar mills of the North, the plantations of the South, and the mines of the interior.

His source of labor assured, the ambitious Portuguese was seized with a fever to discover more gold and diamonds. Those riches bathed him in unsophisticated vanity, exaggerated ostentation, vainglory, and above all else boredom. His women and children dressed in all kinds of velvets, damasks, and silks, often to excess. The landowners delighted in lavish banquets and drank prodigious amounts of wine imported from Portugal. They slept off their excesses in beds of crimson damask trimmed in gold and covered with rich spreads from India. At any rate that is what at least one eyewitness from the period recorded. Added to that luxury were the heavy silver services, the sedan chairs, the pure-blooded horses with banners and saddles of gold. Everything was acquired by the exhausting labor of the hero of work, the African, the diligent and obedient slave. The Portuguese became accustomed to enjoying the fruit of labor without feeling the weight of it.

Suicide, Violence, and the Desire for Freedom

Punishment on the plantations and in the sugar mills, if not generally perfected to the highest degree of perversity, was severe and at times cruel. Society rebuked only those masters who carried punishment to an unusual extreme. Once a runaway slave was captured, he was brought back by the bush captain, who tied the captive's arms securely and forced him to run behind his horse. Then the unfortunate slave was turned over to two strong slaves who, whips in hand, beat their fellow slave, tearing his flesh until he died in the presence of the master, who watched that scene of barbarism with pride in his unchecked despotism. Another method of punishment was to chain the slave to a stake without giving him either food or drink. To increase the torture, a cup of water and some food were placed just beyond his reach. Meanwhile, insects bit his legs and feet. Another fatal punishment was to lash the victim to the back of an animal and send the animal out into the wilderness where the unfortunate slave died for lack of nourishment.

Nostalgia seized the unhappy captive. He remembered the impetuous winds, the soft murmur of the waterfalls, the sleepy echo of the forests of his native land. Anguished by the cruel rigors of slavery, tormented by the demands for more work, he dreamed one dream, thought one thought: liberty. His mind, body, and spirit craved the liberty innate in his soul. Physically he was forced to submit to slavery, but in the inner recesses of his soul, the love of and desire for freedom never submitted. Slavery never succeeded in eradicating either that love or that desire. His constant thought was to free himself. He tried many ways to achieve his freedom.

The most impatient threw themselves into the rushing currents of the rivers or the foaming waters of the sea. Strangulation and poisons were other quick ways to end a painful existence. Desperate, tormented, uncertain, they hoped thus to return to life in their lost and beloved land. David Livington related seeing six captives in Africa singing as if they did not realize their state of degradation or feel the weight of the chains on their body. When he asked them the cause of their happiness, they responded that they rejoiced knowing that after their deaths they would return to torment and kill those who had sold them into slavery. Later, the slaves held that the masters were the ones who deserved to meet violent death. They did not hesitate a moment but began poisoning and murdering the masters, the overseers, and their families. The souls of the slaves screamed for vengeance; the horrors of slavery had awakened a despair crying out for action. The perversity of their treatment tortured the slaves' patience; their spirit resorted to the most extravagant reprisals. They fled the plantations and gathered in the hinterlands to offer collective resistance to recapture. Hidden in the woods, they organized their own society.

Collective Resistance, Uprisings, and Palmares

The spirit of the African race leaped with joy when the slaves deserted the sugar plantations and mills to found the Confederation of Palmares in the early seventeenth century. At Palmares, the blacks defended their liberty. Ancient Rome, the master of so many enslaved peoples, had once witnessed with horror and panic a Spartacus as the head of an army of slaves. In Brazil, too, slavery incited the Africans to revolt and to redress their wrongs. Much blood flowed, but in Palmares, the runaway slaves had not thought of vengeance. To the contrary, their objective was to escape tyranny and to live in liberty, the noblest aspiration of man.

The Greek slaves were instructed in public games as well as literature, advantages which the enslaved Africans in America never had because the rigor of their captivity did not permit the slightest mental preparation. It benumbed their intelligence. Nonetheless, they showed themselves superior to the anguish of their suffering and made memorable attempts to revolt and to organize a society with its own independent government. They organized guerrilla bands in order to defend their citadel of Palmares. When necessary, they made incursions into neighboring territory. They adapted their native songs to war chants.

Abandoning their masters, the Greek and Roman slaves did not attempt to organize a regular society in the land where they found themselves. They either wandered about alone or formed bands to pillage. The devastation wrought by the Roman slaves awoke terror among all those who learned of their proximity. The founders of Palmares did not behave in a similar manner. They sought refuge in the vastness of a virgin Nature and there laid out the basis of a society that imitated those they had left behind in their homeland, Africa, societies much more advanced than those of the American Indians. Their conquest was not motivated by hatred, but rather by the legitimate desire to live as free men. Thus, in Palmares, they enacted the laws necessary for their society. They had severe laws against robbery, murder, and adultery, and among themselves they observed those laws rigorously. Hatred of the white did not preoccupy them. They pardoned. They forgot former griefs. Their inspiration was to be free, and living freely in Palmares they expressed a joy which eclipsed any former rancor. Freedom, not revenge, was their ambition.

In the society of Palmares neither criminals nor loafers flourished; ready and natural comfort replaced the tortures of the slave quarters. When civilized man doubted whether the African or Indian possessed a soul and even the most tolerant conceded that they did only after baptism, the son of the Black Continent gave proof that he possessed one. He revolted with indignation against the unjust oppression of which he was a victim and by force imposed his liberty and independence. The Portuguese historian Oliveira Martins held that of all the protests by the slave throughout history, Palmares remains as the most appealing and heroic. He referred to Palmares as a Black Troy and to its history as an Iliad. An eminent Brazilian historian, Rocha Pombo, described Palmares as the finest page of African heroism and of the great love for independence which that race bestowed on America.

The defeat of Palmares encouraged the masters to tighten their hold on the slaves. It was a reaction prompted by a vision of danger. Slaves in the sugar-rich coastal region of Bahia were very badly treated. They were poorly fed and scantily clothed. The African slaves did not hesitate; they kept their resolve to reconquer their lost freedom by whatever means possible. The Governor, the Conde da Ponte in 1807, decreed severe measures against the *quilombos,* which were multiplying rapidly. The increasing cruelty of the masters intensified the resentment of the slaves and awoke among those unhappy victims a thirst for vengeance. An increasing number of uprisings occurred, some of more, others of less, importance, all followed by slaughter. The courage of the rebels in the service of liberty resulted in unmeasured sacrifices and unjust suffering. It was necessary to fight—and, given the inequality of conditions, to fight heroically. Once the inextinguishable flame of hatred was ignited in the breasts of those miserable slaves by the barbarous punishments and bad treatment inflicted by the masters, it was natural that it would burst into conspiracy. On February 28, 1814 in Bahia, flagelated by hunger and driven to desperation by overwork and by the habitual cruelty of their overseers, the slaves revolted and attacked the plantations around Itapoan. On that same day, the troops battled with the rebels on several occasions in the vicinity of Santo Amaro de Ipitanga. The blacks fought desperately and only gave ground when they fell before the superior firepower of the soldiers. The troops, as was their custom, tried to injure and not to kill in order to save the masters the loss of their slaves. But the blacks preferred to lose their lives fighting for liberty. In those encounters they fought with courage and desperation. In Brazil there arose more than one African Spartacus who preferred death to captivity.

Mutual Aid Societies for Self-Liberation

Exhausted by a series of constant struggles, restricted by all possible measures in their aspirations, yet firm, resolute, and confident in their ideal, the African slaves did not abandon hope or delude themselves. They tried another means: dedication to their work in order to achieve their goal, a means which harmonized with the conservative nature of the society.

Legend has it that an African king and his entire tribe were transported as slaves to Minas Gerais. The masters reduced all of them to the same common level as slaves, but the Africans always revered their king and kept their old customs as much as possible. At the cost of immense effort during the few free hours at his disposal, the slave-king was able to earn enough money to buy his own freedom. He then worked to buy the freedom of a second, and together they purchased the freedom of a third. Each newly freed African contributed toward the purchase of still other members of the enslaved tribe until all were free. Then they erected a chapel to Saint Ifigenia, a princess of Nubia. There, under her patronage, the tribe continued to thrive and pay honor to their sovereign, the black king. Thus was bequeathed to future generations the legend of "Chico-Rei."

The Africans in Bahia did practically the same thing. No savings banks existed in Bahia before 1834; nor was it possible until long after that to count on abolitionist societies for funds; nor were the masters as generous as they would later become in freeing favorite slaves as one means of celebrating a family birthday, anniversary, wedding, or other joyous occasion. Instead, the blacks saved their own money or kept it with some highly trusted person to buy their freedom or that of their descendants. The procedure of saving and loaning the money for the liberation developed into a special institution.

Those slaves who agreed to save money jointly for such a noble purpose organized themselves into an informal society and selected their most trusted and respected member as the leader. The leaders charged with the responsibility of safeguarding the money devised a peculiar way of noting the quantities received, the amounts loaned, and the interest accrued. It was done without written records. The money lender acknowledged the repayments to the fund made by each borrower by making an incision on a wooden baton kept by each. One black took charge of collecting the payments from borrowers who failed to appear at the assigned time with their money. Generally the societies met on Sundays to receive contributions, to count funds on hand, principally in copper coin, and to discuss matters related to loans.

If a member needed a sum of money, he had the right of withdrawing it, discounting the interest for the time borrowed. In case the entire investment was withdrawn, then a certain percentage had to be paid to the guardian of the fund as a reimbursement. As could be foreseen, the lack of bookkeeping gave rise to some difficulties for all parties involved. At times, a member borrowed enough money to buy his freedom, and after all the calculations of interest he generally would repay about double what he borrowed.

At the end of each year, as happens in all business organizations, dividends were distributed to the members. On those occasions heated discussion raged among the members, just barely averting fist fights so that it was not necessary for the police to intervene in their meetings. Despite those disagreements and some irregularities, the slaves were able to band together to reach their goal of freedom. In that way many of those heroes of labor, thanks to their patience, hard work, and mutual cooperation, were able to liberate themselves.

The Role of the Black in National Life

Agriculture was the initial and lasting wealth of the nation. Though encumbered by outmoded, routine, and elementary methods, it still grew and developed from the labor of the slaves. The African exerted all his physical strength in the fields to produce as much as possible, a labor from which the colonists reaped all the benefits. Only after the slave began to weaken from the burden of his field work, from the effect of the climate, and, above all else, from old age was he transferred to duties in the house of the master, a sort of reward for having escaped death while straining and groaning in the fields.

Once transferred to the Big House, the Negro slave with his affectionate nature, his good will, his ability, and his fidelity won the esteem of his master through his sincere devotion and frequent sacrifice. It was in the Big House that the Negro expanded the most noble sentiments of his soul. He collaborated lovingly in bringing up the offspring of his lord and master, teaching them obedience, deference, and respect for age. He inspired good will and even love from all members of the family. The black mother was a storehouse of tenderness and affection for the master's children. Within the conviviality of the Big House, the Negro performed many intimate services. They were the lady's companions, the valets, the wetnurses, pages, bodyguards, and favorite maids.

The African slave was hardworking, thrifty, and provident, qualities which his descendants did not always conserve. He sought to give his offspring a licit occupation, and whenever possible he saw to it that his children and grandchildren had mastered a skill. The work of the Negro for centuries sustained the grandeur and prosperity of Brazil. It was the result of his labor that Brazil could afford scientific institutions, literature, art, commerce, industry, and so forth. He thus occupies a position of importance in the development of Brazilian civilization.

Whoever takes a look at the history of this country will verify the value and contribution of the Negro to the defense of national territory, to agriculture, to mining, to the exploitation of the interior, to the movement for independence, to family life and to the development of the nation through the many and varied tasks he performed. Upon his well-muscled back rested the social, cultural, and material development since without the income which he provided and which made everything possible there would have been neither educators nor educated: without that wealth the most brilliant aspirations would have withered; the bravest efforts would have been in vain. With the product of the Negro's labor, the wealthy masters sent their sons to European universities and later to our own universities, from which, well instructed, came our venerable priests, able statesmen, notable scientists, excellent writers, brave military officers, and all the rest who made of first colonial and then independent Brazil a cultured nation, strong among the civilized peoples.

From the conviviality and collaboration of the races in the formation of this country emerged a large mestizo population of all shades and hues, from which has come so many illustrious men of talent who are the true glory of our nation. . . . It can be concluded that Brazil possesses two riches: the fertility of the soil and the talent of the people of mixed races.

The black is still the principal producer of the nation's wealth, but many are the contributions of that long-suffering and persecuted race which has left imperishable proofs of its singular valor. History in all its justice has to respect and praise the valuable services which the Afro-Brazilian has given to this nation for more than three centuries. In truth, it was the black who developed Brazil. □

Combining European and Local Values into a National Culture

In a rejection of Sarmiento's civilization versus barbarism thesis, the Argentine nationalist Ricardo Rojas (1882–1957) believed that Latin Americans must draw from their own traditions to create national cultures. In this selection from *Eurindia* (1924), he argued in favor of the synthesis of European (exotic) and local (Indian) values. The concept of "synthesis" became fundamental in the nationalists' attempts to define new, unique Latin American cultures.

A CONTINENT IS THE GEOGRAPHIC stage upon which the drama of human culture evolves. After the Europeans disrupted the unique cultures of the Incas and the Aztecs, the Americas began a new cultural process. In fact, we are still in the initial phases of that process, but one thing is certain: that emerging culture will differ from the European.

The differences already are observable. In Argentina, for example, we show scant interest in some of the questions preoccupying Europe, such as religious orientations or monarchy. Militarism, imperialism, and anti-Semitism are absurd concepts for us, although among us live a few who in their stubborn imitation

Source: Ricardo Rojas, *Eurindia* (Buenos Aires, 1924) pp. 14–20.

of all things European would impose them on us. As for literary influences, the European schools denoted as classicism, romanticism, realism, and decadence degenerate here. Like plants transplanted to another climate, they become sterile or produce strange fruits. To those who understand the difficulties of transplanting cultures, nothing seems so ludicrous as our imitative intellectuals who persist in pursuing foreign models. Each civilization springs from a unique culture; each culture reflects its own traditions and values; each tradition arises from the history and spirit of a people.

If we carefully study the history of the Americas, we will see that the city, considered by some as the source of civilization, has always been a fortress for conquest or the depot for economic exploitation. Our cities did not arise spontaneously. Armed men, bureaucrats, and merchants from abroad established them.

Unlike the European "polis," American cities do not reflect local origins and needs. Consequently, our civilization is imposed; hence, our culture is weak. It will remain so until the spirit of the countryside influences the city to counter and alter the now dominant foreign presence. American genius suffers in this environment of self-denial, and European genius cannot flourish in this American environment. This dilemma challenges colonies that want to become nations. They must manifest their own cultures and reject imposed foreign cultures.

Domingo F. Sarmiento witnessed the struggle between the Argentine city and the pampas. He termed it "civilization versus barbarism." He viewed it with European eyes and in political terms. Had he viewed the struggle more philosophically through American eyes, he would have judged it differently. Our cities at that time were then extensions of Europe; our countryside reflected local human and geographical forces struggling to express unique American values and goals. On previous occasions, I, too, have expressed a struggle underway, but I understood it quite differently than did Sarmiento. I saw the essence of our historical dialectic as "Indianism versus exoticism." It explains the Argentine or American process of progress and reaction as well as the changes that European culture undergoes in our environment. This explanation offers greater insight into our political and intellectual history.

The American Indians enjoyed their own cultures when the European conquest imposed new values and demands. Those values and demands radiated from the newly founded, European-oriented cities in the Americas. While the Spaniards hispanicized the Indians, the Indians also influenced the Spaniards. The Iberian conquerors penetrated the American empires, politically destroying them. Yet, three centuries later, the Americans expelled the conquerors. Independence was an American act, that is to say—Indian. It was a revindication. It opposed the "civilizer" of exotic origins. One declaration of independence affirmed, "We wish to expel from the country all Spanish residents." The "hymn" of the Argentine independence movement extolled its accomplishments and evoked the pre-Columbian Incas.

The independence movement, Indian, which is to say American, in its objectives, expressed the ideas of the smaller cities, more intimately linked to the American soil, rather than those of the viceregal capitals closely intertwined with European thought. It liberated the native genius of the countryside with its Indians, gauchos, and caudillos. After independence was achieved, a new group of local "civilizers," once again centered in the capital city, opened the doors of the nation to European immigrants in order to encourage "progress." They imposed a new cycle of exoticism. This cycle gained momentum, and we currently find ourselves well within it. Still, one can discern signs of a new Indianist reaction. It should not take the negative form of xenophobia but rather the positive approach of creating an American culture, expressing intelligently native values, and conquering spiritually by American genius the Europeanized cities. We move toward synthesis. It will be reached through an intellectual and artistic renaissance whose presence can already be seen and felt.

According to the historical processes underway in our own past and present, we can see these trends: First, the Spaniards conquered the Indians; next, the Argentine gauchos influenced the conquerors; later, a new wave of European immigrants conquered the gauchos; and finally, nationalist intellectuals overcome the immigrants. In sum, Indianism conquers exoticism. Our literature repeats those very same cycles: first, indigenous folklore; next, the gaucho poetry; later, positivism and decadence imported from abroad. We now await the absorption of this exotic influence by the Indian traditions into a synthetic, symbiotic expression of national thought and art.

European development occurs through chronological cycles within its own continental tradition, while in the Americas the process of "before" and "after" conquest is intermixed with the realities of "the here" and "the there." The external and internal influences interact, the interplay of the Americas and Europe. I term this process the interplay of Indianism and exoticism. The exotic is needed for our political development just as the Indian is needed for our spiritual development and aesthetic culture. We want neither gaucho barbarianism nor cosmopolitan barbarism. We search out and must give value to a national culture as the base for our national civilization. Our arts must give expression to both that culture and that civilization. *Eurindia* is the name I give to our evolving culture. ☐

La Raza Cósmica:
A New Race and a New Ideal

Fittingly, the optimistic rhetoric of the Mexican Revolution celebrated not just a new political order but the recognition of a unique people with a renovative mission. The thorough mixture of the races in the New World had given birth to a new race, *la raza cósmica* in the imaginative phrase of José Vasconcelos (1882–1959).

Inconsistent, vague, contradictory, even incorrect at times, the message of Vasconcelos in his pithy *La Raza Cósmica* (1924) can perplex the reader. Nonetheless, his statements rank as one of the most innovative nationalist credos of the twentieth century. He debunked the myth of European superiority; he infused pride; he helped to liberate the Latin American spirit; and he projected an ideal complementary to the experience of Latin America.

GREECE LAID THE FOUNDATIONS of Western or European civilization; the white civilization that, upon expanding, reached the forgotten shores of the American continent in order to consummate the task of re-civilization and re-population. Thus we have the four stages and the four racial trunks: the Black, the Indian, the Mongol, and the White. The latter, after organizing itself in Europe, has become the invader of the world, and has considered itself destined to rule, as did each of the previous races during their time of power. It is clear that domination by the whites will also be temporary, but their mission is to serve as a bridge. The white race has brought the world to a state in which all human types and cultures will be able to fuse with each other. The civilization developed and organized in our times by the whites has set the moral and material basis for the union of all men into a fifth universal race, the fruit of all the previous ones and amelioration of everything past.

White culture is migratory, yet it was not Europe as a whole that was in charge of initiating the reintegration of the red world into the modality of preuniversal culture, which had been represented for many centuries by the white man. The transcendental mission fell upon the two most daring branches of the European family, the strongest and most different human types: the Spanish and the English. . . .

It seems as if God Himself guided the steps of the Anglo-Saxon cause, while we kill each other on account of dogma or declare ourselves atheists. How those mighty empire builders must laugh at our groundless arrogance and Latin vanity! They do not clutter their mind with the Ciceronian weight of phraseology, nor have they in their blood the contradictory instincts of a mixture of dissimilar races, *but they committed the sin of destroying those races, while we assimilated them, and this gives us new rights and hopes for a mission without precedent in History.*

For this reason, adverse obstacles do not move us to surrender, for we vaguely feel that they will help us to discover our way. Precisely in our differences, we find the way. If we simply imitate, we lose. If we discover and create, we shall overcome. The advantage of our tradition is that it has greater facility of sympathy towards strangers. This implies that our civilization, with all defects, may be the chosen one to assimilate and to transform mankind into a new type; that within our civilization, the warp, the multiple and rich plasma of future humanity is thus being prepared. This mandate from History is first noticed in that abundance of love that allowed the Spaniard to create a new race with the Indian and the Black, profusely spreading white ancestry through the soldier who begat a native family, and Occidental culture through the doctrine and example of the missionaries who placed the Indians in condition to enter into the new stage, the stage of world One. Spanish colonization created mixed races, this signals its character, fixes its responsibility, and defines its future. The English kept on mixing only with the whites and annihilated the natives. Even today, they

Source; José Vasconcelos, *La Raza Cósmica* (Los Angeles: Centro de Publicaciones, Department of Chicano Studies, California State University, Los Angeles, 1979), pp. 7, 15–17, 32, 36–37. With permission of the publisher.

continue to annihilate them in a sordid and economic fight, more efficient yet than armed conquest. This proves their limitation and is indication of their decadence. The situation is equivalent, in a larger scale, to the incestuous marriages of the pharaohs which undermined the virtues of the race; and it contradicts the ulterior goals of History to attain the fusion of peoples and cultures. To build an English world and to exterminate the red man, so that Northern Europe could be renovated all over an America made up with pure whites, is no more than a repetition of the triumphant process of a conquering race. This was already attempted by the red man and by all strong and homogeneous races, but it does not solve the human problem. America was not kept in reserve for five thousand years for such a petty goal. The purpose of the new and ancient continent is much more important. Its predestination obeys the design of constituting the cradle of a fifth race into which all nations will fuse with each other to replace the four races that have been forging History apart from each other. The dispersion will come to an end on American soil; unity will be consummated there by the triumph of fecund love and the improvement of all the human races. In this fashion, the synthetic race that shall gather all the treasures of History in order to give expression to universal desire shall be created.

The so-called Latin peoples, because they have been more faithful to their divine mission in America, are the ones called upon to consummate this mission. Such fidelity to the occult design is the guarantee of our triumph.

Even during the chaotic period of independence, which deserves so much censure, one can notice, however, glimpses of that eagerness for universality which already announced the desire to fuse humanity into a universal and synthetic type. Needless to say, Bolivar, partly because he realized the danger into which we were falling by dividing ourselves into isolated nationalities, and partly because of his gift for prophecy, formulated the plan for an Ibero-American Federation which some fools still question today.

It is true that, in general, the other leaders of Latin American independence did not have a clear conception of the future. Carried away by a provincialism that today we call patriotism, or by a limitation that today is dubbed national sovereignty, every one of them was only concerned with the immediate fate of their own people. Yet, it is also surprising to observe that almost all of them felt animated by a humane and universal sentiment which coincides with the destiny that today we assign to the Latin American continent. Hidalgo, Morelos, Bolívar, Petion the Haitian, the Argentinians in Tucuman, Sucre, all were concerned with the liberation of the slaves, with the declaration of the equality of all men by natural right, and with the civil and social equality of Whites, Blacks and Indians. In a moment of historical crisis, they formulated the transcendental mission assigned to that region of the globe: The mission of fusing all peoples ethnically and spiritually.

Thus, what no one even thought of doing on the Anglo-Saxon area of the continent was done on the Latin side. In the north, the contrary thesis continued to prevail: The confessed or tacit intention of cleaning the earth of Indians, Mongolians or Blacks, for the greater glory and fortune of the Whites. In fact, since that time, the systems which, continuing to the present, have placed the two civilizations on opposing sociological fields were very well defined. The one wants exclusive dominion by the Whites, while the other is shaping a new race, a synthetic race that aspires to engulf and to express everything human in forms of constant improvement. If it were necessary to adduce proof, it would be sufficient to observe the increasing and spontaneous mixing which operates among all peoples in all of the Latin continent; in contrast with the inflexible line that separates the Blacks from the Whites in the United States, and the laws, each time more rigorous, for the exclusion of the Japanese and Chinese from California.

The so-called Latins insist on not taking the ethnic factor too much into account for their sexual relations, perhaps because from the beginning they are not, properly speaking, Latins but a conglomeration of different types and races. Whatever opinions one may express in this respect, and whatever repugnance caused by prejudice one may harbor, the truth is that the mixture of races has taken place and continues to be consummated. It is in this fusion of ethnic stocks that we should look for the fundamental characteristic of Ibero-American idiosyncrasy. . . .

Each ascending race needs to constitute its own philosophy, the *deus ex machina* of its own success. We have been educated under the humiliating influence of a philosophy conceived by our enemies, perhaps innocently if you will, but with the purpose of exalting their own goals and annulling ours. In this manner, even we have come to believe in the inferiority of the mestizo, in the unredemption of the Indian, in the damnation and the irreparable decadence of the Black. Armed rebellion was not followed by a rebellion of the consciences. We rebelled against the political power of Spain and yet did not realize that, together with Spain, we fell under the economic and moral domination of a race that has been mistress of the world since the demise of Spanish greatness. We shook off one yoke to fall under a new one. This displacement to which we fell victims could not have been avoided, even if we had been aware of it sooner. There is a certain fatality in the destiny of nations, as well as in the destiny of individuals, but now that a new phase of history has been initiated, it becomes necessary to reconstruct our ideology and organize our continental life according to a new ethnic doctrine. Let us begin, then, by making a new life and a new science. If we do not first liberate the spirit, we shall never be able to redeem matter.

We have the duty to formulate the basis of a new civilization, and for that very reason, it is necessary that we keep in mind the fact that civilizations cannot be repeated, neither in form nor in content. . . .

On the other hand, the joy-creating faculty is contained in the law of the third period, which is a feeling for beauty and a love so refined that it becomes identified with divine revelation. A quality assigned to beauty since ancient times, in the *Phaedro,* for example, is that of being pathetic. Its dynamism is contagious, it moves the emotions and transforms everything, even destiny itself. The race best qualified to discover and to impose such a law upon life and material things will be the matrix race of the new civilization. Fortunately, such a gift, necessary to the fifth race, is possessed in a great degree by the mestizo people of the Ibero-American continent, people for whom beauty is the main reason for everything. A fine aesthetic sensitivity and a profound love of beauty, away from any illegitimate interests and free from formal ties, are necessary for the third period, which is impregnated with a Christian aestheticism that puts upon ugliness itself the redemptive touch of pity which lights a halo around everything created.

We have, then, in the continent all the elements for the new Humanity: A law that will gradually select elements for the creation of predominant types; a law that will not operate according to a national criterion, as would be the case with a single conquering race, but according to a criterion of universality and beauty; and we also have the land and the natural resources. No people in Europe could replace the Ibero-American in this mission, no matter how gifted they might be, because all of them have their culture already made and a tradition that constitutes a burden for such enterprises. A conquering race could not substitute us, because it would fatefully impose its own characteristics, even if only out of the need to exert violence in order to maintain its conquest. This mission cannot be fulfilled either by the peoples of Asia, who are exhausted, or at least, lacking in the necessary boldness for new enterprises.

The people that Hispanic America is forming in a somewhat disorderly manner, yet free of spirit and with intense longings on account of the vast unexplored regions, can still repeat the feats of the Castilian and Portuguese conquerors. The Hispanic race, in general, still has ahead of it this mission of discovering new regions of the spirit, now that all lands have already been explored.

Only the Iberian part of the continent possesses the spiritual factors, the race, and the territory necessary for the great enterprise of initiating the new universal era of Humanity. All the races that are to provide their contribution are already there. . . . We have all the races and all the aptitudes. The only thing lacking is for true love to organize and set in march the law of History.

Many obstacles are opposed to the plan of the spirit, but they are obstacles common to all progress. . . . All the tendencies of the future are intertwined in the present, . . . [including] the emergence of the fifth race that will fill the planet with the triumphs of the first truly universal, truly cosmic culture.☐

Liberating the Spirit of the Artist

The artists of Mexico responded to the call of José Vasconcelos for "spiritual liberation." They turned their backs on European tutelage to paint, depict, and dissect Mexico. Their art radiated the vibrant nationalism of the new Mexico. Splashing their colors imaginatively across canvas and wall, José Clemente Orozco, Diego Rivera, and David Alfaro Siqueiros emerged as artistic giants of the twentieth century. With eyes focused inward on Mexico and "spirits" liberated from the colonial obsession to copy, Mexican genius soared. In his autobiography, as well as in other essays, the highly articulate José Clemente Orozco (1883–1949) recorded the emotions of an artist on the threshold of that new creativity. These selections from his writings illustrate both the practical application of Vasconcelos' ideas to the arts and the essence of Latin American cultural nationalism. Orozco was the quintessential cultural nationalist.

My Life and Art

IN THE PAST, the Mexican had been a poor colonial servant, incapable of creating anything or even of thinking for himself. Everything had to come ready-made from the great European metropolises, since we were an inferior and degenerate race. If we were permitted to paint, well, we had to paint just as they did in Paris, and, furthermore, the critics had to be Parisians who would judge our art and give the final verdict. Our architecture, too, was just a copy of French styles. All the marble and statues of our public and private buildings were imported from Italy.

It was utterly inconceivable that a humble Mexican would even dream of being the equal of a "foreigner." He had to go abroad in order to prepare himself for a career in art, and if he ever gave a thought to his backward country it was just to seek financial help in some moment of need.

The consecrated ideas of the academy reigned supreme: The ancients had achieved perfection. They had accomplished everything that was worthwhile artistically. It only remained for us to copy them slavishly. Florentine drawing, Venetian coloring, they were supreme. And if attracted to modernism, then the painter had to go to Montparnasse to get his orders.

In those night classes where we listened to the enthusiastic voice of Doctor Atl, the agitator, we began to suspect that the colonial mentality foisted upon us was another trick of imperialism. We had our own personality, and it was as valid as anyone's. Certainly we should take lessons from the old masters and from foreigners, but at the same time we were perfectly capable of making our own judgments and contributions that were just as good as theirs. This conclusion manifested no arrogance but rather an expression of confidence in ourselves, a new consciousness of our own being and our own destiny.

For the first time, painters began to look around them and take stock of their own environment. They learned something about the country in which they lived. Saturnino Herrán was painting the Mexican people as he saw them, not aping foreign perceptions of them. Doctor Atl went to live on Popocatépetl, inspiration for so many of his paintings, and I set out to explore the poorest suburbs of Mexico City. Like the awakening of dawn, our canvases slowly began to show Mexican scenery, forms, and colors, the ones we were most familiar with. The first step was being taken. We were freeing ourselves from foreign tyranny. We also drew on another strength—our thorough preparation and rigorous training.

Why did we always have to be on our knees before Kant and Hugo? Hooray for those great masters! But we ourselves are perfectly capable of producing our

Sources: José Clemente Orozco, *Autobiografía* (Mexico City: Ediciones Era, 1970), pp. 31–32, 56, 58, 60, 61; *Textos de Orozco* (Mexico City: Universidad Nacional Autónoma de México, 1983), pp. 41, 42, 67–69. With permission of the publisher.

own Kants and Hugos. We can extract the iron from our own soil to make our own machines and ships! We know how to build prodigious cities, create nations, and explore the universe. Were not the two races from which we sprang Titans? . . .

Mexico was prepared and ready for the mural movement that burst forth in 1922. The very idea of creating murals, as well as other ideas and the fervor that go into making an artistic movement, already existed. They had been germinating, developing, defining themselves between 1900 and 1920, a period of twenty years. Of course such ideas had their origins in earlier centuries, but they acquired their distinctive form during those two decades. Everyone knows all too well that no historical event appears out of nowhere, isolated and without origins.

It is possible to summarize Mexican thoughts on art in 1920 as follows:

1. In those days we came to believe that anybody could paint. Indeed, the greater the ignorance and stupidity of the practitioner the higher the merit of the art.
2. Many believed that the pre-Cortés art was our true tradition and they spoke of the "renaissance of Indian art."
3. Excitement over the handicraft art of the Indians reached a fever pitch. Mexico was awash with woven straw objects, ceramics, sandals, dancing figures from Chalma, serapes, and rebozos and began to export these items. Tourists inundated Cuernavaca and Taxco.
4. Folk themes, in all their varieties, appeared in painting, sculpture, theater, music, and literature.
5. Extreme nationalism appeared. Mexican artists considered themselves the equal or superior to foreigners. The themes depicted in art had to be Mexican.
6. The place of the worker in art became clearer. "Art glorified the working class." It was thought that art ought to be an essential weapon in the social struggle.
7. The attitude of Doctor Atl favoring direct, active, and militant participation of artists in politics became a school of thought.
8. Artists took up history and sociology with a passion.

It is worth noting that at the same time Mexican musicians came to similar conclusions. In 1913, Manuel M. Ponce discovered before anyone else the value and significance of popular music. In a concert which he gave in the Wagner Theater featuring songs such as "Estrellita," he was highly criticized for taking seriously what, until then, had been considered trivial.

All these ideas flowed together to shape the mural movement. Ideas were one thing, techniques another. The aspiring muralists had to experiment and slowly, through trial and error, develop their own techniques. During that preparatory period, muralists created some work that was largely decorative, only timidly relating to the drama of our history, philosophy, and other themes. Once the muralists mastered technique, they used it to express themselves well, and since they were a small, organized group each learned from the other's experiences.

Later, some became so impassioned by the themes of their art that they totally abandoned art to participate in other revolutionary activities that had nothing to do with their artistic training.

What differentiated the mural painters from any other artistic group was their critical skills. Because of the extensive training most of them enjoyed, they understood the artistic challenge and rose to meet it successfully. They understood perfectly the significance of the historical moment in which they painted and the relationship of their art to the world around them. Fortuitously, a group of talented artists and revolutionary leaders came together with a common goal, the one facilitating the other, each understanding the role he was to play in that happy coincidence and historic moment. José Vasconcelos was the statesman with the greatest vision of the role the artist could play in the revolution.

In 1922, a revolutionary Ministry of Education was organized. Its building was nearly completed, and everywhere the State was building new schools, stadiums, and libraries, all with vast walls inviting murals. The Government Printing Office, also a creation of Vasconcelos, published large editions of the classics, which were sold at less than cost to the public. The revolutionary government called on all artists and intellectuals to participate, and the painters found a golden opportunity, unavailable to them for many centuries. I do not know how or why Diego Rivera returned from Europe. Vasconcelos called Siqueiros from Rome, and the two artists joined the colleagues resident in Mexico. . . .

Mural painting began under excellent auspices. Even the errors committed were useful. It broke the routine into which painting had fallen. It overcame many prejudices and served as a means to view social problems from new perspectives. It brought to a close a whole period of Bohemian mindlessness populated by charlatans who lived listless lives in ivory towers—really, dingy little rooms—with a drink in one hand and a guitar in the other, while they feigned some absurd idealism, beggars in a putrid society on the verge of extinction.

In the revolutionary society, painters and sculptors will be people of action, sane and educated; they are prepared to work eight or ten hours a day like a good laborer. They frequent factories, universities, barracks, and schools, eager to learn and understand. Dressed in overalls, they mount the scaffolding to do everything possible as quickly as possible to contribute to the creation of a new society.☐

New World, New Race, and New Art

THE ART OF THE NEW WORLD cannot take root in the old traditions of the Old World nor in the aboriginal traditions represented by the remains of our ancient Indian peoples. Although the art of all races and of all times has a common value—human, universal—each new cycle must work for itself, must create, must yield its own production, its individual share to the common good.

To go solicitously to Europe, bent on poking about its ruins in order to import them and servilely to copy them, is no greater error than is the looting of the indigenous remains of the New World with the object of copying with equal servility its ruins or its present folklore. However picturesque and interesting these may be, however productive and useful ethnology may find them, they cannot furnish a point of departure for the new creation. To lean upon the art of the aborigines, whether it be of antiquity or of the present day, is a sure indication of impotence and of cowardice, in fact, of fraud.

If *new* races have appeared upon the lands of the *New World,* such races have the unavoidable duty to produce a *New Art* in a spiritual and physical medium. Any other road is cowardice. . . .

The highest, the most logical, the purest and strongest form of painting is the mural. In this form alone, it is one with the other arts—with all the others.

It is, too, the most disinterested form, for it cannot be made a matter of private gain; it cannot be hidden away for the benefit of a certain privileged few.

It is for the people. It is for ALL.□

In Defense of National Dance

THE BEST EVIDENCE OF THE magnificent success of the Mexico City Ballet during its second season is the virulence of the criticism hurled against it. That unjust criticism, a total refusal to see anything positive, misunderstood or overlooked an important reality and contribution.

This ballet company is not improvised but is the result of more than a decade of the continuous, intense, intelligent daily work of the Campobello sisters. They have taught the art of dance to a large group of young people. They were the first to have the idea of outdoor ballet performances and then to carry it out. They made the most profound, complete, and perhaps only technical study of Mexican folk dances. They organized the only formal classical ballet company in the nation. They have been, and continue to be, the most imaginative choreographers and directors, and if those achievements are not enough, one of them, a prima ballerina, is a dancer whose personal gifts and potential could rank her among the finest in the world. Fortunately, our country can boast of some illustrious women in the arts, and there is no doubt that the Campobello sisters will some day rank with them.

Right now we have our ballet; it is their work, it is offering programs of dance, not a promise, not a project, not an experiment, but a reality, a consummated fact, something that should neither be destroyed nor overlooked as the envious would do. The company may well have its defects, as any human product might, but it contains the divine spark of creation, the vital beginning that guarantees a permanent and definitive life for this company.

The old Franco-Russo ballet form has fallen into full decadence after a long and glorious life. The remains of that artistic shipwreck can be found floating hither and yonder like pitiful remnants. The principal cause of that wreckage was capitalism, the insatiable thirst of impresarios for profits that drowned the creative genius of choreographers and dancers. In the midst of that disaster, at least locally, appeared the Mexico City Ballet to rescue the art of dance. It represents the strength of youth, enthusiasm, dedication, generosity, genius, and efficiency.

Those that would have us believe that because it is a Mexican organization the Mexico City Ballet is inferior and untrained come too late with such stupid arguments. Those days are now past. Those responsible for getting rid of such traditional ideas of cultural inferiority are the contemporary painters of this country. We are always eager to take lessons from the art of the rest of the world, anywhere we can find worthy examples to study, but that is absolutely different from considering ourselves inferior to the rest of the world and incapable of creating our own art.

An unmistakable and certain proof that an artist or a group of artists is mediocre and improvising is that, achieving a certain level of development, they ossify and cannot move forward. Although this is only its second season, our ballet has demonstrated its impressive progress and one will see in the near future its dynamic ability to renovate. It will improve, it will correct the errors of detail, it will perfect whichever works need improvement, it will advance the invention, magic, and surprise its art cultivates. The ballet only looks to the past like any good student who learns from old teachers, but it directs its ambitions toward the future in a world shaken to its foundation by an unquenchable thirst for renovation, in an age that is furiously revolutionary.

It is necessary to transcend the old Franco-Russo ballet, and our dance company will do just that. It is already doing it by ending a beautiful but now spent and decrepit chapter of descriptive, romantic dance and reaching for the higher level of poetic and lyric purity already achieved by the plastic arts in our country. □

Reinterpreting the Indian Past

While others talked vaguely in their interpretive studies of the Indians' contributions to the creation of Latin American societies, the Peruvian thinker José Carlos Mariátegui (1895–1930) dwelt on the importance of their agrarian achievements. Within their own communal settings, they once had produced abundantly. In fact, the Andean population ate far better before the arrival of the Europeans than any time thereafter. As the conquerors and their descendants increasingly emphasized commercial and export agriculture, the supply of food diminished, a situation Mariátegui considered an interruption in economic development. He consistently and emphatically linked economic well-being with subsistence agriculture, a connection that most economists neglected in their pursuit of industrialization as the panacea. Among the many provocative ideas he put forth in his *Seven Interpretive Essays on Peruvian Reality,* first published in 1928, was the need to reinvigorate the Indian communities through agrarian reform. Thus, for him, the achievement of an economically viable and developed Latin America, the professed goal of all nationalists, required the re-creation of a part of the Indian past by returning lands to the Indian community.

ECONOMIC INSTITUTIONS, better than any other measurement, demonstrate how the Spanish conquest altered the history of Peru. That aspect of the conquest broke a fundamental historical continuity. Up until the conquest, an

Source: José Carlos Mariátegui, *Siete Ensayos de Interpretación de la Realidad Peruana* (Lima: Biblioteca Amauta, 1928), pp. 7–9, 18–19, 25–27, 29, 34–37, 52–53, 60, 62–63.

economy had developed that spontaneously and freely sprang from the Peruvian soil, people, and experience. Within the Incan empire, the most interesting aspect of the sedentary, agrarian communities arose from their economic behavior. All the historical testimonies conclude that the Incan population—hardworking, disciplined, and simple—enjoyed economic self-sufficiency. Food abounded; the population increased. The empire experienced none of the problems predicated by Malthus. The community life-style directed by the Incas minimized individuality, but it instilled in each a humble and religious sense of social duty that ensured economic development. The rulers took full advantage of that virtue of their people and improved their vast imperial territory with roads and irrigation projects. They constantly expanded their rule into neighboring tribes. Collective work and common effort were fruitfully used for social goals.

The Spanish conquerors disregarded that marvelous productive system without finding an adequate substitute for it. Indian society and the Incan economy were disrupted and then destroyed by the force of the conquest. Once the imperial bonds of unity had been destroyed, the kingdom dissolved into isolated communities. The Indian labor system stopped functioning in its customary, organic manner. The conquerors concerned themselves primarily with the distribution of booty, robbing the temples and palaces of their treasures. They divided up the land and the inhabitants among themselves with no thought of the future except their own individual enrichment.

Once implanted, the viceroyalty began the difficult and complex task of reorienting the economy. The Spanish king set the new economic and political organization of his vast colony. Spaniards began to till the soil and mine the gold and silver. On the ruins of a successful socialist economy, they built the bases of a feudal one.

Spain did not send to Peru, nor to any of its extensive possessions for that matter, many colonists. The weakness of the Spanish empire resided precisely in its character and structure as a military and religious enterprise more than a political and economic one. Contrary to what happened along the coast of New England, few pilgrims or pioneers arrived in the Spanish colonies. About the only ones who arrived in Spanish America were viceroys, bureaucrats, lawyers, adventurers, clergy, and soldiers. In the strict sense of the word, colonization did not take place. The population of Lima consisted of the viceregal court, a complementary bureaucracy, some religious, inquisitors, merchants, servants, and slaves. The Spanish settler lacked the ability to create viable economic communities. Instead of utilizing the Indians, the Spaniards seemed more intent upon exterminating them. The colonizers failed to create a solid and organic economy. The base of the colonial organization revealed a structural weakness: It lacked a coherent population. The Spaniards and the mestizos were too few in number to be able to exploit on any appreciable scale the riches of the territory. They imported Africans as slaves to work the coastal estates, thus mixing into their feudal society the characteristics of a slave society.

Only the Jesuits, with their propensity toward capitalism, demonstrated in Peru, as elsewhere in the Americas, some aptitude in creating a viable economy. The lands they acquired prospered. Traces of their efficient economic organization can still be found. Whoever recalls the vast experiment of the Jesuits in Paraguay, where they cleverly took advantage of and exploited the natural communal instincts of the Indians, will not be surprised that the sons of Saint Ignatius of Loyola succeeded in establishing flourishing economic centers in Peru as well. They accomplished what the nobles, lawyers, and clergymen, given over to the pleasures of Lima, never could.

More than anything else, the colonizers wanted to exploit the Peruvian lodes of gold and silver. The Spaniards preferred to live in the lowlands. They both respected and feared the Andes, over which they never felt they exerted full control. But to exploit the mines, they had to establish some towns in the mountains. Without the greed for the precious metals buried within the Andes, the Spanish conquest of the mountainous region would have been slower and less complete. . . .

Beneath the feudal economy imposed by the Spaniards during the conquest there still exists in the mountains some distinct residues of the indigenous communal economy. Along the coast, a nascent capitalist economy struggles to grow in feudal soil. It gives every indication, most particularly in the mental outlook of the aspiring capitalists, of being hopelessly backward.

Peru remains an agrarian country despite the emphasis placed on mining. Farming employs the vast majority of the population. The Indians, who compose four-fifths of the population, are traditionally farmers. They remain closely linked to the cultivation of the soil. . . . The problems the Indians experience arise from our economy. They have their roots in landowning structures. Any efforts to resolve them through administrative or police methods, through education or through the expansion of communication and transportation, are superficial and secondary as long as the present feudal landowning system exists.

This system, known locally as *gamonalismo,* invalidates any law or ordinance for the protection of the Indians. The large landowner is nothing more or nothing less than a feudal lord. He scoffs at any law that does not suit him. Custom and habit support him. The law proscribes unpaid labor and, yet, unpaid labor and even forced labor exist on the large estates. The judge, local officials, the police, the teacher, and the tax collector are all held in bondage to the feudal estate. No law can prevail against the *gamonales.* Any official who dares to impose the law will receive no support from the central government in which the influence of the large landowners is paramount. One way or another, they control congress. Any new approach to the major problem of the Indians requires attention to the inequities of the landowning system rather than to protective laws. . . .

Any assumption that the Indian problem is ethnic, or "racial," rests on the most pitiful, outdated imperialist ideas. The concept of inferior races well served Western Europe in its conquests and expansions. To hope for the emancipation of the Indians through the active cross-breeding of the native race with white immigrants is an anti-sociological naivete, only conceivable in the primitive mind of the importer of merino sheep. Asians, who in no way are superior to the Indians, have assimilated admirably Western culture without any need of European blood transfusions. The degeneration or incapacity of the Peruvian Indians is a self-serving deception propagated by scientific quacks in the pay of the feudal lords. . . .

To remedy the agrarian problem it is absolutely essential to first eliminate feudalism in Peru. In fact, the first order of business of the democratic-bourgeois governments after independence should have been its eradication. The truth of the matter is that during a century of independence Peru has had neither a bourgeoisie nor capitalism. The old feudal class, disguised as a republican bourgeoisie, preserves its privileges. While an end was declared to entailed estates after independence was won, that legality did not lead to the increase of the small propertied class. The old landowning class retains both land and power. As long as that class holds power, it is fruitless to expect the disappearance of the large estate. However, legal means to disentail and break up the lands of the remaining Indian communities were used effectively. Large estates even grew in size at the expense of those communities. During a century under republican constitutions, the large estates continued to grow and to strengthen themselves despite all the fine liberal theories incorporated into our constitutions and the urgent need for the development of a capitalist economy.

Two major characteristics of feudalism survive: the large estate and forced labor. The two are inseparable. It is impossible to eliminate one without eliminating the other. This analysis highlights the socioeconomic and, consequently, political nature of the problem. In short, the agrarian problems are such that they cannot be resolved by technicians and agronomists.

The liberal solution to this problem would emphasize individuality, the division of the large estate into small individual parcels. Such a solution cannot be labeled revolutionary, vanguard, Marxist, or heretical; it is pure and simple a constitutional, democratic, capitalist, and bourgeois response. It has its origin in that pool of liberal ideas that inspired the constitutions of democratic-bourgeois nations. The nations of Central and Eastern Europe, where a world war destroyed the basis of feudalism, decreed agrarian reforms. Encouraged by the Western capitalist nations opposed to Russia, the reforms limited, in principle, the size of property to a maximum of approximately one thousand acres.

In accordance with my ideology, I believe the time to experiment with the liberal, individualistic solutions has already passed. Peru possesses a unique situation, a peculiar characteristic of an agrarian nature: residues of the Indian communities survive. Still present in Indian life and agriculture are elements of the old Incan socialism.

If those professing the liberal and democratic doctrines really want to solve the Indian problem, a solution that will free the Indian from servitude, they can draw from the recent reform experiences of Eastern Europe rather than from the experience of Mexico, which they seem to regard as dangerous and radical. They still have time to experiment with a liberal solution. They would thus ensure that discussions of the agrarian problems by new generations would include liberal ideas. Liberalism would still be part of the political agenda.

The land problem clarifies the Socialist or more advanced attitudes toward the remnants of the viceregal past. The literary glorification of the colonial past does not interest us except to demonstrate the colonial attitudes and practices still among us. The colonial inheritance that we seek to eliminate consists of the large estate and forced labor. . . . It survives in feudalism, which, in turn, contains the uncultivated seeds of capitalism.

Spain brought us the Middle Ages with its Inquisition and its feudalism. Then, it introduced us to the Counter-Reformation, reactionary, Jesuitic, and scholastic in nature. As we slowly assimilated Western culture, at times filtered through Spain itself, we painfully freed ourselves from those influences. But we have still not freed ourselves from the economic strictures imposed by Spain and allowed to remain intact during the past century of independence. The roots of feudalism still lie buried in our economic soil. Their existence retards the development of our capitalism.

The land-owning system dictates the political and administrative systems of our country. The agrarian problem—which the republic refuses to resolve—dominates all other problems. On a feudal economic foundation, liberal and democratic institutions can neither prosper nor function.

The link of the Indian problem to the land problem is even more pronounced. Indians are farmers. The overwhelming majority of the Incas worked in the countryside as farmers or herders. Even their industries and arts had a rural, domestic character. The link between people and the land was stronger in Incan Peru than anywhere else. The most admirable public and collective works in the Incan Empire were for military, religious, and agrarian purposes. The irrigation systems of the coast and the highlands, the roads, and the terraced agriculture of the Andes stand as the best testimonies of the high level of economic organization achieved by the Incas. In all aspects, Incan civilization can be characterized as an agrarian civilization. The anthologist Luís E. Valcarcel in his study of the Incan economy wrote, "The land, in the Indian tradition, is the common mother. From her womb come not just food but the people themselves. The land provides everything. The cult of Mama Pacha is equal to that of worship of the sun. As the sun belongs to no one individual but rather to everyone who stands under it, so the earth, too, belongs to everyone who stands on it. Together these two fundamental tenets of Indian belief create the agrarian concept of communal access to land and universal worship of the sun."

The Incan system—which can neither be negated nor belittled because it developed under the autocratic governance of the Incas—can be designated as agrarian communism. According to the economic historian César Antonio Ugarte, the fundamental characteristics of the Incan economy were the following: "The *ayllu,* a communal organization of related families, collectively held the land, although part of it was divided into individual but non-transferable parcels; the collective enjoyed equal access to water, pastures, and woodlands for the use of all the community. Likewise, a federation of ayllus settled in and around a village enjoyed the same rights and privileges of the individual ayllu. Cooperative labor existed and so did the individual harvest of produce."

The destruction of this economy—and the culture it nourished—resulted from Spanish conquest and colonization. Not only was this autochthonous system destroyed but Spain offered nothing superior as a substitute. The colonial regime disorganized and annihilated the Incan agrarian economy without replacing it with one that provided as abundantly for the population. Under the Indian aristocracy, the natives composed a nation of ten million inhabitants with an efficient and organic State that exercised all the attributes of sovereignty. Under a foreign aristocracy the natives were reduced to a dispersed, befuddled mass of a million bound to servitude and peonage.

The democratic data are damning. One may censor the Incan system from the point of view of modern liberal concepts of justice and liberty, but the historical reality is that it assured the material well-being and growth of a population that numbered at least ten million when the Spaniards arrived in Peru. After three centuries of colonial rule, that population barely exceeded one million. This reality condemns the colonial system not just from an abstract, theoretical, or moral point of view of justice but from the very practical access to the material needs of life. It inflicted genocide. . . .

The large estates continue their domination of national life. While the liberalism manifested in the republican legislation remains inert before feudalism, it actively opposes any form of community property. If no changes threaten the large estates, many constantly work against the Indian communities. In a society dominated by community traditions, the act of dissolving the community has not served to create a small propertied class. It disorients the Indian. It is difficult to transform society artificially, and that difficulty only multiplies when dealing with a peasant society profoundly attached to its traditions and institutions. Neither a constitution nor a civil code can implant individualism in a traditional community. The formation of the individualism has been both more spontaneous and more complicated. While the destruction of the communities neither converted the Indians into small property holders nor into salaried laborers, it did transfer their land to the large landowners and their clientele. The destruction of the communities also made it easier for the large landowners to recruit Indian laborers and to tie them to the large estate. . . .

The defense of the Indian community does not rest on abstract principles of justice nor on sentimental traditionalist considerations but on concrete and practical reasons of social and economic order. Communal property does not represent in Peru a primitive economy that is being replaced gradually by a progressive economy based on private property. No, quite the contrary. The communities have been dispossessed of their lands in favor of the feudal or semi-feudal estate, organically incapable of technical progress. . . .

The Indian community served society in two major ways. First, it proved to be an effective producer of food. Second, it morally stimulated the Indians to do their best work. The community nourished the well-being of the Indians. Castro Pozo made a very just observation when he noted, "The Indian community encourages two great economic and social principles which neither the sociologist nor the capitalist has been able to duplicate: cooperative work that is performed in a relaxed atmosphere of pleasantry, emulation, and companionship." By dissolving or abandoning the Indian community, the governments of the feudal landowners have attacked an economic institution and, more importantly, a social institution that defended the Indian traditions, protected the rural family, and reflected popular legal philosophy. . . . □

Masquerading Reality

In 1989, Eduardo Galeano pleaded that efforts to define Latin America must take
into account both what it is and what it is not. He differentiated between a "real
reality"—what Latin America is—and an "official reality"—what it is not. A kind
of fantasy reigns, in which governments masquerade as something they are not
and use a language that makes no sense. Oligarchies declare themselves to be
democracies and boast of economic development when it is economic growth
that occurs. In his essay, Galeano provides some scathing examples of these
masquerades. Nearly a century after Martí's "Our America," Galeano, an Uruguayan intellectual, echoed Martí's criticism and advice: Reject the exotic foreign example and explore local realities so that Latin America can achieve its
promising potential.

W E ARE CONTEMPORARIES of an incommunicado world, a world ever more
incommunicado as the technology of communication becomes more developed. It is a world where only rarely does the sound of words coincide with their
meaning, and where the vast majority of the people are condemned to the mute
language of fear and solitude.

I am a man from the South, and Latin American history teaches one to
mistrust words. In 1965, the military dictatorship of Brazil, the military dictatorship of Paraguay, the military dictatorship of Honduras, and the military dictatorship of Nicaragua invaded Santo Domingo, together with the U.S. Marines,
to save "democracy" threatened by the people. In 1961, in the name of democracy, those who longed for the dictatorship of Batista landed on the beaches of
Cuba's Playa Girón. Today, in the name of democracy, those who long for the
dictatorship of Somoza attack Nicaragua. The President of Colombia speaks of
democracy, yet in 1987 more than a thousand political opponents and trade
unionists were killed by the forces of state terrorism, acting with impunity and
in accord with the instructions of the army's counterinsurgency manual, which
teaches how to create paramilitary organizations.

Official language rants deliriously, and its delirium is the system's normality. "There will be no devaluation," say the Ministers of Economy on the eve of
the currency's collapse. "Agrarian reform is our principal goal," say the Ministers of Agriculture as they extend the *latifundios.* "There is no censorship," rejoice the Ministers of Culture in countries where price and illiteracy make books
inaccessible to the vast majority of the people.

For five centuries, Latin American history has been a history of continued
disjuncture between reality and words. The truth of colonial Latin America is
not to be found in the numerous, fat volumes of *Laws of the Indies* but in the
scaffold and pillory erected in the center of every town square. And our countries' independence did not reduce the distance between juridical life and fiction.
On the contrary, the distance multiplied in length and depth, creating the gaping,
immense abyss that currently lies between official reality and real reality. Official

Source: Eduardo Galeano, "Democracy in Latin America: Best Is That Which Best Creates,"
Social Justice 16:1 (Spring 1989), pp. 119–126. With permission of *Social Justice.*

reality today, as much if not more than yesterday, serves the necessary exorcism of real reality. At the end of the 18th century, the "certificates of whiteness" issued by the kings of Spain and Portugal magically made whites out of mestizos—those who could afford to pay for them—no matter how dark their skin. A few years later, the illusionism of juridical formalities reached its greatest splendor in constitutions of the new-born nations, embroidered with great dexterity by the luminaires of Independence. From the beginning our ruling classes were inflicted with copyitis and convinced that no one is better than he who copies best; thus they faithfully reproduced the constitutional models of the metropolis. Consequently, we had bourgeois constitutions without ever having had a bourgeois revolution or a bourgeoisie. The first Constitution of Bolivia, personally drafted by the liberator Simón Bolívar for the country which bears his name, was a beautiful synthesis of the constitutions of the most civilized countries of that era. It suffered from only one defect: It had nothing to do with Bolivia. Among other things, it granted rights of citizenship only to those who knew how to read and write Spanish, leaving out 95% of all Bolivians.

The generals who won independence, and the traders and doctors who profited by it, acted as though the new countries could transform themselves into France simply by repeating French ideas, or could become England by consuming British goods. Today, their heirs act as though their countries could become the United States by virtue of imitating its defects. Those who rule believe that he is best who copies best. Official culture exalts the virtues of the monkey and the parrot. Alienation in Latin America: a circus spectacle. Imports, imposters: Bolivia has no coast, but it has admirals dressed up as Lord Nelson. Lima has no rain, but it has roofs with drain gutters. In Managua, one of Earth's hottest cities, condemned to boil perpetually, mansions were built with ostentatious fireplaces and society ladies came to Somoza's parties draped in silver-fox stoles.

The dominant cultures, cultures of dominant classes dominated from abroad, reveal themselves pathetically incapable of offering either roots or wings to the nations they are said to represent. They are tired cultures, as though they had done a great deal. Despite their deceptive resplendence, they express the opacity of the local oligarchies, still able to copy but ever less able to create. After having covered our lands with fake Parthenons, fake palaces of Versailles, fake castles of Loire, and fake cathedrals of Chartres, today they deplete our national wealth by imitating U.S. models of ostentation and waste. Ensconced in great shelters and Babylonic cities, they ignore and disdain national reality, or all of it that contradicts them, and they are practically reduced to acting as transmission belts for foreign centers of power. Children come from Paris in the beak of a stork, and truth comes from New York or Miami in video cassettes.

Far from an artificial import, democracy sinks its roots into the deepest of Latin American history. When all is said and done, Thomas Moore's Utopia was inspired by the indigenous American communities, which, through the centuries and the massacres and the scorn, miraculously have been able to perpetuate a mode of production and life based on solidarity, equal rights, and collective participation. But the Western "democracimeter" measures the greater or lesser degree of democracy in so-called Third World countries by their greater or lesser ability to imitate.

The democracimeter is located in the international centers of power—a handful of countries in the North where increasing wealth, in large part a result of the growing poverty of the rest of the world, allows for internal political freedom without risk of surprise attacks. In measuring underdeveloped countries, the democracimeter forces them to demonstrate a devotion to form, even though such devotion implies a betrayal of content. Little does it matter that the developed world's caricature of democratic institutions disguises a fear of real democracy, of any genuine expression of the popular will; little does it matter that almost all of the Latin American military dictatorships of the 20th century have been careful to pay taxes on their vices in order to finance the appearance of virtue. Nearly all of the dictatorships have held elections, financed parliaments, judges, political parties, and even an opposition press; they have paid homage to a tradition that places all importance on the husk and none on the grain. In reality, the international code of good democratic conduct not only condemns the less presentable dictatorships—generals skilled in the craft of carnage; it also disqualifies any experience that attempts to escape the stifling confines of capitalism and that does not adjust to the institutional norms of European liberalism.

Thus the vigilant democracimeter rejects Nicaragua, which has reduced infant mortality by half during the years of its revolution. Yet it accepts, for example, Brazil, where the military dictatorship has been survived by a social dictatorship and where the economy annihilates even more people than the police, who annihilate many.

The truth of democracimeter, which is the truth of the system, can be a lie for the victims of the system. I don't think the eight million abandoned children who roam the streets of Brazilian cities believe in democracy. I don't think they believe in it, because democracy doesn't believe in them. They have no democracy in which to believe; Brazilian democracy wasn't made by them, and it doesn't function for them, even though it meets certain of the formal requisites demanded by the democracimeter before granting its nod of approval.

Democracy is not what it is, but what it appears to be. We live surrounded by canned culture. Canned culture scorns content. Importance is given to what is said, not what is done. Canned culture: The marriage contract matters more than love, the funeral more than the dead, clothes more than the body, and Mass more than God. The spectacle of democracy matters more than democracy itself. The death penalty doesn't exist in Brazil, nor will it, according to the new Constitution. But Brazil continuously applies the death penalty: every day it kills a thousand children by starvation and who knows how many more by the bullet in its violent cities and its *latifundios* invaded by desperate peons. Slavery supposedly has not existed for a century, but a third of Brazilian workers make little more than a dollar a day, and the social pyramid is white at the top and black at the base. The richest are the whitest and the poorest are the blackest. Four years after abolition, around 1892, the Brazilian government burned all documents related to slavery, books and accounts of the slave companies, receipts, regulations, statutes, etc., as though slavery had never existed.

For something not to exist, it is sufficient to declare that it does not exist. On July 14, 1789, French men and women stormed the Bastille, and King Louis

XVI wrote in his diary: "Nothing of importance." The Guatemalan dictator, Manuel Estrada Cabrera, decreed in 1902 that all of the country's volcanos were calm, while an avalanche of lava and mire erupting from the Santa María volcano razed more than a hundred villages in the outskirts of Quezaltenango. In 1905, the Colombian Congress approved a law establishing that Indians did not exist in San Andrés de Sotavento and other territories where streams of oil had suddenly sprung up; the Indians who existed were made illegal, and the oil companies were therefore able to kill them with impunity and keep their lands.

In Uruguay, a law was enacted in late 1986 ordering that the tortures, kidnappings, rapes, and assassinations committed by the recent military dictatorship be forgotten, as if these acts of state terrorism had never taken place. The Uruguayan people call it the Law of Impunity, and more than 600,000 signatures were gathered in opposition to it. Shortly before the promulgation of this law absolving the torturers, Uruguay signed and ratified the International Convention Against Torture, which obliges signatories to castigate torturers. The same thing happened in Argentina. This Convention explicitly denies as a defense the claim that torture was carried out under orders given by superiors. The Argentine government signed and ratified the Convention and then proceeded to legalize tortures that had been carried out in obedience to higher orders. In our countries, international conventions are equivalent to national laws. But it so happens that while some laws demand respect for human rights, others authorize the violation of those rights; some laws *appear* to exist while others exist in reality.

Last year Colombia celebrated the centennial of its national Constitution. During 50 of those 100 years, Colombia was under a state of siege. Which of these anniversaries is more representative of Colombian reality? The century since the adoption of the Constitution, a work of pretentious jurists and copy cats, or the half century lived under a state of siege? A military assault was carried out against Colombia's Palace of Justice very shortly before the Constitution's anniversary, and this unpunished crime made more evident than ever the high degree of militarization of Colombian democracy. Representative democracy of liberals and conservatives does not impede the ravages of structural violence: One of every three children in the Colombian countryside suffer mental retardation from malnutrition, and more people die from gun shots in Cali and Medellín than in Beirut. Death squads linked to the armed forces kill more people than the drug traffickers or terrorists, but not one of their members has been arrested or prosecuted, much less convicted.

The system applauds infamy if it is successful and castigates it if it fails. It rewards those who steal a lot but condemns those who steal little. It invokes peace and practices violence. It preaches to love thy neighbor, but it forces you to devour your neighbor in order to survive. The system's schizophrenic language reaches one of its most perfect moments of insanity when it confuses freedom of money with freedom of the people. The system's own language thus reveals what is in contradiction—open contradiction understandable by simple common sense—and anyone can see that this insanity is not innocent.

However, there is no shortage of intellectuals ready to fall into the trap, as was made evident by the nationalization of the private banks in Peru. There are those who place the poets' freedom of expression on the same level with the bankers' freedom of speculation. But in Latin America, as throughout the Third World, freedom of business has nothing to do with freedom of people; indeed, they are incompatible. To give complete freedom to money, the military dictatorships jail the people. It has taken much too much spilled blood over the centuries to force open our eyes to this reality.

We are trained not to see. Education uneducates, the communications media incommunicate. And education and the media induce us to accept a cat for a hare.

Even the map lies. We learn world geography from a map that doesn't show us the world as it is but as its owners order it to be. In the traditional planisphere, the one used in schools everywhere, Ecuador is not in the center: the north occupies two-thirds and the south one. Scandinavia looks larger than India, when in reality it is three times smaller. The Soviet Union looks twice the size of Africa, when in reality Africa is considerably larger. Latin America takes up less space on the world map than Europe, and much less than the total of the United States and Canada, when in reality Latin America is twice the size of Europe and considerably bigger than the United States and Canada.

The map, which shrinks us, symbolizes everything else. Geography stolen, economy sacked, history falsified, a daily usurpation of reality: The so-called Third World, inhabited by "third class" people, encompasses less, eats less, remembers less, lives less, says less.

And not only does it take up less space on the map; it also takes up less space in the dailies, on the television, on the radio. Less, to say the least; it takes up almost no space at all. Sometimes Latin America becomes fashionable, as fugaciously fashionable as any fad. Then the intellectuals of the north cast fleeting glances of adoration. At the end of the 1950s it was Cuba's turn. At the end of the 1970s, Nicaragua. Between one or another hallucination, illusions of unblemished revolutions, were Che Guevara's guerrilla war and other romantic exploits. Such fulminating passions have given way, fatally, to disenchantment and public abomination. As in the 16th century, reality spoils the illusory promises of El Dorado. Reality is what it is, not what it is wished to be by those who first confuse it with heaven and then assume the right to confuse it with hell, to condemn it to hell for ever more: a hell of silence, a hell of contempt. Fascination and condemnation are two sides of the same attitude that ignores and disrespects reality. And the reality is that Latin American democracies want to be real democracies. They will not resign themselves to being "dictamocracies," democracies mortgaged by the dictatorships, although the Western democracimeter doesn't give much importance to this detail. But any dynamic democracy, transformer of reality, is dangerous to the structure of impotence. We well know what happened to Salvador Allende and thousands of Chileans when Chile took democracy seriously.

Writer Gabriel García Márquez has defined in very harsh terms the unleashing of the Chilean process which culminated in the tragedy of 1973. Chile had lived through a cycle of affirming democracy—people power—and of affirming sovereignty—the recuperation of usurped resources and the power of national decision making. But Chilean democratic institutions were designed to function against democracy, not for it. Referring to the Supreme Court of Justice, which legitimated the assassins, and to the Congress, which groveled before them, and to the newspapers and parties which encouraged the *coup d'état,* García Márquez wrote that destiny had offered Salvador Allende "the rare and tragic greatness to die defending with bullets the grotesque anachronism of bourgeois rights, all of the moth-eaten paraphernalia of a shitty system."

Fifteen years after the tragedy in Chile, Nicaragua resists. Feet firmly on the ground, Nicaragua's experience with popular participation and the collective will of national dignity endures against mean winds. In Nicaragua not only does a people's army confront rented soldiers who invade the country; the energy of human creation also confronts the damned inheritance of underdevelopment, ignorance, passivity, irresponsibility, the fear of change, the fear of being, the fear of doing. And fear, as Argentina's Mothers of the Plaza de Mayo have said so well, is a jail without bars.

Against all odds, against the wind, against all fear, the Uruguayan petition campaign to collect signatures to put the law of "forgetfulness" before a plebiscite has recently ended. The recent military dictatorship, which castigated any act of human solidarity with torture, imprisonment, exile, or death, had experimented with a society of deaf mutes: hearing prohibited, talking prohibited. And this experiment appeared to have its democratic continuation in collective amnesia: remembering prohibited. But more than 600,000 Uruguayans have signed a petition against forced forgetfulness; in terms of population, that would be the equivalent of eight million Spaniards, or eleven million French or Italians. And each signature affirms: affirms the dignity and the will to change, and affirms the memory of dignity and the memory of the will to change. And thus each signature affirms the certainty that, sooner or later, another time, a new time, will come.

More than half a century ago, a writer from the Dominican Republic, Pedro Henriquez Urena, asked that the blood spilled throughout the centuries not have been spilt in vain. He asked, or, rather, demanded, that the tragedy of Latin America be productive. "If our America is to be nothing more than a prolongation of Europe," said Henriquez Urena,

> . . . if the only thing we do is offer new soil for the exploitation of man by man, if we haven't decided that this shall be the promised land for a humanity tired of seeking it in all climates, then we have no justification. It would be preferable to see our highlands and our pampas turned into deserts rather than let them serve to multiply human pain: not the pain born of love and death, which can never be avoided, but the pain inflicted by greed and arrogance.

The memory of pain is forcing us to struggle so that democracy shall be democracy, true democracy, and not the decorative mask of a system which sacrifices all other rights to the right of property and which only grants freedom of expression to those who can pay for it. And this democracy won't be any truer because it looks more like the models of Western Europe or Eastern Europe, or of anywhere else. It will be truer democracy to the extent that it unleashes the participatory will and creative energy of the people, which is an energy for the transformation of reality. Because that which copies best is not best; best is that which best creates, even when mistakes are made in creating.

And the process of creation, with its hits and misses, forebodes of another time, a time in which laws to absolve the crimes of state terrorism will not be written, but rather laws to absolve fear; and no law shall require due obedience, but all laws will require due dignity; and the final word will not be said on justice until the final word has been said about the injustice that reigns in our sad lands. And then humiliation will disappear, not the men and women who fight against humiliation. This is our way of paying homage to these women and men, the thousands upon thousands of disappeared in Latin America, and to the infinite number of combatants throughout the world who have fallen in the fight for human dignity. To create and to fight, against the powerful lie, against the powerful fear: this is our way of saying to each of them, to each of the disappeared, to each of the fallen: "When you died, your death was not." □

6

The Quest for Economic Development

Beginning at varying periods during the last half of the nineteenth century, the nations of Latin America underwent a pronounced acceleration of modernization, industrialization, and urbanization. During the early decades of the twentieth century, nationalism and a greater degree of democratization added to political complexities. Together, those five trends contributed to what appeared to be rapid changes throughout the region. At the same time, demographic and economic growth increasingly characterized all of Latin America. A heavy influx of European immigrants even changed the physical appearance of Latin Americans in some areas.

Latin Americans became acutely aware that as their economies grew, however erratically, development remained elusive. Greater apparent wealth and manifestations of modernization seemed to etch more sharply the poverty of ever larger numbers of the population. Wealth concentrated in few hands. Modernization benefitted only part of the population. While the production of exports displayed commendable efficiency, food for local consumption became scarcer and consequently more expensive. If economic development had anything to do with the economic well-being of the majority of the citizens, then little development was taking place to the apparent frustration of many.

The questions of how and why the concentration of wealth took place and persisted preoccupied thinkers, statesmen, some governments, and many ordinary citizens who felt left out. Inevitably the search for the suitable means to achieve economic development sparked discussions and debates. The enigma of poor people inhabiting rich lands challenged—and taunted—the Latin Americans. Some historians view the search for economic development as the central theme of twentieth-century Latin America.

The first four documents of this chapter discuss the history and consequences of underdevelopment, emphasizing a causation linked to institutional structures and dependency. The succeeding three documents suggest resolutions to persistent underdevelopment. The final documents reveal expressions in art and literature of concern with underdevelopment and modernization.

The Historical Causes
of Underdevelopment

Using his own country, Venezuela, as the example, José A. Silva Michelena summarizes the complex history of Latin America's underdevelopment and dependency. A failure to develop and a reliance on, and subordination to, the stronger and developed economy of a dominate foreign power (the metropolis) intimately entwine throughout the history of Latin America. Silva Michelena indicates that such a relationship became institutionalized during the past five centuries. Consequently, the best that Venezuela, or Latin America, can hope for under present structures is "dependent economic growth," unsteady, unreliable, and therefore undesirable because it can only react to economic demands and decisions made abroad. The Venezuelan scholar characterizes the combination of underdevelopment and dependency as a potent historical force that has shaped and continues to shape Latin America.

THE GENERAL LAW that describes underdevelopment as a process has been briefly expressed as follows:

> Capitalism inserts, in a precapitalist structure, a foreign sector which gives origin to and fosters a deformed and dependent capitalist growth which generates the conditions for its own stagnation or involution.[1]

In order to understand this definition we must review history, though concisely, in order to lay bare the roots of the process. If we know how deep the roots lie, we shall better understand the enormous effort that must go into the uprooting.

What is today called Latin America was discovered when the European capitalist nations were expanding throughout the world in search of new trade routes, new markets, and primary resources. At that time, Spain and Portugal had some industry and carried on minor trade with other European countries, but they were in no sense dynamic centers of capitalism. They were, in fact, quite independent of the European centers of mercantilism. For this reason, the impact of their colonization policies was different from that of the countries which were to control the industrial revolution in Europe.

England and France, for example, permitted sizable emigration to their colonies not only to ensure supplies of raw materials but also to enlarge export markets. These markets could be maintained and broadened only if colonists to the new world were permitted reasonable latitude in the development of the lands they had occupied. Their purchasing power, obviously, depended on their own economic growth.

The economies of the Portuguese-Spanish colonies were organized on a different and extremely rigid pattern. The colonies were viewed by the mother countries as sources of wealth (gold) and raw materials, not as potential markets. Colonial policies were therefore tailored to ensure that the colonies would de-

Source: José A. Silva Michelena, *The Illusion of Democracy in Dependent Nations* (Cambridge, Mass.: The M.I.T. Press, 1971), pp. 268–276.

velop no national sense of their own. The forms of guaranteeing dependency were various. Both Spain and Portugal established intermediary centers (for example, Buenos Aires and Mexico City) between the colonies and the metropolis (the imperial states). This system guaranteed to Spain and Portugal both their monopoly of commerce and an effective control over the colonies.

The Spaniards, in this drive to maintain their colonies separate from, but dependent on, predetermined power centers, granted exclusive rights to carry on commerce to Spaniards sent out from the mother country. This policy was aimed also at maintaining the largest margin of profits possible for Spain. Their second major technique for averting any possible development of independent political structures in the colonies was to appoint only Spaniards in important political positions. Such arrangements effectively shut off the possibility that the criollos would be able to control their own destinies. Despite their Spanish descent and what would seem to have been their logical right to benefit from their economic activities and to control their political destiny, they were limited to agrarian activities—albeit on large plantations—and to minor political offices in the city. The situation might have been altered if there had been large-scale emigration from Spain and Portugal, but there was not. Instead, this dependent and atomized economy was firmly established, affecting not only the ecology of populated centers and the means of communications but also the distribution of products and the exercise of power.

In Venezuela, which was a poor and therefore weak link in the chain of control, the *latifundista* class—criollo owners of large plantations—prospered, principally by cultivating cacao. What other agricultural products were grown were for local consumption. From its base of the cacao plantations, which were concentrated in the central region of Venezuela, the *latifundista* class emerged with enough power to challenge the Spaniards. This class gradually began to demand more participation in the economic and political control of the region. Antagonism between what had by then become two dominant classes therefore had two mutually reinforcing sources: first, hostilities between plantation owners and merchants and, second, those between criollos and Spaniards.

The social structure as a whole was conditioned by the mode of production of the latifundia, which had organizational characteristics similar to feudal modes of production but produced for a world capitalist market. Part of the labor force was slave, but most of it was made up of "free" workers of varying degrees of indenture. Meanwhile, a middle sector developed in the cities, composed of marginal whites and pardos (racially mixed persons) who worked in minor jobs but whose aspiration was to be incorporated into the total structure.

Two significant events helped to sharpen the conflicts between the dominant classes. First, the establishment and operation of the Compañía Guipuzcoana not only centralized and controlled the national market but also fostered the institutionalization of the organs of political control and made them more rigid. Second, at the end of the eighteenth century, the collapse of the cacao market seriously affected the volume of exports. A further factor was the weakening of Spanish control due to the French occupation of Spain.

All of the events just described were among those leading to the wars of independence. With political independence came the possibility of transforming the colonies into autonomous centers, because finally the alternative of an indigenous development of capitalism was open. But this alternative was never adopted, because the criollos retained the economic and political patterns of the past.

The criollos, both during the war of independence and afterward, concentrated on keeping the economy linked with the world capitalist market through the exploitation and export of a new primary product, coffee, which was to substitute for the declining cacao.

First of all, it should be understood that Western political institutions were not created by chance. They were structured to meet the needs to administer, guide, and facilitate the development of the new capitalist relations of production and distribution being established throughout Europe. Thus, the development of industry created not only a new mode of work—"free work"—but also a new form of organizing production—a hierarchical system. This system is ultimately imposed on society through state bureaucracy. Along with the consolidation of markets, national boundaries were defined.

In Venezuela, as in most of Latin America, these stages of nationalization were not reached until the twentieth century, when an integrated national market had been established. Consequently, until recently Venezuela was not a nation in the conventional historical sense, because there had been no socioeconomic requirement for it to become one. Throughout the nineteenth century the region was basically an exporter of primary products; this condition helped to maintain the "islands" or regional centers, economically dependent on a world market but ruled by local caudillos who were constantly struggling with one another to gain central control.

At this stage, three dominant classes had developed: the *latifundistas,* the importers and their administrators, and the *latifundista* generals. Although they held considerable local control, they were still under a dependent structure, subordinate to decisions they did not control. The backwardness of the productive forces made organization of the masses almost impossible. Instead, they were used alternatively as soldiers or as semifree workers. The lowest classes, then, were subjected to both internal and external domination and profited not at all from their own work.

Toward the end of the nineteenth century a crisis in the world coffee market created a new and profound political crisis in Venezuela. The Andean region, where most of the important coffee plantations were located, suffered the most. Logically, the Andeans began a military invasion to the center. By the turn of the century they had gained national power. Meanwhile, foreign loans and investments increased, although not at the same pace as in other Latin American countries such as Argentina and Brazil. Nevertheless, the blockage of Puerto Cabello by foreign navies, as well as other international incidents, were political symptoms that the nature of dependency was changing.

Like the criollos after the wars of independence, the new Andean elite too showed no interest in changing the economic structure of the country; the entrepreneurs of those days were economically and culturally incapable of launching an industrialization program. Conditions such as this are perfect for establishing an economy of enclave. In Venezuela it was oil, which requires an accumulation of capital and a technological capacity well beyond that of the local entrepreneurs. Every Venezuelan petit bourgeois individual tried to grab a share of the enormous benefits the oil business was producing. Because of these factors the oil industry in its initial stages developed almost without national control. The companies exploiting the oil resources were able therefore to take advantage of all the facilities offered by an agrarian-based government elite and a dependent bourgoisie that saw, in urban land speculation and financial operations, unlimited opportunities for easy profit taking at small risk.

The peculiar character of the Venezuelan economic pattern of growth stems from this history. Its special consequence was that during the economic crisis of the 1930s, when other Latin American countries were pushing industrialization forward by means of import substitution, Venezuela kept growing outward. Its economic infrastructure was built on an untransformed dependent urban economy and agrarian structure. This phase of "simple growth," as Armando Córdova and Héctor Silva Michelena call it, had as its principal motive power the export sector of the economy.

Only during World War II did a few Venezuelan entrepreneurs, spurred by the trade limitations imposed by the war, begin to establish import-substituting industries. Thus, by 1950, when the world oil market was beginning to diminish its rate of growth, both national industry and the bourgeoisie were still at the primary level of development. The decision of the military dictator Pérez Jiménez to modernize the country through a program of public works—building magnificent highways, hotels, and so forth—was simply a variation of a system of dependent economic growth. The policy not only failed to generate a national, independent bourgeoisie but further engendered a bourgeoisie linked with and subordinated to the bourgeoisie of the dominant countries, especially of the United States.

Even so, what economic growth occurred did transform the conditions of existence of many Venezuelans of the middle sector, workers, and peasants. It also created a new phenomenon, a marginal population that was gradually but swiftly occupying the most visible—and least adequate for living—sites in and around the cities. Contrary to what had happened in the advanced capitalist countries, where the growth of the cities followed the growth of industry, Venezuelan cities took form before, and faster than, industry.

These economic facts, however, only rose to the surface, and therefore to the common consciousness of Venezuelans, between 1956 and 1959, when oil exports, and consequently fiscal revenues, decreased from 9 to 4 percent per year. This crisis forced both government and business to recognize the need to industrialize the country. With the inauguration of the democratic regime that deposed Pérez Jiménez, a crash program of import substitution was begun. This euphoric phase is already approaching its end. Almost all consumer goods, which are easy to substitute, are being produced internally. The process is now beginning to enter a new and more complex phase that requires more highly developed technology and more capital.

It is still too early to predict exactly what will happen. There are signs, however, that Venezuela is following the same course that was taken by Brazil and Argentina, that is, domination of industry by foreign capital—denationalization. Yet the key question here is why the Venezuelan bourgeoisie—now supposedly stronger and more class conscious—is incapable of conducting an autonomous national process of industrialization. There are several answers to this question, but we shall deal with the two crucial ones: the first is politicoeconomic; the second, technical.

The main thesis proposed here is that, as the process of import substitution continues, Venezuelan entrepreneurs are becoming weaker and less "Venezuelan." They are less Venezuelan in the sense that, with the increasing participation of large U.S. corporations in providing both capital and technology, control of the whole process of industrialization is moving into the hands of North Americans. Venezuelan entrepreneurs are less strong, because they lack the technical capacity, entrepreneurial spirit, and nationalism essential for an autonomous leadership. These are fatal weaknesses at a time when the industrializing process is becoming ever more complex and requires ever more complex technical training.

Again using Brazil and Argentina, where the process of denationalization is more advanced, as models for prediction, what can be anticipated for Venezuela? In the first phase, Venezuelan capital will merge with North American capital, with the latter rapidly gaining control of all light industries, such as rum, tobacco, and food. In a second phase, which might even be simultaneous with the first, medium and heavy industries will be established with more or less equal participation between local government and North American capital but relying heavily on North American technology. With such arrangements, we must assume that in this phase Venezuelan entrepreneurs will remain marginal. In the final phase, it is likely that the state will sell all the industrial complex, industry by industry, to large foreign corporations. Meanwhile, the Venezuelan bourgeoisie will retain control of the financial and commercial sectors, of construction and urban development, and of agricultural enterprises and will increasingly invest its profits in the New York stock market or place them in foreign banks.

Although loss of control of the key economic sector (industry) will make the Venezuelan bourgeoisie weaker as a force for economic nationalism, it will not become less important in internal politics. On the contrary, its own direct economic interests, together with its marginal participation in the heavy industry sector, already are being accompanied by an increasing political activity and class consciousness that is leading toward more open and effective use of special-interest organizations (particularly the Federation of Chambers of Commerce and Production, FEDECAMARAS) to exercise political pressure. These organizations are no longer merely defending themselves against government arbitrariness, as was the case in the late forties and early fifties; they are now geared toward guiding government economic policy. Their political philosophy, which underlies the economic process just described, as Frank Bonilla amply documents, might be expressed in a paraphrase of the statement that once rocked U.S. politics: "What is good for Fedecamaras is good for the nation."[2]

Let us assume, for the moment, that the Venezuelan bourgeoisie is culturally and politically able to confront and undertake the second phase of import
substitution, industrialization, autonomously. What would be the likelihood of
its success? To date, there is little if any capacity within Venezuela to generate
the technology required to establish such industrial complexes. Inevitably, then,
under the present form of political organization, it would have to adopt methods
of production and forms of organization and control imposed by those who own
the technology. Hence, it would continue to be subordinate to foreign capitalists.

Although a number of theorists recognize the risk of adopting technology
produced in advanced countries, they feel that such use also has great advantages. Brazilian economist Celso Furtado recently pointed out the fallacy in this
assumption.[3] Latin American entrepreneurs (assuming they have accumulated the
capital and have the cultural disposition to do so) may choose from a wide spectrum of ready-made technology, which makes it unnecessary for them to invest
in creating it. But how real is this advantage in the light of the needs of society?
The technology of advanced countries is developed primarily around the goals
of saving both labor and raw materials—perhaps the only abundant resources in
underdeveloped countries. Thus the adoption of the technology tends only to
worsen unemployment structurally—in terms of the classes in which it is the
greatest problem—and to diminish the overall impact of new investments on the
national economy. Furthermore, almost inevitably the adoption of a foreign technology is linked to dependence on those foreign groups that produce it, leading,
in the end, to the denationalization of the economy.

Adoption of alien technology, however, has further consequences for
underdeveloped societies. Armando Córdova, for example, points out that foreign technology imposes alien patterns of consumption, which, in turn, brake the
development of national productive forces:

> Production not only provides materials to fulfill needs; it also provides needs for
> materials. . . . The need for an object that consumers experience has been created
> by perception of such object. . . . Thus production not only produces an object for
> a subject but also produces a subject for an object.[4]

Interdependently and dynamically, then, both processes reinforce the dependency
of the peripheral country on a technologically and economically dominant one.

Furthermore, within the dependent country, the local bases of science and
technology and, in general, of the culture consequent on developments in the
productive process are judged according to foreign patterns and standards. This
consequence not only reinforces the use of alien technology but also gradually
closes down the possibility of developing an autonomous mechanism for producing the technological innovations that would liberate the potentialities for an indigenous technical structure of production. Moreover, because increments in productivity and therefore in personal income of the workers are linked to
technological advances made in other countries, the workers tend to perceive
dependency as necessary to their personal betterment. This idea is generally reinforced by the alien culture that is diffused through mass media. In this way the

effects of alien—and alienating—technology are propagated through the productive process to social classes, culture, and society.

Dependency is thus revealed as a particular form of relationship between advanced dominant capitalist centers and peripheral dependent capitalist economies. The foregoing analysis of this relationship was made from the standpoint of dependent countries. □

[1]Adicea Castillo, "EL sector agrícola y el desarrollo económico," mimeographed (Caracas: Facultad de Ciencias Económicas y Sociales, UCV, January, 1969), p. 6.

[2]Frank Bonilla, *The Failure of the Elites.*

[3]Celso Furtado, *Subdesenvolvimento e estagnação na América Latina* (Rio de Janeiro: Civilização Brasileira, 1968), chap. 2.

[4]Cited by Héctor Silva Michelena, "Neocolonialismo y universidad," unpublished manuscript, p. 14.

The Web of Exploitation: State and Peasants in Latin America

When import-substitution industrialization gained momentum after 1930, many Latin Americans believed it would spark real economic development. They viewed it as the cure for the region's economic ills. During the remainder of the twentieth century, several of the nations built impressive industrial parks, boasting of sophisticated capital-goods industries. Yet, poverty remained.

In the following essay, the Brazilian social scientist Glaucio Ary Dillon Soares discusses the puzzling anomaly of nations experiencing "dynamic" industrial growth while retaining large impoverished populations. Focusing attention on the relationship between agriculture and industry, he concludes that peasants and rural workers subsidize the urban population and industrialization. Latin America's industrialization has taken place, at least in part, at the expense of further impoverishment of the rural poor.

L ATIN AMERICAN COUNTRIES have a relatively low income per capita; nevertheless, most of them industrialized at an accelerated pace during the past decades. Growth, especially in the larger countries, is based on industry; within industry, the automotive, home appliances, chemical, and electronic subsectors are among the fastest growing. This growth is based mainly on the internal market. This is the paradox: how can countries with annual per capita incomes around $1,000 or even less base their growth on automobiles or color TVs? Obviously, if income were equidistributed, not a single individual could afford to buy a luxury car. Conservative economists brush off these considerations and often try to solve the problem to their own satisfaction simply by labelling these industries "dynamic" as if this were a quality intrinsic to the industries.

Source: Glaucio Ary Dillon Soares, "The Web of Exploitation: State and Peasants in Latin America," *Studies in Comparative International Development,* 7:3 (Fall 1977), pp. 3–11, 13–14, 22. With the permission of the publisher.

But the same countries that display these dynamic, modern industries also show a depressed rural sector, low agricultural incomes, and high mortality and illiteracy rates. Again, conservative economists solve the problem to their own satisfaction by dualistic explanation: development has not gotten there yet, they say. Actually, it has, and this is why life in the rural and agricultural areas is what it is.

This paper suggests that there are intimate relations between import-substitution industrialization and the misery of the rural poor. It further suggests that institutional arrangements play an important part in these relations. Although the processes involved are socioeconomic, the parameters are political.

The agrarian sector should not be analyzed independently from the rest of the society and economy. The exploitation of the agricultural worker and of the peasant is not an isolated phenomenon; on the contrary, it is part of an intricate web that sustains society and economy in their present form.

If agricultural wages experienced a substantial real increase, the costs of food production would be far higher than at present. A sharp increase in food prices would affect substantially the budget of almost the entire population, as food expenditures account for a large share of the total. The surplus of urban families of low and middle income levels, which is used for the consumption of nonagricultural products and services, would be seriously reduced, with drastic consequences for the consumption patterns of these families. Correspondingly, the internal market for these products and services would be reduced. At the same time, there would be an increase in the demand for products and services of lower cost, due to the entrance in the consumer's market of low income agrarian sectors that are at present excluded from the market.

Studies conducted in Latin America show that the share of food expenditures in total family expenditures is extremely high in all sectors of the population, except at the very top. In Mexico, The Secretaría de Industria y Comercio studied family expenditures and income in 1963–64, based on a sample of the total Mexican population; below the top 5 percent, food expenditures require over 40 percent of the total family expenditures; therefore, a substantial increase in food prices would seriously affect most social sectors, including the urban middle classes. Obviously the nonagricultural sectors with the lowest incomes would be most seriously hit by a hypothetical substantial increase in food prices.

Another study in 1963, on the Argentinian urban population, shows that food accounted for a substantial share of all expenditures of the total Argentinian population, over 50 percent of all expenditures of the families with median income or less. These results are similar to those obtained in the city of São Paulo, where the vulnerability of several social sectors to a substantial increase in food prices was substantiated. In the city of Recife, in the Brazilian Northeast, at all ordinal income levels the population is even more vulnerable to an increase of food prices than in São Paulo. In Recife, even at the top 5 percent with the highest incomes, food expenditures are substantial and weigh heavily in the family budget. The significance of food expenditures for the marginal urban population is strategic, even in countries with a moderately high per capita income: a study of Puerto Rican slum dwellers shows that those who make approximately

$700 a year spend some 89 percent of their income on food, compared with 59 percent among those whose income is $1500 a year and 46 percent among those whose income is $2500. The diet of the families with the lowest incomes is almost exclusively rice and beans, and the consumption of meat, eggs, and vegetables is due exclusively to the fact that several families keep a small back yard vegetable garden and raise chickens (some even raise pigs).

These populations are very dependent on holding food prices low. In Puerto Rico, as elsewhere in Latin America, many poor families that are under a strong income squeeze resort to an "urban subsistence economy" to alleviate the pressure on food consumption, to increase income, and to use productively the family surplus labor that the market economy cannot productively allocate.

All studies show that food expenditures in Latin America represent a very high share of the total family expenditures in the lower income brackets and in the middle income brackets as well. Taking the 30 percent immediately above the median in the urban areas, we see that they spend 45.7 percent of their total income on food in Argentina, 52.9 percent in Mexico, 41.9 percent in São Paulo, and 58.7 percent in Recife. Middle sectors, therefore, would also be drastically affected by a substantial increase in food prices.

A major conclusion emerges from these studies: a substantial increase in food prices could not be tolerated by at least 80 percent of the Latin American urban population; it would provoke serious political problems and strong pressures on the part of different social groups to increase their own income. First of all, wage and salary earners would bargain for increases, but honoraria, commissions, percentages, participations, and so on would also have to be renegotiated. It is unnecessary to underline that this general increase would be strongly inflationary.

Secondly, and most important, a substantial increase in the percentage that workers spend in food would bring about political unrest in the working class. In Latin America, the urban working class is far better organized than the agrarian working classes. Even in highly repressive countries, such an increase could spark political turmoil and disrupt the artificial social peace that they have; obviously, there would be pressures towards substantial increases in industrial wages, with

TABLE 1   Food Expenditures by Income Levels, Selected Latin American Countries, Around 1969

	MEXICO 1963–4	ARGENTINA, 1963 (URBAN POPULATION)	SÃO PAULO 1960*	RECIFE 1960*
Top 5%	23.5%	25.2%	24.5%	37.6%
Next 15%	40.8%	36.2%	33.8%	47.6%
Next 30%	52.9%	45.7%	41.9%	58.7%
Next 30%	61.7%	51.8%	49.3%	63.4%
Lowest 20%	65.8%	56.5%	53.4%	68.1%

*Food, beverages, and tobacco
Source: (ECLA: 1970)

serious repercussion in the cost of industrial products, maybe generating a reduction in the potential market and the loss in the ability to compete with foreign products; low food prices, therefore, have far-reaching consequences for the political system.

Low agrarian wages allowed Latin American countries to undertake industrialization policies in which the share of labor in total production costs is substantially smaller than those of the more advanced industrial countries. The purchasing power of industrial wages is increased by keeping agricultural products at artificially low prices, as well as certain urban services of low qualification, especially personal and domestic ones; this allows the urban working class to get by with low wages.

. . . This precarious balance would be totally disrupted with a substantial increase in food expenditures. Part of the wage squeeze is passed on to low-cost personal services and to the agrarian sectors. This web of exploitation allows the Latin American industrialist to pay low wages and to increase the rate of capital accumulation in spite of the fact that he often has to transfer some surplus abroad in the form of royalties, technical assistance, patent rights, high interest rates, and so on. Foreign subsidiaries participate in the web of exploitation and are able to show high profits in spite of remittances, under and over billing and technical assistance paid to the parent enterprise. Although the budget of the industrial bourgeoisie would be relatively unaffected by a substantial increase (say 100 percent) in the cost of agricultural labor, in most other classes, including the middle ones, such an increase would bring about serious difficulties, reducing the surplus that is being used in the acquisition of industrial products. There are, therefore, intimate relations between the exploitation of the agricultural worker and the preservation of a pattern of industrial development that is uneven, unequal, and inefficient, being based on an artificially expanded market for middle and high price industrial products, such as automobiles and domestic appliances. . . .

The web of exploitation is uncovered when certain revolutionary changes in the social relations of production in the agrarian sector take place. Serious agrarian reforms have brought about a scarcity of agricultural products in urban centers that was not provoked by a reduction of production, but by a drastic increase in the consumption of agricultural workers, peasants, and their family members. Food scarcity directly affected many social sectors that had not perceived that there was a relationship between their high standards of living (relative to the countries' average), their comfort, their consumption patterns, and the agrarian question. Several social sectors were forced to perceive that, *malgré eux,* they were part of a complex web of exploitation and that their standard of living depended on a freeze on the social relations of production in the agricultural sector. Many reacted in defense of their immediate interest. In Chile, after the first redistributive measures by the Frei government, middle and upper urban sectors that had supported the Christian Democrats joined Alessandri and the Partido Nacional; later on, under Allende, they were joined by some sectors of the lower middle class, and even fractions of the urban industrial class, forming a strong conservative alliance that supported the military coup. Industrial workers, who might face starvation with the demand crisis, as a rule did not join this opposition because there were other public policy measures that favored them, increasing their purchasing power: their wages were increased and food products were distributed at low prices. The efficiency of these egalitarian measures is apparent in a survey published in 1972 by *Ercilla,* between September 13 and 19: whereas only 19 percent of the lower-class members said that it was difficult to obtain essential goods, 77 percent of the middle classes and 99 percent of the upper classes did so.

The political behavior of the Chilean middle and upper classes allows three conclusions: (1) they realized that their high standard of living was dependent on the exploitation of peasants, agricultural workers, and the lower urban classes; (2) they were willing to sacrifice these classes to regain their high standard of living; and (3) they realized that the control of the state was crucial to achieve their goal.

An egalitarian social policy implies an egalitarian sectoral policy. The distri-bution of resources, investment, income, and social priorities along the rural/urban and the agrarian/nonagrarian axes is a necessary component of egalitarian social policies. It is mistaken to present the latifundist as the only historical villain who exploits peasants and keeps Latin American countries underdeveloped. Other social sectors also benefit, to a greater or smaller extent, from the exploita-tion of peasants and agricultural workers. In many Latin American countries the state supported a national development project based on import substitution in-dustrialization; in these countries the urban industrial sectors are active partici-pants in this exploitation and appropriate part of the surplus produced by the artificial reduction of the peasants' and agricultural workers' income. This allows these Latin American countries to increase capital accumulation in spite of the fact that they are themselves victims of a constant transfer of resources to the hegemonic countries. This growth is achieved at little or no cost for several social strata. To analyze rural poverty separately, as if it were a problem that begins and ends within the agricultural sector, is a serious mistake. It is a grotesque reification of analytical categories as if they were separate realities, autonomous, independent, unrelated to each other. The compartmentalization of knowledge in disciplines leads to the compartmentalization of analysis, and the resulting inability to grasp the web of exploitation. This web does not conform with aca-demic frontiers. The transfers of surplus cut across sectors of economic activities, administrative boundaries, and national frontiers. Various Latin American coun-tries have undertaken development policies that would have to be completely revised if the elimination of rural misery were a serious goal.

In most Latin American countries, income inequality artificially reduces the demand for some essential goods and services. The "balance" between internal supply and demand for food that some of these countries display is dependent upon income concentration: an end of the wage squeeze alone would be sufficient to show the incapacity of the agricultural sector to satisfy a demand for food products in a market in which the entire population participated. If the social classes and sectors that are most exploited were to consume the same quantity and quality of food as the urban middle sectors do, the present agricultural production of nearly all Latin American countries would be insufficient to satisfy the added demand. The artificially reduced demand of the poor sectors contributes to the relative abundance enjoyed by the middle and upper classes. These classes pay moderate prices for a privileged diet. The food consumption of urban middle and upper sectors in Latin America is not much inferior to that of equivalent sectors in countries with a much higher per capita income.

Most Latin American countries have adopted policies oriented towards industrialization-based growth. This decision and its execution came first in Argentina and in Chile, later in Brazil and Mexico, being even more recent (post–World War II) in other countries. In the industrialization-based growth, the state has been called upon to play an important role in the planning and execution of growth policies, and in recent decades this role has been greatly increased. These policies concentrate the largest part of public resources in urban areas and in the construction of an infrastructure for industrial growth. In recent decades, the state has moved into the productive process and has established several publicly owned industries. Political priorities determine that the social cost of these projects should fall mainly on the poor rural classes. The middle and upper urban classes went unscathed through industrialization, avoiding the payment of their sacrifice quota, which was transferred to the already overburdened poor sectors. The urban working class, often effectively organized and unionized, managed to keep their quota at a tolerable level. The bulk of the sacrifice was passed on to agricultural workers, peasants, and minifundists. These social sectors were unable to pass further on the costs of industrialization. They were illiterate, seldom unionized, without political organization and class consciousness, often geographically distant from the decision-making centers. In extreme circumstances they reacted with violence in the defense of their previous rights, however meager they might have been. The rule, however, was acceptance; rebellion was the exception. Furthermore, rebellion took the form of sporadic spurts of violence, rather than of organized partisan and revolutionary action. The concern with industrialization drove the Latin American states through historical roads that were very different from those followed by Western European states. The state grew when the agricultural sector employed the majority of the population. This made it possible to transfer to the rural poor the social costs of development. In Latin America, the state never accepted the responsibility for the welfare of these sectors; in Latin America, the state devoted itself to industrial growth, without concerning itself with social development.

The Latin American state made a drastic choice when it decided to base national development on import-substitution industrialization. It downgraded the agricultural sector and abdicated from promoting social development and the welfare of the majority of the population. It mobilized vast resources for industrialization and, as a result, the economic functions of the state were increased. Public enterprises were created to develop an adequate infrastructure for industrialization (oil, transportation, energy monopolies, roads, railroads, development banks, and so on), whereas central government expenditures stagnated. . . .

Relations between industry and agriculture in Latin America have a history of conflict but also of supplementary functions. Conflict, historically, has concentrated on two major issues: (1) exchange controls, for rates were often manipulated to favor industrialization; (2) credits, incentives, and taxation.

Traditionally, industry and agriculture collided in these areas. Given that in Latin America import substitution industrialization took place under conditions of historical dependence and technological inferiority, native industry as a rule cannot compete in the world market. Therefore, Latin American industries do not produce their own foreign exchange. Latin American industry depends on imports that are paid with the exports of primary products: "In 1966 primary products represented almost 87 percent of the total exports (from Latin America), a proportion that reached 95 percent if we computed non-ferrous semielaborate minerals, which were included in the category of other manufactured products. On the other hand, approximately 72 percent of imports are industrial products" (ECLA, 1969:68).

In 1968, food represented 44.8 percent of all Latin American exports but only 9.3 percent of all imports. Thus, the growing need to import provoked by industrialization has been financed by the export of primary products: coffee, cotton, iron ore, cocoa, and sugar (and, more recently, soy beans) in the case of Brazil; meat, leather and wheat in Argentina and Uruguay; copper in Chile; oil in Venezuela; tin in Bolivia; coffee in Colombia, etc. Import-substitution industrialization did not reduce the need to import. On the contrary, it increased imports substantially but failed to increase industrial exports. Import-substitution industrialization requires the continuous import of capital goods, raw materials, intermediate products, and fuel. The growth of these imports was sharp, and in the case of the more industrialized Latin American countries it was accomplished largely at the expense of consumer goods. In 1968, 83.8 percent of the value of all Latin American imports were accounted for by these items.

Industry competes with the agricultural sector for credits, fights with it for favorable exchange controls, but ultimately is dependent upon it to produce the foreign exchange that it needs. In this struggle, industry must win, but may not kill. It is the dilemma of the golden egg goose. It is for this reason that the interpretation of Latin American development based exclusively on intersectoral conflicts is false, although the conflicts are real. . . .

When industrial interests gain control of the state and through various mechanisms transfer surplus from the agricultural sector to the industrial one, the web does not stop there. Certain institutions and legislation, or lack thereof, allow the large exporting farms to pass the burden on, partly or wholly. Of crucial importance are institutional arrangements that allow an extremely unequal land distribution, creating a large number of unlanded agricultural workers and of minifundists, whose land is insufficient to absorb productively the family labor. This creates a labor surplus that must be sold. The excess labor thus created has a negative effect on agricultural wages. This low-wage level is guaranteed by other institutional arrangements, or lack thereof. One of the commonest is the lack of minimum agricultural wages, or the existence of differential minimum wages, higher for urban-industrial workers and lower for agricultural ones.

Union legislation and regulations often restrict the bargaining power of peasants and agricultural workers, thus ensuring that part of the burden will in fact be passed on to them.

Internal food price controls also bring about transfers, but this time the immediate impact is not on large export farms, but on small and medium farms which produce for the internal market.

In underdeveloped countries, income concentration in any sector, rural or urban, if it reduces the income at the lower classes below a certain point, limits the demand for food. This artificially lowers food prices, and other social sectors reap the benefits, buying food at lower prices, at the expense of food producers and of those classes that had to reduce their food intake.

Thus, the exclusion of the peasantry and small owners from the benefits of economic development is not a "natural," spontaneous economic phenomenon. Exploitation does not exist in a political and legal vacuum, nor is it limited to those cases involving a direct social relation of production, as between capitalist and worker. Exploitation is a complex, weblike, structural phenomenon, affected by institutional arrangements, that must be dealt with in order to understand class and sectoral relations in Latin America.□

Dependency Theory

For much of the twentieth century, the ideas discussed in Latin America to promote development sprang from the capitalist theory of "diffusion," the so-called trickle down theory, although Karl Marx also enjoyed a popular following. By means of outside investment and foreign trade, diffusionists argued, capitalist development could be transferred, in stages they carefully delineated, from the major North Atlantic capitalist nations to the underdeveloped nations of Latin America.

Increasingly, economic nationalism prompted Latin Americans to question those ideas, at least to lament the tardy pace of the transfer. They acknowledged rapid economic growth, while lamenting the scanty and spotty evidence of economic development. Even if the diffusionist theory was working on its own protracted schedule, the Latin Americans grew impatient. Many called for a more immediate development. After 1960, intellectuals seemed to be drawn increasingly to the idea that a combination of internal institutions and external trade patterns perpetuated dependency, one condition responsible for underdevelopment. In their thinking, underdeveloped nations required structural changes, both of national institutions and of external trade patterns, to hasten the end of dependency and the advent of development. No amount of "trickle down" could spawn development without basic structural changes.

Theotonio dos Santos, one of the early theorists of dependency, cogently expounded his ideas from the Center for Socioeconomic Studies of the Faculty of Economic Science of the University of Chile. In this brief essay, he repeats his "classic" definition of dependency and then sums up his concept of replacing dependency and underdevelopment with greater independence and development.

THIS PAPER attempts to demonstrate that the dependence of Latin American countries on other countries cannot be overcome without a qualitative change in their internal structures and external relations. We shall attempt to show that the relations of dependence to which these countries are subjected con-

Source: Theotonio dos Santos, "The Structure of Dependence," *The American Economic Review,* 60 (May 1970), pp. 231–236. With permission of the publisher.

form to a type of international and internal structure which leads them to under-development or more precisely to a dependent structure that deepens and aggravates the fundamental problems of their peoples.

I. What Is Dependence?

By dependence we mean a situation in which the economy of certain countries is conditioned by the development and expansion of another economy to which the former is subjected. The relation of interdependence between two or more economies, and between these and world trade, assumes the form of dependence when some countries (the dominant ones) can expand and can be self-sustaining, while other countries (the dependent ones) can do this only as a reflection of that expansion, which can have either a positive or a negative effect on their immediate development.

The concept of dependence permits us to see the internal situation of these countries as part of world economy. In the Marxian tradition, the theory of imperialism has been developed as a study of the process of expansion of the imperialist centers and of their world domination. In the epoch of the revolutionary movement of the Third World, we have to develop the theory of laws of internal development in those countries that are the object of such expansion and are governed by them. This theoretical step transcends the theory of development which seeks to explain the situation of the underdeveloped countries as a product of their slowness or failure to adopt the patterns of efficiency characteristic of developed countries (or to "modernize" or "develop" themselves). Although capitalist development theory admits the existence of an "external" dependence, it is unable to perceive underdevelopment in the way our present theory perceives it, as a consequence and part of the process of the world expansion of capitalism—a part that is necessary to and integrally linked with it.

In analyzing the process of constituting a world economy that integrates the so-called "national economies" in a world market of commodities, capital, and even of labor power, we see that the relations produced by this market are unequal and combined—unequal because development of parts of the system occurs at the expense of other parts. Trade relations are based on monopolistic control of the market, which leads to the transfer of surplus generated in the dependent countries to the dominant countries; financial relations are, from the viewpoint of the dominant powers, based on loans and the export of capital, which permit them to receive interest and profits; thus increasing their domestic surplus and strengthening their control over the economies of the other countries. For the dependent countries these relations represent an export of profits and interest which carries off part of the surplus generated domestically and leads to a loss of control over their productive resources. In order to permit these disadvantageous relations, the dependent countries must generate large surpluses, not in such a way as to create higher levels of technology but rather superexploited manpower. The result is to limit the development of their internal market and their technical and cultural capacity, as well as the moral and physical health of their people. We call this combined development because it is the combination of these inequalities and the transfer of resources from the most backward and dependent sectors to the most advanced and dominant ones which explains the inequality, deepens it, and transforms it into a necessary and structural element of the world economy.

II. Historic Forms of Dependence

Historic forms of dependence are conditioned by: (1) the basic forms of this world economy which has its own laws of development ; (2) the type of economic relations dominant in the capitalist centers and the ways in which the latter expand outward; and (3) the types of economic relations existing inside the peripheral countries which are incorporated into the situation of dependence within the network of international economic relations generated by capitalist expansion. It is not within the purview of this paper to study these forms in detail but only to distinguish broad characteristics of development.

Drawing on an earlier study, we may distinguish: (1) Colonial dependence, trade export in nature, in which commercial and financial capital in alliance with the colonialist state dominated the economic relations of the Europeans and the colonies, by means of a trade monopoly complemented by a colonial monopoly of land, mines, and manpower (serf or slave) in the colonized countries. (2) Financial-industrial dependence which consolidated itself at the end of the nineteenth century, characterized by the domination of big capital in the hegemonic centers, and its expansion abroad through investment in the production of raw materials and agricultural products for consumption in the hegemonic centers. A productive structure grew up in the dependent countries devoted to the export of these products. (3) In the postwar period a new type of dependence has been consolidated, based on multinational corporations which began to invest in industries geared to the internal market of underdeveloped countries. This form of dependence is basically technological-industrial dependence.

Each of these forms of dependence corresponds to a situation which conditioned not only the international relations of these countries but also their internal structures: the orientation of production, the forms of capital accumulation, the reproduction of the economy, and, simultaneously, their social and political structure.

III. The Export Economies

In forms (1) and (2) of dependence, production is geared to those products destined for export (gold, silver, and tropical products in the colonial epoch; raw materials and agricultural products in the epoch of industrial-financial dependence); i.e., production is determined by demand from the hegemonic centers. The internal productive structure is characterized by rigid specialization and monoculture in entire regions (the Caribbean, the Brazilian Northeast, etc.). Alongside these export sectors there grew up certain complementary economic activities (cattle-raising and some manufacturing, for example) which were dependent, in general, on the export sector to which they sell their products. There was a third, subsistence economy which provided manpower for the export sector under favorable conditions and toward which excess population shifted during periods unfavorable to international trade.

Under these conditions, the existing internal market was restricted by four factors: (1) Most of the national income was derived from export, which was used to purchase the inputs required by export production (slaves, for example) or luxury goods consumed by the hacienda- and mine-owners, and by the more prosperous employees. (2) The available manpower was subject to very arduous forms of superexploitation, which limited its consumption. (3) Part of the consumption of these workers was provided by the subsistence economy, which served as a complement to their income and as a refuge during periods of depression. (4) A fourth factor was to be found in those countries in which land and mines were in the hands of foreigners (cases of an enclave economy): a great part of the accumulated surplus was destined to be sent abroad in the form of profits, limiting not only internal consumption but also possibilities of reinvestment. In the case of enclave economies the relations of the foreign companies with the hegemonic center were even more exploitative and were complemented by the fact that purchases by the enclave were made directly abroad.

IV. The New Dependence

The new form of dependence, (3) above, is in process of developing and is conditioned by the exigencies of the international commodity and capital markets. The possibility of generating new investments depends on the existence of financial resources in foreign currency for the purchase of machinery and processed raw materials not produced domestically. Such purchases are subject to two limitations: the limit of resources generated by the export sector (reflected in the balance of payments, which includes not only trade but also service relations); and the limitations of monopoly on patents which leads monopolistic firms to prefer to transfer their machines in the form of capital rather than as commodities for sale. It is necessary to analyze these relations of dependence if we are to understand the fundamental structural limits they place on the development of these economies.

1. Industrial development is dependent on an export sector for the foreign currency to buy the inputs utilized by the industrial sector. The first consequence of this dependence is the need to preserve the traditional export sector, which limits economically the development of the internal market by the conservation of backward relations of production and signifies, politically, the maintenance of power by traditional decadent oligarchies. In the countries where these sectors are controlled by foreign capital, it signifies the remittance abroad of high profits, and political dependence on those interests. Only in rare instances does foreign capital not control at least the marketing of these products. In response to these limitations, dependent countries in the 1930's and 1940's developed a policy of exchange restrictions and taxes on the national and foreign export sector; today they tend toward the gradual nationalization of production and toward the imposition of certain timid limitations on foreign control of the marketing of exported products. Furthermore, they seek, still somewhat timidly, to obtain better terms for the sale of their products. In recent decades, they have created mechanisms for international price agreements, and today UNCTAD and ECLA [Economic Commission for Latin America] press to obtain more favorable tariff conditions for these products on the part of the hegemonic centers. It is important to point out that the industrial development of these countries is dependent on the situation of the export sector, the continued existence of which they are obliged to accept.

2. Industrial development is, then, strongly conditioned by fluctuations in the balance of payments. This leads toward deficit due to the relations of dependence themselves. The causes of the deficit are three:

   a. Trade relations take place in a highly monopolized international market, which tends to lower the price of raw materials and to raise the prices of industrial products, particularly inputs. In the second place, there is a tendency in modern technology to replace various primary products with synthetic raw materials. Consequently, the balance of trade in these countries tends to be less favorable (even though they show a general surplus). The overall Latin American balance of trade from 1946 to 1968 shows a surplus for each of those years. The same thing happens in almost every underdeveloped country. However, the losses due to deterioration of the terms of trade (on the basis of data from ECLA and the International Monetary Fund), excluding Cuba, were $26,383 million for the 1951–66 period, taking 1950 prices as a base. If Cuba and Venezuela are excluded, the total is $15,925 million.

   b. For the reasons already given, foreign capital retains control over the most dynamic sectors of the economy and repatriates a high volume of profit; consequently, capital accounts are highly unfavorable to dependent countries. The data show that the amount of capital leaving the country is much greater than the amount entering; this produces an enslaving deficit in capital accounts. To this must be added the deficit in certain services which are virtually under total foreign control—such as freight transport, royalty payments, technical aid, etc. Consequently, an important deficit is produced in the total balance of payments; thus limiting the possibility of importation of inputs for industrialization.

   c. The result is that "foreign financing" becomes necessary, in two forms: to cover the existing deficit, and to "finance" development by means of loans for the stimulation of investments and to "supply" an internal economic surplus which was decapitalized to a large extent by the remittance of part of the surplus generated domestically and sent abroad as profits.

      Foreign capital and foreign "aid" thus fill up the holes that they themselves created. The real value of this aid, however, is doubtful. If overcharges resulting from the restrictive terms of the aid are subtracted from the total amount of the grants, the average net flow, according to calculations of the Inter-American Economic and Social Council, is approximately 54 percent of the gross flow.

      If we take account of certain further facts—that a high proportion of aid is paid in local currencies, that Latin American countries make contributions to international financial institutions, and that credits are often "tied"—we find a "real component of foreign aid" of 42.2 percent on a very favorable hypothesis and of 38.3 percent on a more realistic one. The gravity of the situation becomes even clearer if we consider that these credits are used in large part to finance North American investments, to subsidize foreign imports which compete with national products, to introduce technology not adapted to the needs of underdeveloped countries, and to invest in low-priority sectors of the national economies. The hard truth is that the underdeveloped countries have to pay for all of the "aid" they receive. This situation is generating an enormous protest movement by Latin American governments seeking at least partial relief from such negative relations.

3. Finally, industrial development is strongly conditioned by the technological monopoly exercised by imperialist centers. We have seen that the underdeveloped countries depend on the importation of machinery and raw materials for the development of

their industries. However, these goods are not freely available in the international market; they are patented and usually belong to the big companies. The big companies do not sell machinery and processed raw materials as simple merchandise: they demand either the payment of royalties, etc., for their utilization or, in most cases, they convert these goods into capital and introduce them in the form of their own investments. This is how machinery which is replaced in the hegemonic centers by more advanced technology is sent to dependent countries as capital for the installation of affiliates. Let us pause and examine these relations, in order to understand their oppressive and exploitative character.

The dependent countries do not have sufficient foreign currency, for the reasons given. Local businessmen have financing difficulties, and they must pay for the utilization of certain patented techniques. These factors oblige the national bourgeois governments to facilitate the entry of foreign capital in order to supply the restricted national market, which is strongly protected by high tariffs in order to promote industrialization. Thus, foreign capital enters with all the advantages: in many cases, it is given exemption from exchange controls for the importation of machinery; financing of sites for installation of industries is provided; government financing agencies facilitate industrialization; loans are available from foreign and domestic banks, which prefer such clients; foreign aid often subsidizes such investments and finances complementary public investments; after installation, high profits obtained in such favorable circumstances can be reinvested freely. Thus it is not surprising that the data of the U.S. Department of Commerce reveal that the percentage of capital brought in from abroad by these companies is but a part of the total amount of invested capital. These data show that in the period from 1946 to 1967 the new entries of capital into Latin America for direct investment amounted to $5,415 million, while the sum of reinvested profits was $4,424 million. On the other hand, the transfers of profits from Latin America to the United States amounted to $14,775 million. If we estimate total profits as approximately equal to transfers plus reinvestments we have the sum of $18,983 million. In spite of enormous transfers of profits to the United States, the book value of the United States' direct investment in Latin America went from $3,045 million in 1946 to $10,213 million in 1967. From these data it is clear that: (1) Of the new investments made by U.S. companies in Latin America for the period 1946-67, 55 percent corresponds to new entries of capital and 45 percent to reinvestment of profits; in recent years, the trend is more marked, with reinvestments between 1960 and 1966 representing more than 60 percent of new investments. (2) Remittances remained at about 10 percent of book value throughout the period. (3) The ratio of remitted capital to new flow is around 2.7 for the period 1946-67; that is, for each dollar that enters $2.70 leaves. In the 1960's this ratio roughly doubled, and in some years was considerably higher.

The *Survey of Current Business* data on sources and uses of funds for direct North American investment in Latin America in the period 1957-64 show that, of the total sources of direct investment in Latin America, only 11.8 percent came from the United States. The remainder is in large part, the result of the activities of North American firms in Latin America (46.4 percent net income, 27.7 percent under the heading of depreciation), and from "sources located abroad" (14.1 percent). It is significant that the funds obtained abroad that are external to the companies are greater than the funds originating in the United States.

V. Effects on the Productive Structure

It is easy to grasp, even if only superficially, the effects that this dependent structure has on the productive system itself in these countries and the role of this structure in determining a specified type of development, characterized by its dependent nature.

The productive system in the underdeveloped countries is essentially determined by these international relations. In the first place, the need to conserve the agrarian or mining export structure generates a combination between more advanced economic centers that extract surplus value from the more backward sectors, and also between internal "metropolitan" centers and internal interdependent "colonial" centers. The unequal and combined character of capitalist development at the international level is reproduced internally in an acute form. In the second place the industrial and technological structure responds more closely to the interests of the multinational corporations than to internal developmental needs (conceived of not only in terms of the overall interests of the population, but also from the point of view of the interests of a national capitalist development). In the third place, the same technological and economic-financial concentration of the hegemonic economies is transferred without substantial alteration to very different economies and societies, giving rise to a highly unequal productive structure, a high concentration of incomes, underutilization of installed capacity, intensive exploitation of existing markets concentrated in large cities, etc.

The accumulation of capital in such circumstances assumes its own characteristics. In the first place, it is characterized by profound differences among domestic wage-levels, in the context of a local cheap labor market, combined with a capital-intensive technology. The result, from the point of view of relative surplus value, is a high rate of exploitation of labor power. . . .

This exploitation is further aggravated by the high prices of industrial products enforced by protectionism, exemptions and subsidies given by the national governments, and "aid" from hegemonic centers. Furthermore, since dependent accumulation is necessarily tied into the international economy, it is profoundly conditioned by the unequal and combined character of international capitalist economic relations, by the technological and financial control of the imperialist centers by the realities of the balance of payments, by the economic policies of the state, etc. The role of the state in the growth of national and foreign capital merits a much fuller analysis than can be made here.

Using the analysis offered here as a point of departure, it is possible to understand the limits that this productive system imposes on the growth of the internal markets of these countries. The survival of traditional relations in the countryside is a serious limitation on the size of the market, since industrialization does not offer hopeful prospects. The productive structure created by dependent industrialization limits the growth of the internal market.

First, it subjects the labor force to highly exploitative relations which limit its purchasing power. Second, in adopting a technology of intensive capital use, it creates very few jobs in comparison with population growth, and limits the generation of new sources of income. These two limitations affect the growth of the consumer goods market. Third, the remittance abroad of profits carries away part of the economic surplus generated within the country. In all these ways limits are put on the possible creation of basic national industries which could provide a market for the capital goods this surplus would make possible if it were not remitted abroad.

From this cursory analysis we see that the alleged backwardness of these economies is not due to a lack of integration with capitalism but that, on the contrary, the most powerful obstacles to their full development come from the way in which they are joined to this international system and its laws of development.

VI. Some Conclusions: Dependent Reproduction

In order to understand the system of dependent reproduction and the socioeconomic institutions created by it, we must see it as part of a system of world economic relations based on monopolistic control of large-scale capital, on control of certain economic and financial centers over others, on a monopoly of a complex technology that leads to unequal and combined development at a national and international level. Attempts to analyze backwardness as a failure to assimilate more advanced models of production or to modernize are nothing more than ideology disguised as science. The same is true of the attempts to analyze this international economy in terms of relations among elements in free competition, such as the theory of comparative costs which seeks to justify the inequalities of the world economic system and to conceal the relations of exploitation on which it is based.

In reality we can understand what is happening in the underdeveloped countries only when we see that they develop within the framework of a process of dependent production and reproduction. This system is a dependent one because it reproduces a productive system whose development is limited by those world relations which necessarily lead to the development of only certain economic sectors, to trade under unequal conditions, to domestic competition with international capital under unequal conditions, to the imposition of relations of superexploitation of the domestic labor force with a view to dividing the economic surplus thus generated between internal and external forces of domination.

In reproducing such a productive system and such international relations, the development of dependent capitalism reproduces the factors that prevent it from reaching a nationally and internationally advantageous situation; and it thus reproduces backwardness, misery, and social marginalization within its borders. The development that it produces benefits very narrow sectors, encounters unyielding domestic obstacles to its continued economic growth (with respect to both internal and foreign markets),and leads to the progressive accumulation of balance-of-payments deficits, which in turn generate more dependence and more superexploitation.

The political measures proposed by the developmentalists of ECLA, UNC-

TAD, BID [International Development Bank], etc., do not appear to permit destruction of these terrible chains imposed by dependent development.

Everything now indicates that what can be expected is a long process of sharp political and military confrontations and of profound social radicalization which will lead these countries to a dilemma: governments of force, which open the way to facism, or popular revolutionary governments, which open the way to socialism. Intermediate solutions have proved to be, in such a contradictory reality, empty and utopian. □

The Need for Structural Changes

Observing with dismay the deteriorating condition of the Latin American economy and its failure to develop, the Mexican journal *Comercio Exterior de México* concluded in 1978 that only basic institutional changes could reverse the dismal trends. The journal made a convincing case for its recommendations. However, in the twentieth century, such changes have eluded reformers and revolutionaries alike.

IN THE FINAL INSTANCE, the structural deficiencies are the root cause of the critical situation of the region's economy. They help to transmit the crises in the developed capitalist nations and reinforce the inequitable character of the current international economic order.

The structural defects of the Latin American economy have been accentuated in recent years in a cumulative process that sees the agricultural sector increasingly less able to satisfy the needs of the population; industry increasingly dependent on exporting and more oriented toward satisfying the demand for luxury consumer goods; real wages decreasing or only very slowly rising while, by contrast, profits shoot up, a feature that, together with the rising unemployment rate, is responsible for an increasing concentration of income; exports continuing to rely on a narrow range of products and imports being utilized fundamentally for the maintenance or expansion of economic activity; and the foreign debt growing and direct foreign investment controlling a significant proportion of the basic sectors of the manufacturing industry. By giving priority to the effort to stabilize, the structural defects of the economy have been accentuated in most of the countries of the region. With very few exceptions, the peoples of the continent have not received the benefits of the stages of recovery and expansion; nor has sustained growth been generated.

It is perhaps the agricultural sector which is the most affected by this kind of development. In effect, over the 1970–1976 period, agriculture grew at an average rate of 2.9%, while the population went up at a 2.8% rate. Agricultural production per inhabitant thus remained virtually static. All of this would suggest

Source: Editorial, "The Need for Structural Changes in Our America," *Comercio Exterior de México* (Mexico City), October 1978, pp. 416–418. With the permission of *Comercio Exterior de México*.

the standard of living suffered no significant change, but there were features which make it possible to claim that, in reality, a deterioration occurred, particularly the fact that a growing proportion of the cereal crop went to producing cattle-feed. Thus, in the 1972–1974 period, Latin America utilized an average of 26.1 million tons of cereals to feed cattle (40% of the grain availability, as opposed to the 32% utilized in the 1961–1963 period). The amount of grain available for foods accessible to the masses is thus reduced. Meanwhile, cattle products are mainly consumed by those in high-income brackets and undernourishment among the poor is augmented by both factors.

At the Fifteenth Regional Conference of the Food and Agriculture Organization for Latin America, held this year in Montevideo, the Director General of the organization emphasized the need for a "world food reserve system to face up to the situations brought on by poor harvests," which should necessarily form part of the Integrated Basic Products Program, and of the New International Economic Order. In this regard, the Director General claimed that in Latin America "the proportion of the population having available less food than the critical minimum was 15%," which means that malnutrition affects more than 46 million people.

The same international body asserts that protein-energy deficiency in children from 0 to 4 is 32.1% in Guyana; 26% in El Salvador; 32.4% in Guatemala; and 25.2% in Brazil. There is no need to remark on the fact that almost all these children belong to the low-income groups that live in conditions of the utmost misery and that for the rest of their lives—if they survive—they will carry with them the burden of poor physical and mental development. Throughout Latin America malnutrition is a problem that cannot be hidden. While it may be true that the extreme cases are to be encountered in the countries mentioned, together with Haiti, Bolivia, and Colombia, recent estimates suggest that "40% of all Mexicans have a food deficiency so great that, in the majority of cases, not even the calorie needs are satisfied.". . .

There is general recognition that in Latin America, "with few exceptions, no real programs of agrarian reform have been carried through to their full extent." This has resulted in the agricultural sector having decreasing capacity for generating employment. Similarly, the deterioration of the standard of living in the countryside compared with that in urban areas goes on uninterruptedly.

Within such a perspective, State action acquires increasing importance. In most cases, it regulates the nature of agricultural credit, fixes the guaranteed prices for agricultural produce, orients production and consumption, strengthens certain types of organization and discourages others, etc. Faced with this, only the transnational corporations and the local oligarchic groups possess the power and organization necessary to oblige the State to take particular action which will favor them.

Capitalist development in Latin America has generally produced a progressive weakening of agrarian movements. Unlike what happened in the fifties and sixties, today campesino mobilization is centered on the temporary, unstable workers, the so-called semi-proletariat. However, the action of the State, which could counteract the worst effects of a trend that it encourages, more often than not is only manifested in "the setting up of great bureaucratic apparatuses, . . . with no corresponding increases in the effective participation capacity of the great masses of the rural population."

The socioeconomic situation in Latin America is already too complex for any solutions. Such complexity characterizes the region as a whole and, more particularly, certain countries within it, which either cannot break the chains of backwardness, dependence, and domestic social injustice for the majority of their inhabitants (immersed, as they are, in a negative process that feeds upon itself), or else, at the other extreme, which appear to be at a stage of "forced landing in disaster conditions" rather than at stages of "take off" or of "sustained growth," to imitate the curious terminology of an economist [Walt W. Rostow] who was very much in fashion in the sixties. Thus, the traditional economic policies are inadequate to provide proper response to the great challenges of Latin America. . . .

The problems of Our America should be tackled not just with a willing spirit and a tenacious determination, but also—and above all—with the unwavering goal of transcending solutions and approaches whose failure is shown by history, and by carrying out to this end the great structural transformations in the social and economic spheres that reality demands. Only thus will the dearest hopes of our nations' forefathers prove capable of fulfillment.

The structural transformation of Latin America must be fundamentally oriented toward changing the norms and conditions of production: the types of goods produced, how they are produced and who produces them, so that a consistent economic policy may be applied that will benefit the mass of the population. It is clear that such economic changes must be accompanied, or even preceded, by political changes that would give a wider popular base to the region's governments.☐

An Early Statement of Economic Nationalism

In the twentieth century, nationalists increasingly focused attention on the problems of underdevelopment and dependency, economic realities they regarded as inseparable. An early contributor to the ideas of economic nationalism, the Brazilian intellectual Alberto Tôrres (1865–1917) wrote a series of books between 1909 and 1915 equating economic development and nationalism. To exercise "real sovereignty" and express "true nationalism," he affirmed, the nation-state must control its own sources of wealth, its industry, and its commerce. This pioneer economic nationalist argued that Brazil had turned over its economic destiny to foreigners, who had sown their capital without restriction and were in the process of reaping an abundant harvest. He convincingly put forth those ideas in his book O Problema Nacional Brasileiro (The National Brazilian Problem), published in 1914.

OUR NATION has renounced its own heritage. Foreigners seize it. Foreign companies, recently arrived foreign immigrants, foreign businessmen without any headquarters in our country, foreigners in transit or with a residence just long enough for them to enrich themselves take advantage of our vast regions, our soil, our railroads, and our natural sources of wealth. They purchase our property; they take advantage of the credit extended by our banks. They seem to have future projects that would divide our country into spheres of influence. It is impossible to disguise the fear provoked by the contrast between these undeniable facts and the benign, even permissive attitude of our governments toward the growing reality of foreign domination.

The Brazilian people have no idea of the national danger that suddenly confronts them, even threatens them. Foreigners control the national patrimony as well as the exports. Our territorial integrity, our independence, and our sovereignty exist at the mercy of the great economic and military powers. . . .

There can be no doubt about the present alarming economic situation of our country with its disequilibrium between production and consumption and the commercial and industrial inflation. Powerful foreign businesses, whose activities conflict with the best interests of our nation, exploit us mercilessly. The economic ideas that come to us from abroad are adverse and always alien to our best interests. Indifferent to our priorities and needs, foreigners view Brazil exclusively as a source of profits.

Their interests do not complement ours. They persuade some Brazilians with their logic to the extent that they have come to favor foreign exploitation to the detriment of their own Brazil.

Our financial crises further expose us to foreign domination. Absorbed in matters of foreign credit and crushed by the pressure of debts, the governments descend to the lowly status of subordinates, showing real fear of foreign creditors and capitalist pressures. They are unable to give the nation the direction needed to serve its own best interests. They are slaves to foreign interests. They compromise the nation. Above all else, the independence of a people is founded on their economy and their finances. . . .

In order for a nation to remain independent, it is imperative to preserve the vital organs of nationality: the principal sources of wealth, the industries of primary products, the instrumentalities and agents of economic vitality and circulation, transportation and internal commerce. There must be neither monopolies nor privileges, but there must exist ample guarantees and protection for free labor, individual initiative, small-scale production, and the distribution of wealth. . . .

A people cannot be free if they do not control their own sources of wealth, produce their own food, and direct their own industry and commerce.□

Source: Alberto Tôrres, *O Problema Nacional Brasileiro: Introdução a um Programma de Organização Nacional* (Rio de Janeiro: Imprensa Nacional, 1914), pp. 111–113, 115–116, 122, 123– 124.

Goals for Development

During the final decades of the nineteenth century, El Salvador became an efficient producer, processor, and exporter of coffee. By the opening of the twentieth century, coffee production dominated the economy of that small Central American nation. It not only monopolized increasing amounts of the best land but also tended to absorb a lion's share of capital, technology, and labor. Because coffee plantations encroached on lands that once grew beans, rice, and corn, staples of the diet of the ordinary citizens, food production for local consumption began to lag. By the end of the 1920s, El Salvador had to import food for the first time in order to feed its population.

The critical eye of the intellectual and nationalist Alberto Masferrer (1868–1932) observed prosperity and progress amid dependency, poverty, and hunger. In the first selection that follows, he assessed the reality of hunger in El Salvador in 1928. In the second, he offered in 1929 a revolutionary Doctrine of a Guaranteed Minimal Quality of Life.

The Problem

T HERE ARE NO longer crises; instead, there are chronic illnesses and endemic hunger. . . . El Salvador no longer has wild fruits and vegetables that once everyone could harvest, nor even cultivated fruits that once were inexpensive. . . . Today there are the coffee plantations and they grow only coffee. . . . Where there is now a voracious plantation that consumes hundreds and hundreds of acres, before there were two hundred farmers whose small plots produced corn, rice, beans, fruits, and vegetables. Now the highlands support only coffee plantations and the lowlands cattle ranches. The cornfields are disappearing. And where will the corn come from? The coffee planter is not going to grow it because his profits are greater growing coffee. If he harvests enough coffee and it sells for a good price, he can import corn and it will cost him less than if he sacrifices coffee trees in order to grow it. . . . Who will grow corn and where? . . . Any nation that cannot assure the production and regulate the price of the most vital crop, the daily food of the people, has no right to regard itself as sovereign. . . . Such has become the case of our nation. □

The Solution

D EFINED PRECISELY, the Doctrine of Guaranteed Minimal Quality of Life means the permanent and complete satisfaction of primary necessities for everyone. The lack of those primary necessities undermines the health and vigor of the individual and inevitably causes an early death. Health, happiness, an ability to work, good will, selflessness, and strength all depend on the permanent and complete satisfaction of minimal needs.

Sources: Alberto Masferrer, *Patria* (San Salvador: Editorial Universitaria, 1960), pp. 179–182; *El Minimum Vital* (San Salvador: Ministerio de Educación, 1968), pp. 15–21, 32–33, 35–36.

Ignoring those basic needs, society actually encourages illness, apathy, weakness, unhappiness, pessimism, idleness, and vice. People without proper food, shelter, clothing, and rest cannot serve society either as citizens or workers. They can neither defend their country nor sustain their families.

The full satisfaction of primary needs is the base and prerequisite for life and health. This conclusion serves the interests of no particular caste, class, or privileged group. Rather, it is in the best interests of the entire nation, which draws its own dynamic from the health, strength, vigor, happiness, courage, and well-being of each citizen. Strong citizens make a strong nation.

Reduced to their absolute minimum, what are the basic necessities that constitute the Minimal Quality of Life? They can be summarized in nine categories:

1. *Work:* safe, permanent, honest, and justly paid.
2. *Food:* sufficient, varied, nutritious, and healthy.
3. *Shelter:* ample, dry, well ventilated, and sunny.
4. *Water:* safe and plentiful.
5. *Clothing:* clean, correct, and protective.
6. *Medical care and proper sanitation.*
7. *Justice:* prompt, easy, and equally accessible for all.
8. *Education:* free and primary to help create an informed and contented population of good workers and conscientious heads of family.
9. *Rest and Recreation:* sufficient and adequate to restore the vigor of mind and body.

Is it possible to promise and, more importantly, to guarantee to every citizen of this nation a minimal quality of life without incurring bankruptcy? Yes, of course it is. Let the nation take its example from the family. Every normal family seeks to obtain and maintain for each of its members these same basic goals of quality of life. The family wants to feed, dress, shelter, instruct, and provide work to all its members so that they can grow, develop, and live equally and happily. If the family, subordinated as it is to the social environment in which it exists, struggles against innumerable obstacles in its efforts to satisfy to a greater or lesser degree the needs of family members, then how can the nation do any less? The nation, after all, enjoys many more advantages than the family. It is sovereign, the owner of great wealth, the arbiter of laws and institutions; it is able to regulate work and finances, to encourage new ideas and trends, and to initiate experiments it considers prudent for a better and more just life.

The nation enjoys considerable power and advantages. Its strength surpasses that of a single family. It can coordinate the efforts of all its citizens. Nature has given the nation resources and a varied population capable of every form of production and labor.

If nations thus far have not implemented this simple and just Doctrine of Guaranteed Minimal Quality of Life, it may well be because they have not thought enough about it. In their multiple activities, nations have opted to support other goals, assigning to last place a concern with the quality of life of the majority. Thus, they have failed to give this goal the consideration it merits. Once a nation changes its priorities, once it understands that its fundamental and elementary duty is to satisfy the basic needs of each and every citizen, then what once appeared to be utopian and complex becomes feasible and easy.

A change of priorities constitutes the decisive step in the transformation of society. This new faith in collective well-being is the seed we plant to produce the tree of a new life. If we do not embrace the change, if we fail to endorse the new faith, it is clear that we will continue in old patterns to the further ruin of the nation and its people.

Among the most important principles contributing to the Doctrine of Guaranteed Minimal Quality of Life are:

1. The State, the Province, and the Community have as primary goals and obligations to work first and foremost to implement the Doctrine so that all citizens of this country will benefit from it.

2. All other activities are secondary; indeed, they are illegal if they tend in any way to detract from or postpone the primary goal.

3. The constant and foremost ideal of the State, Province, and Community will be to fulfill first and to the fullest extent possible the feeding, clothing, and sheltering of everyone.

4. Medical assistance, justice, and education always must be free and accessible since they are vital to the well-being of everyone.

5. The availability of a job for everyone is indispensable for individual and community well-being. That well-being is understood as physical, moral, and mental, and it is the key to social happiness, harmony, and progress. Thus, the highest duty and aspiration of each citizen is legitimate, honest, and productive work that benefits the social community.

6. No work can be considered legitimate if it is in any way detrimental to the individual, family, or society. . . .

Essentially the Doctrine of Guaranteed Minimal Quality of Life is a statement of faith, a new, simple, and just way to understand and experience human relations. It is a new concept of life, a new form of consciousness, a new configuration of institutions.

What once was given mere lip service now becomes the foundation for institutions; what once people received as charity now becomes their right; what once was treated as purely secondary—figuring in budgets, laws, and morality after matters of sovereignty, progress, enlightenment, international affairs, and public displays—will now rise to the primary plane of consideration.

We now declare that the right of each person to at least a minimal quality of life is an *absolute right*. The duty of the collective to ensure that each individual enjoys a minimal quality of life now becomes an *absolute duty*.

If these concepts capture and move the consciences of every person—the oppressed and the oppressors, the exploited and the exploiters—then the Doctrine of Guaranteed Minimal Quality of Life will flourish within our institutions, laws, and customs. It will renovate our patterns of life. Our nation and society will transform themselves slowly and surely under its moral influence. . . .

How can we make this Doctrine a reality? Let us use every means possible, those already known and those still to be improvised. We can ask ourselves where do we get the money to make wars, to build roads, to send ambassadors abroad, to finance an infinity of institutions that sometimes are not only useless but harmful? If we are able to find money to build theaters, barracks, hospitals, and schools, if we can purchase cannons, war planes, and thousands of other similar items, it is because we give them priority, believing them to be both useful and necessary. Belief and faith dictate our priority of expenditures. People imagine that it is both good and necessary to establish embassies abroad, to asphalt streets, to open conservatories, to organize exhibitions, to purchase war machinery, to build radio stations; they believe that a failure to do so contravenes duty, destiny, and faith in progress and civilization. Once they believe that the Doctrine of Guaranteed Minimal Quality of Life is correct, just, and necessary, they will reprioritize laws, regulations, and budgets in order to put it into effect. To carry out that goal, they will reorganize property, work, production, and consumption in such a way that with a job every person of good will can enjoy a minimal quality of life. In that way, the Doctrine, like the present pursuit of progress, will rank first in priorities and achievements. Let us undertake the obligation of redirecting our energies, talents, and finances.□

Nationalism and Development

Reacting after 1930 to the economic dislocations brought about by the Great Depression, nationalists honed their prose in favor of accelerating industrialization, limiting foreign penetration and control of local economies, and repossessing foreign-owned natural resources. While vigorously proclaiming programs designed to encourage economic development, they accused foreign investors, allied with part of the native oligarchy, of perpetuating the colonial past in order to preserve their power, privileges, and profits.

Intellectuals like the Brazilian Nelson Werneck Sodré promoted nationalism as the ideological force to destroy the colonial past, to diminish foreign control, and to redeem Latin America. Thus, he built on the ideas of his compatriot Alberto Tôrres. An articulate spokesperson for developmental nationalism, he boldly asked in 1959, "Why Nationalism?" and then proceeded to offer a convincing response.

WHY NATIONALISM? Because now foreign economic forces are the most powerful obstacle to our development and their internal allies decline in resistance, they no longer tutor the nation. For any country with a colonial past, with an economic structure subordinated to foreign interests, to create itself nationally is to accomplish a task in many ways identical to what the European nations accomplished at the dawn of the Modern Age with the defeat of feudalism and the advance of capitalism. What for them were feudal relations, restrictions on development, are for us all that still remain of the colonial past. Nationalism thus presents itself as liberation. From its possibilities as a liberating force arises the impassioned atmosphere which surrounds it and which causes its enemies to

Source: Nelson Werneck Sodré, *Raízes Históricas do Nacionalismo Brasileiro* (Rio de Janeiro: Ministério da Educação, 1960), pp. 30–35.

consider it more passion than politics. It is proper to emphasize that passion in the abstract does not exist and that Nationalism interprets a truth—truth within the historical context, and that truth is concrete.

To those who find difficulty in placing Nationalism in the economic realm, who judge false the declarations by which it is presented as a shield against various forms of real foreign aggression, perhaps it is more easily understood within its political framework where the lines are more precisely drawn. In that framework, Nationalism represents the democratic ideal, supported solely by the rising classes, which need liberty as the human body needs oxygen, which live by the enlightenment of opinion, which need to discuss and to debate publicly. More than anything, they need popular support and only that reveals the essential democratic character of the nationalist position. The opposition forces, quite to the contrary, have lost the conditions for open life and exercise varied and repeated attempts to limit freedoms, to restrict opinions, to reduce politics to the old formulas of the combinations of a few, of clandestine decisions, of summit statements with a characteristic horror of anything that smacks of the masses.

Nationalism appears, then, on the historic scene as the escape from a difficult situation whose symptoms appear in day-to-day life. It answers the present demands, concrete necessities—it was not invented, it did not come from the imagination of a few, it does not live in theory but in practice. It is a spontaneous solution, and this seems to be one of its limitations because it is difficult for it to take on organized forms in the political struggle. Organized it is invincible. The feeling of passion which accompanies it, a positive sign of its force and not a symptom of its weakness, points out the generality and profundity of its effects: it reveals that Nationalism is popular, which should not surprise anyone, seeing that everything that is national is popular.

Inaccurate are the comparisons, slyly put forward as accusations, that Nationalism is historically outdated—so is colonialism—and that it can lead to what happened recently in other countries, particularly in Germany and in Italy. It is clear that Nationalism can lead to anything, but there is no relationship whatsoever between the situation presented by a country like Brazil with an economic structure still strongly contaminated by colonialism and the nations, like those mentioned, in which the capitalist system was fully installed. Likewise, it would be simple to establish other distinctions by an easy comparison: the economic forces which aided nazism and fascism are the same which here oppose the growth of Nationalism.

Nationalism springs from the necessity of creating a new scheme of coordinating class interests, or reducing them to a minimum common denominator, for the struggle in defense of what is national in us. It is imperative to overcome the disagreement between the national bourgeoisie and the working class which adopts Nationalism as an opportune political expression. It is understood that only by minimizing, without denying or obscuring, the contradiction between the class which furnishes the labor and increases its consciousness every day and the class which needs to strengthen itself through capitalization of the national resources and their proper use, we will be able to endure as a nation which presents Nationalism as the natural solution and gives to it that force, that penetration, and that catalytic power which the simple observation sees in it.

To set up all the obstacles to the creation of a framework in which the forces interested in national development are harmonized becomes the essential task of those who oppose Nationalism, of those who see in it the direct menace to what they represent, of those who see and fear the existence of a possibility for Brazil to overcome the remnants of colonialism by making itself into a nation. The simplest process is to divide those forces by establishing as fundamental the contradiction which separates them, by aggravating the conditions of life to force to desperation those who work and to distress those who compose the varied range of the middle class. For these reasons we see the dangers of an economic and financial policy which generates the conditions of uncertainty and propitiates those of subversion and the anomalies of a country famished for capital exporting capital, of creating difficulties for the equipping of factories which use national capital, of systematizing the desperation of those who have the right of expecting equal treatment when they do not receive preferential treatment for the simple fact that they live, invest, and work here.

Then, what is old and what is new in this phase [of the growing Brazilian Revolution which began in 1930]? Old doubtless are the semi-feudal relations which impede the amplification of the internal market; old is the policy of spreading the economic setbacks among all the classes by reducing the acquisitive power of the masses; old is the orientation of relegating the State to inertia; old is the mercantilism which requires us to ship more abroad and to receive less for it; old is the rule which imprisons us in the role as a tropical producing plantation of primary materials for foreign industries; old is our subordination to foreign reasoning, no matter how valid it might be abroad; old, particularly, is the idea that Brazil can only develop with outside aid and principally with foreign capital.

And what is new? New is the social composition which includes a bourgeoisie capable of becoming a class and beginning to understand that its opportunity is now or never and that it is a middle class attentively and ideologically receptive, through the major part of its elements, to the clamor which is raised in the depths of history in the sense that we must organize ourselves for the task we have to fulfill, and a working class which acquired a political conscience and mobilizes itself for the purpose of sharing the national undertaking, seeing thereby the opening of perspectives to its historical role. New are the people. Nothing more will occur without their participation. New is the national industry, which has passed the stage of consumers' goods to producers' goods, limited, however, by the backwardness in the acquisitive capacity of the internal market and burdened by a policy of obstacles and doubts. Volta Redonda [Brazil's first steel mill] is what is new that is altering the Brazilian scene and Petrobras is what is new which affirms our capacity for progress without interferences. New, in short, is Nationalism, which corresponds to what pushes us forward and breaks with what held us back.

Between the new and the old the choice is not difficult. Between the past and the future, no doubt exists. We choose the future. We do not intend "to lose the continuity of history." □

Artistic and Literary Reactions to Progress

The type of selective modernization evident during the last half of the nineteenth century also dominated the twentieth century. The inescapable result was that manifestations of modernization—or progress as it was denoted in the nineteenth century—coexisted with traditional modes, often of pre-Columbian origins. The inevitable contrasts and contradictions of dual societies emerged; in fact, they became dominant characteristics of Latin America.

Many of the experts saw development as the means of resolving the duality in favor of the modern, the up-to-date, too often the imported and foreign. First the onset of modernization and then the drive toward development raised fundamental questions. What kind of modernization or development and for what ends? And what were the results? As these were tabulated, did they always indicate positive achievements, development in the sense that the quality of life for the average citizen improved? The questions asked and the tabulations themselves aroused controversy.

To provide another insight into that controversy, this section draws on artistic and literary responses: first, representational and symbolic visual depictions of perceived reality; next, a poem; finally, a short story. Art, poetry, and fiction share the characteristic of being able to encapsulate and distill "reality." A perceptive artist, poet, or writer offers insight and understanding, opening a dialogue with the reader/viewer who imaginatively interprets the art, poetry, or prose. The following selections constitute exceedingly rich intellectual documents. They elicit varying interpretations and probably convey different understandings, depending on the imagination of the reader/viewer.

Art as Historical Document

The two etchings, two paintings and linoleum cut that follow are visual documents of a reality at a given moment as perceived by an artist. The viewer can enjoy them for obvious aesthetic reasons but can also read them for social insight.

Economic Protest

This etching by José Guadalupe Posada from the very early twentieth century depicts a primary socioeconomic issue: the cost of living. Housewives along with a male chef protest to a merchant about the high prices of food products. Indeed, as the long administration of Porfirio Díaz lengthened in Mexico, prices of basic foodstuffs rose in absolute terms. Irate women played an active role in voicing a basic economic complaint. In this etching, they strike a threatening pose. The clothing of the merchant suggests he might be a foreigner or foreign-born, an implied criticism of foreign control of the Mexican economy and, thus, of dependency.

Poverty Prevails

This etching by Posada contains rich iconography. By one interpretation—and the print lends itself to many—it seems to reflect hope amid poverty. Clearly the mother, the three children, and the empty table, the central grouping in this Mexican working-class home, signify poverty. The burning candle and the Virgin of Guadalupe on the right and the stalwart husband with a trade on the left suggest hope. The husband and wife stare at each other solemnly, questioningly. Between them a crying, naked child raises a supplicating hand. For her part, the mother grasps the table with one hand and a child with the other; her domestic responsibilities/cares immobilize or imprison her. For his part, the father holds a mallet or hammer in one hand, a symbol of his trade, and his hat in the other, recognition of his spatial mobility and link to the outside world. Posada made a strong statement about the impoverished family. He provides no resolution, only hinting of hope.

2nd Class

An important contributor to the Modernist art movement and cultural nationalism, the Brazilian artist Tarsilia do Amaral (1886–1973) depicted on this canvas, titled "2nd Class," migrants on the move from the Northeast, the most impoverished region of Brazil. They search for a promised land, their redemption. Quite probably they will end up in a large city, contributing to the phenomenal growth of places like São Paulo or Rio de Janeiro. They possess no skills to contribute to the technologically oriented cities. Their hope may lie in the success of their children in the new environment. Yet, the hunger and malnourishment of the young ones, depicted by thin limbs and overly large heads, taunt that hope. The painting links human misery with the train, the universal symbol of "progress." Although "2nd Class" refers directly to the coach in which the migrants travel, the artist also implies that these Brazilians are "second class" citizens. Amaral makes a powerful statement about Latin American development and the future.

Still Life

Brazilian migrants are also the subject of the painting "Still Life," by Quirino Campofiorito (1902–). While the title seems innocuous enough, the combination of title and image resounds with irony. The distant families trek across the barren land—both scenery and the situation again reflect the Brazilian Northeast—but the viewer cannot make out whether the families move toward or away from the display of corn and tropical fruits, basic foods that Brazil is capable of producing abundantly. Which is "still," the landless, impoverished inhabitants of the Northeast in the background, the foods displayed in the foreground, or both? And what are the implications of "still"?

The Dinner

The very title of this linoleum cut contradicts the image. There is no food. The doleful look of expectant children dominates this picture, created by Mauricio Lasansky in 1937, when he served as director of the Fine Arts School in Córdoba, Argentina. Children figure predominately in visual documentation because the majority of Latin Americans are under sixteen years of age and because children symbolize the future. Lasansky's image, like those of Posada, raises the question of whether economic development is taking place in Latin America. Images such as these indict the form that modernization took.

"Economic Protest," etching, Mexico, c. 1900 (José Guadalupe Posada, 1852–1913).

"Poverty Prevails," etching, Mexico, c. 1905 (José Guadalupe Posada, 1852–1913).

"2nd Class," oil on canvas, Brazil, 1931 (Tarsilia do Amaral, 1886–1973).

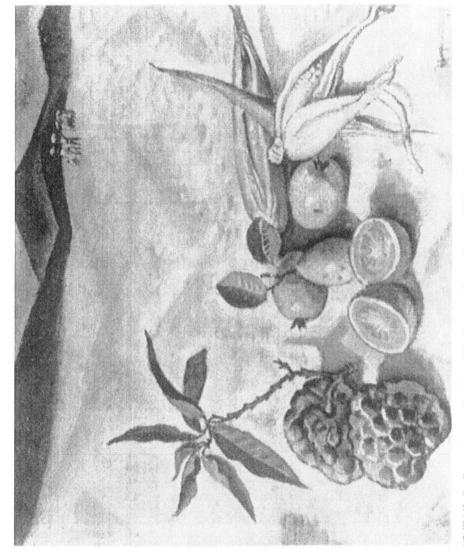

"Still Life," oil on canvas, Brazil, c. 1950 (Quirino Compofiorito, 1902–   ).

"The Dinner," linoleum cut, Argentina, 1937 (Mauricio Lasansky, 1914–   ).

"An Appeal to Some Learned Doctors"

A childhood spent among the Indians of Andean Peru instilled in José María Arguedas (1911–1969) a profound respect for their beliefs and life-styles. His fiction, poetry, and ethnographical accounts all testify to that respect. The ubiquitous development plans circulating in the Latin American capitals aroused his suspicions. He criticized them as mere copies of foreign models alien to local reality and disrespectful of people, inevitably harmful to them. In turn, the "economic experts" and the "learned doctors" ridiculed Arguedas as a hopeless romantic. On one occasion, he replied to their taunts with a poem in Quechua, the major Indian language of Peru in which he wrote nearly all his poetry. He reminded his critics that the Indians boasted of a noble history of their own, filled with accomplishments and satisfactions, not least of which had been an ability to feed themselves satisfactorily. He alluded to their admirable harmony with and respect for nature. He firmly believed that no plans for the Indians' future—or any formula for their development—can be made without consulting them.

T HEY say that we don't know anything, that we are backwardness, that they'll exchange our heads for others, better ones.

They say that our heart also does not match the times, that it is full of fear, tears, like the calendar lark; like the heart of a huge, butchered bull; and thus (saying) we are impertinent.

They say that some doctors tell this about us; doctors who multiply in our land, who grow fat here, get golden. . . .

What are my brains made of? Of what the flesh of my heart?

The rivers run roaring in their depth. Gold and night, silver and the fearsome night shape the rocks, the walls of the canyons the river sounding against them; of that silver and gold night-rock are my mind, my heart, my fingers.

What's there, at river's edge, unknown to you, doctor?

Take out your binoculars, your best lenses. Look, if you can.

Five hundred kinds of flowers of as many kinds of potatoes grow on the balconies unreached by your eyes; they grow in the earth; mixed with night and gold, silver and day. Those five hundred flowers are my brains, my flesh.

Why did the sun stop for an instant, why have the shadows disappeared? Why, doctor?

Start your helicopter and climb here, if you can. The condor's feathers, those of smaller birds, light up, are now a rainbow.

Source: From *Deep Rivers,* by José María Arguedas; Frances Horning Barraclough, translator. Introduction by John V. Murra. , pp. xiii–xv (Austin: University of Texas Press, 1978). By permission of the publishers.

The hundred flowers of *quinua* which I planted at the summit bubble their colors in the Sun; the black wings of the condor and of the tiny birds are now in flower.

It is noon; I am close to the lord-mountains, the ancestor-peaks; their snow now yellow flecked, now with red patches, is shining in the Sun. . . .

Don't run away from me, doctor, come close! Take a good look at me, recognize me. How long must I wait for you?

Come close to me; lift me to the cabin of your helicopter. I will toast you with a drink of a thousand different flowers, the life of a thousand crops I grew in centuries, from the foot of the snows to the forests of the wild bears.

I will cure your weariness, which clouds you; I will divert you with the light of a hundred *quinua* flowers, with the sight of their dance as the winds blow; with the slight heart of the calendar lark which mirrors the whole world;

I will refresh you with the singing water which I will draw out of the black canyon's walls. . . .

Did I work for centuries of months and years in order that someone I do not know and does not know me, cut off my head with a small blade?

No, brother mine. Don't sharpen that blade; come close, let me know you; look at my face, my veins; the winds blowing from us to you, we all breathe them; the earth on which you count your books, your machines, your flowers, it comes down from mine, improved, no longer angry, a tamed earth. . . .

We know that they want to misshape our face with clay; exhibit us, deformed, before our sons.

We don't know what will happen. Let death walk towards us, let these unknown people come.

We will await them; we are the sons of the father of all the lord mountains; sons of the father of all the rivers. . . . □

"Rosaura"

Published in 1922, the brilliant short story "Rosaura" by the Argentine master Ricardo Güiraldes (1886–1927) serves as a kind of counterpoint to Domingo F. Sarmiento's thesis of civilization and barbarism. If Sarmiento proclaimed in 1845 the birth of the future, Güiraldes chronicles the death of a past.

For both intellectuals, the railroad serves as the symbol of change, progress, and an imported European civilization. For both, the train, an instrument of the city, penetrates the countryside, considered by Sarmiento as the citadel of barbarism but by Güiraldes in a more nationalistic vein as the stronghold of *argentinidad,* the being and soul of Argentina. Whatever the interpretation of the symbols, the expansion of the railroad ordained a clash of cultures. For good or for bad, modernization extracted its toll. Whether the benefits outweigh the costs remains unresolved. Questioning modernization, or the civilization of Sarmiento, Güiraldes helped to propel a debate, which still continues, over how much "civilization" should be borrowed from abroad and how much should be nurtured from within.

Through the eyes of Güiraldes, the reader of this tightly constructed short story glimpses life in an Argentine provincial town in the early twentieth century. The impact of the railroad, what it brings and what it takes, becomes quickly apparent. The ending, with its broad symbolic meaning, arouses emotions that rivet the story to the mind. Among the broadest questions this tale raises is whether the type of modernization (progress or development) imposed by Latin American leaders served the best interests of the majority.

I

LOBOS IS A TRANQUIL TOWN, in the middle of the pampa.
An indifferent boredom drifts through its tree-fringed streets.

Few passersby sound on its pavements, steps tell-tale as hoof-beats, and except at the train-hour or during the summer promenades on the plaza, fresh with evening quiet, nothing stirs the sober siesta which a spinster conscience seems to impose on the town's friendliness.

Like all our towns, Lobos possesses a plaza whose blunt brick enclosure, exposed by a recent sacrifice of old vines, stretches across from the Church, and daily flaunts an artificial sleekness renewed by the long and flexible nozzle of a hose.

The Church is colonial style, its great courtyard of red flags rimmed with a single zig-zag marble parquet. In front, the plaza between, is the police station with its coat-of-arms and its chief in view, while his orderly takes the air to the count of *mates* prepared by an ex-felon policeman, who trades retail in pardons.

A two-story branch of the Banco de la Nación overlooks one of the corners of the square. On the second corner, counting by display, the gastronomic windows of the *Jardin* confectionery, known by residents familiarly as "the Basque's," spread out an invitation for the afternoon. And while on the third, the store smiles percaline brightness, on the fourth the pharmacy reminds that there are ills in this world.

Here is all the community needs: justice, money, clothing, self-indulgence, and ideals, in moderate doses.

The main artery of the town's life, one of the streets opening into the plaza, is called *Calle Real* and is cobblestoned. Ornate souvenirs of some Louis nth on its houses are tempered by massive old elms in danger of being felled by a progressive administration which might not consider them fine trees.

In a row, monopolizing the privilege of the pavement noisy under wheels and hoofs, stand the Hotel de Paris, the Club Social, the *Globo* jewelry, the clothing store, and the *Modelo* shoe-shop.

Five or six blocks from this center, the squares of monotonous colourless structures built adjoining are brightened here and there by a bush or a tree whose

Source: Waldo Frank (ed.), *Tales from the Argentine* (Freeport, N.Y.: Books for Libraries Press, 1970), pp. 181–235.

serene crown looks out over the dusty bricks of the walls, flat and angular as a house of cards. The façades begin to glow yellows, greens, and sky-blues, blotting-paper tones. Doors and windows are framed in deeper hues. Through the doorways a glimpse of vines is caught reflected in polished tile floors.

On the fringe, the grocery store, once the headquarters for the alley, sleeps deserted, despite the mildly domestic air lent by a sorry team of hacks (one grey, the other dappled) dozing harnessed to a spring-wagon.

Villas scatter the town into a vast horizon of ranches, to which summer visitors bring the only glitter of wealth in the district.

The soul of Lobos was simple and primitive as a red bloom. Lobos thought, loved, lived, in its own way. Then came the parallel infinities of swift rails, and the train, marching armoured to indifference from horizon to horizon, from stranger to stranger, brushed its passing plume over the settlement.

Lobos fell ill of that poison.

II

In a car of the National Railways that afternoon rode a young man dressed in European style, irreproachably: collar and tie, soft hat, and country-suit that, though worn, retained in the lining of an inner pocket the label and date of delivery from Poole. His legs were encased almost to the knee in boots impeccably curved. Beside him balanced a suit-case from a great London house, colorfully patched with stickers that recorded stays at fashionable hotels and beaches. His coat hung from the clumsy rack. And the thick-seamed gloves lay like a pair of amputated Indian hands on the dusty table in the middle of which a litre of water danced spherically within a round-bellied jug of long and pretentious neck.

The youth's clothing proclaimed an education abroad. His dark skin, evenly laid either side of a lean nose, his high cheek-bones and rigidly correct bearing, revealed Castilian descent; something silent and searching in his pupils told several generations of watchful pampa life; and the native zest of a new race braced his easy laughter.

The inspector called him Don Carlos when he asked for the tickets. His age might have been gauged roughly as somewhere between twenty-five and thirty. With leisure, he glanced through a daily, at the cattle-market quotations.

The cars jarred abruptly, the asthmatic gasps of the locomotive died down, a yellow lantern illegibly flashed past, the earth-level rose to a platform outlined by a row of banana trees; the train stopped in front of the lighted corridor of that station that shut out the night.

"Lobos"

People descended, people ascended. The boiler hissed like a deflating balloon. The buzz of a beehive rose from the crowd: politicians out campaigning, fashionable youths in gray felts and light shoes, personages displaying their official personalities, sheiks with straw hats about to slide off their greasy foreheads and stickily pomaded skulls, coachmen waiting for fares, *peons* for mail or on errands, while like perfume-blossoms in the jungle, the exuberant girls of Lobos came and went, shyly discreet or laughing excessively, nervous—who knows why.

Three went, arm in arm, slowly: one in sky-blue, another in pink, another in yellow. Toward Carlos' window they glanced with such bold curiosity that he was annoyed, squared his shoulders, breathed high, and flushed aggressively and violently as a turkey. In defense he fixed his eyes upon one of them, thinking to intimidate, but instead the girl held that gaze as wood does a plug.

They passed. Two or three times they promenaded the station from end to end, walking with the careless ease of coquettes. Carlos, no longer offended, took the play and gazed after the swaying little figure retreating as if in anger, or bored with his eyes into the pupils that became penetrable and docile.

And she with surprise felt her eyes opened like that, as if they had been careless windows, and her body overcome by a strange wave of languor.

But it was all play and when the train jerked out after a blazon of whistle and bell, as the elegant youth half bowed, they laughed openly, correcting that rudeness with a bare and almost involuntary dip of the head to the shoulder.

The car passed quickly, striking from the station windows a vibrant echo.

III

Her name was Rosaura Torres and she was the daughter of old man Crescencio, owner of the wealthiest livery-stables in town, an estate which counted no less than five cabs drawn by horses splendid for work, God willing.

It was large, half a block, this place of brick and unwhitewashed clay.

The hallway, dining room, kitchen and bedrooms faced front. Inside they were backed by a porch from the eaves of which hung, like slim and long sensual boas, intricate vines embracing hungrily. A tiny orchard containing one flower-tree, three fruit-bearers, and four small cottonwoods, flourished either side of a grape-arbor.

Enclosing this quiet ensemble, where the women trailed their skirts as they went about their homely tasks, a wire fence upheld the subtle rustle of honey-suckles and climbing roses.

The corral was nearly open field, with its light zinc roof to protect the vehicles, harness and fodder, its little yard with stalls for the horses, its chicken-coop which used up the trough-waste, and its adopted cur, not so harmless, despite the whimperings and snugglings of the little fellow.

Her name was Rosaura Torres and she was pretty. Her slippers slapped at her heels indolently like oriental sandals; her hands were skilled, her laughter eager, her dreams simple; life waited curious within her inviolate lips.

For her, every waking was gay, to live a daily boon, all flowers beautiful, the afternoons smiling and tranquil with something that cradled and soothed.

Rosaura was pretty and waiting to plunge her skilled hands into life, as into her morning basket of flowers.

IV

She had two blocks to go along the narrow sidewalk a meter above the dusty road, to reach the main street.

Rosaura walked out about five-thirty in her yellow dress, generously powdered, enjoying to the full all the usual incidents of her pilgrimage to the station, where she waited like the others for the six-thirty-five express.

At five-thirty Rosaura would leave, unaware of the miracle of youth that went with her. She crossed the end of the street, careful not to make a misstep in her Louis XV heels, and not to smudge with sandy soil the mirror perfection of her shoes. Half a block down she exchanged a good afternoon with old Petrona, who always stood on the threshold of her white house, her arms pillowed on the soft mound of her stomach, shaken with deep laughter.

"Hello, Doña Petrona."

"God bless you, child . . . why, you're a regular doll . . . poor boys! . . ."

Rosaura never heard the end, always crude banter, and she hurried the swift patter of her bright little shoes, knowing that at the corner masculine eyes would manage better to convey those flattering, but repellent, thoughts.

She was on the main street. Fashionable Lobos promenaded between station and plaza, its greetings and laughter ruffling the earlier silence of the streets.

The minutes flicked by spent in chatter, salvaged by charming or important ends. Words cloaked the feelings of the men and women who brushed each other—the women with the air of jewels on display, the men like wary customers concealing their tastes.

The afternoon would be winding itself out in dark corners, when the promenade, aimless heretofore, turned toward the station. Planks creaked in the floor of the waiting-room, through which the platform was gradually invaded.

And it was always the same, from the Bois de Boulogne with its tide of coughing motors to the modest echo of village heels, there in this last corner of the world, where tiny hopes waver up in a piteously simple society.

The station is to Lobos what Hyde Park is to London, the Retiro to Madrid, the Sweet Waters of Asia to Constantinople. If a slight, unknown guilt exists, it does not fall there.

But the first train is in. It is six o'clock, highest pitch of excitement till six-thirty-five, when the really important one, dealer of emotions from Buenos Aires, is due.

People passed, people criticized, and a web of romanticism entangled the youth of the town.

The minutes scrambled down the restless clock.

Rosaura saw that fashionable young man many times. Her friends teased her because of the insistent glances that they perhaps wished for themselves, and the girl felt something agreeably clouding her reason, when Carlos looked at her smiling, watching for recognition.

An emotion, greater than the little breast in the yellow dress, welled in Rosaura.

Through the restless days that speed too, the hours come again and again, and among them the moment when the express is due. The initials of an idyll can be traced on the dusty haunch of the cars, and Rosaura wrote her name on the diner, in which travelled the fashionable youth of the glance.

Oh, evil influence of the indifferent locomotive to whose monster eye the horizon presents no ideal! Pitiless train that passed on, abandoning to the monotonous boredom of the village those fanciful dreams of the sentimental Rosaura who wrote her fate on its cars!

But the enamoured child was too much a part of today's amazement to sense the disharmony between stable people and the great forces that pass. And one afternoon, when Carlos got down, ostensibly for a walk, and passed beside her very near, she felt she would fall, strangely drawn as if by the slight breath in his wake.

V

Little garden with your arbour, your odorous jasmine, your white and cold laurel and sexual carnations, something stirs there to fill you so tenderly. In Rosaura the simple provincial of pastoral soul, blooms the miracle of a great love.

Rosaura lives closing her eyes to possess more completely her intense emotion. Her coquetry is wasted no longer: for him her arms drop in consent; for him her pupils suffer this concentrated feeling; for him her body yields unknown surrender, when she walks wrapped in disturbing day-dreams; and for him too, her breast fills to the size of an entire world.

How enormous is this unsuspected world! At times Rosaura thinks and fears: What will be of her life now? Is this love? Does that incredibly elegant and distinguished youth love her too? She thinks and fears and leaves unsolved those impossible elusive problems.

Rosaura closes her eyes to possess more completely her intense emotion.

The days are no longer monotonous nor the hours leaden in that tiny unsuspected garden, there in the pampa that sings its endless song of the unending spaces.

And the spring that is not illusion brings the lilacs to bloom, clinging twined in clustered embraces, falling splendid in violet sprays; and in the vines that drooped from the eaves like slim and sensual boas, timid gleams of white jasmine appear. The honeysuckle too breathes a hint of the tropics, vibrant as a ringing bell; and the potted carnations burst into pride.

The soul of Rosaura wells an odour of troubled love like the perfumed wave of the honeysuckles. Her cheeks are like jasmine, her eyes become pooled to a sheen of grape, and her blood ripens her mouth so that she strangely needs to bite her lips.

The soul of Rosaura slowly is inhaled by her body.

VI

Restlessly wandering about, Rosaura awaits the unrealized idyll of those glances. Will he come? Won't he come?

She pictures beforehand, in the square of light framed by the car window, that fine profile hastily looking up from the paper to seek her alone, among all the girls of the crowded platform.

Always it is his tense eyes that pierce her, fixed on her black locks, on her shoulders, on her walk which suddenly shifts with mysterious languor.

To look into his face is a physical shock and just to think of his face flushes her cheeks, and makes her mind grow dangerously wild. She fears then she may walk crookedly, may fall absurdly on account of a misstep, or because of that moment's blindness may run blankly into someone who would guess her disturbance.

Carrying these painfully intense visions, Rosaura walks arm in arm with her friends, and plunges into dreadfully flat talk to hide and disguise them.

But the green tranquil light becomes a red, color of blood and passion. Two meters above the rails the monster eye of the locomotive runs flaming brighter, and then passes beyond, as the steely forehead of the engine turns to the horizon. There is the shock of yielding metal. Rosaura suffers, arm in arm with her friends indifferently lost in Sunday laughter.

And one afternoon—strange!—when she sought in the frame of the window that profile which had been to her an intangible, fugitive ideal calling forth dreams, and no more, she saw the man descend with his great suitcase; stride across the crowd on the platform, and take a cab of old Torres, with the gesture of a landlord returning to his estate.

Rosaura felt her soul pierced by the anguish of a virgin possessed.

She was displeased by the active, direct, now justified teasing of her friends. She left them with scant caresses to flutter the streets with their stale and flat chatter, and fled home in amazement, fearful and dazzled as a quail.

VII

Rosaura slept badly all that night, pursued by a vague event whose influence would definitely change her life.

Already roused she heard her father in the kitchen, splitting wood for the morning *mate*.

She joined the old man, surprising him with that unnecessary rising.

"Where will the sun come up?"

"It's you, daddy, that woke me."

"Well, go on out to the hen-coop and bring in some kindling."

Dawn lighted the yard when Rosaura in quest of the chips saw Lucio's coach ready to leave.

"I'm going to the hotel, *niña,* to get a stranger who's come to look at *haciendas.*"

"And why the extra harness?"

"Seems we're goin' to go far . . . maybe till tonight."

Lucio twisted his half-open mouth and clapped his tongue on his palate, clucking the horses to start: the uneven team disappeared through the gate, the coach seemed to drop in a hole, comical and shameless as a street wench.

"Good-bye, *niña!*"

The coachman had exaggerated; when Rosaura went down toward the main street that afternoon, after speaking to Doña Petrona, she was struck with surprise upon seeing Carlos seated at a small table in front of the hotel, accompanied by the political leader Barrios, the cattle-auctioneer Gonzalez, the representative Iturri and other gentlemen of the hour.

Naturally Carlos bowed to her like the rest and Rosaura answered courteously though she felt naked in her blushes. How hard to maintain a natural walk and how awful to linger like that before ten staring men!

Rosaura's pride suffered and the susceptible little creole, hurt by that supposedly betraying blush, hated the stranger violently. Why couldn't things remain as they were, easy?

She was overcome by a fear of having to talk to Carlos in public. She believed her platform flirtation so flagrant. . . .

Oh, indeed! she would make him pay for that humiliation doubtless already glossed by the clumsy words of that shameless crowd in front of the Hotel de Paris; nobody should have a peg on which to hang a tale about *her* favours.

And that afternoon at the glory hour of Lobos, Rosaura, wounded in the privacy of her romantic passion, became singularly talkative and attentive to the chatter of her friends, returned their shafts charmingly, and cruelly, suicidally ridiculed the elegant youth, who followed her with his eyes fixed steadily as the headlights of an automobile on the road.

When Rosaura went home she was exhausted and convinced that she had been uselessly a coward; she threw herself on the bed and, pathetically dishevelled, wept great sobs of pain for her blighted passion.

VIII

Fortunately that state of affairs did not last. Rosaura would have died of grief. It was not possible to weep so, days and days, accusing herself bitterly.

Carlos had left on the morning following that, to him, incomprehensible afternoon.

No actions proved, and no words even, that the saucy flirtation of the girl on the platform meant anything more than a few moments' diversion. Hurt by the impudence of the staring little chit in the yellow dress, he thought no more of the matter, unaware that he left a great passion tortured into a sorrow, as the train jerked from the station in the biting chill of that windy morning.

In the garden that smelled of jasmine, honeysuckle and carnations, little Rosaura wilted like a flower bruised by some casual humming-bird which flitted on, once it had sucked the savor.

Ended for ever, the gay starts every afternoon at five; the hellos to Doña Petrona; the coquettishly careful crossings; the fastidious resentment at the brutal stares of the loungers in front of the Hotel de Paris, the meetings with her friends and the glorified walks on the platform, before those eyes that kindled her and pierced her.

There was nothing left but to weep, weep forever, for these memories of her broken life.

Rosaura would have died had she thought that the fashionable youth of the dining car would never come back, or would pass in the train as indifferent to her as the monster eye of the locomotive to the ideal of the horizon.

It was five. Rosaura recalled even the slightest movements of her habit of years and years. Impatience pulled her to the dressing-table, but a presentiment of martyrdom dropped her on her knees before the niche adorned with palms crossed ovally, where her little blue madonna spangled with gold prayed, in mystic stance, through the centuries.

Oh, that he might be returned to her with a smile of forgiveness; that she might receive only two affectionate lines so as not to die strangled by this thing so much bigger than herself!

Three dry little knocks of somebody's knuckles on the door announced a discreet visitor. Rosaura hurriedly arranged her pitifully disordered self, and in came Carmen, the friend of the pink dress who had been deserted so long, in the distress of that wrecked loved. And as Rosaura's arms passionately convulsive about her were a confession, Carmen, charmingly comforting, spoke openly:

"Holy Mother, be still! . . . why, I've a piece of news that will just make you laugh!"

Rosaura, turned to the wall to hide her tears, quivered from head to foot and her shoulders shook with deep, painful sobs.

"Don't cry like that. . . . You'd do better to start making a peach of a dress for the dance that the Club is giving next week. . . . Or don't you care?"

"Don't joke with me, Carmen."

"Joke? Sit down and listen to real information. . . . I know who he is, what he thinks of you, what he came for and a lot of other things."

"And who told you all that?"

"Gonzalez, who showed him the cows for Lorenzo Ramallo."

"And what's he got to do with Ramallo?"

"Nothing much, he's his son, that's all."

Far from being overcome by that name known far and wide as one of the cream of landholders, Rosaura's passion rose with this new impossibility. So long as Carlos passed through on the train, so long as he came now and then to the isolated little village of Lobos, so long as he looked at her as he had, her love would seek more impulses to grow.

"What else did he say?" she murmured tremblingly.

"That you're a marvel and that he's coming to the dance at the Club to meet you. Now cry if you want!"

Rosaura did not weep but she paled unbelievably. She suffered a torment of pleasure and that fulfillment was as painful as a pregnancy.

More than ever the rings deepened under her eyes, beneath her drooped eyelids; and while Carmen ran merrily on, a smile rose to her lips from the calm depths of her love in contemplation.

IX

Came a tranquil time to the Torres place. The little garden sprouted under the caress of the sun. The orchard bore amply either side of the arboured vine. The red-crested ceibo tree scattered fine glints in the shimmering air. The dog chased mischievously around the edges of feminine skirts, balancing the silver notes of its little whimper like a tune rehearsed in a nightingale's nest.

On the porch enclosed by the fresh bloom of its vines. Rosaura sewed leaning back in her chair. Patches of sunlight dropped on the dress through the vines and the leaves overhead; and when with an indolent foot she would start the chair rocking, those imperceptible wavelets of warmth ran carelessly over her body.

At her right a bent-legged sewing-basket spread out like a split nut, its contents brimming, and on the left a little table unevenly set on the flags, threatened to drop a fashion review lent by a friend on one of the estates for the occasion of the Club dance.

Happy, the lovely Rosaura, absorbed in her work, threaded promises of her love on the porch shaded by the quiet garden stirred in the spring.

Rosaura had chosen from among the models a pattern of muslin embroidered with buds and sprays of fern fine as cobwebs. It opened a bare timid triangle at the neck and a great sash with a bow on one side fluffed like a full rose.

How much she knew now of the Carlos heretofore so mysterious and so untold! Carlos had been educated in Europe. On his return Don Lorenzo, his father, had given him the place at General Alvear to manage, which, however, did not hinder later travels into countries fabulous to Rosaura.

What a new wreath of glory all of this laid upon him, in the heart of the romantic little provincial!

She would go with him as in the fairy-tales, to enchanting and beautiful lands where everything is as easy as dreaming and where to love is to fulfill the most sacred duty. Her hand would be held in his and he would tell her about everything, knowing everything. Then they would return to the little garden, and would live in the neighborhood that reminded them of other days.

Rosaura ran the needle into her finger. One of the buds on the muslin blushed deeper, and she, annoyed at this stupid break in her rhythmic trance, pressed the tip of the hurt finger, making a tiny crimson source.

The dress was finished on time.

X

The greyish façade of the Club Social occupied twenty yards of the cobble-stoned street; from its windows streamed a blaze of festive light, promising gaiety.

At nine that night the hearts of the Lobos girls beat fast, this being the hour to put the last touches on the frocks that would mean scorn or envy. Only Rosaura, pale as a bride, shivers running over her body in its spring-time festoon of sprays and buds, remained indifferent to such petty social successes.

She had arrayed herself with the delicate care of a miniaturist, drawing on the long stiff silk hose, finished off by the bright patent-leather pumps; her skin had quivered at the touch of the fine white undergarment spangled with yellow bows, fitted snugly to her torso by the girdle, rose-faint as a blush. And she had called her mother to gaze as she slipped into the rustling folds of the frock.

It was time. She walked toward the mirror tasting, at the measured swing of her step, the barely tangible subtlety of her airy garments; she walked profiled, light as an apparition; smiled faintly, lifting in quick amazement her mobile eyebrows; and she thought she might please because of that shade of docility in her eyes, messengers of miracles.

It was time and she was ready, pure and vibrant as a crystal shivered by the distant note of a bronze bell. She swooned almost, with virginal ripeness of sacrifice, sensing herself worshipped by the intact garments, adorned with the solemn splendours of an offering. "Oh, yes, all his." And a momentary loss of consciousness sent her swaying for support to the bureau, where her hand, limp and cold, lay like marble on the red glamour of the mahogany.

"Come on, come on! . . ."The door opened filling the room with brief clamour. The Gomez girls had arrived to fetch her, as agreed, and Rosaura folded in on herself, like a sensitive plant.

In the dance-hall of the Club Social, revealed inconsiderately by the hard, blinding lights, the reception committee, self-conscious and solemn, fenced opportunely.

Carlos, acquainted with the gloved punctiliousness of such parties, had come early, to settle himself comfortably in a private corner.

An air of naïve cordiality already reigned, and they had all become more used to the gala dress, when the auctioneer Gonzalez, waving a hand from left to right, spoke their names softly:

"Señor Carlos Ramallo, Señorita Rosaura Torres."

To Rosaura, that coupling of their names attained the significance of a question before the altar.

"Very pleased, señor," she said, and she thought this was everything.

He gave her his arm properly.

"As to me I confess it was almost absolutely necessary to speak to you, since I look upon you as an old friend."

Rosaura blushed:

"It is true, we have seen each other so often."

Oh, the melodious enchantment of walking thus, arm in arm, with their words moving close to confession!

And all Lobos looking on!

"Shall we sit down?"

"If you like."

They went out through the corridor, toward a bench glimpsed in the patio, suddenly glorified by the luminous glitter of stars, in a sky framed by the naïve grey cornice.

"This is nice."

They sat down, relieved of pretense; night knows nothing of etiquette and love is everywhere, naturally.

They were silent. Rosaura, quiet, looking at the button of her glove and in the comradely tone that the night required, queried:

"Tell me about yourself. Would you mind? I have lived so alone here."

Carlos did not reply. To tell the child, simple as a red bloom, of his intricate fashionable adventures would be the irreverent action of a cheap Don Juan.

"Please believe my amusements don't amount to anything."

"But—and all you have travelled in this wide world?"

"I have some pleasant memories."

And carried away in the mood of Rosaura, who intently waited for wondrous tales, he seemed to have just discovered the true charm of things past.

He was surprised to hear himself saying sincerely:

"Those journeys are saddening when one makes them alone."

With what further absurdities would he continue?

But Rosaura, surmising an indirect allusion, toyed more intently with her glove, purchased for the ball.

Scenting a new fad, other couples followed Carlos and Rosaura toward the patio, and the night, its silence broken, was dethroned. Carlos recalled other scenes trilled too with laughter and dizzied with perfumes.

"Will you dance?"

But another youth claimed that polka from Rosaura. Carlos found himself alone and near his friend the auctioneer, so he begged to be presented to other girls, saying to himself that thus he would mask his reason for coming to the dance.

The daughter of Barrios was a lovely wench of excited voice, from whose pouter-pigeon bosom gushed a tangle of the most astonishing speeches.

What a relief, what a pleasure, when he found himself again with the simple Rosaura, love entire, on a bench in the patio now emptied by the greed that free refreshments awakened!

"Oh, señorita, how your friends weary me!"

"Don't call me señorita."

"Thank you, Rosaura, how all these little Sunday girls bore me. If I couldn't feel myself a friend of yours, I would dash out at a gallop. Stay with me awhile, as long or as short as you please, and I shall be grateful."

"You see how quickly we understand each other," laughed Rosaura. "But unfortunately I would have to hear tales if I stayed as long as I'd like."

"Would it be very long?"

Rosaura turned again to the button of her glove, and they were silent, overcome by discoveries mutually guessed.

One must, when one cannot speak from the soul, touch on simple things to hear undisturbed the song within.

"Are you always bored, Rosaura?"

"Not before. I had enough with my work and my walks to the station or to the plaza, where I met my friends and we would amuse ourselves with our jokes and our foolishness. Now I want more. The town seems so dreary, and I think of how you travel so much, have seen so many things. . . ."

"And yet you see I come here."

To say something, terrified by the consequences of her own words, Rosaura murmured:

"You must have a reason."

"Don't you know it?"

"Why should I know it?"

Rosaura was suffering now. Carlos' eyebrows were drawn tightly together, hardening his expression. Something vaguely in his smile prophesied who knows what dreadful phrase.

"Please, Carlos, be still."

The eyebrows were calmed, the forced smile disappeared:

"We do not need to say much."

It was true, and as the fraternally begun conversation had turned difficult, Carlos again told stories of his restless life to the little provincial so childishly attuned with her trustful eyes.

This intimate chat bridged a long time easily, and then Carlos with the air of a guardian said:

"Well, go and dance now with your friends, or they'll be saying that we are sweethearts."

"Oh, heavens!"

"Anyhow we are good friends."

"Yes, . . . but now, who knows when you'll come back."

"You'll see. . . . I have it arranged so that it won't be so seldom."

Rosaura went back to the hall, leaving Carlos without thinking to ask him to explain.

And thus ended the first meeting of the provincial girl with the elegant youth of the diner, now a cordial friend: which is not little for an ideal that passes, rousing great dreams that can never come true.

XI

From then on, after that night so brimful of lover's portent, the six-thirty-five express no longer carried an intangible ideal, the youth of the diner in his frame of light. Carlos had found a better solution and sacrificing the sluggishness of a bad sleeper, took the train at five in the morning to spend the day in Lobos.

The pretexts, though weak, would suffice: To see his friend the auctioneer Gonzalez, to go uselessly to his sales, or simply to shorten the six monotonous hours of the usual journey.

But what are pretexts when two lives are drawn to each other?

The sun was high when Carlos descended hampered by his London suitcase checkered with hotel labels.

Scarcely anybody stood on the platform, so crowded in the half-hour between the two express-trains, the six o'clock and the six-thirty-five. One of old Torres' cabs took him to the Hotel de Paris where he "made the morning" with Gonzalez, Iturri, and other personages of the hour. He lunched with the appetite of a traveller and slept a restful siesta till four, when he took tea facing the cobble-stoned street which fluttered already in prospect of the daily promenade.

And all this just for the little half hour in the afternoon, in the teeming confusion of the crowded platform: politicians out on campaign, young men in gray felts and light shoes, personages displaying their official personalities, sheiks with straw hats about to slide off their greasy foreheads and stickily pomaded skulls, coachmen waiting for fares, peons for mail or on errands. While like aromatic blooms in a virgin forest, the Lobos girls passed flirtatious and mocking.

From end to end of the platform, flanked by her friends, the one in pink and the one in sky-blue, Rosaura walked with the tread of a coquette, returning the glances of Carlos, her affectionate friend, with smiles that opened like flowers.

And Carlos filled his eyes with that dainty loved figure which retreated as if in anger, or gazed into those docile pupils open and penetrable as windows wide to a tryst.

But the cars of the express clanked unevenly in. The asthmatic gasps of the locomotive died down.

The blazing train drew up in front of the covered station and shut out the night.

People ascended, people descended, the minutes scrambled down the restless clock; on the dusty haunch of the diner, while speaking her last shy words of farewell, Rosaura traced the initials of an idyll. And suddenly, tearing a great wound through the soul of the little enamoured provincial, a brutal screech announced the departure. The cars flew apart like the vertebrae of a reptile in flight; the iron of joints and bumpers clanged from locomotive to caboose. Carlos bowed, quickly smaller at a sudden distance. The caboose passed rapidly, striking from the station windows a vibrant near echo.

And before Rosaura rose the deep indifference of the spangled night, painfully stifling the fugitive blare of the train which flies with the blind gaze of its monster eye toward the horizon whose attraction it does not comprehend.

Poor little Rosaura, abandoned thus to that passion too large for herself, in the deadly boredom of the village lost in a pampa that ignores the way of romance in its children.

XII

Nevertheless, except for the disconsolate parting that wounded as if it were forever, Rosaura's life overflowed happiness.

In her garden now heightened beyond springtime budding, the lilac dropped great fragrant sprays and the fresh porch flourished green, spattered with morning-glories, jasmines and honeysuckle.

Yielding to the soft breath of summer, Rosaura dreamed warmly through the stream of hours.

Seated in her rocking-chair, bathed in the odour of flowers, she works without ceasing, the needle quick in her skilled hands.

At her right, the sewing-basket on its bent legs spreads open like a split nut, its contents brimming. To her left, a little table unevenly set on the flags holds scattered colourful fashion books borrowed from that friend who had sent her the first for the dance at the Club Social.

Happy beyond explanation, the little Rosaura intent on her work lives with memories of meetings with her beloved Carlos so worthy of all the passions.

Rosaura had many patterns because she had quickly found herself deplorably provincial in her country clothing. And what feminine delight to devote all her days thus to sheathing herself in chaste caressing undergarments. Oh, the bows and the weaves white as holy wafers around her virgin body, all an offering to the mysterious rites of adoration! Gentle murmurs of future bliss steal into her dreams. She would be worthy of him, simple and naïve but still passionate and tender in the radiant fire of a love all immolation.

Elusively identical the days passed in the little garden of the Torres stables, idealized by the intense soul of Rosaura, always certain that her Carlos would come tomorrow, day after tomorrow, or next week, to tell her with his eyes that he loved her,put in her hand a nosegay of strange country blossoms, and in the afternoon to take a departure as painful as if forever, but to return because that was fate.

XIII

Night knowing something of sorcery transformed the insipid plaza of the town. Night, the blue, the stars; reducing the visible world to a few pools of light wept by the lamps, immobile, isolate and sad, condemned to stay forever, although they aspire desperately to be stars: a desire aroused by the springtime infinity of the depthless sky.

The people, limited to their bodies, tread the slavery of the plaza paths made to walk on, and cannot escape in perishable desires.

And so their souls fling themselves into mad impossible futures and migrate from love to love, as does light from star to star, drilling through the spaces that bar the victory of matter.

But it is the same plaza. The bushes and hedges clipped like thick manes shape greenish-black geometric figures curiously similar to human forms. The paths curve, lacking space in which to be true roads that know where they are going. A few trees, newly green, have become thus tender in response to the benison of spring, on time as always.

The groups of girls are like displays under glass of souls that will love, and the men long impossibly to clasp a bunch of them with feverish hands.

Carlos comes when he can to this holiday parade on the plaza stretched out under the stars, beneath the holy watch of the colonial bell-tower, where with infinite forgiveness God blesses his straying sentimental lambs.

In that luminous scene of fans, skirts and blouses, the most beautiful is Rosaura and also the farthest from herself; for she is carried off by great dreams of a heroine of romance, pining for the hero who has appeared from an unbelievable land, with a halo of the glamorous unknown.

Oh! . . . To be thus chosen among all!

Night, that knows something of sorcery, filters its temptation into the hearts of those people, who, God be thanked, have their morals; that is why this tale does not end here, with the most natural of love's solutions.

XIV

Thus Rosaura reached the height of her glory. Carlos' intervals of absence were brief, in which to savour every word, every gesture; and their meetings were fulfillments whose intuitive comprehensions made vows superfluous; rapture floated around them, as if exhaled by their emotions.

But that state of their souls perhaps called disaster upon them, as lightning is drawn by the crosses that pray on cupolas.

Carlos, pretending to take the matter lightly, told her he was leaving shortly for Europe:

". . . Oh! For a very short time; three or four months at the most . . .

through the summer . . . I can't avoid it; my father would be very much surprised and he might even be angry. . ."

Rosaura, mortally wounded, listened with anguish.

"Tell me, Carlos. Isn't Señor Ramallo sending you away?"

"What an idea, child! And why should he?"

"Don't know . . . maybe they've told him that you're wasting your time in some little village."

"No, Rosaura, what a notion!"

Carlos explained again. Who would know and if they did, who would think anything bad of his visits to Lobos? But it meant much to his father for him to make this trip to England, where he would learn a great deal studying the best-known model farms under a competent person.

"Three or four months . . . it seems so long, Carlos!"

He answered her, for the first time with a plain meaning:

"Rosaura, believe me, even if I were gone six, they would be too few to erase certain things."

"Sure?"

"Very sure."

Life sprang again in the little village girl. Carlos spoke with so much assurance that his absence seemed more bearable, and the especially tender pitch of that beloved voice was deceptive balm to her sensitive soul. Furthermore, Rosaura possessed the greatness of noble trust, and an extraordinary feminine delight in sacrificing herself to the will of her idol. In her eyes Carlos could do nothing wrong. And that poor night they parted; their hands more than ever revealed their love, despite all human obstacles.

XV

It was summer, and of Carlos nothing remained in Lobos except the increasing passion of his Rosaura and a brief note of farewell in her hands.

Life went on as usual in the Torres household, except for the lengthened burdensome days, the greater fatigue of the horses and the always perspiring peons, the sleepy inertia of the throbbing siesta hour, and the sadness of the poor girl, drooping now like a flower prostrated by the full blaze of the sun.

Nevertheless, her faith firm in her Carlos, Rosaura laboured to embellish herself. Her provincial wardrobe disappeared totally and no one, by her clothing, could have distinguished the former showy little country girl in yellow from a fashionable urban young lady.

This clothing that wove its knowing charms around her was born of the wish to seem elegant to him, and its contact filled, though imperfectly, the void left by the want of other caresses.

How daring dreams are; and how, by sheer familiarity with her more and more definite visions of what might happen, Rosaura grew to feel that she had been incredibly timid.

She did not know how, but she was certain that on Carlos' return their love would take a more natural course, and this prodded her anxious count of the long days.

But time passed with all its apparent slowness, while Rosaura worked to make herself beautiful, cared for her person as for an idol that belonged to someone else, and for whose pricelessness she was responsible. At this stage she never doubted the love of her Carlos.

XVI

An incurable sadness floated in the little garden of the Torres place, breathed off by the approaching winter that blighted the flowers so merrily brought by the spring.

The autumn petals were seared by the cold, the last stunted peaches dropped from their boughs, the arbour was stripped of its grapes and the little garden so piteously rifled bore a seal of arid harshness.

A mild patch of sunlight filtered on the porch, overhung by once matted vines, gilding the withered leaves. Rosaura, pale with her first woman's sorrow, had lost her youthful jasmine smoothness and her honeysuckle lushness; and abetted by sleepless outpourings of tears, the violet rings under her eyes triumphantly deepened to the transparent sheen of grapes.

Poor little Rosaura, tender aimless fancy; the fragrance of whose love was worthy of immortalizing a whole town's prosaic staleness.

Poor little Rosaura, victim of a moment of fateful evolution; incurable longing of simple things for the meshes of splendor; on her simple faith in the promise of a beyond, turned all her disaster.

Her fate was to suffer and no other, because thus says a homely proverb: "Who looks too far upward may break his neck."

Her grief was as fatal as the race of melting snow downward.

Immensely sad is the little garden of the Torres place. From the soul of its small mistress disconsolate dreams ebb, while autumn falls like a shroud upon that corner of the world, lost in the middle of the changeless pampa that knows nothing of romantic loves.

XVII

A nervous anxiety aroused Rosaura from the dejection in which she lived. Carlos might come any moment.

The daughter of Crescencio Torres returned to her old habits and except for Carmen or whoever in the village possessed the gift of divination, Lobos ignored the change in the spirit of its lovely child.

About five-thirty Rosaura went out in an airy blouse, cut triangularly at the neck, dark blue skirt, and calf pumps, though bareheaded so as not to be too conspicuous among her friends. Half a block down she stopped to speak to old Petrona unweariedly standing on the threshold of her white house, her arms pillowed on the soft mound of her stomach shaken with deep laughter.

"Hello, Doña Petrona."

"God bless you, child. . . . My, the poor boys, you're a regular poster! . . . Holy Mary! why you're right up to the minute! . . ."

But Rosaura would not hear.

On the main street, fashionable Lobos promenaded, fluttering with chatter the paths shaded by hoary elms.

Afternoon would be winding itself out in the corners when they gradually invaded the crowded platform.

What an unbearable emotion, this waiting; what torment and overcoming reminder arose in Rosaura at the gleam of the headlight of the locomotive on the rails!

Yes, he will come this afternoon. She will spy him in his window, meeting her with brilliant joy in his eyes. Her soul will divine his presence and all her old delight will burst forth like a radiant dawn.

"Oh, to fall in his arms!"

But in the glaring frame of that window which once gave life, no face appeared.

XVIII

The leaves fell, the first chill crept out, and Rosaura suffered like the red autumn blooms that freeze in the flight of the sun.

Was all that romance an illusion?

The poor girl almost believed so, with the daily disappointment of the vacant space in the window of the diner.

But it was not an illusion, because one afternoon when her heart was breaking, Carmen took her by the arm and trembling at the enormity of her announcement said:

"Come here, child, come, I've seen him in another car."

Oh, Rosaura! How to keep a scream from escaping? Her legs refused to advance, though her friend dragged her by the arm. It was true, he was there.

Carlos! . . . Oh, to fall on his beloved breast and to tell him that she never doubted his return, and then so many, many things more! She recognized him through a dim window. Nearly swooning, and almost stretching out her arms, there before them all, her upper-lip rose smiling faintly; and he bowed merely, as if there had never existed between them anything beyond a passing word.

XIX

Rosaura fell into a coma of intense pain. Everybody in the house knew that something unusual had happened to her and the mother learned of the drama on the delirious night that followed the incident unperceived by others.

The love of Rosaura, rooted in her like an organism inseparable from her own, was killing her with its death.

Carmen, the friend who had once brought the first-fruits of her love, brought her the gravestone as well:

"Listen, child . . . it isn't worth while, suffering for that wicked man."

"Please, Carmen, let's not speak of it any more."

"It's that I wanted to tell you . . . if you want to notice next time he passes, you'll see that he is with another woman, all dressed up in those things that you like."

"For God's sake be still, Carmen."

So she swallowed the details which her friend brought to be close to her; livid, her lips quivering childishly but with her eyes dry, she burst into sobs long and painful as if her very bowels were being dragged from her slowly.

XX

Rosaura has come to the station, in her frock of flowered muslin, reminder of that unforgettable night in the Club Social. She has tucked the brief note, the only one from Carlos, in her bosom, the note of farewell, and her convulsive hands crumble to dust the dry petals of the flowers she had kept because he had given them to her.

Rosaura must be a little mad to come dressed like that to the platform. But what does she care what they say?

Carmen is with her, caring for her like a nurse, troubled by those strange fancies, and dressed as always in pink, not having suffered, like her friend, the intense influence of outside things.

Suddenly, Rosaura's hand sinks into the soft flesh of her friend's arm.

"Come on, Carmen, come on for God's sake, I can't stand any more."

Thus together they walked to the end of the platform. Carlos (oh, horrible unconsciousness!) rides in a compartment with the unknown woman and Rosaura does not want to see him.

"Oh, I can't bear any more, I can't bear any more . . . and leave me now, I beg you for the sake of what you love most . . . leave me and go back with the rest, I'm going home."

"But, child, you don't want me to leave you, and you in that state and crying like a lost soul?"

"Yes, for the sake of what you love most, leave me."

What powerful influence made Carmen obey?

The shrill locomotive announces departure. Carmen goes back to the station.

There is a shock of steel, the locomotive snorts its great poisonous crests out upon Lobos, gasping a strenuous start. The train will continue its journey from unknown to unknown, from horizon to horizon.

Then the little Rosaura, overcome by a terrible madness, screams, grinding incomprehensible phrases between her teeth that clamp convulsively with pain. And like a springtime butterfly she flashes out, running between the parallel infinities of the rails, her arms forward in useless offering, calling the name of Carlos, for whom it is passionate joy to die, on the road that takes him away, far from her forever.

"Carlos! . . . Carlos! . . ."

The steely din nears her. The swift victory of the train knows nothing of the cries of a passion that knew how to die.

"Carlos! . . ."

And like a snowy feather, the dainty figure in flowered muslin yields to the march of the gigantic locomotive, for whose monster eye the horizon holds no ideal. □

7

The Revolutionary Option

Despite dramatic changes during the twentieth century, Latin America failed to develop economically. Many advocated institutional reforms to induce development gradually. Favorable periods in the histories of Chile, Costa Rica, Uruguay, and Venezuela seemed to fulfill some expectations from reform. But reform both tantalized and eluded most of Latin America. Frustrations rose. Mixed with hope, these frustrations prompted some Latin Americans to advocate revolution, the sudden, often violent, substitution of new institutions for old and discredited ones.

During the twentieth century, Latin America experienced five significant revolutions: Mexico, 1910–1940; Guatemala, 1944–1954; Bolivia, 1952–1964; Cuba, 1959 and continuing; and Nicaragua, 1979–1990. Highly nationalistic in tone and objective, these revolutions hoped to reduce dependency and induce development. They tried to involve the majority of the citizenry in the modification or eradication of institutions that thwarted development. For the benefit of the majority, they succeeded in opening doors of access to land, education, and health care. The Cuban Revolution has attempted and achieved the most profound changes.

For a variety of reasons, not least of which was overt and covert U.S. intervention, those revolutions struggled against formidable odds to meet expectations. With the possible exception of Cuba, the revolutions, like the reforms, seem incapable of bringing about meaningful long-term change. At the end of the twentieth century, most Latin Americans still seek a means by which to develop economically in order to improve the quality of life of the majority of the people.

A Theory of the Natural History of Revolution

Drawing on his historical investigations, the sociologist Lyford P. Edwards attempted to chart the commonalities and course of revolutions. He suggested that all of them moved through distinct stages from "the overture" to "the return to normality." His theory provides an organizational means to study the complex revolutionary process. It facilitates comparing and contrasting revolutions.

THERE IS A POPULAR OPINION that revolutions are sudden, unpredictable, and exceedingly rapid in their development. This opinion is mistaken. It is even ludicrously mistaken. A revolution, in certain respects, resembles an elephant. The elephant is the slowest breeding of all living creatures, and a revolution is the slowest forming of all social movements. There is not, so far as the writer is aware, a real revolution in all human history which developed in less than three generations. . . . In the great majority of cases it is in the fourth generation, or later, that the overthrow of the old institutions occurs. . . .

The earliest symptom of a coming revolution is an increase of general restlessness. A certain amount of restlessness is normal and socially healthy. There is no method of quantitative measurement by which it is possible to determine just how much restlessness indicates a pathological social condition. With the progress of time, any established social order tends to become stiff and rigid. Its institutions ossify. The elementary human wishes for new experience, security, recognition, and response are thwarted. Opportunities for their realization become less and general restlessness results. But for a long time the situation is not understood. The feeling of restlessness is at first very vague and indefinite. . . . The next preliminary symptom to be noted is a marked increase of wealth, intelligence, and power in the repressed portion of society. . . . A smaller degree of repression is felt as more intolerable when one is "coming up in the world." People "on the make" are especially sensitive to any discrimination against themselves. So it often comes about that revolutions overthrow repressive institutions at the very time that those institutions are milder and less repressive than ever before. Similarly, people become most revolutionary and most resistant of oppression when the actual degree of oppression is least. That is to be expected, because under those conditions the people are best able to revolt and there is the most likelihood that a revolution will be successful. The emotion which furnishes the driving power to revolution is hope, not despair. . . .

Revolutions do not occur when the repressed classes are forced down to the depths of misery. Revolutions occur after the repressed classes, for a considerable time, have been in the enjoyment of increasing prosperity. A marked increase of

Source: Lyford P. Edwards, *The Natural History of Revolution* (Chicago: University of Chicago Press, 1927), pp. 16–17, 23, 33, 34–35, 36, 38, 40–41, 69–70, 90–91, 98, 99, 105, 107, 118, 120, 121, 127, 150, 151, 156, 174–175, 184, 192–193, 194, and 212. © 1927 by University of Chicago Press. With permission of the publisher.

power, intelligence, and wealth in the repressed portion of society is a phenomenon invariably found in the period preceding any great revolution. It is one of the most important symptoms of future upheaval. . . .

The first master-symptom of revolution is the "transfer of the allegiance of the intellectuals." The authors, the editors, the lecturers, the artists, the teachers, the priests, the preachers, and all those whose function it is to form and guide public opinion become infected with the discontent of the repressed classes of society. . . .

The small minority of "repressors" can maintain the system of repression only so long as they have the willing support of the publicists. The repressed class, in a society that is ripe for revolution, always outnumbers both of the other classes combined. They can dominate either or both of the other classes whenever they have become sufficiently class conscious and sufficiently organized and disciplined to act collectively. The position of both repressors and publicists is therefore precarious unless the publicists maintain sufficient confidence in the existing regime to give it their loyal support. . . .

When the institution becomes repressive, the inarticulate masses feel the repression first but do not understand the causes of it. An interval, generally a long one, occurs between the time any institution is first felt to be repressive and the time the publicists lose their faith in it. During such intervals (which cover most of the years of recorded history) the publicists support repressive institutions. But sooner or later the publicists become infected with the prevailing unrest and begin to sympathize with the repressed class. Frequently, after a time the publicists feel the repression themselves. . . . When the publicists are sure that an institution, which they had supposed to be good, is really repressive, they attack that institution with a zeal proportionate to their anger at having been deluded as to its nature. In other words, they desert the cause of the existing institution and support the cause of the institution that is, as they hope and believe, to replace it. . . .

No great historical revolution has ever succeeded without the assistance of the economic incentive. Human cupidity must be appealed to in order to arouse the energy, the aggressiveness, and the sustained interest of masses of people— without which no revolution can succeed. This is true of the most idealistic, religious revolutions no less than of the most frankly economic ones. Revolution involves the disintegration of society. The evils of this disintegration are so many and so obvious that men are willing to incur them only under stress of the strongest incentives. Whatever may be thought about the power of different incentives, it must be admitted that the economic incentive is not the weakest one. . . .

A master-symptom is one which, in a marked degree, conditions others and without which a great revolution is impossible. According to this analysis, two master-symptoms appear in pre-revolutionary society. One is the "transfer of the allegiance of the intellectuals"; the other is the "social myth." . . . Without a super-rational "theological" dynamic no great revolution is possible—at any rate, none has ever occurred. It would even seem that a revolution is only great and important in the degree to which this element is present. . . . The French philosopher Sorel named this spiritual dynamic of revolution the "social myth."

The social myth arises from a fusion of the ideas propounded by the revolutionary intellectuals with the elemental wishes of the repressed class of the society concerned. Out of the innumerable criticisms of "things as they are" and the equally innumerable hopes of "things as they might be" there gradually emerges a new ideal. This ideal is all embracing. It includes in a new totality the strongest as well as the weakest inclinations and desires of the discontented, repressed class. It so frames an indeterminate future as to give an aspect of complete reality to the hopes of the present. . . .

The outbreak of revolution is commonly signaled by some act, insignificant in itself, which precipitates a separation of the repressors and their followers from the repressed and their follwers. . . . The mental and emotional preparation for revolution is only complete when any casual crowd of members of the repressed class can be depended upon to act in a revolutionary capacity consistently and over a long period of time. . . . There is one important reason why some quite ordinary act of mob violence generally proves to be the start of revolution. It is helpless incompetence revealed by the governing class in the emergency. . . .

The outbreak of revolution is due as much to this revelation of the inability of the ruling class to handle even an ordinary riot as to anything else. A ruling class which cannot perform even the common duties of police at once reveals itself as impotent. It invites repeated attack and receives it until it is destroyed. This invokes the disintegration of society. But revolution is much more than the disintegration of society. It is at the same time the reintegration of society along different and more efficient lines. A revolution is not a period of anarchy; that is the last thing it is. It is a period of despotism, with instant destruction to everyone opposing that despotism. Caesar and Cromwell, Robespierre and Lenin, were not anarchists; they were autocrats. There is not less government during a revolution, there is more government. . . .

A revolution passes through its first phase with the moderate reformers in control of affairs. In this phase much good and necessary reform work is accomplished, but there is nothing which can be described as really revolutionary. . . . The real revolution, when it comes, is not a fight between the conservatives and the combined moderate reformers and radicals. It is a fight between the moderate reformers and the radicals, after the emigration of the conservatives, who then function only by means of foreign armies and futile internal plots. The radicals win because the counterbalancing power of the conservatives has been destroyed, so far as the internal situation in the revolutionary society is concerned. . . . By deserting their posts these refugee conservatives really throw the victory to the radicals. They realize this themselves but they care little about it. They trust to foreign military power to crush both the moderate reformers and the radicals and to reinstate the old regime. . . .

Revolutions are all very much alike in their preliminary symptoms and in their early stages of development. Up to the actual outbreak of violence and even for a short time after the seizure of power by the moderate reformers the progress of events is strikingly similar in all of them. But very soon after the moderate reformers obtain control of affairs, differences in the development of revolutions begin to appear. These developments no longer conform to one type. From the era of optimism onward any individual revolution shows more and more evidences of differentiating itself into one of three classes. These three classes are: the abortive revolution, the moderate revolution, and the radical revolution. The underlying reason for these three forms of revolution is plain enough. There are three main factions in a revolutionary society which has arrived at the era of optimism. These three factions are the conservatives, the moderate reformers, and the radicals. At the outbreak of revolution the moderate reformers obtain control of the society. But it is evident that three different developments are thenceforth possible. The moderate reformers may retain power, or they may be overthrown by the conservatives, or by the radicals. . . .

The last and most important thing to be here noted about the period of the moderate reformers' government is the uncontrollable swing of the masses of the people toward radicalism. Radical leaders gain enormous influence during this interval. They become the most prominent and most trusted persons in the society. Their radical ideas excite popular enthuasism; their slogans are repeated everywhere. Though the radicals are a minority, they have the genuine backing of public opinion. . . . The motive which leads the public to allow the radicals to seize power is the hope that real leadership—the one desperate need of the society—may come from them. The swing of the people toward radicalism and the rise of the radical leaders, it is all one process. . . .

When the radicals obtain supreme power they have three main difficulties to face. These difficulties are foreign invasion, domestic insurrection, and their own inexperience in government. They have, however, certain great advantages. In the first place, they are a select group. They are the ones who have proved fittest in a very ferocious struggle for existence. They are the victors in the civil war, the strongest men that the revolutionary society possesses. They are likely to be bolder, abler, and more determined than any rulers that the country has had within living memory. They are willing to act. As excitement increases, the demand for action is intensified. The reformer fails because he is limited in the action that he takes or that he is able to imagine. The indecision and caution of the moderate reformers have brought the revolution to the point of failure. The decisiveness and enthusiasm of the new rulers snatch victory from the very jaws of defeat.

The essential characteristics of the radical rulers are physical and mental courage, boldness, determination, an absolute faith in the righteousness of their cause and in their own ability to govern, despite lack of experience. . . . Some avenue of release for this accumulated nervousness must be provided. The avenue of release is the reign of terror.

A reign of terror is psychologically akin—in some of its aspects at least—to an old-fashioned Methodist revival meeting. Its primary function is to serve as a safety-valve for the discharge of wrought-up emotions. It is the phase of revolution which most strikes the popular imagination because of its dramatic qualities. This is natural, for the terror—so far as it is planned and executed with definite purpose—is deliberate melodrama acted in real life. Like the melodrama of the theater, however, the performance that goes on behind the scenes is quite different from the show as the audience sees it. The terror presents itself as a wild orgy of unrestrained passion. Actually, it may be an elaborately planned and carefully worked-out stage show for purposes of emotional catharsis, which, according to the best authorities on such matters, is the purpose of all stage tragedy. The terror is not so bloody as is often assumed. . . .

The terror furnished a necessary avenue of release to the overwrought nerves of people in extreme danger. It is at the same time the revenge of a social class for what it regards as a social injustice long endured submissively and in silence. It is the eruption of the volcano. . . .

It is a difficult thing to say just when a revolution ends. After the terror and the end of revolutionary warfare the radical party undergoes a transformation. The nature of this change can best be understood by considering the radicals in their aspect as a sect. A sect is a "religious" organization with four chief characteristics: It is at war with the existing moral order. It seeks to establish a new social system different from the one in the midst of which it lives. It makes great use of isolation devices and shibboleths which isolate it from the rest of the world. It is highly evangelistic and displays marked missionary zeal. During the time of revolutionary war the right of the radical faction to exist at all is denied by the rest of the world. . . . After the new sect has made good its right to existence, by winning its revolutionary wars, a process of accommodation sets in. The new sect has to be tolerated. . . . The radicals become tolerant when they have won toleration for themselves. . . . When the process of accommodation has advanced to the point where all the chief factions concerned have compromised enough to make ordinary intercourse between them normally peaceable, the revolution may be said to be at an end. . . .

We may take it for certain that revolutions, even violent revolutions, will occur periodically for a long time to come. We hear some talk about substituting peaceable evolution for violent revolution, but such talk is only what the theologians call "pious opinion"—laudable, but imaginative. No technology is being developed for the purpose of translating this talk into action.□

The Visual Presentation
of Popular Protest

In his linocut "The Torches," 1948, Leopoldo Méndez, one of Mexico's leading graphic artists, preserved on paper the intensity of feeling and determination of villagers in local revolt. They set out to avenge the murder of the village school teacher by the *cacique*, the local political boss. Questions of modest change and desired improvement triggered the conflict. The school teacher represented the hope for such improvement; the cacique enforced repressive institutions of the past, ensuring their continuity. The torches of the villagers announce hope, enlightenment, and justice in the dark night of oppression. All the body language, most certainly the facial expression of the peasant in the foreground, bespeaks anger and determination. This powerful print by Méndez strongly suggests that ordinary people can control their own destiny. In Latin America, that message is revolutionary.

"The Torches," linocut, Mexico, 1948, (Leopoldo Méndez, 1903–1969).

Such popular art doubtless evoked a variety of responses. At one extreme, the humble might extract empowerment from it; at the other extreme, the elites might disdain or even fear it as a threat, a form of rabble-rousing.

Land and Revolution

Land, along with its ownership and use, serves as the basis for Latin American society and economy. In no region of the world is land concentrated in fewer hands. The contrast between the wealthy few with access to land and the large number of impoverished rural inhabitants with no land stands as a major characteristic of Latin America. It generates tensions that often provoke violence. Furthermore, failure of owners to cultivate their land, misuse of the land, and underuse of it contribute significantly to underdevelopment.

All revolutions turned their attention to the rural inequities. Basically they tried to put unused or underused land into the hands of people desiring to cultivate it as the first step toward economic development.

The Plan of Ayala

On November 28, 1911, the popular agrarian leader Emiliano Zapata proclaimed his Plan of Ayala. He advocated transferring land to the landless. His slogan "Land and Liberty" resounded throughout Mexico. Symbolically it remains Latin America's most fundamental and popular revolutionary message.

THE REVOLUTIONARY JUNTA of the State of Morelos will not sanction any transactions or compromises until it secures the downfall of the dictatorial elements of Porfirio Díaz and Francisco I. Madero, because the nation is tired of traitors and false liberators who make promises and forget them when they rise to power . . . as tyrants.

As an additional part of the plan that we proclaim, be it known: that the lands, woods, and water usurped by the hacendados, científicos, or caciques, under the cover of tyranny and venal justice, henceforth belong to the towns or citizens in possession of the deeds concerning these properties of which they were despoiled through the devious action of our oppressors. The possession of said properties shall be kept at all costs, arms in hand. The usurpers who think they have a right to said goods may state their claims before special tribunals to be established upon the triumph of the Revolution.

. . . [T]he immense majority of Mexico's villages and citizens own only the ground on which they stand. They suffer the horrors of poverty without being able to better their social status in any respect, or without being able to dedicate themselves to industry or agriculture due to the fact that the lands, woods, and water are monopolized by a few. For this reason, through prior compensation, one-third of such monopolies will be expropriated from their powerful owners

Source: James W. Wilkie and Albert L. Michaels (eds.), *Revolution in Mexico: Years of Upheaval, 1910–1940* (New York: Knopf, 1969), pp. 45–46.

in order that the villages and citizens of Mexico may obtain *ejidos,* colonies, town sites, and rural properties for sowing or tilling, and in order that the welfare and prosperity of the Mexican people will be promoted in every way.

The property of those hacendados, científicos, or caciques who directly or indirectly oppose the present plan shall be nationalized, and two-thirds of their remaining property shall be designated for war indemnities—pensions for the widows and orphans of the victims that succumb in the struggle for this plan. □

Agrarian Reform Begins

In the mid-1930s, Ramón Beteta (1901–1965), a distinguished Mexican econo-mist and lawyer, outlined the early history of his nation's agrarian reform. The government's effort to reduce the size and number of the large estates in favor of the Indian *ejidos* was a major revolutionary action. In addition to being an act of social justice, the reform promised, in Beteta's judgment, a better diet for the farmers and greater agrarian production for the nation. He offered some impressive statistics to buttress his conclusions. At any rate, Latin America's first agrarian reform was underway.

I SHALL not go into the details of the background of the Mexican Agrarian Reform. There are two points, however, which I shall mention. First, one must try to understand what the deprivation of their lands meant to the Mexican natives. It was not only an economic blow. Psychologically it was more than that. It was condemning them to exile, depriving them of their fatherland, tearing them away from the origin of all power and all life: land, a very real God!

To say that Mexico has been conquered more than one time, is not a meta-phor. The "moving of the land marks"; the "denuncios" of the surveying and colonizing companies; the "punishing" by the Federal troops of supposed rebel-lious tribes and all the various other means by which the natives were forced to abandon their fields and work as "peons" for the *hacendados* have been so many deeds of conquest which, from the standpoint of the Indians, cannot be distin-guished from the arrival of Cortez to the fertile Valley of Tenochtitlán.

The second point I want to insist upon is the fact that the "hacienda" system of land holding is not only unjust, as it creates peonage which is slavery without legal protection; harmful, as it breeds political abuse; damaging to the country, because it forms an absentee ownership; but besides all this it is a very primitive, backward, inefficient method of production. Agronomically the "hacienda" which cultivates solely the best part of the land, which uses no system of crop rotation, which employs no artificial fertilizers, which has no equipment besides a few oxen and some wooden plows, represents the middle-age method of agricul-tural production. It is a system of manpower and land instead of machinery and natural resources.

Few people question today in Mexico the justification or the necessity of

Source: Ramón Beteta, *Economic and Social Program of Mexico* (Mexico City, 1935), selections from pp. 22–46.

the Agrarian Reform. Even the *hacendados* have already accepted the desirability of changing the old system of land holding. The discussion has reduced itself to the method rather than to the principles.

The law of January 6, 1915, which was later incorporated into the Constitution of 1917, provided three systems of land distribution: restitution, donation and ampliation. The first takes place in those cases in which the Indian villages could prove that they had been illegally deprived of their lands. The second is outright donation and follows solely the principle of necessity: all communities needing land have the right to receive it. Finally, ampliation is a new donation to those communities not having sufficient land in spite of previous grants. Following all of these three methods land has been distributed in Mexico with a speed which varies with the zeal of the President of the Republic in the agrarian question because his decision is indispensable in every case.

During the first five years the Agrarian Reform took practically only the form of restitution, and in fact, very few hectares of land were distributed. One may really say that the Agrarian Reform begins in Mexico in 1920. During the Presidency of General Obregón it got well under way and within the following term, that of General Calles, a steady increase in distribution of the land is to be noted. During the ad interim Government of Portes Gil, more land was distributed than during the four years of his predecessor, although his term lasted only fourteen months. Then comes the Government of Ortiz Rubio, during which the Agrarian movement slowed down, and it was even in danger of collapse. The provisional Presidency of General Rodríguez, in spite of the fact that many people thought he was rather conservative, was also fruitful in dividing the land.

President Cárdenas, well known for his enthusiasm in regard to the Agrarian Reform has given new stimulus to the movement. In one single day, May 1, 1935, to celebrate Labor Day and the Chicago incident [the Haymarket riot, 1886], 552,936 hectares of land were distributed to 353 villages and to the benefit of 36,856 heads of families.

The latest and the most reliable statistical figures we have representing the movement are due to the Agrarian Census taken last April 10. The preliminary results of such census show that there were in Mexico 7041 "ejidos," (we call an *ejido* a village which has received land from the Government by any one of the three methods already mentioned) benefiting 895,284 heads of families who have received 11,741,191 hectares of land, of which 3,735,931.14 hectares are crop land. The rest is considered as pasture or as wood land, not suited for cultivation.

This gives a rough idea of the extent of the Reform, so far as the actual distribution of the land is concerned. One must remember, however, to really understand its significance, that Mexico has only 14,517,699 hectares of cultivable land and that according to the Census of 1930, 3,626,278 persons were gainfully employed in agriculture.

It is important in this connection to insist once more upon the necessity of being aware of the fallacy of Mexico's unlimited wealth. In fact, it is the scarcity of arable land that has made the Agrarian Reform so acute. As you know, Mexico is a mountainous country with insufficient rainfall and therefore a large part of its territory is unfit for agricultural purposes.

That considerable progress has been made, however, is shown not only by the figures given above, but also by the tremendous change in the attitude of the people. One cannot judge the Agrarian Reform in terms of economic factors alone. The Mexican people are the children of their land where they have lived for centuries; where they have multiplied and grown; where they resisted the incursion of the Spaniards, the dryness of the desert, the awe of the mountain and the sterility of the jungle. Attachment to the soil is the central factor in the psychology of our people. Having back their lands our native population are again in harmony with nature.

There is one point which always comes to one's mind in connection with the present-day situation of the Agrarian Reform in Mexico: the productivity of the "ejido." Visitors of Mexico have often asked me whether or not it is true that the agricultural production has steadily decreased as the distribution of the land has progressed. This unfortunately is a question that cannot be answered categorically, as there is a complete lack of information of the pre-revolutionary period. An accurate comparison between the pre-revolutionary and the post-revolutionary periods is especially difficult to make, because there has been a change of crops and consequently, while there is a decrease in certain crops, there has been a considerable increase in some others. Besides, as many of the rural communities of Mexico are practically self-sufficient and produce for consumption purposes only, as they live practically in a prepecuniary economy, it is very difficult to calculate the production even through indirect means. We may, however, attempt to get an approximate idea by the comparison of importation statistics. If we take the period 1901–1907 as typical of the Díaz Regime, and we compare it with that of 1929–1934, as an example of the post-revolutionary period, we find that corn, flour, meats, dairy products and cotton, among others, were imported in larger amounts during the period of 1901–1907 than in the second.

The more significant of these products is corn, because that is the most important crop of the Republic, both in the extension of land under cultivation and in the volume of the crop. And yet, there was not one year, even in the most prosperous times of our octavian peace, in which Mexico did not have to import some corn. The same thing could be said about beans, our second most important crop. On the other hand, during 1934 and the first months of this year, Mexico has been exporting both corn and beans in comparatively large amounts.

In 1934, Mexico exported 71,079 tons of corn, and during the first four months of 1935, 65,117 tons. For beans the figures are: In 1934, 12,205 tons, and for the four months of 1935, 4,428 tons.

Those figures seem to indicate that there has not been a decrease in agricultural production. But there is still another way to prove it. The Agricultural Census of 1930 tells us that while the "haciendas" cultivated 48.27% of their crop-lands, the "ejidos" had under cultivation 57.35% of their crop-land. This is especially remarkable in view of the inferiority of the agricultural equipment on the part of the latter.

The question of agricultural production resolves itself in the last analysis into one of the standard of living of the Mexican people. But here again, we have no way to make any accurate comparison. There have been a few studies made in this respect. One of them made by the Department of Statistics last year, a special study of 300 families of the working class in the Federal District, shows the incredibly low standard of living of our industrial workmen, and we have good reason to believe that the situation in the rural districts is still worse. But low as it is, our standard of living today is higher than it was before the Revolution as even a superficial observer cannot fail to see.

But as the leaders of the movement soon realized, the Agrarian Movement to be successful cannot be limited to land distribution. Credit and education are just as essential. . . .

We have chosen the "ejido" as the center of our rural economy. Within its limits "land belongs to him who works it with his hands" as our Indian poet expressed it. New methods of production, machinery and new techniques will be introduced without having to make rugged individualists out of the ejidatarios and at the same time without killing the human desire of progress in those communities. Then, and only then, could national economy be planned, not by directing the conflicting interests of the various individuals, but by conceiving the country as a unit whose needs are to be satisfied by the harmonious working of these villages, agricultural or industrial, in an effort to make the whole country secure and prosperous. □

Is the Mexican Revolution Dead?

Thus far, only the Mexican Revolution offers the opportunity to apply fully to Latin America Lyford Edward's theory of the natural history of revolution. That revolution seems to have moved through all the stages he outlined. The disturbing reality at the end of the twentieth century is that despite the many and monumental achievements of the Mexican Revolution during the first half of the century, the quality of life for the majority seems little different at the end of the twentieth century than before the revolution. Is that revolution dead? Mexicans have debated that question for half a century. Below appear the assessments, tentative answers to the question about the demise of the revolution, of two distinguished Mexican intellectuals.

Mexico's Historical Crisis

Assessing the revolution in the mid-1940s, the Mexican sociologist José E. Iturriaga concluded that it had carried out a significant program. He proudly enumerated the achievements. Nonetheless, he fretted that the Mexican Revolution had lost some of its attraction and perhaps even its direction. He sensed that his nation had shifted from the vibrancy of change to, what Lyford Edwards might have characterized as, normalcy. In short, an historic moment had been reached: the revolution was over. Positive about the past, Professor Iturriaga seemed perplexed about the future.

O NE OF THE MOST pressing problems for Mexicans today is our present historical crisis, one resulting from the great humanistic movement that got underway in this country in 1910. The Mexican Revolution has now reached a certain maturity which allows us to view it over a considerable time perspective. Lately, people of every class, ideology, and age have concerned themselves with the fate of the Revolution and have contributed their insights to discussions of its development and future. . . .

As the people of Mexico contemplate the present crisis in an historical cycle that we call the Mexican Revolution, one major question is asked and it demands a response: Does the phenomenon of the Mexican Revolution still contain within itself sufficient creative power and the ability to stir the enthusiasm of the people to sustain itself, to speak to contemporary needs, and to endure? In the answer to this fundamental question lies the future of Mexico. . . .

One of the answers we have heard, even from men of respected intelligence, is that the Revolution had neither program nor plan, and it also lacks leaders of sufficient wisdom and insight to guide it constructively. If by program one means a single plan which included, anticipated, and summarized each and every unspoken hope of a varied people engaged in a bloody conflict, then it is very clear that the Revolution lacked a program. Obviously the disadvantage of a previously conceived plan would be that the contradictions of popular desires, the variety of demands and hopes, and the fluidity of a prolonged revolutionary struggle would impede the carrying out of any inflexible plan. Historical reality tends to bypass the ideologues with their fixed plans. Of course we do not argue that revolutions have no room for the ideologues. Quite the contrary, we realize the important role these ideologues play in the revolutionary process. They sense social unrest; they articulate the need for change; they arouse the public spirit and mind; they clarify both the causes of discontent as well as the popular goals.

While it is true that the Mexican Revolution lacked a single plan, it is equally true that from the rhetoric, hopes, and multiple plans we can distill a set of common goals that motivate the majority who participated in the Revolution. Such goals included the destruction of the feudal, agrarian society; an end to the re-election of municipal, state, and federal officials by means of dishonest elections; a termination of the exploitation of the workers by imposing the eight-hour workday; and the construction of schools to achieve the goals of universal education and the eradication of illiteracy. . . .

So, in that way, we can say that the Mexican Revolution pursued certain goals that taken together emerged as a program. Now, it is fair to ask whether the Revolution met those goals.

As to the important agrarian goals, we can point out that nearly two million heads of family received more than sixty million acres of land during the period of three decades from the promulgation of the Law of January 6, 1915, until 1945. If the farmers had been provided with cheap and sufficient credit, technical assistance, and modern agricultural tools, the Agrarian Reform would have been

Source: José E. Iturriaga, "México y Su Crisis Histórico," *Cuadernos Americanos,* 33:3 (May–June, 1947), pp. 22, 26, 29–30, 31–33, 35, 37.

perfect. Nonetheless, the impressive delivery of land and the rupture of the feudal system upon which the long reign of Porfírio Díaz was based certainly are sufficient reasons to justify fully the social movement that began in 1910.

Article 123 of the Constitution of 1917 provided the legal base for the Federal Labor Law, which protects the workers and guarantees their rights. Many countries judge it a model law. Here, then, is another major achievement of the Revolution.

In the field of education, progress can be measured by the improvement in the literacy rate. It stood at 28 percent during the last year of the Porfírio Díaz regime; by 1945, it reached 55 percent. Despite the impressive number of schools constructed by the Revolution, their number is still insufficient to meet the demands of the growing school-age population. . . .

In religious matters a new tolerance has recently appeared, similar to the kind that exists in countries where the clergy did not have the custom of intervening in politics. In my opinion, it is a healthy trend, indicating a willingness to forget the bitter experiences of the past. . . .

In contrast to the practices of the Porfirian dictatorship, our Revolution respects freedom of speech and press. . . .

In foreign relations, the Revolution follows its own independent policy that defines for our country an important role in international affairs. . . .

The government continues to invest significant sums in the infrastructure of transportation and communications. The new roads contribute significantly to the economic vigor of the nation, although construction and maintenance of railroads have been insufficient.

On balance, then, the Revolution has accomplished a great deal, although some critics like to argue that without the Revolution, the nation would have advanced even more. To support this contention, these detractors argue that although dictators debase people they are able to justify themselves in history by their attention to public works and by the surpluses they accumulate in the public treasury. This hoary argument has been repeatedly refuted. With regard to the economic successes of Díaz, Francisco Bulnes wryly observed, "The best economic planner Don Porfírio had was the goddess of good fortune who, between 1876 and 1910, smiled on him. His minister of finance, José Ives Limantour, instead of promoting the economy, actually obstructed it."

Some believe that the successes of the Revolution were due more to the natural evolution of society than through the efforts of revolutionary leaders and good planning. I would argue against this point of view. It was the abolition of the feudal estates that promoted modernization. The landowners were incapable of achieving such modernization on their own. The Revolution was essential in order to implement a meaningful agrarian reform.

No one can ignore the constructive force of the revolutionary governments despite some embezzlement and illicit enrichment of not a few government officials. . . .

This summary balance leads us to examine the question of whether the Mexican Revolution is sufficiently creative to be able to guide and serve us in the future. In recent years we can conclude the revolutionary rhetoric has lost some of its appeal. Its capacity to resolve problems seems to have diminished. When we examine the public reactions to key words repeatedly employed by traditional politicians, we can see that they have lost their emotional content and no longer stir the masses as they once did. When I employ the term masses, I refer not to that tiny group of people who for the past decade in the principal cities listened almost mechanically to the political leaders, applauded them, cheered them, and all the time conveyed to them a false sense of the true national consciousness. I refer instead to the vast majority of people throughout this nation.

More and more I sense that this revolutionary rhetoric, besides losing its emotional appeal through overuse and abuse, no longer helps us to see, understand, and take action on pressing current problems. Rhetoric, sadly enough, serves as one way of saying nothing, of avoiding realities. And in this way, the Revolution is losing contact with people, not just the young in our cities but also among the humble folk of the countryside.

I confess that the first time I understood this reality I was shocked. The most intelligent and thoughtful followers of the Revolution, whether they be young, middle-aged, or old, still associate the traditional revolutionary rhetoric with the noble struggles of our movement of 1910. But the sons and daughters of the peasants who fought for their lands, the sons and daughters of the urban workers who shed their blood for better wages and working conditions, and the sons and daughters of the middle class who rallied to the banner of Francisco I. Madero are largely deaf to the rhetoric employed to allude to noble ideals and goals.

This conclusion does not lead me to the assumption that Mexican youth are reactionaries. I just believe that we have reached a period in our national history in which the contrast or difference between the terms reactionary and revolutionary has lost much of its meaning, just as the contrast between insurgent and royalist, centralist and federalist, liberal and conservative, republican and monarchist belong to a definite period of the past, bearing today little more than historical meanings. I do not believe that Mexican youth would opt for any program contrary to the well-being of the vast majority of the people. Fascism or any of its incarnations simply does not attract them.

Setting forth an honest diagnosis of contemporary problems and offering an equally honest solution to them would arouse the enthusiasm of our youth. They would support a just cause. Continuous dependence on a meaningless vocabulary, failure to come to grips with existing problems, and inability to understand new times and conditions will disillusion the youth and work to the benefit of the enemies of the Revolution. But the challenge is not just one of new methods, new words, and new solutions but also of new men who can guide our youth in the search for change. . . .

For some years now, Mexico has been submerged in an historical crisis. Inevitably it will soon emerge. It must be prepared to enter a new period characterized by its own style and direction. The transition does not mean that we deny the past, which will shape that future. To recognize that a monumental historical period of the Revolution with all its fervor, rhetoric, and personalities has drawn to a close does not mean that we are happy to see it end. The natural instinct of people for progress does not have to come to and end. . . . It will be necessary to reconstitute the dialogue between the leaders and the people. The people deserve to have leaders in whom they have confidence. There must be a genuine incorporation of the people into the governance.□

The Revolution Is Dead

In 1960, one of Mexico's most respected historians, Daniel Cosío Villegas, pronounced the revolution dead and in need of a decent burial. While it had vigorously attacked the past, the revolution offered little guidance for the future. That weakness, according to Professor Cosío Villegas, explained its demise. Revolutions do not continue indefinitely. They, too, end.

I SINCERELY BELIEVE that the Mexican people have long known that the Mexican Revolution is dead, although they do not know, or only half understand, why this fact is concealed instead of being proclaimed. Therefore, the question arose some time ago: If it is dead, why have the death notices not been circulated? Why, more exactly, has the Mexican Revolution not been buried in the Rotunda of the Great, or perhaps in the Monument to the Mexican Revolution, where two of its heros, Francisco Madero and Venustiano Carranza, already lie?

This lack of good manners in a people who boast of being paragons of courtesy—"as polite as a Mexican Indian," said Vicente Espinel in 1618—may be easily explained and even justified. Making public the death of someone arouses everyone's curiosity as to the inheritance left by the dead person, and excites his relatives—legitimate or spurious—to mistrust and resentment, if not to a battle to the death, a manner of speaking appropriate to a discussion of a dead person and of a death. The Mexican Revolution actually gave to the country, and especially to its leaders, an ideology and a language, and, so long as no new ideas and expressions appear, it is easier—and perhaps it has been indispensable—to continue governing with the old ideology and language. A popular saying is that it is better to endure a known evil than to risk an unknown good; so here it may perhaps be said that it is better to endure a known dead person than to risk an unknown live one.

Two attitudes very common among today's old-time Mexicans could have led to the suspicion that there was some truth in the rumors that the Revolution was dead. One of these is a tendency to proclaim to high heaven the virtues of the Mexican Revolution and to bury as deep as possible its faults. The other is to assert that it burst out of nothing, thus magnifying the breadth of its accomplishments and the brilliance of its eminence. Apart from the fact that it is very normal, very healthy and very human to find consolation in recalling lost felicity, it may be truly maintained that the Mexican Revolution was a social, economic and political movement of extraordinary magnitude and depth, in addition to

Source: Daniel Cosío Villegas, "The Mexican Revolution, Then and Now," *Change in Latin America: The Mexican and Cuban Revolutions,* 1960 Montgomery Lectureship on Contemporary Civilization (Lincoln: University of Nebraska Press, 1961), pp. 23–37.

having a good deal more originality than the Mexicans themselves grant it. And it is also largely true that its origins were very modest, so much so that hardly any ideologists were responsible for its conception.

In order to estimate the magnitude and originality of the Mexican Revolution it will suffice to recall, on the one hand, the scope of its destructive force, and, on the other hand, comparable movements in other places.

In effect, it totally swept away not only the political regime of Porfirio Díaz but all of Porfirian society, that is, the social classes or groups together with their ideas, tastes and manners. Not only the commanders-in-chief of the army but their officers and all the soldiers disappeared without exception. Landholders, urban and especially agricultural, were almost entirely replaced by new ones. Not one of the great newspapers survived. Only two out of about fifty banks continued into the new regime. Official bureaucracy—federal, state and municipal— was wholly reformed. Moreover, let us remember that in no other Latin American country has an event of such magnitude occurred in the last hundred years, except now in Cuba. Strictly speaking, I believe that the only three changes to surpass it in extent and depth are the communist revolutions of Russia and China, and perhaps in Cuba. But even as regards these three, it may be stated that the Mexican Revolution was the first political regime to achieve power and deny the validity of liberal political philosophy in order to give to the State the role of principal promoter of the nation's material and moral well-being. Speaking broadly and somewhat ironically, liberalism supposes that if you allow rich people to become richer, and richer people the richest, the poorest people may in time become simply poor—just as when it rains heavily at the top of a mountain, the valley far below will eventually receive some additional humidity. The Mexican Revolutionists believed in the early stages that rich people should not be allowed to become richer, and that all the power and resources of the State should be applied to the benefit of the poor.

Its humble origins may be expressed in a word. The Mexican Revolution, in reality, lacked great ideologists to shape it intellectually. The contribution of the so-called forerunners—especially, Flores Magón and his associates—and even of later figures such as Luis Cabrera, was of far greater moral than ideological value. . . .

As a matter of fact, the Mexican Revolutionists first tried to define their goals formally when the 1917 Constitution was drawn up. The history of this episode is all the more interesting in that the Carranza government offered the Constitutional Congress of Querétaro, as an aid in preparing its work, Francisco Zarco's *History of the Constitutional Congress of 1857* in a new edition which omitted Ponciano Arriaga's views on the bad distribution and worse use of land in Mexico. These two facts suggest that at least the Carranza group, then the most powerful, hoped that the new Constitution would simply be a revision of the old one, a revision that would be justified by the experience of the country during the sixty years the 1857 Constitution had been in force.

Nonetheless, two events took place in the Querétaro Congress which Carranza and his group apparently did not foresee. The Revolution's lack of ideologists is confirmed by the fact that the greatest technical-juridical influence on the writing of the new constitutional text turned out to be the book *The Constitution and the Dictatorship*. Its author, Emilio Rabasa, was beyond doubt a great jurist, a good writer and a persuasive and intelligent person. But he was also a bitter critic of the 1857 Constitution, a liberal who was committed to the reactionary regime of Profirio Díaz, and he certainly lacked any revolutionary ideas or inclinations.

The predominant influence of Rabasa resulted in the enlarging of the powers of the executive branch at the expense of the many powers which the previous Constitution had given to the legislative branch. In this way, Mexico passed into a presidentialist regime, but not precisely because the revolutionaries believed that their idea of the State as principal promotor of public well-being required a strong and alert executive endowed with the legal authority to take prompt and direct action. The form of the new regime was actually suggested by a reactionary who wished to give posthumous justification to the dictatorial government of Porfirio Díaz. The other result of Rabasa's influence was perhaps beneficial. The critical tone of his book made the 1917 constituents see less merit in the work of their colleagues of 1857, so they felt fewer scruples at drawing away from it. . . .

. . . The constitutional text drawn up by those men of Querétaro was to serve as a pattern for the immediate future life of the country, and the pattern could channel, but also limit or shackle, any new, revitalizing—in short, revolutionary—force. A small group of constituents was determined to insert something new into the Constitution. Against an apparently general wave of feeling, it finally achieved the approval of Articles 3, 27, 123 and 130.

The essential meaning of Article 27 is that the economic interests of the State or of the Nation are above the interests of individuals or of groups, and therefore must prevail in case of opposition or conflict. This principle is obviously antiliberal, very modern and nevertheless also very old. It was, after all, the order in New Spain during its three hundred years as a colony. But this article gave a formal legal base to agrarian reform and, in general, to the relations of the State with the exploiters of the Nation's natural resources, particularly minerals and oil. The fact that the majority of these exploiters were foreign reveals the nationalistic and antiforeign tone of the Mexican Revolution. But this is confirmed and broadened by other provisions of the same article such as that which states that only Mexicans and Mexican corporations may acquire possession of lands, water or mining and oil resources, and that if foreigners want to obtain them, they must agree to consider themselves as Mexicans and not invoke the protection of their governments under penalty of losing their acquired wealth to the Nation. This same Article 27—but also Article 3 and even more Article 130— is anticlerical and very much in keeping with an old Mexican tradition; and it is so to a degree of insistence and detail which is truly surprising.

Article 123 is, in reality, a complete law. Rather than being new in itself, it raised labor legislation to the rank of a constitutional law, while even today it is an ordinary law in most countries. . . . The constitutional character of this Mexican labor legislation unquestionably makes Article 123 an innovation; but at the same time it raises doubts as to whether the Mexican constituents so distrusted the protection which an ordinary law might afford their revolutionary convictions that they preferred to shield them with the constitution, which is more difficult to amend and politically impossible to abolish.

It does not seem to me that the Mexican Revolution found its best expression in the spoken or written word, but in the psychology and morale of the whole country. By 1920 the Mexican Revolution had no longer a single enemy within the country, and although the United States did not recognize the government of Obregón, the government and the country at large were self-confident. For the first time in ten long years it was felt that there was order and presence of an accepted authority. The world was going through a period of prosperity which reached Mexico. But above all else, naturally, there was enormous expectation of the great reconstruction work to be initiated by the Revolution. Not "everybody" but certainly large numbers everywhere felt that exalted sensation of man turned into a god, of man with creative genius and will, with the faith that from his hands may come a new, great, brilliant, harmonious and kind world; faith, also, that nothing is impossible and that anything may be achieved by simply willing it.

The explanation of how the Mexican Revolution passed from that initial stage—exalted, secure, generous—to the one in which we now find ourselves is complicated and difficult. Although I believe that this explanation is necessary in order to know where the Revolution stands now and even in order to imagine where it may go, I shall barely attempt to sketch it.

It is a generally accepted observation that a revolution always produces a corresponding reaction; but in our case there is a particular circumstance to be considered. The drive and the energy of the Revolution were consumed much more in destroying the past than in constructing the future. As a result, the past certainly disappeared, but the new present came into being and began to develop haphazardly, so that, for lack of another image to imitate, it finally ended by becoming equal to the destroyed past. From this standpoint the reaction won a complete victory over the Revolution, since it has succeeded in taking the country back to the exact point where it was when the Revolution broke out. I mean "the exact point" where Mexico was before the Revolution in the sense of the general mental outlook prevailing now in the country, but not in the sense that the country itself is like the Mexico of 1910, and much less in the sense of what Mexico will be like in ten or twenty years.

Why has this happened, or why has it happened to this extent? Many factors would have to be taken into account in order to give a complete picture, but one seems to be outstanding: the lack of ideologists to formulate the Mexican Revolution, to indicate its course and, once it was under way, the unavoidable but deplorable fact that the people who were youngest, most prepared, intelligent and honest joined the government in only minor posts. Therefore, they neither truly inspired the policy or the plans of the Revolution, nor served it by criticizing them, as they would have done had they been outside the government, in congress or the press, for example. The press, for its part, from the beginning took a stand opposed to the government until the government ceased to be revolutionary and became conservative. Since then, they live as harmoniously as partners in a business enterprise.

The fact is that, in one way or another, the present situation has been reached. What is this situation?

The economy is sound, judged from a classical liberal point of view, so much so that it is often commented that Mexico has made phenomenal progress in recent years. More strictly examined, it is possible to find rather weak points in this economy, such as the fact that some official and semiofficial enterprises depend ultimately on the fiscal resources of the federal government. Mexico likewise faces the serious problem of an unpromising future for its visible exports. A declining market for its metals and principal agricultural exports, together with ever-increasing imports, placed it in a difficult situation. However, it may be stated that the present economic conditions of Mexico do not create insoluble problems and that they are no more serious than those of, for example, the Latin American countries and, in general, any country in the world with similar resources and history.

Nor is the apparent social situation bad. The constant improvement of communications since 1925 has given the Mexican population a mobility which it formerly lacked, making it easier to move to places where there are prospects of better work and salaries. The general level of public health has risen, as is shown by the fall in the general mortality rate and the increase in life expectancy. A worthy effort has been made in the field of education, although not proportionate to the headlong increase in our population and the greater needs of today's children and young people. The social security services although not as broad and general as would be desired, have been extended to a notable and promising extent.

Strictly speaking, the only problem of great magnitude is the rate at which the population and the national product grow. Since demographic trends change only very slowly, it seems better to look at it from that angle, and not, as it is quite possible to do, from the point of view of readjustment of investments and production. The rate of population growth is all the more serious because, alongside a high and sustained birth rate, the infant mortality rate tends to decline slowly but surely. It is possible that this population increase may very well strain the country's physical, human and economic resources, and that if energetic measures are not taken, it may present a very serious problem. Until now, the rate of economic growth has surpassed, generally speaking, that of population. But there is more than one reason to suspect that this situation cannot be indefinitely maintained, and that even the more or less normal ups and downs of the economic development of any country may produce disproportionate disequilibria, precisely because of the lack of a margin which permits time to act during years of pause or recession.

The political situation is decidedly less satisfactory than the economic and social. The only tangible progress is the periodic and regular renewal of the Mexican rulers: the president of the Republic, the governors of the States and the municipal authorities and federal and local legislative bodies. But their election is far from popular, being decided by personalist forces that rarely or never represent the genuine interests of large human groups. The economic and political power of the president of the Republic is almost all-embracing and is exercised in the designation of public servants of almost all categories and areas of the country. And since it is impossible for one man to know the special needs of each city or town, and which person or persons are most suitable to resolve them, most of the choices of the great elector are deplorably inadequate, and in any event they do not please anyone, because they are not the result of the free play of the political interests and aspirations of the groups concerned. . . .

On Mexico's horizon, nonetheless, there is a black cloud that few Mexicans and foreigners have noticed until now. . . .

It seems to me that the essential characteristics of the Mexican Revolution were these: to entrust to the State, and not to the individual nor to private enterprise, the promotion of the general welfare of the country; to make this general welfare the principal or only goal of the action of the State so that its economic and technical resources as well as its moral influence would be used to better the lot of the farmers and laborers, the teachers and the bureaucracy, and so forth. The Mexican Revolution had, moreover, a strong popular flavor, not only in the sense already described, in attempting to satisfy first the needs of the poor, but in believing that the people, the Indians, themselves, have virtues which must be recognized, respected and enhanced. The dominant idea during the good years of the Revolution, let us say 1920–1925, was that the Mexican Indian had so many natural qualities that the problem of education lay in teaching him modern work techniques, but without contaminating him or modifying his general way of life: his traditional courtesy and reserve, his artistic sensitivity and capacity, etc. And it was also a revolution that exalted the national at the expense, naturally, of the foreign.

What is left of all this? In truth, little or nothing.

In the first place, let us look at the situation of the government in Mexican society. Its political power is almost unlimited: that of the president in all the Republic; that of the governors in their respective States as regards local matters; and that of the municipal authorities in their respective jurisdictions as regards the minor matters that they manage. . . .

In the sphere of economic action, the authority and force of the State have become less and less vigorous and decisive, to the extent that it is now possible to say that the State is the prisoner of private enterprise. If it wanted to fight, the government would win, even using only legal means, such as, for example, fiscal measures. But the government does not want to fight nor even to disagree with private enterprise. It is already remarkable—and this in itself describes the situation—that a considerable increase in the number and size of public needs— which would have to be reflected in an increase in budget expenditure—has not been matched by a change in tax rates or by the creation of new taxes.

The situation has developed broadly in this way. The state rightly considered at a certain moment that Mexico could not progress very much if it relied on agriculture and mining, its two traditional occupations; therefore, the country should industrialize, at least until it would be one-third agricultural, one-third mining and one-third industrial. To achieve this goal, the State took the initiative in the establishment or expansion of certain industries. But in most cases, it waited for private enterprise to carry out the undertakings. For this purpose, and in accordance with classical liberal reasoning, the State proposed to create "a favorable climate" for private enterprise, and this was to be done, naturally, by the classical means: political and social stability; inflexible wage rates; low taxes; easy credit and other secondary aids.

The State was not mistaken either in its initial reasoning or in the methods it used to achieve industrialization, for it is estimated that in effect 60% of industrial investment to date comes from private sources. But the State made several important errors which have finally led to the situation in which we now find ourselves. One was that it never drew up a general framework of the industrial activities which were most suitable for the country, so that private enterprise would only undertake those that fitted into that general framework. In the second place, the State has been unsuccessful in restricting inflation so that the real wages of the labor force have clearly diminished, and it is the workers who ultimately are paying for the industrial progress of Mexico. In the third place, as an inevitable consequence, economic influence has begun to be converted into political influence, so that the State today would have difficulty in taking a fundamental economic policy measure without consulting the country's great banking and industrial firms or, in fact, without counting on their approval beforehand. For these reasons and some others quite as important, the final outcome is that while 16% of the Mexican families get 50% of the national income, 46% of those families got only one-seventh of such income.

I must add one word, not about the political or economic strength of the government, but about its moral authority. It has been at a low point for several years, and for many reasons. One of them is the most important, however. All men participating in the country's public life, all politicians, as they are commonly named, talk as if we were living in 1920, 1928 or 1938 at the latest. They talk as if the Mexican Revolution were very much alive, as if its original goals were still prevailing, as if large and small government policies were inspired and adopted to reach those goals in the shortest possible time and to the fullest possible measure. It seems, however, that moral authority usually rests on the man whose deeds match his word and whose words do not go beyond his deeds.

This situation explains why there has been a considerable weakening of the popular meaning and nationalist note found in the Mexican Revolution during its best period.

It is difficult to give an opinion, even a very tentative one, on whether Mexico can go back to a course more in keeping with the original objective of the Revolution, and what means it should employ to achieve this, short of a new revolution. This is perhaps the principal concern of Mexico's leading men, although I do not know whether there is an agreement, at least as to the principal points toward which the country should direct itself. It may be that the real dilemma for Mexico—as for so many countries in the world—lies in whether to grow faster at the top only, or at a slower pace, but benefiting the lower levels of the social pyramid. Whatever may be the proper way, I am quite confident that Mexico will find it soon, for my country has a real genius for getting out of a mess . . . and for getting into a mess.☐

The Cuban Revolution

By the early 1990s, Cuba boasted of the only extant revolution in the Americas. It traces its roots to the quixotic attack led by Fidel Castro on the Moncada army barracks in 1953 and particularly to the guerrilla movement that began in the Sierra Maestra Mountains in 1956. The revolutionaries led by the charismatic Castro triumphed and came to power in early January 1959. The long duration of the revolution can find some explanation in Lyford Edward's theory: The revolution has not been accepted either by the many Cubans living in exile or by the metropolis; not finding tolerance, the revolution has displayed none; the road to "normalcy" remains blocked.

The Cuban revolution achieved much, particularly in education, health care, food production, and cultural identification. Thus far, it has failed to achieve a satisfactory degree of economic independence and individual self-expression. After three decades, it remains as controversial as ever. For many it kindles the embers of hope for change; for others it fans the flames of fear of change.

Program Manifesto of the 26th of July Movement

The 26th of July Movement, an organized effort to overthrow the dictatorship of Fulgencio Batista and to renovate Cuba, issued its program of goals in 1956. It carefully linked revolutionary objectives with historical precedents, thus integrating the proposed revolution with long-standing Cuban desires. Essentially the program emphasized three basic goals, all nationalistic, with which most Cubans, and most Latin Americans for that matter, could identify: These goals were sovereignty, development, and the affirmation of local culture.

T HE REVOLUTION is the struggle of the Cuban nation to reach its historic goals and accomplish its complete integration. That "integration" consists in the harmonious development of three elements: *political sovereignty, economic independence, and a differentiated culture.* The first defines the condition of the state, the second affirms the necessity for its own maintenance, and the third relates to the character and appropriate mental attitude of the people. . . .

The Revolution simply seeks *the establishment of a state of affairs in which man will have justice and dignity, in which he will find well-being, and in which all legal and necessary aspects of life will be agreeable.* In this case, of course,

Source: From *Cuba in Revolution* by Rolando Bonachea and Nelson Valdés. Copyright © 1972 by Rolando Bonachea and Nelson Valdés. Used by permission of Doubleday, a division of Bantam Doubleday Dell Publishing Group, Inc.

we will realize this ideal in the island of Cuba and for the benefit of the Cuban people.

The revolutionary ideal is composed of political, economic, social, and cultural aspects. Therefore, it covers all areas where the *human person* lives. Man has as much right to a free land as he has to his bread. He has the right to live in a society directed by norms recognizing his rights, and to enjoy cultural opportunities compatible with his particular character.

Taking this concept as a basis, the essential aims of the Cuban Revolution are the following: (1) a free and sovereign fatherland, (2) a democratic republic, (3) an independent economy, and (4) a culture of its own.

None of these goals can exist in isolation from each other. There is no fatherland without economy, no republic without culture, nor the opposite. Each is a part of the others, and the integral presence of all is necessary if the national goal is to become a tangible reality.

Ideology

"A Constitution is a lively and practical law that cannot be constructed with ideological precepts."

Martí.

With regard to ideological definitions, the 26th of July Movement prefers to avoid abstract formulations or pre-established clichés. The ideology of the Cuban Revolution must arise from its own roots and the particular circumstances of the people and the country. Therefore, its ideology will not be something imported from other places, nor will it be discovered by a mental process that will later be applied to reality. On the contrary, its ideology will come forth from the land and the Cuban people.

Nonetheless, beginning from the stated principle and taking into consideration the essential goals already expressed, the 26th of July Movement can be defined as guided by the *ideals of democracy, nationalism, and social justice*. . . .

With regard to *democracy,* the 26th of July Movement still considers valid the Jeffersonian philosophy and fully identifies with Lincoln's statement, "government of the people, by the people and for the people." Democracy cannot be the government of a race, class, or religion, it must be the government of *all* the people. The Cuban Revolution is also democratic due to the tradition established by our forefathers. "All men are equal," stated the proclamation of October 10, 1868. And the same idea was later maintained in the Montecristi Manifesto [of 1895], and in all the documents and Constitutions of the Republic.

Nationalism is the natural outcome of geographic and historic circumstances which from the outset determined Cuba's independent status. It refers to "wanting to be a nation" of a people that has been capable of conquering its own freedom. Cuba achieved nominal independence in 1902, but it has not yet accomplished its economic independence. The land, mines, public services, credit institutions, the transportation sector—in other words, the most important sectors of the national economy—send the greatest percentage of their profits abroad. The nationalist position, in this case, consists of rectifying that unjust situation so that the country will benefit from its own wealth and economic resources. As an adequate complement to that task, the nation will also have expression in education and culture.

With regard to *social justice,* the 26th of July Movement foresees the establishment of an order in which all the inalienable rights of a *human being*—political, social, economic, and cultural—will be fully met and guaranteed.

That premise established, some considerations relative to material well-being are necessary because they constitute the *sine qua non* of any other human right. The experience of the economic development of other nations in the nineteenth and twentieth centuries has demonstrated that the capitalist system of free enterprise inevitably leads to the accumulation of wealth in a few hands, while the majority is exploited. This experience has forced the most advanced nations, including the country most representative of the capitalist system—the United States—to resort to economic planning techniques that will guarantee the production and consumption of goods in accordance with the needs of the social order.

The 26th of July Movement favors a system of economic planning that will be capable of freeing the country from the ills of monoculture, concessions, monopolist privileges, latifundia, and other expressions of a colonial economy.
. . .

In summary, the 26th of July Movement declares that the above-stated principles emanate from the political thought of José Martí, who once stated that the essential principle was that of the *full dignity of man.* All human relations—fatherland, politics, economy, education—converge at that point. In that position, in the following of Martí's ideas, the philosophical base of our struggle must be found.

This ideological position can be divided into the following points.

1. National Sovereignty
    "If the family of American republics have a specific function it is not to be servants of any other." (Martí)

Sovereignty is the right of a nation to orient and shape its own destiny. Without it, everything else—state, government, culture—lacks national meaning; it is false. The first objective of the Revolution, therefore, is to assert the full sovereignty of Cuba. . . .

The nation must be fully sovereign with regard to its territory, form of government, national and international political decisions, economic orientation, education, culture and any other activities related to its historic process. . . .

2. Economic Independence
    "The only fruitful and lasting peace and freedom are those accomplished by one's own effort." (Martí)

Economic independence is understood as the capacity of a country to take care of itself within the natural system of international relations. This independence is the indispensable foundation for political sovereignty. Cuba possesses sufficient resources to aspire to its economic independence like any other sovereign nation in this world. This aspiration does not hinder in any way; rather it aids the development of a rich, productive, and satisfactory trade for all. . . .

. . . The state will exert a policy of controls over natural resources, public services, banks, insurance, capital investments, and all other forms of production and credit. It will also reserve for itself the right to orient and plan, within international common understanding, the conditions of foreign trade.

3. Work
"The general happiness of a people depends on the individual independence of its inhabitants." (Martí)

Although the 26th of July Movement does not defend the doctrines of economic determinism, it proclaims that there cannot be democracy or social justice if man does not have the means to satisfy in an honorable way his material needs. Consequently, we maintain that the state is obliged to provide those means, principally in the form of adequate production instruments and well-paid opportunities to work.

Hence, work is considered a right and a way to achieve individual progress. More than a pretext to fragmentize the social unity of alien groups, it will be a factor indispensable for production and national unity. Work should be guaranteed at all times by a just and progressive compensation, and by a body of legal measures that will regulate its conditions, having as its point of departure the full dignity of every human being. . . .

4. Social Order
"We must impede the distortion or exploitation of Cuba's interests by the interests of one group, the excessive authority of a military or civil organization, a given region, or of one race over another." (Martí)

The 26th of July Movement takes its ideas with respect to social problems from Martí. Its ideal about this is the *organic unity of the nation.* According to this concept, no group, class, race, or religion should sacrifice the common good to benefit its particular interest, nor can it remain aloof from the problems of the entire social order or one of its parts. Ancient civilization recognized this principle in the expression *salus populi suprema lex,* which meant that the commonweal was the norm guiding the practice and spirit of the law. . . .

Social unity rests on what can be considered the supreme goal of the Revolution: *the moral and material welfare of man.* This implies all human rights, including the natural right to a dignified standard of life. In that manner, when promoting the happiness of the individual and his harmony in relation to the community, the necessary conditions are established for the ideal of *national integration* and the subjective values of the fatherland are affirmed.

5. Education
"The measure of responsibility is related to the extent of one's education." (Martí)

Education is the radical solution to be implemented by the Revolution (the immediate or urgent one is political insurrection). Since we cannot have a fatherland without a national consciousness, nor democracy without citizens, it is necessary to have a thorough and systematic instrument dedicated to provide the people with those indispensable instruments. . . .

. . . Education cannot be simply reduced to a pedagogic technique. In a country like Cuba, still struggling to achieve its *national* fulfillment, education must be aimed toward the achievement of important goals, some of which are *subjective,* while others are *objective.* The subjective goals are the values of freedom and fatherland, both of which are complemented by the basic principle of the *dignity of man.* Among the objective goals can be found, at the forefront, the cultural, vocational, and technical preparation of the citizen which will make him a capable and aggressive instrument in the face of the country's social and economic problems.

All this explains the great revolutionary importance of the educational process. It also shows why the state must pay special attention and interest to the philosophy that will guide this process.

If education pretends to have national and civic ends, it cannot limit itself to a technical function, but requires a certain moral and philosophic content; this content cannot be of a sectarian or confessional type, because it will gravely endanger the democratic freedoms. The morality that will animate our education will be universal in character, common to all men in spite of belief differences. It will be a natural ally of the principle of freedom. Also, the essential characteristic of the democratic state demands that public education be *absolutely secular,* so that there will be no room, due to reasons of conscience, for undesirable discriminations or distinctions among the future citizens. . . .

6. Politics

"To govern is to direct the national forces in such a manner as to allow each man to fulfill himself in a dignified way, and to make good use of public prosperity." (Martí)

The 26th of July Movement is determined to achieve the ideal of a democratic republic, inspired in the credo of freedom and founded in the character and capacity of its citizens. It aspires to establish in Cuba a form of government and a system of public and individual rights that will be fully practiced in real life and not forgotten in written Constitutions and laws.

To reach that end, however, it is first necessary to carry out a thorough eradication of arbitrary procedures and evils that debase Cuban politics. The principal causes for this particular situation are: *political parties without doctrine, immoral politicians, personalism, the low level of civic consciousness among the masses, abstentionist neutralism; and all their consequences, such as: electoral mercantilism, the mocking of elections, police power, military hegemony, providentialism, and dictatorship.*

The eradication of all these ills supposes a twofold task: on the one hand, revolutionary action in the form of a series of decrees directly aimed at severely punishing crimes committed against political freedom or against human rights; and on the other hand, a systematic campaign of civic education capable of giving the masses the indispensable minimum of political education acquired in a democratic system. . . .

7. Civil Authority
    "Governmental power should be only in the hands of civilian men. . . . A nation is not established as one runs a military camp." (Martí)

All the guarantees of the democratic system contained in essence in all the great historic documents of the West, from the Declaration of Independence (1776) to the Déclaration des Droits de l'Homme et du Citoyen (1789) to the Present Declaration of Human Rights of the United Nations, are based on the establishment of a firm civil authority that will assure their fulfillment. . . .

8. Freedom of Conscience
    "Freedom is the right every man has to be honest and to think and speak without hypocrisy." (Martí)

The Revolution considers as one of the essential elements of democracy the principle of freedom of conscience. Each citizen will be free to sustain whatever creed or religion he might want, or none at all, as long as his attitude does not diminish human dignity or endanger the rights and freedoms of others. . . .
On this matter, the 26th of July Movement adopts and proclaims the ideas of Martí, declaring that it will fight at all times for those conditions which would make the principle of freedom of conscience effective. In political terms this means a secular state.

9. Public Morality

The Republic was born carrying the colonial germs of political corruption. At the same time it lacked the moral or philosophical strength to counteract corruption, and time has done nothing but aggravate the evil. It is not surprising, therefore, that public matters in Cuba constantly fall prey to profiteers and thieves for whom the institutions of democracy are only a profitable market. That is why the Cuban Revolution must complement its ideology with serious ethical concerns. . . .

10. International Position

The Cuban Revolution is historically situated within the purest American tradition. The common ideals and interests which necessarily unite the republics of the hemisphere—both north and south—are a reality that should be developed and maintained cooperatively by all the nations of the continent.
The independence of Cuba, therefore, as well as that of all the other countries of America, cannot be taken as an isolated event. It is part of a process

whose supreme objective must logically be the integration of all in a higher unity of freedom and mutual understanding.

That is, then, in a few words, the international position (mainly inter-American) that the 26th of July Movement adopts. Therefore, in its relations with the other American republics, including, of course, the United States, Cuba's attitude is not one of separation but rather friendship. This attitude, as long as the common historical ideals demand it, will have priority over the rest of our international relations, that is, extracontinental.

Having laid down certain basic points, we must now make some other clarifications. Just as it is true that independence can be considered a step toward plural integration (not yet realized), this does not mean that it can or should be omitted or reduced at any time. On the contrary, this desirable state of harmonious unity for all could never be attained without the full maturity of all its parts— a maturity that in this case is *national integration*. In other words, independence is not an obstacle but a path. It is conceived as good and beautiful, a possible fraternity among homogeneous republics, not as colonies or satellites.

With regard to the specific matter of the relations between Cuba and the United States, the 26th of July Movement formulates a doctrine of *constructive friendship*. By this we mean mutual respect, particularly in the economic and cultural areas.

In good political terminology, it is improper in America to utilize the word "imperialism"; but forms of economic penetration still persist, accompanied generally by political influence. These cause irreparable damage to the moral, as well as material, well-being of the country that suffers them.

Fortunately, such a situation can be overcome without damage to any legitimate interest. Through *constructive friendship,* Cuba can truly become, as is indicated by a multitude of geographical, economic, and even political factors, a loyal ally of the great country to the north, yet at the same time preserve its ability to control its own destiny. Through new and just agreements, without unnecessary sacrifices or humiliating sellouts, it can multiply the advantages that are derived from our neighborhood.

Constructive friendship can be expressed fully in one simple formula: combine the process of national integration with an increase in relations on a scale of equity and justice. That is, in reality, a "healthy Americanism." On the one hand, it gives reality to the postulates of the national Revolution, and, on the other hand, it opens the door to a reasonable, profitable, and lasting understanding.

. . . Cuba is undergoing the most critical juncture of its history. Either the Revolution triumphs—thanks to the effort, almost the only one, of the youth reserves—and inaugurates a new order of dignity, freedom, and national reconstruction, or the banditry of Batista prevails (even though it dissimulates its appearance by a false change of façade in complicity with elements of the pseudo-opposition) and adds new frustration to the destiny of the fatherland, obliging itself to continue the struggle indefinitely.

As a revolutionary force, born and baptized with blood in the midst of the tragedy, the 26th of July Movement aspires not only to the overthrow of govern-

ment banditry and the renovation of the rotten political atmosphere that nour-
ishes and supports it, but also to the development of the indispensable program
of transformations that constitute the positive part of the Revolution. □

Causes of the Cuban Revolution

Addressing the United Nations General Assembly in 1960, Fidel Castro outlined
some of the basic causes of the Cuban revolution: poverty, underdevelopment,
dependency, and exploitation. He also suggested how Cuba intended to make
fundamental social changes. In reality, most of the Third World suffered from
the same problems and sought viable solutions to them. By implication, then,
most of the Third World could embrace revolution. That reality provided Castro
and Cuba an unprecedented opportunity for international leadership.

THE PROBLEM OF CUBA? Some representatives are perhaps well-informed;
some of them not so well—it depends on your sources of information—but
there is no doubt that for the world as a whole the Cuban problem is one that
has arisen in the last two years; it is a new problem. Formerly the world had little
reason to know that Cuba existed. To many people it was rather like an appendix
to the United States. Even for many citizens of this country, Cuba was a colony
of the United States. It was not so on the map. On the map we were shown in a
different colour from the United States; in reality, we were a colony.

How did our country come to be a United States colony? Not through its
origins; the United States and Cuba were not colonized by the same people. Cuba
has a very different ethnic and cultural background, built up over several hundred years.

Cuba was the last country in America to free herself from Spanish colonialism, the Spanish colonial yoke, if the representative of the Spanish Government
will forgive me, and because it was the last, it had to struggle much more desperately. Spain had only one possession in America left and she defended it obsti-
nately and with every means at her disposal. Our little people, numbering hardly
more than one million at that time, had for nearly thirty years to fight alone
against an army which was regarded as one of the strongest in Europe. Against
our small national population the Spanish Government mobilized a force as large
as all the forces which had fought against the independence of all the nations in
South America put together. Nearly half a million Spanish soldiers fought against
our people's heroic and single-minded determination to be free. The Cubans
fought alone for their independence for thirty years; thirty years which laid the
foundation for our country's love of freedom and independence.

But in the opinion of John Adams, one of the Presidents of the United
States in the early years of last century, Cuba was a fruit, an apple, as it were,
hanging from the Spanish tree, destined, as soon as it was ripe, to fall into the

Source: United Nations, *Official Records of the General Assembly. Fifteenth Session (Part I).
Plenary Meetings. Volume 1: Verbatim Records of Meetings, 20 September–17 October 1960* (New
York: United Nations, 1960), pp. 118–120, 121, 126.

hands of the United States. Spain's power had wasted away in our country. She had neither men nor money left to continue the war in Cuba. Spain was routed. Apparently the apple was ripe and the United States Government held out its hands. It was not one apple that fell into its hands but several: Puerto Rico fell, heroic Puerto Rico, which had begun its fight for freedom together with the Cubans; so did the Philippine Islands and a number of other possessions.

However, some different pretext had to be found for subjugating our country. Cuba had fought a tremendous fight and world opinion was on its side. The Cubans who fought for our independence, those Cubans who at that time were laying down their lives, trusted completely in the Joint Resolution of the United States Congress, of 20 April 1898, which declared that "The people of the island of Cuba are, and of right ought to be, free and independent." The people of the United States sympathized with the Cubans in their struggle. That joint declaration was an Act of Congress of this nation under which war was declared on Spain.

That illusion ended in cruel disappointment. After two years of military occupation of our country, something unexpected occurred. Just when the Cuban people, through a Constituent Assembly, were drafting the basic law of the Republic, another act was passed by the United States Congress, an act proposed by Senator Platt, of unhappy memory for Cuba, in which it was laid down that a rider was to be attached to the Cuban Constitution whereby the United States Government would be granted the right to intervene in Cuban political affairs and, in addition, the right to lease certain parts of Cuban territory for naval bases or coaling stations; in other words, under a law enacted by the legislative authority of a foreign country, the Cuban Constitution had to contain this provision, and it was made very clear to the members of our Constituent Assembly that if no such amendment was made, the occupation forces would not be withdrawn. In other words, our country was forced by the legislature of a foreign country to grant that country the right to intervene and to hold naval bases or stations. . . .

The new colonization of our country then began: the best agricultural land was acquired by United States companies; concessions were granted for exploiting our natural resources and mines, concessions for the operation of public utilities, commercial concessions, concessions of every kind which, combined with the constitutional right, based on force, to intervene in our country transformed it from a Spanish into a United States colony.

Colonies have no voice. Colonies are not recognized in the world as long as they have no opportunity to make themselves heard. That was why the world knew nothing of this colony or of its problems. Another flag, another coat of arms, appeared in the geography books. Another colour appeared on the maps; but there was no independent republic in Cuba. Let no one be deceived because if we are, we shall only make fools of ourselves. Let no one be deceived. There was no independent republic in Cuba. It was a colony where the orders were given by the Ambassador of the United States of America. We have no shame in proclaiming this because any shame is offset by the pride we have in saying that today no embassy rules our people because our people are governed by the people.

Once again the Cuban people had to resort to strife to win their independence and they achieved it. They achieved it after seven years of bloody oppression. By whom were they oppressed? By those in our country who were merely the tools of those who dominated it economically. How can any unpopular régime, inimical to the interests of the people, remain in power except by force? Do we need to explain here to the representatives of our fellow countries of Latin America what military tyrannies are? Do we need to explain to them how they have remained in power? Do we need to explain to them the history of some of these tyrannies which have already become a byword? Do we need to explain to them on what strength these tyrannies rely, from what national and international interests the military group which oppressed our people drew its support? It was supported by the most reactionary circles in the country and most of all by the foreign economic interests which dominated our country's economy. Everyone knows—and we believe that even the United States Government admits this—that is was the type of government preferred by the monopolies. Why? Because by force any demand by the people can be repressed; by force strikes for better living conditions were repressed; with force peasant movements for ownership of the land were repressed; with force the dearest aspirations of the people were repressed.

That is why governments of force were preferred by those directing United States policy. That is why governments of force remained in power for so long and still remain in power in America. . . .

The Government of Fulgencio Batista was a typical government of force, a government which suited the United States monopolies in Cuba. But it was not, of course, the type of government which suited the Cuban people. With great loss of life and much sacrifice the Cuban people overthrew that Government.

What did the revolution find after it succeeded in Cuba? What wonders did it find? If found, first of all, that 600,000 Cubans fit for work were permanently unemployed—a figure which is, in proportion, equal to the number of unemployed in the United States at the time of the great depression which shook this country and almost led to disaster. Three million people, out of a total population of a little over 6 million, had no electric light and enjoyed none of the benefits and comforts of electricity. Three and a half million people, out of a total population of a little over 6 million, were living in hovels and huts unfit for human habitation. In the towns rents accounted for as much as one third of family incomes. Electricity rates and rents were among the highest in the world.

Thirty-seven and a half per cent of our population were illiterate, unable to read or write. Seventy per cent of the children in the rural areas were without teachers. Two per cent of our population were suffering from tuberculosis, that is to say, 100,000 people out of a total of a little over 6 million. Ninety-five per cent of the children in rural areas were suffering from diseases caused by parasites. Infant mortality was consequently very high. The average life span was very short. In addition, 85 per cent of small farmers were paying rent for their lands amounting to as much as 30 per cent of their gross incomes, while 1½ per cent of all the landowners controlled 46 per cent of the total area of the country. The proportion of hospital beds to the number of inhabitants of the country was ludicrous when compared with countries with average medical services. Public utilities, electricity and telephone companies were owned by United States monopolies. A large part of the banking and import business, the oil refineries, the greater part of the sugar production, the best land, and the chief industries of all types in Cuba belonged to United States companies. In the last ten years, the balance of payments between Cuba and the United States has been in the latter's favour to the extent of $1,000 million, and that does not take into account the millions and hundreds of millions of dollars removed from the public treasury by the corrupt and tyrannical rulers and deposited in United States or European banks. One thousand million dollars in ten years! The poor and underdeveloped country of the Caribbean, with 600,000 unemployed, contributing to the economic development of the most highly industrialized country in the world!

That was the situation which confronted us; a situation which is not unknown to many of the countries represented in this Assembly because, in the final analysis, what we have said about Cuba is merely a general X-ray photograph, so to speak, which is valid for the majority of countries represented here. What alternative was there for the revolutionary government? To betray the people? Of course, in the eyes of the President of the United States, what we have done for our people is treason to our people; but it would not be so, for sure, if instead of being loyal to our people we had been loyal to the great United States monopolies which were exploiting our country's economy.

Let note at least be taken here of the wonders which the revolution found after it succeeded, wonders which are no more and no less than the usual wonders associated with imperialism, the wonders of the free world for us colonized countries.

No one can blame us if Cuba had 600,000 unemployed, 37½ per cent of its population illiterate, 2 per cent suffering from tuberculosis, and 95 per cent of the children in rural areas suffering from diseases caused by parasites. No; until the revolution none of us had any say in the future of our country; until then the rulers who served the interests of the monopolies controlled its destinies; until then it was the monopolies which determined the fate of our country. Did anyone try to stop them? No, no one. Did anyone place difficulties in their way? No, no one. They were allowed to go about their business and in Cuba we are now enjoying the fruits of their work.

What was the state of the national reserves? When the tyrant Batista came to power there were $500 million in the national reserves—a goodly sum for investing in the industrial development of the country. After the revolution there were $70 million in our reserves. Does this show any concern for the industrial development of our country? None at all; that is why we are so astonished and we continue to be astonished when we hear in the General Assembly of the United States Government's great concern for the future of the countries of Latin America, Africa and Asia. We cannot overcome our astonishment because, after fifty years of such a régime, we now see the results in Cuba. . . .

The Revolutionary Government began to make its first reforms. The first thing it did was to reduce rents paid by families by 50 per cent. A very just measure, since, as we said earlier, there were families paying as much as a third of their income. The people had been the victims of large-scale speculation in housing, and there had been tremendous speculation in urban land at the people's expense. But when the Revolutionary Government reduced rents by 50 per cent, there were some who were not pleased, to be sure: those few who owned the apartment buildings. But the people rushed in to the streets rejoicing, as would happen in any country, even here in New York, if rents for all families were reduced by 50 per cent. But this did not involve any difficulty with the monopolies; some United States companies owned large buildings, but they were relatively few.

Then came another law; a law cancelling the concessions which the tyrannical Government of Fulgencio Batista had granted to the telephone company, which was a United States monopoly. It had taken advantage of the people's defencelessness to obtain very favourable concessions. The Revolutionary Government cancelled these concessions and restored the rates for telephone services to the previous level. This was the beginning of the first conflict with the United States monopolies.

The third measure was the reduction of electricity charges, which were among the highest in the world. Thus arose the second conflict with United States monopolies. By this time we were beginning to look like communists. We began to be painted red, simply because we had clashed with the interests of the United States monopolies.

There followed another law, an inevitable and indispensable law, inevitable for our country and inevitable, sooner or later, for all the peoples in the world, at least for all those peoples of the world who have not yet carried it out: the land reform law. Of course, in theory, everyone is in favour of land reform. No one dares to question it; no informed person dares to deny that land reform is an essential condition for economic development in the underdeveloped countries of the world. In Cuba too, even the big landowners were in agreement with land reform, provided it was a kind of land reform which suited them, like the land reform proposed by many theorists: a land reform which would not be carried out, for just as long as it could be avoided.

Land reform is something recognized by the economic organs of the United Nations, something which is no longer in dispute. In our country it was indispensable; more than 200,000 families lived in the rural areas of our country without any land on which to grow essential food crops. Without land reform our country would not have been able to take the first step toward development. Well, we took this step. We instituted a land reform. Was it radical? It was a radical reform. Was it very radical? It was not particularly radical. We carried out a land reform appropriate to the needs of our development, appropriate to our capacities for agricultural development; that is to say, a land reform which would solve the problem of landless peasants, solve the problem of the supply of these essential foodstuffs, remedy the fearfully high level of unemployment in rural areas, and put an end to the appalling poverty which we found in our countryside.

Well, it was at that point that the first real difficulty arose. The same thing had happened in the neighbouring Republic of Guatemala. When land reform was carried out in Guatemala, difficulties arose there. And I must in honesty warn the representatives of Latin America, Africa and Asia: when they plan to carry out a just land reform, they must be prepared to face situations similar to ours, especially if the best and largest estates are owned by United States monopolies, as was the case in Cuba. . . .

Despite these difficulties the Cuban revolution is changing what was yesterday a country without hope, a country of poverty, many of whose people could not read or write, into a country which will soon be one of the most advanced and highly developed in the Americas.

In a scant twenty months the Revolutionary Government has opened 10,000 new schools, that is, double the number of rural schools which had been built in the previous half century, and Cuba is today the first country in the Americas to meet all its school needs, with teachers even in the most remote mountain villages.

In this short space of time the Revolutionary Government has built 25,000 houses in rural and urban areas. Fifty new towns are under construction. The most important military fortresses are being used to house tens of thousands of students and next year our people propose to launch an all-out offensive against illiteracy, with the ambitious goal of teaching every illiterate person to read and write. Organizations of teachers, students and workers—the entire people—are preparing themselves for an intensive campaign and within a few months Cuba will be the first country in the Americas to be able to claim that it has not a single illiterate inhabitant.

Our people now benefit from the services of hundreds of doctors who have been sent to the country districts to fight diseases caused by parasites and improve sanitary conditions in the nation.

In another field, that of the conservation of natural resources, we can point with pride to the fact that in a single year, in the most ambitious plan for the conservation of natural resources being carried out in this continent, including the United States and Canada, we have planted approximately 50 million timber-producing trees.

Young people, for whom there were no jobs or schools, have been organized by the Revolutionary Government and are today being employed in work that is of value to the country and at the same time are being trained for productive employment.

Agricultural production has increased from the very outset. This virtually unique achievement was possible because the Revolutionary Government made over 100,000 small tenant farmers into landowners and at the same time maintained large-scale production by means of agricultural producers' co-operatives. By using co-operatives to maintain large-scale production it was possible to apply the most modern agricultural techniques, and from the very outset production increased. And we have carried through this programme of social betterment and provided teachers, houses and hospitals without sacrificing resources for development.

The Revolutionary Government is already carrying out a programme of industrialization and the first factories are now being built. We have used our country's resources rationally. Thus, Cuba used to import $35 million worth of cars and $5 million worth of tractors. A predominantly agricultural country was importing seven times as many cars as tractors. We have reversed the figures and are importing seven times as many tractors as cars.

Close to $500 million has been recovered from the politicians who had enriched themselves during the tyranny. We have recovered a total of close to $500 million in cash and other assets from the corrupt politicians who had been plundering our country for seven years.

By making proper use of this wealth and these resources, the Revolutionary Government is able to implement a plan for the industrialization of the country and the expansion of agricultural production and at the same time to build houses and schools, send teachers to the most remote villages and provide medical services, in other words to carry out a programme of social development.□

Agrarian Reform

Agrarian reform, introduced on May 17, 1959, ranked among the foremost goals and achievements of the Cuban revolution. While on the one hand distributing land to small farmers to cultivate food crops, the reform, on the other hand, expropriated the *latifundios,* the large estates. The law turned cattle ranches into state farms (called *granjas*) and sugar plantations into cooperatives. Later, those cooperatives became state farms as well, in accordance with the goal to curtail private ownership and maximize state ownership, which, in the newly socialized state, meant the property of the people. The Cuban experience remains unique in the Americas in its insistence on state ownership and administration of most of the land. Thus, as the Cuban revolution consolidated, it further restricted, although it did not abolish, private ownership.

Ever since the origin of the revolutionary struggle, Fidel Castro has emphasized the importance of agrarian reform. A speech in 1962 reiterated that emphasis.

W HEN THE REVOLUTION TRIUMPHED, it was a fact that the first step taken was the Agrarian Reform. You will remember when we began to speak of the Agrarian Reform, how the people immediately began to be interested, even the workers in the cities.

It is possible that many people heard of the Agrarian Reform, without, nevertheless, understanding what this meant. But finally everyone realized that the reform was necessary, that the situation in the countryside could not continue, that a complete change was needed in the conditions of life, work, and cultivation of the land, that such a change would be beneficial to the *campesinos.*

The Agrarian Reform is one of the most far-reaching tasks to which the Revolution set itself. It has also been one of the most difficult tasks. The problem of ownership and means of exploitation of the land is far more complex than the

Source: Castro delivered this speech at the closing of the National Congress of Sugar Cane Cooperatives, August 18, 1962. Reprinted in *Fidel Castro Speaks,* edited and translated by Martin Kenner and James Petras, pp. 34–35, 36–37, 40, 41, 47–49. Copyright © 1969 by Martin Kenner and James Petras. Used by permission of Grove Press, Inc.

same problem in industry. The revolution of the system of industrial production, for example, is always much simpler than the revolution in the countryside.

In our countryside, two types of production centers existed: the large *latifundios* and the small farmers. The large *latifundios* exploited a considerable number of workers, especially the large cane *latifundios*. Among the small farmers there were certain distinct characteristics. The small farmer who was the owner of land was in the minority. Then there were the squatters, the cultivators of coffee and cocoa in the mountains, who, although they did not pay rent, always lived under the threat of eviction. There was also the farmer who paid rent, who, together with the squatters, constituted the great majority.

We were, therefore, confronted with two types of ownership of the land. There was the small farmer who worked his own land and there was the landlord who lived, in many cases, far from his lands and who employed at times hundreds of workers. The large *latifundios* like those of the United Fruit Company employed thousands of workers.

The basic outlines of the first revolutionary law that changed the system of production in the countryside were as follows; first, the liquidation of the *latifundios;* second, the liquidation of the rent system, that is to say the liberation of the *campesinos* from the rents that they were paying; third, to guarantee to the squatters the ownership of the land that they were occupying.

There remained the problem of how to make the great *latifundios* productive. It was talked about a great deal, and it was on everybody's tongue in a period when we could aspire only to partial triumphs, to partial solutions. It was a period when we could not move forward with the Revolution on all fronts, but had to move in stages. In this period, much was said of the Agrarian Reform as simply a distribution of the lands. Many people saw the Agrarian Reform as nothing more than the distribution of land.

Fortunately, our revolution had the good judgment and sufficient audacity to adopt a progressive system of cultivation of the land. Today that is very easy to understand.

The division of the *latifundios* could have destroyed the Revolution. Dramatic problems would have resulted from the division of these lands. First of all, there is the practical problem of dividing these lands, since all the lands have distinct characteristics. With any *latifundio* some land is more fertile than other, some is used for one thing, some for another. From the political point of view, the easiest solution would have been the division of those lands; from the practical point of view, this would have been an inferior solution. Often what at one moment appears easiest is in the long run not the best.

The results that would have followed the division of these lands are understood by everyone. In the first place, there isn't enough land for everyone. We remember that when the agrarian law was proclaimed, someone suggested printed forms for those who wanted land. Why? Because everyone wanted land, even the people who lived in the cities.

If the *latifundios* had been divided, many workers would have been left without land, or on the other hand, the lots would have been too small for a family to subsist on. . . .

If the *latifundios* had been divided, each one would have built his own *bohío* [squatter's shack] on his own little piece of land; the school would have remained several kilometers from where the children live; the possibilities of electricity, suitable roads, sewage, recreation sites, and shopping centers would not have been realized.

None of the many towns that have appeared, that nevertheless are only a small part of what is really needed in the countryside, could have been built either. Bringing the comforts of city life to the countryside would never have been possible, i.e., the large school centers, artistic and cultural activities, running water, electricity, sewage, streets; in a word, everything that is done in a small town would have been impossible in the countryside, since such small towns can be built only when the land is cultivated collectively.

Besides this, the division of the land would have had other economic, political, and social consequences. It is a fact that today there is a great demand for products which as a result of drought, poor administration, and errors, agricultural production did not increase in proportion to the demand. We see, as a result, some speculation in agricultural products and more or less exorbitant prices.

Where does it occur and how does it happen? Why? Why does meat keep its price? Why do these staple articles not vary in price? Why do pork products keep their price? Why aren't three turkeys worth fifty pesos? Why don't they sell four chickens for twenty pesos in the cities? Why? Because those products come from the *Granjas* [state-owned farm]. Because the beef which is used in the cities was raised on the *Granjas!* Because those fowl were raised on the *Granjas!* Because the agricultural products of the *Granjas* come to the towns and cities, to the workers, at reasonable and stable prices.

The nation can count on those products because they go from the production centers to the distribution centers. What are the products which become objects of speculation? They are the products cultivated on the small isolated plots. . . .

From every point of view, and today we see it with total clarity, it was a great thing, a great step, when the Revolution turned the *latifundios* into collective centers of production; in spite of all the difficulties, all the deficiencies at every turn, it was a great step.

You know that rural unemployment has been liquidated. You know that the problem now is a shortage of labor in many parts of the country. . . .

The Revolution resolved the fundamental problem of unemployment in the countryside, resolved it because it neither distributed nor divided those *latifundios*, thereby permitting the mechanization of agriculture. . . .

Thus we see that despite the many shortages, and they are many, something has been done, changes have been made. As we look back on our difficulties and errors, we must apply new means. We are not yet beginning to ascend, but already we have walked part way uphill. Now we do not have the problems of the first days, the problems there were in the beginning. There are problems, yes, but problems that correspond to a stage where we have overcome many of the past evils.

How did we go about organizing production in the countryside? What did we do? The *latifundios* were not divided, but collective centers of production were established. Two types appeared: the co-operatives in the cane fields; and *Granjas* in the cattle and rice *latifundios,* and on the virgin lands.

The Revolution took a bold step when it did not redistribute the *latifundios.* The two types of collective agricultural organization, the co-operatives and the *Granja,* have developed side by side.

From the cane *latifundios,* more than six hundred Cane Cooperatives have been organized. From the cattle *latifundios* and virgin lands, more than three hundred *Granjas* have been organized or constructed. . . .

There are many things about which we ought to think seriously and responsibly. There are many evils, defects, vices against which we still must struggle in order to merit a better future, which can be accomplished only by sacrifice. We will not accomplish it by sleeping in the shade; we will not accomplish it if we are like vagabonds or loafers. Abundance of all that we wish, of all that we need, can be attained only with sweat, with work, and with sacrifice.

For that reason, *compañeros,* we must take the spirit of the Revolution and of truth to all the workers of our country. We must make them conscious of the duty of work, and of the fact that work is not a punishment but a necessity in the life of man. That which makes a man a man, and distinguishes him from the others, and makes him lord and master of nature, is work.

The vagabonds do not progress. The vagabonds will not help us to liberate ourselves from want and misery. For that reason, it is necessary to create a devotion to work, to see work as it is and not as a punishment. In the past, work was an instrument of exploitation of man. Today, it is an instrument for the redemption of man, for the progress of man.

We know that there are many things to overcome, many deficiencies, many things which grieve us, errors which grieve us, weaknesses which grieve us, carelessness which grieves us, as, for example, uncultivated lands and shortages of agricultural products caused by carelessness, because those in the front line have not been attentive, have not listened, have not paid attention to plans.

With an attentive eye on all problems, we fight to conquer them the way we resolve the problems of supplies, without stepping backward. We use as an example the problem of the supplies of those products themselves. We have thought much about this problem and have discussed what should be done. Should we give a plot of land? No. Because he who has a small plot wishes a larger plot later; his animals multiply and he no longer has three, he has ten or twenty or fifty, and the worker turns into a *latifundista,* because every herdsman must have pasture for his particular herd. No! We must not use these methods which encourage the abandonment of the obligations of work. We must not go to individualism which encourages egotism, which encourages inequalities among men; we must go to the collective.

How do we resolve the problem of housing? It is impossible now to build houses for all. It is necessary then, in order to resolve this problem, not to be too ambitious. We must spend whatever we can to resolve the problem of a place to live at least, even though that dwelling is not as good as the houses being constructed in the towns, because the housing problem cannot be solved in one year.

Each and every one of these problems must be looked after. But how? By thinking of the future, thinking of the interests of the nation, thinking of the interests of all the workers. This is how we must think, because if we are all dependent on others, if no one can depend only on himself, then we must always think of the interests of all. If one concerns himself not only with his own needs, but with the needs of others, then others will look out for the needs of the individual.

Thus, we must discuss, not with orders and commands, but with reason and truth; because faced with the truth, faced with what is reasonable, no one can oppose; faced with what is just, no one can be opposed. Always with reason, always with what is just, always discussing, always teaching, never imposing, but persuading, with you participating.

From among you must come your union leaders. Now, at last, we can reply to the question, which has been asked many times: "Why don't we have a union?" Indeed, you will have unions, your union leaders, the Technical Advisory Councils will come from among you. In the future, more and more of you will become leaders. And finally, from you, from the mass of the proletariat, will come those who will advance the countryside. You will display the maximum interest, responsibility, sense of duty, patriotism; thinking of the nation, thinking of our great people, who, united, must march forward, who, united, must conquer their future. Thus, each time we are more aware of our social debts; each time less egotistic; each time more brotherly; each time more stripped of the dead weight of the voices of the past, to continue adapting our thinking and our actions to the present and to the future.

We trust in you, cane workers; we trust in the revolutionary spirit of the great masses. We know that you will put forth the maximum effort in the face of the present difficulties. We know that you will assert yourself in the face of weakness, the spirit of laziness, and before those who do not feel a sense of duty, those who do not understand the great truth; that work is the most honorable activity of man, the most fundamental necessity of man; that work makes men out of us.

Let us work for all, so that all will work for each one of us.

Patria o muerte! Venceremos!□

Women in the Cuban Revolution

The Cuban revolution set high goals for itself, none more so than the formation of the new individual. A better human being, less selfish, more industrious, motivated by ideals, was to emerge from the difficult challenge of revolutionizing society. The eradication of racism and sexism constituted two primary objectives.

Vilma Espín, an industrial chemical engineer and former guerrilla, held higher positions than any other woman in Cuba. She served as a member of the Central Committee of the Cuban Communist Party and the head of the Federation of Cuban Women (FMC). In the following excerpts from an interview in 1972, she reveals some of the goals, achievements, and aspirations of Cuban women.

O NE OF THE SOCIAL THEMES which has been debated throughout history is without doubt that of the woman and her role in society. However, in recent years, during which the revolutionary movement has gained ground throughout the world, the liberation of women is one of the questions that is being discussed by sociologists, psychologists, politicians, economists, that is all those who in one way or another have something to do with the development of society. We should also say that it is a problem which first and foremost, interests woman herself.

In my opinion, the liberation of women cannot be separated from the liberation of society in general. There can be no liberation for a social group constituting half of humankind, as long as exploitation of man by man continues, as long as the means of production are owned by an exploiting minority.

A woman cannot have any political, economic or social rights in a capitalist society where she suffers from class oppression and discrimination because of sex and race.

Historically, the feminist movement has put forth partial solutions, struggling for political rights—as did the suffragettes—but in my opinion, it has not attacked the roots of the problem, which is the capitalist society.

Of course, the feminist movement as such was progressive in its time, at the start of this century, because it helped to create consciousness in the woman, to take her out of the narrow confines of the home. Even now it can play an agitating role, channel dissatisfactions, but its fundamental weakness is that it strays from the real road which is the struggle for the liberation of the peoples and confuses many women desirous of struggling for a better life.

This feminist movement is quite strong in the United States and in western European countries. There are dozens of groups that have different aims, many of them positive. Of course, the woman is attracted to them in societies that grow increasingly corrupt, where the use of drugs and juvenile delinquency constitute veritable terror for mothers, where the woman is discriminated against as a worker, receiving a lower salary than men, with few possibilities of highly-qualified jobs or posts. Societies which in some cases are very economically and culturally developed but where truly backward laws exist discriminate against women.

We don't deny that sometimes through this way some women join the struggle, in the measure that they grow in consciousness, acquiring a political development. But unfortunately many feminist groups take away forces that could strengthen the genuinely revolutionary movement.

We even know of some capitalist countries where the ruling class stimulates those movements, they do not persecute them, they let them grow because to a

Source: June E. Hahner (ed.), *Women in Latin American History: Their Lives and Views* (Los Angeles: UCLA Latin American Center, 1976), pp. 165–171. With permission of UCLA Latin American Center Publications, University of California, Los Angeles.

certain extent these movements are playing into the hands of the so-called democracies. Let's not forget that women make up half of the electorate.

The problem of the liberation of women is a class problem and we can't speak of women's liberation as long as the oppressed classes do not free themselves from the exploitation of the oppressing classes. Women's struggle is intimately linked to the struggle of their peoples.

On the other hand, for the peoples who have succeeded in eliminating the exploitation of man by man, the women's problem is one of society in general, a society which must work to incorporate women into active life, into social production. In our country where since the triumph of the Revolution, a tenacious struggle is being waged to overcome underdevelopment, we are creating institutions, services, all the conditions to free women from domestic problems, although we still don't have all the resources we need to do this. We are also waging an intense ideological battle aimed both at women and at the rest of society to eliminate all vestiges of backwardness, the prejudices about women and the role they must play in society. Even in socialist countries with developed economies, where the woman already occupies an important place, there are still problems in the material and ideological aspects, which are being analyzed by society in general, while serious efforts are being made to find the proper solutions.

I mentioned the liberation of women as being a problem not only of women but of all society. Her incorporation into social work is essential for her incorporation into society. Women must play their rightful role in the world.

In Cuba the woman is aware that society needs her, that she is part of the productive forces fighting against underdevelopment to build the material base which will make it possible to create all the institutions, services and industries which will alleviate her domestic workload.

Moreover, work gives new perspectives to women, it broadens their horizons, it takes them out of the home and helps create a social consciousness, but, as is logical, just working itself will not solve all the problems. All society must be aware of this problem and be willing to solve it.

In all new societies vestiges of previous practices subsist for a long time. It is very difficult to change man's mentality, that's why we still have some vestiges of discrimination and prejudice toward the woman. In woman herself these vestiges have their roots in the centuries of colonial and imperialist exploitation to which we were subjected and to the place which woman occupied in that society: woman in the home and man in the street. Of course, woman in the home means that she was reduced to her role of mother and housewife, for which she did not need a high level of education, according to that idea. Ideas which, on the other hand, served the interests of the exploiting classes, which used the woman as cheap labor reserve whenever necessary.

Let us recall the two world wars when women were needed to work in factories to replace the male workers that went into the armies. Then all pre-established schemes were broken, the woman had to go out of the home and take a place in production.

We can say that the situation of the Cuban woman after the triumph of the Revolution is totally different and that during these thirteen years the political consciousness of men and women has grown and created a totally new situation, although, as I've said, there are still some prejudices. Perhaps the most deep-rooted are the ones referring to the fact of women working.

Not everyone understands the necessity for woman to work, to meet her social duties and raise her cultural and political level.

This is most frequent in the case of men, although there are women who do not understand the problem either.

Sometimes there are some expressions of discrimination in men who lead a certain branch of the economy, who do not consider the woman worker on a fully equal basis. Of course, this is a mental attitude and is not general, they're just manifestations of discrimination which sometimes are evident and other times are not.

However, the Revolution has systematically struggled against this, we can say, right from the start.

In February 1959 Fidel spoke of the exploitation and discrimination of women. The very fact that our organization was created with the aim of incorporating women into the revolutionary process, educating her culturally and politically, implies a struggle to eliminate these vestiges of the previous society.

Our Communist Party and the FMC and all the mass and political organizations have waged and are waging a systematic campaign, because evidently the elimination of even the most minimum discrimination requires a process of political and cultural education.

We have also taken other measures to incorporate women and to create the best conditions for them to change their status from housewife to full-fledged workers. The Party, the Cuban Workers' Federation, the Ministry of Labor and the FMC had made efforts to help women adapt to their new status of workers.

We should mention that this political work is also aimed at explaining the responsibilities that the human couple should assume in this stage of intense struggle for economic development. There is not only the social responsibility of sharing in the education of the children, but also the responsibility of facing all types of practical problems involved in incorporating women into social work.

This is something that the young people, especially the students, work on in common. Since we don't have all the resources we need to alleviate domestic tasks, the fact that the couple share them helps out.

The sharing of important social responsibilities such as the duty of working and of educating children, evidently tightens the bonds uniting the couple and gives a genuine and deep meaning to conjugal love.

The work of our organization [the Federation of Cuban Women, FMC] is eminently social and political since we are trying to prepare ideologically a social group that constitutes half the population and incorporate it in full into the revolutionary process so that it will occupy the role it rightfully has in the new society, be it in state administration or in all the other tasks regarding political, cultural, social and economic work in our country.

A truly important achievement of the FMC is the incorporation of women into work. Moreover, the qualitative change has been extraordinary. Women have taken jobs which before they couldn't have. They do so in better conditions since in general their educational and technical level has been raised and they are protected by a more just labor legislation.

Women in work have no limitations at all, except for the problems we mentioncd bcforc regarding child care centers, services, etc., which still are not enough to cover the growing demand. Even so, woman, without being part of a work center, fulfills her social duty through voluntary work in agriculture, industry or services. She has made an extraordinary contribution in voluntary work during these years.

Another important achievement has been in education, in educating adult women at the triumph of the Revolution and the possibilities the woman has today to study any career she wants. In this sense, the FMC is making a gigantic effort, creating special adult courses, directing specific plans for the training of organizational cadres, opening technical courses according to the needs of production, studying material on social research and attention, etc.

During 1961, in addition to taking part in the literacy campaign, the FMC had the responsibility of creating massive educational courses. The first thousand attendants for the nursery schools were trained in that year, as well as 17,000 peasant girls who learned to sew and received a general primary education. Thousands of women who had been servants in the homes of the bourgeoisie who had left the country took courses preparing them for administrative work. Later different technical courses were organized by the FMC in coordination with organizations that needed skilled labor. We also worked hard to help out the primary and secondary schools.

In regard to social work, we have developed vast plans in coordination with different ministries, including health education and projects, especially concerning the health of the child, pregnant women and new mothers, children with behavior problems, community services, recreation facilities, etc.

We can say that the FMC has achieved its objectives, the woman is an integral part of the process of transformation going on in our society.

In regard to future tasks we are trying to develop the plans we have today to the maximum, plans which are headed by our secretariats of Production, Social Work, Foreign Relations, Education, Ideological Orientation, Nursery Schools and the organizational and financial work of our organisms, because it should be known that the mass of women in our organization, in addition to doing voluntary work on all fronts, pay all the expenses of the FMC with their dues.

We are convinced that woman must, and will, play a very important role in the fight for full national independence. Moreover, in our great Latin American homeland there is a deep-seated historic tradition of women's struggles. In the battles for our first independence, together with the popular and internationalist armies of San Martín and Bolívar, women were present. Outstanding fighters such as Colonel Juana Azurduy de Padilla who fought in the area then called Upper Peru; Manuela Saenz, the companion of Bolívar; Remedios Escalada de San Martín; and our own Ana Betancourt who in 1869 demanded that women's rights be included in the new constitution; Mariana Grajales, the mother of the Maceo brothers, the heroes of our independence; Captains of the Liberating

Army, Adela Azcuy and Rosa Castellanos, the Bayamesa, and many others who not only helped the combatants but were also combatants themselves.

Thus, with these examples which we have inherited and the awakening of consciousness on the part of the Latin American woman, we know that women will make their enormous renovating and patriotic force felt in the struggles for the liberation of their peoples and for their second and definitive independence. □

The Twenty-Fifth Anniversary
of the Cuban Revolution

On January 1, 1984, Cubans celebrated the twenty-fifth anniversary of their revolution. Fidel Castro summed up what he perceived as its major achievements. Sharing a salient characteristic of Latin America's demography—youthfulness—the majority of the Cubans listening to the Maximum Leader's assessment never lived under any other Cuban government. They had neither experience with nor memory of pre-revolutionary Cuba.

THE ROAD THAT HAS LED us to this twenty-fifth anniversary of the victorious Revolution has been long and hard, glorious and heroic.

The Revolution did not tremble or waver before the colossal task of doing away with unemployment, illiteracy, ignorance and the calamitous state of public health in our country, creating work centers; child care centers; primary, secondary and high schools; technical schools; universities; special schools for handicapped children; rural hospitals; pediatric, maternal-infant, and clinical-surgical hospitals; polyclinics; dozens of specialized research and medical care centers; and numerous cultural and sports facilities for the mental and physical development of our youth and our people.

It did not tremble or waver in resolutely undertaking the long and difficult road of economic and social development, starting with a backward, deformed and dependent economy, inherited from colonialism, and in the midst of a brutal economic blockade by those who had been our suppliers of equipment, technology, plans and raw materials. A long and difficult road was begun demanding countless efforts, perseverance and sacrifice: the drawing up of five-year and annual plans; the creation of construction, industrial assembly and design enterprises, the building of a solid infrastructure of roads, highways, railways and ports; the creation and development of the merchant and fishing fleets; the mechanization of the sugar harvest and all agricultural activities; the electrification of the countryside; the building of dams and irrigation and drainage canals; the introduction of fertilization and chemicals in general, cattle improvement, artificial insemination and numerous other techniques in our backward agriculture; the beginning of the industrialization of the country; the training of hundreds of thousands of workers, middle-level technicians and university graduates; the

Source: Reprinted by permission of Greenwood Publishing Group, Inc., Westport, CT, from *Cuba: Twenty-Five Years of Revolution 1959–1984,* edited by Sandor Halebsky and John M. Kirk. Copyright © 1985 by Praeger Publishers.

founding of dozens of scientific research centers and the development of solid economic relations with the socialist camp; a thoroughly new road in which at the beginning we had no experience whatsoever.

Along this road we have built thousands of industrial, agricultural and social projects over the years. As a result of this, the profile of our countryside and cities has changed drastically. Work in all the basic spheres of production has been humanized through technology and machines. Many highly important works are under construction or near commissioning in the sphere of energy, including the first nuclear power plant, a new oil refinery, large nickel processing industries, important textile factories and spinning mills, the geological survey of the country, oil prospecting and extraction, big iron and steel works and plans pertaining to basic industry and the light and food industries. New sugar mills are being built with 100 percent of the design and over 60 percent of the components produced in Cuba. Intensive and methodical work is being done on future plants and economic and social development lines until the year 2000.

Proof of the way work productivity has been increased is that whereas only 12 years ago 350,000 canecutters were employed in the harvest, today fewer than 100,000 are used in producing much more sugar without entailing any unemployment. The same has happened in other branches of agriculture, industry, construction and transportation, while increasing the quality and quantity of jobs in the various branches of production and services. Can any other country in Latin America say the same?

Today the whole world—including our enemies—acknowledges that our public health and education are impressive achievements, never before attained by any other country of the so-called Third World, or even by several of the countries listed as industrialized. Our enemies, nevertheless, dare to question the success of our economic development. The truth is that our economy, in spite of the brutal Yankee economic blockade, has grown at an annual rate of approximately 4.7 percent—higher or lower in given years—since the triumph of the Revolution, one of the highest growth rates in Latin America for this period. Otherwise, how could we afford an educational system that costs more than 1,500 million pesos per year and a health system whose cost surpasses 500 million pesos, which is dozens of times more than what was spent in these areas during capitalism? How could we have become a country without unemployment, with an advanced social security system that benefits all workers without exception? How could we be—after Argentina, with its huge expanses of agricultural land and herds of cattle—the second best-fed country in Latin America, with almost 3,000 calories and almost 80 grams of protein per capita a day, as was recently acknowledged by an institution that is an enemy and a detractor of the Cuban Revolution? How could we hold an outstanding place in sports, culture and scientific research? How could we be a country without destitute children, without beggars, without prostitution, gambling or drugs? Are not many of these activities the bleak livelihood for countless individuals, not only in underdeveloped countries, but in almost all the industrialized capitalist countries? How could we take on and technically train more than 20,000 young people from Asia, Africa and Latin America and cooperate with more than 30 Third World countries?

This is all possible, of course, not only because our economy has grown, but also because our trade with the socialist countries, which today accounts for more than 80 percent of Cuba's foreign trade, is not subjected to the growing unequal and arbitrary prices the Third World faces in its economic relations with the developed capitalist countries; it is possible because our wealth is better distributed, because the fruits of our economy do not go into the hands of the monopolies or the pockets of the rulers; because there is no capital drain, and because we have a hard-working, enthusiastic, generous people, full of solidarity, who are equal to any task, any mission, at home and abroad. That is, we have a priceless treasure, unknown in capitalist societies: a new man with new values and a new conception of life, for whom there is no difficult or impossible task. Speaking of our internationalist spirit, we recently said to some foreign journalists that when teachers were requested for Nicaragua, almost 30,000 volunteered; when some months later, some Cuban teachers were murdered in Nicaragua, 100,000 volunteered. The United States has its Peace Corps; the churches have their missionaries; Cuba alone has more citizens ready to fulfill these tasks voluntarily anywhere in the world than the United States and all the churches put together. This spirit is reflected in our work, both at home and abroad.

Further proof of the soundness of our development may be added. In spite of the huge resources we are forced to invest in the defense of our country, the budgets for education, health, culture, sports, science and technology are growing every year; every year we invest more resources in the maintenance and construction of housing; every year we invest a greater amount in industry, agriculture and in the economic infrastructure. This year, 1984, the budget for science and technology will grow by 15.6 percent; public health by 14.3 percent; housing and community services by 14.1 percent; sports by 10.8 percent; culture and art by 9.1 percent; education by 5.1 percent; and social security and welfare by 4.2 percent. In spite of this, our budget income and outlays will be balanced. In the rest of the countries of this hemisphere, one only hears news of increased unemployment and decreased budgets for education, health and other social expenditures.

In the midst of a world economic crisis, while the Latin American economy as a whole decreased by 1 percent in 1982 and by 3.3 percent in 1983, the Cuban economy grew by 2.5 percent in 1982 and 5 percent in 1983. A similar growth to that of the past year is forecast for 1984.

I recently explained how the Revolution had begun its successful health program with only 3,000 doctors, that now we had almost 20,000, and that in the next 16 years, 50,000 more would graduate. In just 15 or 20 years, the selection, previous training and work of these doctors, their adequate use and our health system will make Cuba rank first in the world in this field.

We have said that production and defense are our main slogans today. They are not in the least contradictory; they complement each other. The greater the fighting spirit of a people, the more they are aware and ready to fight for their homeland, all the more will they work, all the more will they devote themselves to the work of the Revolution and the development of their country; the more production and services are developed, the more we struggle for the well-being, future and happiness of our countrymen, the better we care for children in the schools and the sick in the polyclinics and hospitals, the better will be our attention in all other services in the country; the more brilliant our writers, artists and scientists, more outstanding our athletes, more efficient and vigorous our Party and our State, all the more determinedly and heroically will our people defend our homeland and our Revolution. □

The Nicaraguan Revolution

Overthrowing a brutal dictatorship, the Nicaraguan revolution entered into power on July 19, 1979, with the gun of victory in hand; it exited on February 25, 1990, through the ballot box. Although the revolution terminated almost half a century of tyrannical rule of the Somoza dynasty—father and two sons— and opened access for every Nicaraguan to medical care, education, and land, the revolutionary party, the Sandinista Front for National Liberation (FSLN), lost the 1990 national elections to a heterogeneous political coalition, the National Opposition Union (UNO). The tally astonished the world, possibly the Nicaraguans as well. Nicaragua provides a unique Latin American study of the electoral demise of revolution. Lyford Edwards probably would classify events as the triumph of the combined forces of counterrevolution and foreign intervention to truncate the revolution.

Sandino to Sandinistas: Historical Revolutionary Continuity

The FSLN originated in 1961, drawing its inspiration from the thoughts and struggle of Augusto César Sandino (1893–1934), who waged a protracted guerrilla war, 1927–1933, against an even longer U.S. occupation of Nicaragua, 1909– 1933. Sandino never enumerated his economic, political, and social programs in one document, but they clearly emerge from the totality of his writings. He sought a popular, independent government, the revision of all treaties that limited Nicaragua's sovereignty, and the recovery of the nation's riches and resources for the benefit of all Nicaraguans. To raise the quality of life of the people, he wanted them to have access to the nation's riches and resources, most importantly the land itself, then owned by the few to the impoverishment of the many. Although the land should belong to the state, it should be available to anyone willing and able to work it. Sandino reasoned: "I believe the state owns the land. . . . I favor a system of cooperatives to work the land." Pointing to foreign capital and businessmen as a barrier to Nicaragua's prosperity, he encouraged the growth of national industry and commerce. In 1933, he called upon all the nations of the hemisphere to sign a treaty "to outlaw intervention in the internal affairs and to respect the sovereignty and independence of each nation." Brief as always, Sandino summarized his life and some of his ideals in the following document. His example and ideals inspired the young founders of the FSLN. Their goals coincided with Sandino's: political independence, economic development, and national dignity.

I WAS BORN at four in the morning on May 18, 1895, in the town of La Victoria in the Department of Masaya, Nicaragua. Two young people, both 18 years old, were my parents. I attended a primary school built under the government of General José Santos Zelaya, the constitutional president during that period.

At 12 years of age, I left my parents and set out in the world. I visited some of the principal cities of Central and North America, as well as some of the major industrial centers. Much of that time I spent in Mexico.

I keep a large number of recommendations from different companies for which I have worked testifying to my skills. I was a mechanic, a job at which I excelled.

I have always been inclined to read whatever in my judgment is moral and instructive. According to my latest observations and way of thinking, one of the things that I have learned most clearly is that men, endowed by God with fertile minds but for some reason often forgetting that they are mere mortals, frequently take pride in participating in the unpardonable crime of trafficking in justice and in human lives, behaving as though they were a pack of animals. Alas, about 95 percent of my fellow citizens have fallen to that level of debasement.

I have also come to understand that men without scruples and without regard for Humanity or God are not above evoking worthy ideals just to achieve their own unworthy goals. In short, from the knowledge I have acquired, I conclude that man can no longer live with dignity if he separates himself from reason and honor.

Because of that belief and also because I can see that the United States of America, with no other right than that derived from brute force, intends to deprive us of our Fatherland and our Liberty, I denounce the unjustifiable threat it poses to our land and sovereignty, and assume before History responsibility for my acts. To remain inactive or indifferent like the majority of my fellow citizens would be to join ranks with those who betray the nation. Thus, my action is justified since my ideas spring from the basic concepts of accepted international behavior.

I respect Justice. I am willing to sacrifice myself for it. Material desires hold no sway over me. The treasures I seek to accumulate are spiritual.□

The Historic Program of the FSLN

In 1969, the Sandinista revolutionaries issued their program. It detailed their vision of a new Nicaragua and guided their governance after July 19, 1979.

Although this Historic Program arises from situations within Nicaragua, many of its transcendental goals speak to broader desires and needs of many Latin Americans. It is, in short, the program of an underdeveloped and dependent society in search of change.

Source: "In His Own Words: Sandino's Autobiography," *Nicaraguan Perspectives,* No. 16 (Winter 1988/89), p. 4.

THE SANDINISTA NATIONAL LIBERATION FRONT (FSLN) arose out of the Nicaraguan people's need to have a "vanguard organization" capable of taking political power through direct struggle against its enemies and establishing a social system that wipes out the exploitation and poverty that our people have been subjected to in past history.

The FSLN is a politico-military organization, whose strategic objective is to take political power by destroying the military and bureaucratic apparatus of the dictatorship and to establish a revolutionary government based on the worker-peasant alliance and the convergence of all the patriotic anti-imperialist and anti-oligarchic forces in the country.

The people of Nicaragua suffer under subjugation to a reactionary and fascist clique imposed by Yankee imperialism in 1932, the year Anastasio Somoza Garcia was named commander in chief of the so-called National Guard (GN).

The Somozaist clique has reduced Nicaragua to the status of a neocolony exploited by the Yankee monopolies and the country's oligarchic groups.

The present regime is politically unpopular and juridically illegal. The recognition and aid it gets from the North Americans is irrefutable proof of foreign interference in the affairs of Nicaragua.

The FSLN has seriously and with great responsibility analyzed the national reality and has resolved to confront the dictatorship with arms in hand. We have concluded that the triumph of the Sandinista people's revolution and the overthrow of the regime that is an enemy of the people will take place through the development of a hard-fought and prolonged people's war.

Whatever maneuvers and resources Yankee imperialism deploys, the Somozaist dictatorship is condemned to total failure in the face of the rapid advance and development of the people's forces, headed by the Sandinista National Liberation Front.

Given this historic conjuncture the FSLN has worked out this political program with an eye to strengthening and developing our organization, inspiring and stimulating the people of Nicaragua to march forward with the resolve to fight until the dictatorship is overthrown and to resist the intervention of Yankee imperialism, in order to forge a free, prosperous, and revolutionary homeland.

I. A Revolutionary Government

The Sandinista people's revolution will establish a revolutionary government that will eliminate the reactionary structure that arose from rigged elections and military coups, and the people's power will create a Nicaragua that is free of exploitation, oppression, backwardness; a free, progressive, and independent country.

The revolutionary government will apply the following measures of a political character:

A. It will endow revolutionary power with a structure that allows the full participation of the entire people, on the national level as well as the local level (departmental, municipal, neighborhood).

B. It will guarantee that all citizens can fully exercise all individual freedoms and it will respect human rights.
C. It will guarantee the free exchange of ideas, which above all leads to vigorously broadening the people's rights and national rights.
D. It will guarantee freedom for the worker-union movement to organize in the city and countryside; and freedom to organize peasant, youth, student, women's, cultural, sporting, and similar groups.
E. It will guarantee the right of emigrant and exiled Nicaraguans to return to their native soil.
F. It will guarantee the right to asylum for citizens of other countries who are persecuted for participation in the revolutionary struggle.
G. It will severely punish the gangsters who are guilty of persecuting, informing on, abusing, torturing, or murdering revolutionaries and the people.
H. Those individuals who occupy high political posts as a result of rigged elections and military coups will be stripped of their political rights.

The revolutionary government will apply the following measures of an economic character:

A. It will expropriate the landed estates, factories, companies, buildings, means of transportation, and other wealth usurped by the Somoza family and accumulated through the misappropriation and plunder of the nation's wealth.
B. It will expropriate the landed estates, factories, companies, means of transportation, and other wealth usurped by the politicians and military officers, and all other accomplices, who have taken advantage of the present regime's administrative corruption.
C. It will nationalize the wealth of all the foreign companies that exploit the mineral, forest, maritime, and other kinds of resources.
D. It will establish workers' control over the administrative management of the factories and other wealth that are expropriated and nationalized.
E. It will centralize the mass transit service.
F. It will nationalize the banking system, which will be placed at the exclusive service of the country's economic development.
G. It will establish an independent currency.
H. It will refuse to honor the loans imposed on the country by the Yankee monopolies or those of any other power.
I. It will establish commercial relations with all countries, whatever their system, to benefit the country's economic development.
J. It will establish a suitable taxation policy, which will be applied with strict justice.
K. It will prohibit usury. This prohibition will apply to Nicaraguan nationals as well as foreigners.
L. It will protect the small and medium-size owners (producers, merchants) while restricting the excesses that lead to the exploitation of the workers.
M. It will establish state control over foreign trade, with an eye to diversifying it and making it independent.
N. It will rigorously restrict the importation of luxury items.
O. It will plan the national economy, putting an end to the anarchy characteristic of the capitalist system of production. An important part of this planning will focus on the industrialization and electrification of the country.

II. The Agrarian Revolution

The Sandinista people's revolution will work out an agrarian policy that achieves an authentic agrarian reform; a reform that will, in the immediate term, carry

out massive distribution of the land, eliminating the land grabs by the large landlords in favor of the workers (small producers) who labor on the land.

A. It will expropriate and eliminate the capitalist and feudal estates.
B. It will turn over the land to the peasants, free of charge, in accordance with the
    principle that the land should belong to those who work it.
C. It will carry out a development plan for livestock raising aimed at diversifying and
    increasing the productivity of that sector.
D. It will guarantee the peasants the following rights:
    1. Timely and adequate agricultural credit.
    2. Marketability (a guaranteed market for their production).
    3. Technical assistance.
E. It will protect the patriotic landowners who collaborate with the guerrilla struggle,
    by paying them for their landholdings that exceed the limit established by the revolu-
    tionary government.
F. It will stimulate and encourage the peasants to organize themselves in cooperatives,
    so they can take their destiny into their own hands and directly participate in the
    development of the country.
G. It will abolish the debts the peasantry incurred to the landlord and any type of
    usurer.
H. It will eliminate the forced idleness that exists for most of the year in the country-
    side, and it will be attentive to creating sources of jobs for the peasant population.

III. Revolution in Culture and Education

The Sandinista people's revolution will establish the bases for the development
of the national culture, the people's education, and university reform.

A. It will push forward a massive campaign to immediately wipe out "illiteracy."
B. It will develop the national culture and will root out the neocolonial penetration in
    our culture.
C. It will rescue the progressive intellectuals, and their works that have arisen through-
    out our history, from the neglect in which they have been maintained by the anti-
    people's regimes.
D. It will give attention to the development and progress of education at the various
    levels (primary, intermediate, technical, university, etc.), and education will be free
    at all levels and obligatory at some.
E. It will grant scholarships at various levels of education to students who have limited
    economic resources. The scholarships will include housing, food, clothing, books,
    and transportation.
F. It will train more and better teachers who have the scientific knowledge that the
    present era requires, to satisfy the needs of our entire student population.
G. It will nationalize the centers of private education that have been immorally turned
    into industries by merchants who hypocritically invoke religious principles.
H. It will adapt the teaching programs to the needs of the country; it will apply teaching
    methods to the scientific and research needs of the country.
I. It will carry out a university reform that will include, among other things, the fol-
    lowing measures:
    1. It will rescue the university from the domination of the exploiting classes, so it
        can serve the real creators and shapers of our culture: the people. University

instruction must be oriented around man, around the people. The university must stop being a breeding ground for bureaucratic egotists.

2. Eliminate the discrimination in access to university classes suffered by youth from the working class and peasantry.
3. Increase the state budget for the university so there are the economic resources to solve the various problems confronting it.
4. Majority student representation on the boards of departments, keeping in mind that the student body is the main segment of the university population.
5. Eliminate the neo-colonial penetration of the university, especially the penetration by the North American monopolies through the charity donations of the pseudophilanthropic foundations.
6. Promotion of free, experimental, scientific investigation that must contribute to dealing with national and universal questions.
7. Strengthen the unity of the students, faculty, and investigators with the whole people, by perpetuating the selfless example of the students and intellectuals who have offered their lives for the sake of the patriotic ideal.

IV. Labor Legislation and Social Security

The Sandinista people's revolution will eliminate the injustice of the living and working conditions suffered by the working class under the brutal exploitation, and will institute labor legislation and social assistance.

A. It will enact a labor code that will regulate, among other things, the following rights:
    1. It will adopt the principle that "those who don't work don't eat," of course making exceptions for those who are unable to participate in the process of production due to age (children, old people), medical condition, or other reasons beyond their control.
    2. Strict enforcement of the eight-hour work day.
    3. The income of the workers (wages and other benefits) must be sufficient to satisfy their daily needs.
    4. Respect for the dignity of the worker, prohibiting and punishing unjust treatment of workers in the course of their labor.
    5. Abolition of unjustified firings.
    6. Obligation to pay wages in the period required by law.
    7. Right of all workers to periodic vacations.
B. It will eliminate the scourge of unemployment.
C. It will extend the scope of the social security system to all the workers and public employees in the country. The scope will include coverage for illness, physical incapacity, and retirement.
D. It will provide free medical assistance to the entire population. It will set up clinics and hospitals throughout the national territory.
E. It will undertake massive campaigns to eradicate endemic illnesses and prevent epidemics.
F. It will carry out urban reform, which will provide each family with adequate shelter. It will put an end to profiteering speculation in urban land (subdivisions, urban construction, rental housing) that exploits the need that working families in the cities have for an adequate roof over their heads in order to live.
G. It will initiate and expand the construction of adequate housing for the peasant population.
H. It will reduce the charges for water, light, sewers, urban beautification; it will apply programs to extend all these services to the entire urban and rural population.

I . It will encourage participation in sports of all types and categories.

J . It will eliminate the humiliation of begging by putting the above mentioned practices into practice.

V. Administrative Honesty

The Sandinista people's revolution will root out administrative governmental corruption, and will establish strict administrative honesty.

A. It will abolish the criminal vice industry (prostitution, gambling, drug use, etc.), which the privileged sector of the National Guard and the foreign parasites exploit.

B . It will establish strict control over the collection of taxes to prevent government functionaries from profiting, putting an end to the normal practice of the present regime's official agencies.

C. It will end the arbitrary actions of the members of the GN, who plunder the population through the subterfuge of local taxes.

D. It will put an end to the situation wherein military commanders appropriate the budget that is supposed to go to take care of common prisoners, and it will establish centers designed to rehabilitate these wrongdoers.

E . It will abolish the smuggling that is practiced on a large scale by the gang of politicians, officers, and foreigners who are the regime's accomplices.

F . It will severely punish persons who engage in crimes against administrative honesty (embezzlement, smuggling, trafficking in vices, etc.), using greatest severity when it involves elements active in the revolutionary movement.

VI. Reincorporation of the Atlantic Coast

The Sandinista people's revolution will put into practice a special plan for the Atlantic Coast, which has been abandoned to total neglect, in order to incorporate this area into the nation's life.

A. It will end the unjust exploitation the Atlantic Coast has suffered throughout history by the foreign monopolies, especially Yankee imperialism.

B . It will prepare suitable lands in the zone for the development of agriculture and ranching.

C. It will establish conditions that encourage the development of the fishing and forest industries.

D. It will encourage the flourishing of this region's local cultural values, which flow from the specific aspects of its historic tradition.

E . It will wipe out the odious discrimination to which the indigenous Miskitos, Sumos, Ramas, and Blacks of this region are subjected.

VII. Emancipation of Women

The Sandinista people's revolution will abolish the odious discrimination that women have been subjected to compared to men; it will establish economic, political, and cultural equality between woman and man.

A. It will pay special attention to the mother and child.

B . It will eliminate prostitution and other social vices, through which the dignity of women will be raised.

C. It will put an end to the system of servitude that women suffer, which is reflected in the tragedy of the abandoned working mother.
D. It will establish for children born out of wedlock the right to equal protection by the revolutionary institutions.
E. It will establish day-care centers for the care and attention of the children of working women.
F. It will establish a two-month maternity leave before and after birth for women who work.
G. It will raise women's political, cultural, and vocational levels through their participation in the revolutionary process.

VIII. Respect for Religious Beliefs

The Sandinista people's revolution will guarantee the population of believers the freedom to profess any religion.

A. It will respect the right of citizens to profess and practice any religious belief.
B. It will support the work of priests and other religious figures who defend the working people.

IX. Independent Foreign Policy

The Sandinista people's revolution will eliminate the foreign policy of submission to Yankee imperialism, and will establish a patriotic foreign policy of absolute national independence and one that is for authentic universal peace.

A. It will put an end to the Yankee interference in the internal problems of Nicaragua and will practice a policy of mutual respect with other countries and fraternal collaboration between peoples.
B. It will expel the Yankee military mission, the so-called Peace Corps (spies in the guise of technicians), and military and similar political elements who constitute a bare-faced intervention in the country.
C. It will accept economic and technical aid from any country, but always and only when this does not involve political compromises.
D. Together with other peoples of the world it will promote a campaign in favor of authentic universal peace.
E. It will abrogate all treaties, signed with any foreign power, that damage national sovereignty.

X. Central American People's Unity

The Sandinista people's revolution is for the true union of the Central American peoples in a single country.

A. It will support authentic unity with the fraternal peoples of Central America. This unity will lead the way to coordinating the efforts to achieve national liberation and establish a new system without imperialist domination or national betrayal.
B. It will eliminate the so-called integration, whose aim is to increase Central America's submission to the North American monopolies and the local reactionary forces.

XI. Solidarity among Peoples

The Sandinista people's revolution will put an end to the use of the national territory as a base for Yankee aggression against other fraternal peoples and will put into practice militant solidarity with fraternal peoples fighting for their liberation.

A. It will actively support the struggle of the peoples of Asia, Africa, and Latin America against the new and old colonialism and against the common enemy: Yankee imperialism.
B. It will support the struggle of the Black people and all the people of the United States for an authentic democracy and equal rights.
C. It will support the struggle of all peoples against the establishment of Yankee military bases in foreign countries.

XII. People's Patriotic Army

The Sandinista people's revolution will abolish the armed force called the National Guard, which is an enemy of the people, and will create a patriotic, revolutionary, and people's army.

A. It will abolish the National Guard, a force that is an enemy of the people, created by the North American occupation forces in 1927 to pursue, torture, and murder the Sandinista patriots.
B. In the new people's army, professional soldiers who are members of the old army will be able to play a role providing they have observed the following conduct:
   1. They have supported the guerrilla struggle.
   2. They have not participated in murder, plunder, torture, and persecution of the people and the revolutionary activists.
   3. They have rebelled against the despotic and dynastic regime of the Somozas.
C. It will strengthen the new people's army, raising its fighting ability and its tactical and technical level.
D. It will inculcate in the consciousness of the members of the people's army the principle of basing themselves on their own forces in the fulfillment of their duties and the development of all their creative activity.
E. It will deepen the revolutionary ideals of the members of the people's army with an eye toward strengthening their patriotic spirit and their firm conviction to fight until victory is achieved, overcoming obstacles and correcting errors.
F. It will forge a conscious discipline in the ranks of the people's army and will encourage the close ties that must exist between the combatants and the people.
G. It will establish obligatory military service and will arm the students, workers, and farmers, who—organized in people's militias—will defend the rights won against the inevitable attack by the reactionary forces of the country and Yankee imperialism.

XIII. Veneration of Our Martyrs

The Sandinista people's revolution will maintain eternal gratitude to and veneration of our homeland's martyrs and will continue the shining example of heroism and selflessness they have bequeathed to us.

A. It will educate the new generations in eternal gratitude and veneration toward those who have fallen in the struggle to make Nicaragua a free homeland.
B. It will establish a secondary school to educate the children of our people's martyrs.
C. It will inculcate in the entire people the imperishable example of our martyrs, defending the revolutionary ideal: Ever onward to victory! □

The Minister of Agriculture Discusses Agrarian Reform

Falling heir to the lands of the Somozas and their closest associates in 1979, the revolutionary government controlled as much as 20 percent of Nicaragua's richest land. For that reason, it did not get around to promulgating an agrarian reform until 1981. To nationalize unused land, to put it into the hands of people who wanted to cultivate it, and to exploit it for food and exports constituted the goals of that law. Only later, in 1986, did the revolution expand the reform to permit the expropriation of acreage in production in those areas where rural workers demanded land from the government.

Throughout the revolutionary period, Jaime Wheelock Román served as Minister of Agriculture. In this 1983 document he discusses some of the characteristics of agrarian reform in Nicaragua.

AFTER PRACTICALLY four years of agrarian reform we can say, in general terms, that we have completed a quite acceptable process of transformation of the property structure we inherited from Somozaism. At the same time, the drastic revolutionary measures that we have taken have not resulted in a decline in agricultural production. To the contrary, year after year there has been an increase in the recovery and growth of the agricultural sector.

In my opinion, it's not always so easy to combine two such sets of circumstances. It is the result of applying the fundamental political principles of our revolutionary program to agrarian reform and of a program of transformations that has taken into account the socioeconomic conditions that characterize Nicaragua. Nicaragua's agrarian reform is, for that reason, peculiar to it.

I will explain, first, the main political factors.

We worked out a program based on pluralism and the mixed economy, but with a content that is profoundly popular, revolutionary, and anti-imperialist. That is the framework from which all our practical steps in agrarian reform flow. Agrarian reform, therefore, is a means, an instrument for attaining these objectives, and not an end in and of itself. To understand this, it is important to see how its different phases developed.

There was a first phase that I would call anti-Somozaist, in which we recovered all the land that Somozaism had accumulated through robbery, extortion, eviction, etc. Our first agrarian reform law was in fact a decree—the now-famous Decree No. 3 of the Junta of the Government of National Reconstruction—that confiscated the Somozaists. It was complemented by Decree No. 38, which extended the measure to Somoza's associates.

That gave us about a million hectares, nearly 20 percent of the land owned in the country. These properties had to be organized in the form of state enterprises because the great majority of farms were in reality agro-industrial plantations. They included sugar refineries, coffee plantations, and modern rice planta-

Source: An Interview by Marta Harnecker in Institute for the Study of Militarism and Economic Crisis, *Jaime Wheelock Román on the Nicaraguan Revolution* (San Francisco: ISMEC, 1985), pp. 42–46.

tions that were not susceptible either to being distributed among small producers or ceded to cooperatives.

In this first phase there arose what we call the People's Property Sector, which had in particular the task of initiating a process of incorporating agricultural workers into the administration of the enterprises. Formation of this sector gave the state an important control over the strategic section of the economy.

We quickly realized that what we had recovered from Somozaism, given its technological nature and its territorial magnitude, left us rather limited in terms of resolving the problem of peasants without land. To be sure we issued laws forcing landlords to rent out land, and at lower prices—a measure that benefited thousands of peasants, squatters, and small renters. We also initiated a credit policy that was so extensive that, in comparison with the last year of Somozaism, it multiplied by ten the amount of agricultural loans given to peasants.

These measures, however, were insufficient, and we began to work on a more integrated agrarian reform law. The aim of this law, which was to mark the second phase, was to take idle or insufficiently exploited land out of the hands of the big landowners and turn it over to landless peasants, so as to form small units of property, in some cases individually owned but fundamentally cooperative. I would call this the *antilatifundist* phase. In applying this law we expropriated some 600,000 hectares for the benefit of both the peasantry and the state enterprises.

The overall result of these two phases was a very important change in the structure of agricultural property in Nicaragua. Before the triumph of the revolution, 2,000 landowners owned 50 percent of the land while 120,000 peasants owned barely 3 percent of national territory.

Because we acted fundamentally against the Somozaists and owners of idle land, those 2,000 have been drastically reduced, to the point that today they control no more than 13 percent of the land. The state controls 23 percent, and the cooperatives and small producers another 20 percent. We have succeeded in establishing a vast cooperative movement, made up of more than 2,500 associative groups, including nearly 70,000 peasants.

There is an extremely broad layer of medium-sized producers—made up in its majority of humble peasants, but including some who are relatively well off—that owns more than 30 percent of the land. There are also properties of 100, 200, and 300 hectares that belong to big private landowners. They are modern plantations, generally are irrigated, and have certain characteristics of landed property. But because of their efficiency and their size, they have not been brought under the agrarian reform. Finally, the state owns the national land—that is, land that has not been claimed or parceled up—which amounts to half the total area of the country.

We are working today on the third phase, oriented toward consolidation and rationalization of what has already been accomplished. This phase gives particular emphasis to cooperative development and to answering the demand for land on the part of peasant communities in various parts of the country.

I spoke first of the political principles because of the importance they have had in guiding—and in the last analysis, conditioning—our program of transformation. Our agrarian reform, while taking into account national unity and the mixed economy, has struck a blow at Somozaism and at ownership of idle land. But it has also left space for private producers if they are efficient and, of course, if they assume a role that is consistent with the revolution. At the same time poor and landless peasants have benefited from a series of policies aimed at helping them and providing them with incentives such as cheap credit, subsidized inputs, advantageous prices for corn and beans, grocery supply centers in the countryside, social and housing programs, rural electrification, health care, literacy instruction, road construction, etc.

To be sure, we have segregated what had to be segregated—the cancer that had to be cut out. We are working within a model of agricultural development in which the state, acting as the spearhead of production and the pacesetter of norms, is backed up by efficient private production, by the cooperatives, by the thousands of peasants, today with land, who are together increasing national production, both for domestic consumption and for export.

That doesn't mean the job is finished. We have much further to go, not only in regard to the process of transformation of agrarian structures, but also in establishing a new economic development that will have as its axis precisely this agricultural sector. It is certain that this last task is going to be very hard.

First, because the socioeconomic formation of Nicaragua is very uneven. There is a pole of modernization, formed by the extensively upgraded plantations. But this coexists alongside considerable holdovers from the aristocratic economy of colonial origin that functions under a pattern of land use that involves extensive idle terrain. This is especially true in the case of primitive cattle raising of the kind that dominates great expanses of land in the center of the country. Alongside these big cattle ranches there exists a minuscule, subsistence peasant economy that is in a certain sense an annex or tributary to the aristocratic *haciendas*. This peasant community is made up of settlers, squatters, and so forth.

Second, because Nicaragua is a poor country, with weakly developed forces of production and does not have its own technological base for carrying out a project of development based on mechanization and irrigation, which is what we would like to promote.

However, on the basis of international cooperation and the support of the socialist countries and of countries friendly to Nicaragua—such as Mexico, the Arab countries, the Netherlands, France, and Spain—we are carrying out projects that could be characterized as ambitious and whose completion will represent a qualitative leap for the country. In the agricultural sector we are carrying out more than 20 projects totalling some $1.2 billion. These include a sugar refinery, two African palm plantations, four projects for production of blond tobacco, a project to provide 20,000 manzanas of irrigated land for basic foodstuffs, two modern dairy projects that will provide 100 million liters of milk a year, big poultry complexes, rice fields, etc.

We are making all these investments in the midst of an international economic crisis. For us, this is not anything unusual. We have to rebuild what was destroyed and cover the basic necessities that were never covered under Somozaism. Moreover, we have to take into account the future needs of a population that is increasingly demanding. □

A Peasant Discusses Agrarian Reform

Thirty-one-year-old Gregorio Váez of Juigalpa reveals the satisfaction of the new peasant with the agrarian policies of the revolutionary government. His contrast of past with present experiences suggests the support the revolution garnered from the humble people of the countryside.

DURING THE DICTATORSHIP of Somoza we worked even though it was difficult to get land to work, not like now. To get land then first one had to make a labor commitment to the owner of the *hacienda*—the landlord. The landlords had a system. The landlord would let you live on the land, but you had to agree to do his work first; to clear and prepare the land and all of that. And when you finished all of his work then you could do your own. So you had to work quickly to have time to do some work for yourself.

In the planting, we worked up to the last minute. First we had to plant for the landlord, corn, *frijoles* [beans], etc., and then we could plant for ourselves. At times we would be late in our own plantings and the best time for planting would have passed. So often our small plots of land didn't yield much corn or beans because we had planted late. The landowner, however, had a large amount of land planted and therefore a large harvest. So the landlord would give me corn or beans to pay me for my work. That's the system that was used. He gave me corn and beans in exchange for my work—always. We were paid with a little rice and beans. We were always exploited by this system. The landlord would always make a profit, but we never received more even if he had a very good harvest.

But now it's not like that. We are in different times. We make our own decisions about what to plant and when to plant. It's a great change. We have the right to get land from the government. Now the campesinos have land that before could only belong to the rich and the military. Now the majority of campesinos of Nicaragua all have land. The government is giving people title to the land through Agrarian Reform to make cooperatives. It's been three years since the government gave us the right to work this land, and two years since we have had title to it through the Agrarian Reform. I believe that with work and struggle and new methods and equipment, we campesinos will move forward.

In the time of the dictatorship there was little. There was hardly anything one could earn with his work. It was enough to try and feed the family. There was nothing left over. Now we have help because the government guarantees the prices of basic necessities for the whole population—so that no matter what happens we will all have the necessities. Before, it was often impossible to even find basic necessities. Now there is a perfect distribution of these basics.

Source: Gregorio Váez, "Working the Land," in Philip Zwerling and Connie Martin (eds.), *Nicaragua: A New Kind of Revolution* (Westport, Conn.: Lawrence Hill, 1985), pp. 120–121. Copyright by Philip Zwerling and Connie Martin, 1985. Reprinted by permission of the publisher, Lawrence Hill Books (Brooklyn, New York).

Today all of the campesinos support the Revolution. We see the changes and we continued going forward with the struggle and in support of the Revolution. The aggression cannot change things here now because the entire people of Nicaragua would struggle to prevent a return to the past. This would become a country without people because all of us would struggle and die before we would return to the past. We would never give up our land. This is now *our* land. We would go to jail or fight in the mountains. We would never think of returning to the way things were in the past.□

Elections Derailed the Revolution: What Happened?

Clearly the effects of an exhausting decade of war against the U.S.-sponsored counterrevolutionaries and the aid given and promised by Washington to the National Opposition Union offer some explanation for the electoral defeat of the FSLN. Still, as the Argentine social scientist Carlos M. Vilas points out, causation is far more complex than that. After 1980, Vilas held a variety of posts in the revolutionary government and thus speaks as an insider.

Antonio was with me in the militia back in 1981 and 1982, when we used those ancient VZ rifles with their devilish bolts. He had taken part in the insurrection in Managua's Monseñor Lezcano barrio and was a point man for the Sandinista Defense Committees. He was one of the "data" I relied on when I began studying the insurrection for my book *The Sandinista Revolution*. After I moved out of the barrio I did not see him as often, but two or three times a year I would visit him at his house, next to his carpentry shop where he had organized his books into a small library for the students of the neighborhood.

Antonio was a good example of the Sandinista rank and file; combative, quick to protest, well-liked by everyone in the barrio, the first to volunteer for any activity. He was in his early fifties back then, with more political experience than most. That helped him make balanced judgments and keep sectarianism at bay. I liked to talk to him, or to hear him talk, to hear his version of the progress of the revolution in the micro-world of the barrio. He would give his opinion, but his was also the opinion of the many Antonios of Managua. He also liked my visits and would challenge my points of view; he would usually end up telling me I was too intellectual.

I hadn't seen him for a couple of years when we ran into each other in February, two weeks before the elections. He looked older—I did too—and thinner. We greeted each other with affection, but the old enthusiasm was gone. "What's this, *hermano*? You're still driving the same car!" he said. I didn't know whether he was scolding or praising me. He added, "You're one of the few."

"That's right Antonio, and how are things going?"

Source: Carlos M. Vilas, "What Went Wrong." Reprinted from *NACLA Report on the Americas* Vol. 24, No. 1 (June 1990), pp. 10–15, 18. With the permission of North American Congress on Latin America.

"OK, *hermano,*" he answered laconically.

"What do you think about the elections? Who's going to win?"

"Well, you can't tell with these things."

"Yes, I know," I insisted, "but in the barrio, what do people think?"

"Who knows? You know you get all kinds. . . ."

"All right, there are all kinds, but who are you going to vote for?"

"Ah, *hermano,* the vote is secret!"

I froze. "Antonio, that's what people say who are going to vote for Violeta. But you and I, we've known each other for ten years. We've been through a lot together. Don't give me this. . . ."

"Yes, *hermano,*" he cut in, "but democracy is democracy, and the vote is secret."

Despite this and other omens, on Monday February 26, the morning after the elections, all Nicaragua was in shock. Nicaraguans, as well as proponents and detractors of the revolution throughout the hemisphere, are still trying to explain why over half the electorate chose to reject the Sandinistas and support an option ostensibly linked to Washington's policy of aggression. And everyone wonders where—between the ingenuous extremes that Sandinismo is an eternal universal power, and that the United States, the Contras and UNO are omnipotent—the future of the revolution lies.

Elections are extremely complex phenomena, because their outcome depends on a host of simultaneous micro-level, individual decisions. The knee-jerk reaction of the Left that points exclusively to external forces (the U.S. war and financing of the UNO campaign) is as incomplete an explanation as its counterpart on the Right (the people's repudiation of corrupt Sandinista leadership). There were elements of both and more.

The outcome of the elections was conditioned in its most fundamental aspects by a decade of counterrevolutionary war that left thousands dead, wounded and crippled, the economic and social infrastructure in ruins, hundreds of thousands of people displaced—drafted into military service, relocated to refugee camps, forced to flee to the cities to escape attack—and basic goods in desperately short supply. The people voted against that. This decade of harsh and insecure existence was not the creation of the Sandinistas, but the Sandinista government did administer it.

Both Daniel Ortega and Violeta Chamorro presented themselves as candidates of peace. Long before the campaign began, Doña Violeta staked out this turf by promising to end the war and immediately abolish the draft. Though on this point the most the FSLN could promise was to "study the issue," Ortega's U.S. and Nicaraguan handlers did all they could to wipe out anything that would remind voters of his guerrilla past, of the war, and eventually of the revolution itself. He doffed his spectacles and olive green uniform, switching to jeans and cowboy boots—a youthful, debonair image, known by all as the "Danny look." He took to demonstrating his Catholic devoutness by attending mass and referring to "the Lord" in his speeches. The Sandinista slogan was upbeat: *Todo será mejor* (Everything's Going to be Better); and their program claimed all the country's problems would be solved through foreign assistance once the elections were won and the Contras were demobilized. The party called its candidate *el gallo ennavajado* (the knife-bearing fighting cock) to portray him as a man of the people (cock fights are a popular sport) and a macho man, superior to his female opponent.

The Sandinista campaign sought to link UNO to the counterrevolution and to the National Guard of ex-dictator Anastasio Somoza. A number of the UNO candidates had in fact been Somoza functionaries, and at least two close advisers to Doña Violeta were indeed connected to the National Resistance: her son, Pedro Joaquín Chamorro Barrios, and her most prominent adviser, Alfredo César. Several candidates for municipal posts in some departments had recently been members or collaborators of the Contras.

But UNO made no attempt to hide the presence of former Somocistas in their ranks, nor did they try to paper over their status as Washington's favorite. Their leaders believed the former to be a matter of indifference to the population—and in some zones, on the contrary, it could be a positive factor—and that the latter was actually an asset. If, as the Sandinistas claimed, the U.S. government was responsible for the war, then, UNO reasoned, voting for Washington's choice afforded an infinitely greater possibility for ending it than continuing with a party and a ticket notoriously hostile to the United States. In case anyone doubted that this was the case, President Bush, his secretary of state and the Contra leaders bombarded the population with an unvarying litany of messages and declarations to the effect that as long as there are Sandinistas there will be war.

The government did not always help to dispel people's fear and insecurity. On Dec. 27, for example, following the U.S. invasion of Panama, the General Command of the Sandinista Popular Army issued a public directive to all its units and to "state and government institutions at all levels": "Upon initiation of a Yankee intervention, all units of the regular armed forces, reserves, Sandinista People's Militia, and organs of military counterintelligence, in close cooperation with organs of State Security, shall carry out neutralization plans of arrest and execution of all the most diehard traitorous elements who have been either overtly or covertly abetting the Yankee intervention."[1]

Since the Sandinista media had consistently identified UNO with the Somoza National Guard, the White House, and even with the interventionist troops in Panama, it is no surprise that the image of a bloodbath was on the minds of many.[2] UNO complained to the Supreme Electoral Council, but it took no action other than to ask the Ministry of Defense almost a week later for an "explanation of the scope and meaning" of the paragraph in question and to express concern that it "restricts the rights and guarantees set forth in our Constitution."[3]

The possibility that UNO could win the elections, it seems, was rejected a priori by the Sandinistas, since it implied that the people's sympathy lay with the foreign aggressor. What the FSLN viewed as a kind of treason to the fatherland was perhaps no more than a simple instinct of self-preservation: Parents did not want their sons sent to war, and the boys themselves did not want to go.

The economic panorama at the time of the February elections was the worst in Nicaragua's history, and of course it became the main topic of electoral debate. Over the last three-year period, gross domestic product declined 11.7%, a per capita drop of 21.5%; the trade balance showed a deficit of $1.2 billion and the balance of payments was a negative $2 billion; in 1989, foreign debt amounted to over $7.5 billion or $2,300 per capita.[4]

A drastic adjustment program, characterized by the U.N.'s Economic Commission on Latin America as "Draconian," brought hyperinflation down from over 33,000% in 1988 to somewhat less than 1700% in 1989, reduced the fiscal deficit from 25% of GDP in 1988 to just under 5% in 1989, and provided some stimulus to exports[5] The adverse effects included a severe slump in productivity, lack of liquidity, and further deterioration of social services. Nearly 35% of the population was unemployed or underemployed. The shrinkage of consumption, the rising debt burden on the peasantry, and the plummeting of wages—all normal effects of such strategies—followed on years of negative economic developments for the poor. Real wages fell from an index of 29.2 in February 1988 (1980 = 100) to 6.5 in June 1989 and to 1 by December. During 1988, milk consumption fell by 50%. Sugar consumption fell from 200,000 hundredweight per month in 1988 to 124,000 at the beginning of 1989. Tuberculosis and malaria spread widely, and during the first trimester of 1989 infant mortality due to diarrhea was double that of a year earlier.[6] According to estimates made by officials of the Ministry of Education, the illiteracy rate in Region III (Managua) was 30% among the adult population at the end of 1988. At the same time, young people who received scholarships to study abroad were returning after five or six years of college and graduate school to join the ranks of the unemployed.[7]

Nearly a decade of counterrevolutionary war and five years of U.S. trade embargo are certainly to blame for the extremely precarious state of the Nicaraguan economy. But so are the very socioeconomic transformations brought on by the revolution (which caused unavoidable dislocations) and not a few errors in economic policy—not so much in the overall macroeconomic context as in their impact at the microeconomic level, in the day-to-day life of the people.

Unending lines for food and fuel, the lack of basic supplies in hospitals and health centers, the collapse of the educational system, were all part of the daily horizon for an enormous number of people. In July 1989 one of my children cut himself on a rusty can while swimming in Lake Xiloá, and the public health center could not give him a tetanus shot because they had no cotton or alcohol! A few months earlier, the public elementary school my youngest child attends dropped geometry from the curriculum because practically none of the children (that is to say, their families) could buy a compass or a ruler.

War and crisis, in turn, brought about a slowdown of the process of revolutionary change and the reversal of some of the initial measures of the strongest popular impact. In order to keep the national political front united against the Contras and the United States, the Sandinistas offered broad economic concessions to large private farmers, while attempting to hold back worker and peasant demands. Policies favoring middle-income and wealthy people had been introduced years ago, but their impact sharpened after the middle of 1988. One recent and vivid example took place on April 20 of last year, at an assembly of businessmen, peasants and rural workers held by the Agrarian Reform Ministry to promote a policy of *concertación* ("working together"). There the cotton magnates were awarded a subsidy of one million córdobas per manzana of land (1.75 acres)—something they had not actually requested—while the workers' demand for a wage that could cover a minimum supply of eight basic foodstuffs was rejected. At the time a million córdobas amounted to $250.

As the economic crisis worsened, subsidies to middle-class and wealthy entrepreneurs were increasingly financed by cutting back the consumption, income, and living conditions of the revolution's natural base of support, the workers and peasants. Physical rationing of basic commodities, which guaranteed access for everybody, was eliminated in favor of market rationing by making prices affordable only to the richest and plunging peasants into debt.

Furthermore, economic policy was couched in rhetoric that rubbed salt in the wounds of those who got the short end of the stick. When construction and automotive workers went on strike for higher wages during the first half of 1988, the government's answer was to accuse them of being at the service of the United States and to set the police on them. When teachers and health workers called for higher pay, President Ortega lectured them on their moral obligations to the people.[8] A year later, when certain members of the education sector went on strike for the same reason, the usual accusation of being pawns of the United States was leveled at them. When production cooperatives—which represent 50% of industrial employment and 21% of production—protested exorbitant interest rates, the Ministry of Finance responded that unless they adjusted to the new policy, many of the cooperatives would "irremediably disappear."[9]

In other words, the Sandinistas' program of structural adjustment was no different from anyone else's: It favored the rich and hurt the poor. And it gave official confirmation that there was no legitimate room in the revolutionary economy for a good part of Sandinismo's social underpinnings. To make matters worse, the rich accepted these considerable concessions while always demanding more before they would abandon their anti-Sandinista stance. There was no "Managuazo" comparable to the "Caracazo" riots last year in Venezuela, but there was a decline in social participation and, finally, a "domingazo" on Sunday, February 25.

The belief that an adjustment program could meet with popular acquiescence turned out to be a technocratic fantasy that cost the revolution dearly. Some of the opinion polls taken at the end of 1989 reflected a marked drop in participation in government-sponsored community development programs, which are run by the Sandinista mass organizations. A poll taken in Managua in October, for example, showed that two-thirds did not participate in activities such as environmental hygiene, vaccinations, or community gardens.[10] This may have resulted from government policies that used the mass organizations to control popular activity and demands whenever these threatened to go outside state channels. Increasingly, these once-autonomous pressure groups came to act as part of the state apparatus, as mechanisms of control subordinate to the FSLN. The demobilization of the mass organizations and the gradual drop-off in the level of social participation were noted at the time by Sandinistas and observers, and pointed to as indicators of the weakness of the revolutionary process. However, simply mentioning this type of problem more often than not evoked aggressive attacks from those, inside the FSLN and out, who preferred to see the world through rose-colored glasses, and interpreted any critical stance as something close to treason.

During the campaign, the FSLN candidates wooed the vote of the business community. They floated the possibility of rescinding land expropriations under the agrarian reform, and offered renewed guarantees to private property and foreign investment.[11] Any references to the nationalizations carried out during the initial phase of the revolution disappeared from the Sandinista media, even from calendars of anniversaries published in the newspapers. For example, in December the FSLN's official organ *Barricada* referred to the commemoration of the nationalization of foreign trade, as the "tenth anniversary of the nationalization of certain exportable products."[12]

Under these conditions, at the very moment when the Sandinistas' turn to the Right was most evident, references by the government to its socialist orientation, even democratic socialist, were semantic curiosities that seemed to move very few. These proclamations did not evoke reactions from the politicians of the Right, nor the agencies of the U.S. government. Sandinista policies spoke louder than their words. However, the official line did have a significant impact on certain groups within the progressive Church, who took the official rhetoric at face value, assuming that in fact the Sandinista experience was a socialist one.

The UNO campaign held the Sandinista government responsible for the economic disaster because of its "communist" leanings, administrative corruption, and what they considered excessive military expenditures. Their own economic proposals were relatively moderate and generally vague—except for the ravings of certain advisers—particularly in reference to the agrarian reform and properties confiscated or expropriated by the Sandinistas. They promoted above all the figure of their presidential candidate, painting her with maternal and religious overtones. Photographs of Cardinal Miguel Obando y Bravo blessing Doña Violeta were published profusely in *La Prensa,* leaving no doubt as to the preferences of the Catholic hierarchy. If warm relations with the White House showed UNO to be on the side of the mighty, Cardinal Obando's open sympathy for Doña Violeta lent a spiritual legitimacy to the opposition which, for many Nicaraguans, was much more convincing than the support shown by base communities or liberation theologians for the Sandinistas.

The choice of candidates must also have played a part in the results. Despite all his efforts, cool shirts, and groovy campaign style, Daniel Ortega was never able to shake off his *comandante* image. UNO, on the other hand, presented a candidate who was a housewife, a mother, the widow of an eminent figure. She had no noteworthy political experience nor sought to make it appear as though she did. Her style appealed to and drew on all facets of Nicaraguan collective identity, and triggered, perhaps unconsciously, the deepest mother-associations of a macho society. What better symbol for a peace proposal? Where the FSLN saw limitations and absurdity, it is possible that a large segment of the population saw merit and virtue.

The FSLN's personal attacks on Doña Violeta may have only reinforced this feeling. The Sandinista media, including the daily *Barricada,* edited by her son Carlos Fernando, attempted to divest Doña Violeta Barrios de Chamorro of her married name whenever she was mentioned (an implicit recognition of the reverence many Nicaraguans have for her dead husband). Carlos Fernando Chamorro published open letters written by his sister Claudia, an official of the Sandinista government, in which she criticized her mother's association with the Contras and former officers of the National Guard, like Enrique Bermúdez, reminding her that they were the ones involved in Pedro Joaquín Chamorro's assassination.[13] *El Nuevo Diario,* published by her brother-in-law, Xavier Chamorro, ran a series of denigrating cartoons in which Doña Violeta appeared dressed in a long priest-like gown with the initials "GN" (for the National Guard), laden with grenades and ammunition belts, and wearing an ugly, evil expression. This smear campaign must have provoked reactions of solidarity with Doña Violeta among people who saw this as a typical case of a mother being mistreated by her children.

At the beginning of September 1989, in her first speech—which the right-wing Costa Rican daily *La Nación* termed "very modest"—Doña Violeta answered the campaign being waged by *Barricada* and *El Nuevo Diario.*[14] She pointed out that no matter what the newspapers claim, all of Nicaragua knows that she is "marked with the Chamorro brand."[15] Over the following weeks, the Sandinista media used the phrase to ridicule the UNO candidate, suggesting that the brand only shows to whom the cattle belongs.[16] *La Prensa* later published an editorial which, after reciting the illustrious role of the Chamorros in Nicaragua's history, listed 25 family members who were at the time high-level officials of the Sandinista government. It concluded: "This is the irony of fate . . . in the government I did not find as many Sandinos or Fonsecas as I did Chamorros. Like it or not, we all still carry the Chamorro brand."[17]

In the same order of ideas, the Sandinista strategy of organizing a rollicking election campaign inspired by the youth-oriented symbolism of the mass media seemed out of key with the mood of many Nicaraguans. In particular, the lavish handouts of imported presents—articles of clothing, toys for the children, emblems, toiletries, etc.—during campaign rallies and tours by Sandinista candidates, contrasted sharply with the population's deep poverty. In the early years of the revolution such activity was considered "bourgeois" and "sowing ideological confusion." It all lent plausibility to the UNO message that linked the penury of the people to the enrichment of government officials.

There may also have been an element of "getting even"—what is known as "spite voting." The free and secret ballot became for many voters a means for repudiating specific aspects of the Sandinista administration that were personally irritating: the overbearing bureaucrat; the illicit enrichment of a Sandinista neighbor; the boss' sexual harassment; the lack of textbooks in the schools while novels, declarations, and speeches by the leaders abounded; dilapidated public buses alongside the manager's air-conditioned car.

Such things were not introduced by the Sandinistas, but are part and parcel of the traditional perks of the state and army in power in most if not all societies, especially underdeveloped ones. But the Sandinistas did little to do away with them, and in many cases encouraged them. To the degree the revolutionary process became ensnarled in its own ambiguities and inability to defend earlier advances, such manifestations became more notorious and reprehensible.

Under these conditions—aggression, economic crisis, adjustment policy, increasing estrangement between the Sandinista line and the de facto political climate—the trumpeting of the slogan "Everything's Going to be Better," by FSLN hopefuls must have sounded like mockery to many, or rather like "more of the same" after eleven years of Daniel Ortega and Sergio Ramírez in power. Why expect anything new from them? And not only from them, but from the whole pyramid of authority which reaches down and spreads out ever farther as it comes closer to people's daily lives. It is possible that for many the issue wasn't so much the re-election of the president and vice president, as the certainty that this re-election would ensure that everything would remain as it was: the overbearing boss, the parvenu neighbor, the high cost of living, unemployment, the daily suffering. It was not anticommunist ideology or sympathy with the counterrevolution and the United States that drove many of those who took part with such enthusiasm in the extraordinary FSLN closing rally on the night of February 21, to vote for UNO on the morning of the twenty-fifth. It was because when they returned home they had to face the empty rice dish, the vacant place of the son recruited into the army, the photo of the son killed by the Contras, or the neighbor's shiny new car.

Finally, the Sandinistas' decision to run Ortega and Ramírez violated a deep Nicaraguan sentiment against re-election, which grew out of the inveterate electoral practices of Anastasio Somoza and his son. This feeling was reinforced by the inclusion of numerous relatives of Sandinista leaders as candidates for the National Assembly. Running on the Sandinista slate, for instance, were the father of Commander Luis Carrión Cruz (a member of the National Directorate), the daughter, wife and brother of Sergio Ramírez, and the wife of Commander Carlos Núñez (another Directorate member).

Unquestionably, the greatest error was placing disproportionate importance on external factors—U.S. aggression, the world crisis, the reluctance of international and governmental agencies to finance economic development. Observers and analysts, above all those closest to the FSLN, projected the rationality of the Sandinista line onto the electorate, assuming voters would choose on the basis of general ideological reasoning rather than on the concrete and specific issues of living conditions. To assume this was all the more ludicrous considering the recent history of the revolution. Not a few population groups joined the Contras in response to aspects of government policy they considered negative—sectors of the peasant and Indian populations of the Atlantic Coast, for example. Moreover, these subsequently chose to return to civilian life, not because of external factors, but as a consequence of changes in government policy and Sandinista political style.

Before we break down in tears and breast-beating, due note should be taken of the fact that despite the many adverse circumstances surrounding the electoral process, 40% of the Nicaraguan people opted in spite of everything to continue on the difficult path of revolution. Some undoubtedly did so because the hard course was sweetened with not a little honey, but the majority unquestionably did so out of conviction and hope. This 40% makes the FSLN the strongest single political party in Nicaragua, and constitutes a necessary if not sufficient basis for remaking the party for a comeback in the 1996 elections. . . .

What then is left of the Sandinista Revolution? The outlook is not unlike that which Nicaragua faced at the moment the revolution triumphed on July 19, 1979. Then, large sectors of Nicaragua's elite, along with their liberal U.S. allies, were advocating a system of limited mass participation via electoral democracy—a system that would support an economic strategy of bland reforms and entrepreneurial leadership, together with a weeding out from the National Guard of the most corrupt repressive elements. At the time it was pejoratively dubbed "Somocismo without Somoza" by some, or more enthusiastically "scientific Somocismo" by others.

The correlation of forces that achieved the Sandinista victory made this unfeasible, but a good part of what was accomplished and the way in which it was accomplished during the second half of 1979 was fused into this approach of limited confrontation with the internal and hemispheric established order. This will be the common ground for negotiations between the group of advisers around Doña Violeta and their Sandinista cousins.

Eleven years after that famous July 19, Nicaragua bears little resemblance to the society envisioned by Carlos Fonseca and the other founders of the FSLN, or by those who led it at the time and still do. We have to recognize that the revolutionary process got stuck in its own internal tensions and ambiguities long before the Sandinistas were defeated at the polls. By then, the rank and file were already weakened and demobilized.

But neither is it the Nicaragua of July 18. It represents an undeniable advance over the ways and styles of the traditional political culture of families and relationships, even though these are coloring the spectrum of national politics more and more in the case of both UNO and the upper reaches of the FSLN. The changes are considerable and have transformed more than the nation's facade.

The level of consciousness and experience in labor rights that workers and peasants enjoy today was unknown ten years ago, in spite of the restrictions which the state tried to place on them in order to win the support of the business community. Their access to basic resources, land first of all, is incomparably broader than before the revolution, and if this is not irreversible, the political and social cost of an agrarian counter-reform would be greater than what the UNO government could bear. The ethnic communities of the Atlantic Coast have come an enormous way toward the establishment of autonomous government. A decade of Sandinista rule has developed a sense of political empowerment and popular participation which constitutes one of the greatest achievements of this period. This was no gift from the revolutionary state. It was won through great struggle against Somoza, against the ruling circles who joined the revolution, and sometimes against the agencies of the revolutionary state itself.

The possibility for the revolution to survive this electoral defeat will depend on the solidity and depth of the social and political transformations the revolution wrought. It will depend on the capacity of the society to resist attempts to turn these back or neutralize them. And on the capacity of the FSLN to reassume leadership of the people's aspirations, which Doña Violeta's government is unlikely to satisfy.

When revolutions are authentic, and the Sandinista Revolution certainly was, they stamp an indelible seal on society's entire expanse. Even when they do not come out victorious, or suffer reverses, nothing reverts to what it was before, notwithstanding the nightmares of the vanquished or the fantasies of the victors.□

1. Broadcast nationwide on Cadena Nacional the evening of Dec. 27, 1989, and published in *Barricada* and *El Nuevo Diario,* Dec. 28, 1989.

2. See, for example, *El Nuevo Diario* (Managua), Dec. 28, 1989; Jan. 3, 1990.

3. See *Barricada* (Managua), Jan. 3, 1990.

4. See CEPAL, "Balance económico preliminar de la economía latinoamericana," (Santiago, Dec. 1989).

5. Ibid.

6. *Barricada,* February 15 and 21, 1989; *El Nuevo Diario,* April 27, 1989. They quote figures from the Health Ministry's Epidemiology Department, the state ENABAS sugar corporation, and the state Dairy Industry Corporation.

7. *Barricada,* February 20 and 21, 1989.

8. *Barricada,* June 18 and 19, 1988; May 22, 1989.

9. *Barricada,* June 20, 1988.

10. Nicaraguan Institute of Public Opinion (INOP).

11. See declarations by Daniel Ortega in *Barricada,* Dec. 14, 1989 and by Sergio Ramírez in *La Jornada* (Mexico), Feb. 24, 1990.

12. *Barricada,* Dec. 18, 1989. After the elections *Barricada* named the nationalization of foreign trade as one of the revolutionary achievements of Sandinismo (*Barricada,* Feb. 28, 1990).

13. See *Barricada* and *El Nuevo Diario,* Oct. 26, 1989; *Excélsior* (Mexico), Feb. 12, 1990; *La Jornada,* Feb. 23, 1990.

14. *La Nación* (San José), Sept. 11, 1989.

15. See *El Nuevo Diario,* Sept. 11, 1989.

16. See, for example, the article signed by René Corea in *El Nuevo Diario,* Oct. 13, 1989.

17. Ignacio Fonseca, "'El fierro de los Chamorros' en la era sandinista," *La Prensa* (Managua), Oct. 17, 1989.

The Initial Record of the UNO Government

The experience of Nicaragua after February 1990 posed the question whether an election could resolve problems the revolution could not. Pointing optimistically to its campaign promises for economic prosperity, the new government of President Violeta Chamorro announced it would turn the economy around within a hundred days. Her first year in office demonstrated the need for more than optimism and slogans. Inflation spiraled out of control to reach 13,500 percent. The country's gross national product shrank 7 percent; the amount of cultivated acreage dropped 25 percent. A specter of hunger haunted the land. The 70 percent of the population living in poverty lost price subsidies for basic foods and consequently average daily calorie intake plummeted to 1,550, far below minimum requirements. The following essay analyzes the economic performance of the National Opposition Union government.

Barely one year after the defeat of the Sandinistas in the elections, Nicaragua is a different country, almost unrecognizable.

Although it succeeded in ending the war, the expectations created by the National Opposition Union (UNO) have not been fulfilled, there is a high level of social breakdown, the brunt of the economic crisis is being borne by the poorest sectors of society, discontent and disappointment are growing; the UNO is losing its credibility and popularity and the Sandinista Front has still not completely recovered from the electoral defeat. What will the future be like?

Today it seems that no alternatives or hopes remain. Before, even in the middle of the war, Nicaragua had its own character and dignity. The economic crisis was overwhelming but, one year after the UNO victory, the economy is worse and the chances for improvement are slim.

Today Nicaragua is living off public charity and the economistic policy of the government is pushing the workers aside and favoring foreign investors. The contradiction is that the workers are perhaps the only ones who might be able to resolve the basic problem, and the investors—who could buy the country for their own profit—do not have enough confidence in this government to invest.

The government's "allies" give their support in dribs and drabs and President Violeta Chamorro has to be content with alms.

"What is there to celebrate?" Vice President Virgilio Godoy says with a tone of resignation. "This isn't the UNO government. It's Antonio Lacayo's government presided over by Violeta Chamorro." He doesn't fail to mention that Antonio Lacayo, minister of the presidency and President Chamorro's son-in-law, does not belong to any party, but is, nonetheless, Nicaragua's strongman. He commands more than the vice president himself and the distance separating them is constantly growing.

This crisis within UNO has intensified since they took office, and their differences seem to be irreconcilable. From the outset it was clear that disputes would arise for larger shares of power inside the coalition of the 14 parties which make up UNO. But it was also expected that the aim of destroying Sandinism would predominate above all else. Perhaps it was the way in which the different UNO factions proposed to destroy Sandinism which most influenced its disintegration.

The first symptoms of division inside UNO appeared during the signing of the transition accords between the outgoing and incoming governments. For Virgilio Godoy's sympathizers, who represent the radical right sectors, this agreement damaged and tied the hands of the new government. "It's true," they said, "that the Sandinistas continue to govern from below."

In fact, the incoming government had to make more concessions than it wanted to. It had no alternative at the time, but it also felt strengthened since it

Source: Daniel Flakoll Alegría, "One Year Later," *Barricada Internacional* (Managua), March 1991, pp. 5–6. With permission of Daniel Flakoll Alegría, Barricada Internacional.

would have six years and nine months in which to govern. Time was clearly in its favor and the initial obstacles had to be overcome in order to then impose its ideology and class project. However, in the opinion of the ultra-right wing not one concession should have been made; rather, it was necessary to destroy every vestige of the Revolution and finish Sandinism off. They had to reduce 10 years of Sandinism to one paragraph in the new history books and follow-up on the bourgeois social project—different from that of *Somocismo*—which was cut short by the Revolution.

In short, the period between the elections of Feb. 25, 1990, and the inauguration three months later, was for UNO an epoch of euphoria a bit tarnished by the concessions it had to make to the FSLN. After the inauguration the situation rapidly deteriorated and the euphoria turned into frustration.

Another important agreement was the disarmament of the counterrevolution and its integration into society. This agreement was not easy either, and the government was pressured by the Sandinistas as well as the counterrevolutionaries themselves who resisted the demobilization. Arguing that the Sandinistas were still giving the orders, that Gen. Humberto Ortega's permanence as chief of the army was unacceptable and that they did not believe that the government would give them the lands they had promised, the demobilized ex-contras, stirred up by bourgeois sectors, often resorted to the use of force to take over lands belonging to Sandinista cooperatives. Today there are still thousands of demobilized contras who are demanding, along with campesinos and former army soldiers, that the government comply with the signed accords. The land problem remains unresolved and is a constant point of tension for the government.

Despite 10 years of war and the inevitable polarization, there is greater identification between the ex-contra campesinos and Sandinista campesinos than with the Violeta Chamorro government.

Of course, it cannot be said that this is a "honeymoon" period for the ex-contras and the Sandinistas. Profound differences exist, but their demands with respect to land are the same. At the same time there are irreconcilable differences among the ex-contras themselves. For many who put down their arms, the Sandinistas are no longer the enemy, but for those who support Vice President Virgilio Godoy, the Sandinistas still are and the government is not their friend either. The government they backed is not meeting their basic needs; nor do they see themselves represented by the "technocrats" who dominate the executive branch.

After the May and July strikes in which the National Workers Front (FNT) put the government in a tight spot and it was forced to acknowledge that it had not fulfilled its commitments—but at the same time demanded a certain "flexibility" from the Sandinista Front—, a different dynamic developed and the three power groups had to make concessions. The government recognized Sandinism's strength; the ultra-right wing, excluded from the executive but with belligerent and armed grassroots support, was relegated to a low level of participation and nearly disregarded as a part of the government; the FSLN mediated and agreed to put an end to the strike without substantial concessions to the workers' demands having been made. Everyone lost, we all lost, but a fresh wave of violence was successfully averted.

In October, when after negotiation and disagreement the Chamorro government got to the point of having to sign the social and economic *concertación* agreements, it preferred to acquire the FNT's signature than that of the High Council of Private Enterprise (Cosep)—its class ally. The aim was to give lending agencies the impression that in Nicaragua opposing sectors were in agreement on the need to coincide on some specific points in order to obtain foreign resources enabling the country's development.

This gave rise to the November uprising in Region V, where ultra-right wing groups, sectors of the ex-contras and some sectors of Cosep rioted and demanded that President Chamorro give greater shares of power to the faction of her vice president, Virgilio Godoy, or resign.

Everything seems to indicate that this situation has not been resolved. The vice president remains on the fringes and his support base is unhappy, saying that "their" government is leaderless and inconsistent; the FSLN maintains the government has not even minimally fulfilled the agreements signed at the conclusion of the *concertación* process; the country's most important trade unions (health workers, educators, public employees and construction) are on virtual strike, and if an answer is not found quickly, strikes and protests, such as those of May and July last year, could be repeated. At the same time, the government is shielding itself behind the argument that it has not received the aid it expected from its allies (Japan gave only US$7 million and the United States is caught up in the war in the gulf and has not given more than a part of the promised aid).

The panorama is desolate. If the FSLN does not intervene and reason with the government to defend basic revolutionary achievements, the country could once again be caught up in a spiral of chaos. If the ultra-right wing does not abstain from fomenting violence and revenge, the people's response could be devastating. If the government does not come through on its promises to improve the economic and social situation of the majority, this country will remain ungovernable. □

Women at War

The possibility of revolution exists in two Latin American nations: El Salvador and Peru. A discontented, restless society has characterized both countries for decades, but more significantly a well-defined infrastructure for revolution is firmly in place: ideology, plans, political organization, leadership, and impressive military force. In each case, those advocating revolution occupy and/or control large areas of the countryside. Of the two, Peru's "Shining Path" revolutionary movement ranks as older and more radical. It refuses to compromise with existing institutions. The sociologist Carol Andreas provides insight into another unusual characteristic, namely the predominant role of women. They shape, sharpen, and defend the movement's ideology.

IN JUNE OF 1986, I met with a leader of the Communist Party of Peru (PCP), the movement known as Sendero Luminoso or Shining Path. As we sat in the corner of a small restaurant in a middle-class residential neighborhood near the

Source: Carol Andreas, "Women at War." Reprinted from *NACLA Report on the Americas* Vol. 24, No. 4 (Dec./Jan. 1990–1991), pp. 20–27. With the permission of North American Congress on Latin America.

center of Lima, I was intrigued to see that a leader of this movement commonly characterized by outsiders as "enigmatic," "vicious," "despotic" and "dogmatic," was a soft-spoken young woman, articulate but unpretentious. I'll call her "Lucía."

I had discovered in the course of researching women's organizations among Peru's poor that Sendero Luminoso had, since its inception, attracted women in much larger numbers than men. In fact, its best-known military commanders have been teenage women, such as Edith Lagos, whose oratory inspired peasants throughout the south-central sierra, and whose funeral in the highland town of Ayacucho attracted a crowd of some 30,000 people.

I asked Lucía why a movement that brought so much risk to supporters was gaining its most ardent adherents among women. Did it reflect, perhaps, a reclaiming of female power in this society where village life was once characterized by dual governance by women and men? Our conversation was interrupted by a voice booming over the restaurant radio. It was a spokesman for the armed forces, announcing that uprisings were underway in three Lima prisons. Lurigancho, El Frontón, and Santa Barbara, where a number of suspected Senderistas were held.

A day later, it was revealed that nearly 300 prisoners died in the uprising. Most of these had never been formally charged or brought to trial, though they had implicated themselves as Senderistas by literally taking over sections of the prisons and turning them into schools of revolution. Eventually, the government admitted that many of the prisoners had been summarily executed, after they had turned over hostages and given themselves up. Among those killed at Lurigancho was a young man who had lived with our family for eight months ten years earlier—one among many who over the years had lost faith in "politics as usual."

While the foreign press and foreign academics for the most part avoid the subject of female leadership and predominance in Sendero, the Peruvian press, with its penchant for sensationalism, plays it up constantly. Edith Lagos was Shining Path's first military commander in Ayacucho. She escaped from prison several times before being killed by the military at the age of nineteen. Laura Zambrano Padilla, a former schoolteacher known as "Meche," was arrested with great fanfare in 1984, accused of being the head of Shining Path's military operations in Lima. Brenda Pérez Zamora was identified by one source as the second-in-command of the organization since late 1988. María Parado is said to have directed the assault on a prison in Ayacucho that freed hundreds of prisoners. Marina Loayza, Sonia Rosas, Violeta Quispe, Haydee Cáceres, Filipina Palomino, Hermelinda Escobar, Emma Frida, Patricia Zorrilla, Carla Carlota Kutti and Clementina Berrocal are among the dozens of others cited as "cruel and bloody" guerrilla leaders by the mainstream press.

Eighteen of the 30 people arrested in a government roundup of "party leaders" in Lima, the day before last June's run-off presidential elections, were women, including Sybila Arredondo, the widow of novelist José María Arguedas. Female schoolteachers, lawyers, health workers, college professors (including the president of the faculty of San Marcos University), artists, journalists, and union activists—all have been sought in police raids and accused of "terrorism," "apology for terrorism" or "conspiracy to commit terrorist acts." As many as 600 women have been arrested in a single day.

Sendero's appeal to women is only understandable in the context of the breakdown of traditional Peruvian society, particularly in the highlands over the last thirty years. Large numbers of men have been recruited to work in factories, mines and farm cooperatives oriented toward export, leaving women alone for the most part to defend communal lands and the cultural integrity of rural life. Even those women and children who have entered the money economy are effectively excluded from joining the established avenues for political participation and protest.

Peru's male-dominated legal Left has failed miserably to draw the "marginalized" and disenfranchised female majority into a movement for change. In fact, the Left's apparent inability to resist corruption and cooptation in office, especially at the municipal level, has reinforced women's distrust of all male political posturing. Recognizing this, Sendero's leadership has made special efforts to prepare women to assume positions of responsibility. The party's consistent adherence to the idea that all existing governing structures must be destroyed in order to rebuild society from the grassroots up seems to have special appeal for women.

In the countryside, traditional authority structures that date from post-conquest *reducciones* (settlements) established by the Spanish often overlap with municipal governments that date from the Republican era. Municipal governments are almost always entirely male and tend to represent the commercial interest of the better-off members of the community. (While indigenous community meetings are attended by males and females, women usually sit on the ground in a group and only participate when discussions are conducted in Quechua.)

A central feature of Shining Path's program is the overthrow of village governing structures that promote commercial interests, and the establishment of "people's committees," ostensibly to promote reciprocal rather than competitive relations among villagers. It is in these "committees" that women's predominance is most evident. In effect, this has meant the overthrow of male-dominated local governments and the establishment of female-dominated structures, which has allowed women to "settle accounts" in their own fashion as well as to reorganize social life in a manner they view as more equitable.

Besides redistributing land and promoting collective planting and harvesting, peoples' committees have put an end to delinquency, prostitution, drug addiction and domestic violence. Widows and the elderly receive necessary assistance from the community. Education is made available to everyone. Barter replaces buying and selling in local markets, and ancient rituals connected with the cycles of life are observed by the entire community.

Peruvians have always been adept at surviving by establishing relations of cooperation at the community level; traditions of respect for nature and concern for future generations resonate within communal structures. Such practices are undermined, however, in times of extreme hardship and social dislocation. Through "criticism and self-criticism," Sendero encourages villages to regain confidence in communal values. Government corruption and the breakdown of social life has brought so much frustration to women that many yearn for a dependable authority that can arbitrate disputes and restore continuity in daily life. An alternative such as the Communist Party of Peru—no matter how autocratic—that is understandable, that substitutes actions for words, and that requires unbending discipline and faith, is greatly appealing.

My first awareness of the existence of the PCP student federation, "in the shining path of José Carlos Mariátegui," came when I was a teacher at the Universidad Nacional del Centro in Huancayo in 1974. I read the early publications of this movement, based among students and teachers in Ayacucho. These included the translation of "Love in a Communist Society," the classic statement by Russian revolutionary Alexandra Kolantay, and a booklet written by Shining Path leader Catalina Adrianzén, "El Marxismo de Mariátegui y el Movimiento Femenino." I also heard about students' efforts to organize among women in mining camps; I read reports from a national conference on working women organized by the PCP in 1975; and I attended a forum at which cadre debated other Maoists, defending the primacy of "the woman question."[1]

Alone among political parties of the Left in the 1970s, Sendero's Movimiento Femenino Popular insisted that "the woman question" was not a "secondary contradiction" that could be put aside until after the revolution. They published feminist booklets and tracts, and a magazine, *Rima Ryña Warmi* (Women Speak Out), in Quechua and Spanish. While adherents never saw themselves as the vanguard of a class struggle against men, the movement appeared to be a radical response to the supersubordination of indigenous women in what its representatives described as a "semi-feudal, semi-colonial" society. Abimael Guzmán, the university teacher who became Sendero's undisputed leader, and his wife, Augusta de la Torre (credited with pushing her husband to move beyond armchair theorizing about revolution), never abandoned the emphasis on gender equality within the organization—even when the development and implementation of military strategy began to take precedence over public propaganda.

A crucial difference between Sendero and what they call the "revisionist Left" is the former's emphasis on self-reliance and the development of the subsistence economy, as opposed to one based primarily on export-fueled growth. This is particularly relevant to Sendero's appeal to women, because Indian women are the primary participants in Peru's subsistence economy, and are for the most part excluded from the benefits of "development."

A majority of Peru's people have roots in Quechua-speaking communities of the Andes mountains, where Spanish conquistadors defeated the Inca empire, but never succeeded in destroying Indian culture. Only since the 1950s, with the penetration of capitalist economic "development," has rural community life been consistently threatened. Efforts to develop export industries have disrupted local subsistence economies and stimulated out-migration from the sierra, particularly of men. This separation of men and women by wage-work left women without traditional support systems to maintain subsistence agriculture. In some cases, production and sale of food items traditionally under the control of women, such as meat and potatoes, were displaced by industrialized livestock-raising and mechanized farming controlled by men.

This economic "development" did not increase the standard of living of Indian families. Although overall agricultural production may have increased, the amount of food and other products and services available to poor families, especially women and children, did not.[2] Development did bring massive dislocation of peasants, and peasant mobilization against the usurpation and despoliation of communal lands, forcing the government to initiate agrarian reform in the 1960s. As in a number of other nations, the agrarian reform efforts only sharpened class divisions and accelerated political conflict in the countryside.

One-third of Peruvian families are now headed by women, and this statistic is much higher in most rural areas. Besides assuming the primary burden for maintaining subsistence agriculture, many women are entrepreneurs or contract workers in the "informal economy," or have some income from wages but not on a regular or full-time basis. Neither the government nor the country's major union federations have offered women consistent support in any of these roles. Many poor women, therefore, tend to be skeptical about the possibilities for real change short of rebuilding social and economic life literally "from the ground up." Shining Path provides them with a vehicle for pursuing such a radical vision and has welcomed women's leadership in the process.

While women's economic interests have become sharply differentiated from those of men in many communities, cultural traditions of mutual aid and reciprocity, combined with the instability of export markets and the exploitative nature of work relations in capitalist industries, have made collective resistance possible. No one advocates a female revolt against men as a solution to economic and social crisis, least of all Sendero Luminoso. Nevertheless, as male-dominated efforts at reform have faltered, and as Sendero has begun to challenge the power of the state, the struggle sometimes takes on such an appearance. For example, female members of a pro-Indian group based in Lima leafleted and picketed the male leadership several years ago, accusing them of misappropriating funds and of failing to support their own children. The men lost favor with Sendero and were discredited among their constituents.

The "over-representation" of women in Shining Path is not only based on ideology. It can also be traced to the social independence of women in the region where the movement began. In most of the Peruvian sierra, villages are composed of an upper part and a lower part, allowing for the herding of hardy animals such as alpaca in the higher altitudes, and the cultivation of corn and potatoes below. Under the impact of Spanish conquest, many upper villages in the Ayacucho region became havens for women who were persecuted for "idol worship" (*idolatría*) and subject to rape, concubinage, and forced marriage at the hands of priests and hacendados. Cooperative work relations between the women who lived a semi-nomadic life in the higher altitudes and the men who lived in the more stable agricultural communities below allowed women to develop a certain social and economic independence, while at the same time benefiting from the support of their husbands and older male children.

Women lived in temporary huts and were visited regularly by the men. Even though the distance between the two villages necessitated an all-day walk, men often made the trek every weekend. Women also participated in planting and harvest activities in the lower villages, and took part in community fiestas. Although life was extremely hard, the worst effects of feudalism were resisted by men and women together, and mutual respect generally prevailed.

Some have suggested that Peruvian women are reclaiming an aspect of their "historical personalities" through assertion of political and military leadership in Sendero, drawing on an Andean tradition of women occupying the first line of battle.[3] Iconographic representations found in pre-Inca tombs show female deities with teeth in their vaginas. The fifteenth-century female warrior, Mama Huaco, companion of Inca leader Manco Cápac, was so ferocious, according to legend, that she caused the original inhabitants of Cuzco to flee the advance of the Incas.[4] A number of writers have compared Sendero's female leaders to Micaela Bastidas, the eighteenth-century Indian woman who commanded troops in the rebellion against the Spanish led by her husband, Túpac Amaru II. She reportedly sent him a message shortly before their defeat and death in Cuzco, warning that he had sealed their fate by disobeying her orders and delaying the assault on the city.

Peruvian anthropologist Daniel Malpartida makes what he calls an "ethnopsychoanalytic" analysis of female leadership in Peruvian wars: "Mama Huaco, woman warrior, is the mythical representation of female aggressiveness that is latent in the consciousness of Andean women. . . . Women react aggressively because they suffer a double repression, that of their own sexual companion and of a society governed by men. [Sendero leader] Edith Lagos, like so many other women, is an expression of this drama. . . . Micaela Bastidas, on the other hand, saw more clearly than Túpac Amaru the need to take Cuzco. Her education and her ideology were different from his. She was more Indian and more sensitive to the needs of her people. Putting it more bluntly, Túpac Amaru was afraid of the 'dentured vagina.' Unconsciously, he was unable to free himself from the fear of castration. Above all, he was afraid of losing masculine hegemony. Otherwise, the two would have marched on Cuzco together and, needless to say, our history would have turned out quite differently."[5]

In a similar vein, journalists in Peru have drawn attention to the writings of Flora Tristán, the French-Peruvian revolutionary feminist who wrote about the "rabonas," young women who accompanied male regiments resisting the Chilean invasion in the 1880s. "Indian women embrace this life voluntarily," she wrote, "and confront danger with a courage of which the men are incapable."[6]

While alluding to such historical antecedents, Peru's middle-class feminist publications generally stop short of drawing overt comparisons with Sendero Luminoso. Most denounce all forms of violence and do not consider Sendero to be a friend of "the women's movement." When *La Tortuga,* Peru's most conservative feminist magazine, published an interview with well-known Sendero sympathizer Sybila Arredondo in 1986, it caused quite a stir. Arredondo had been accused of cooperating with the guerrillas and was released after fifteen months in jail when no evidence was presented to support the charges against her.

In the course of the interview, she continually attempted to draw attention to the terrible conditions suffered in prison by young Indian women accused under Peru's "anti-terrorist law." The women were refused contact with lawyers and family members, deprived of medical attention and food, and subjected to torture and rape by officials. When asked why so many women join Sendero, she declared that women are attracted to revolution because they, along with children, are the most oppressed, and because Sendero Luminoso "has a 'correct line,' as the politicians say, and they carry it forward effectively, so it's only natural that these women join the movement with great passion."[7]

In the poor urban neighborhoods, Sendero uses guerrilla theater to educate people about the sources of their misery. The plays often depict family squabbles, ridiculing men who strut around, quarrel with their neighbors, drink, and cheat on their wives. Women who gossip and who try to imitate upper-class Peruvians or characters from soap operas are also ridiculed. Typically, the heroine is a women who rebels, joined by her children or by other youth. In the end, all chant together the Maoist slogan: "Rebellion is justified!" Sometimes the chanting turns into rounds of gunshot fired into the air, accompanied by shouts of "Shining Path is in the trenches! Long live the Republic of New Democracy!"

Social changes in recent decades have made adultery endemic, and this is a source of acute anguish for women. Sendero has been known to threaten husbands who have abandoned their wives and children, and who are habitual womanizers. I asked one of my informants how he thought striking fear into male family members could be reconciled with Shining Path's desire to recruit them. He simply responded, "The men are shaping up."

In 1984, I had the opportunity to live for a time in Apurímac (adjacent to Ayacucho), where I accompanied a female leader of the peasant union, Confederación Campesina del Peru (CCP). Large sections of Andahuaylas (a province of Apurímac) had been taken over by members of the union in the mid-1970s, but as agrarian reform faltered, many peasants left the CCP to join Shining Path. Brutal and arbitrary repression by the government followed. I talked with relatives of prisoners accused of terrorism and with a woman who participated in Sendero's "popular education" programs, directed mainly toward people of high school age. They told me that nearly all the students in these clandestine schools were young women, many of whom had grown up in the high altitudes where life had become too difficult for survival. They saw no hope for reform, either through union activity or government largess, and certainly not through the charade of elections.

I recall being told often by women in the farmworkers' union that they were tired of listening to endless speeches and promises, followed by retreat and betrayal. I had seen women in the union stage a kind of "cultural revolution," insisting (without much success) on female representation. The difference was that they had no arms in hand to guarantee respect, as Senderista women do.

I asked a female leader of Shining Path how she, as a well-educated professional, could submit herself "blindly" to the authority of a powerful individual—and a man at that. She was certainly not submissive in relation to her husband, who was unaware of her clandestine life in Sendero. She said that under the leadership of "El Guía"—or "Presidente Gonzalo," as Abimael Guzmán is also known—the party had made great strides, achieving what no other political organization in Peru had ever been able to achieve: a sustained attack against "bureaucratic capitalism" and the "comprador state." She said the entire organization engaged in self-criticism as part of its ongoing commitment to "cultural revolution." But most importantly, she insisted that having overall leadership that was dependable, not vacillating, was an inspiration.

Shining Path cadre see the centralization of political authority in "Presidente Gonzalo" as a guarantee that grassroots power will not be subverted. Disgusted with the "posturing" of electoral candidates and with the seemingly unproductive rivalry among them, the vertical leadership of "El Guía" appears as a welcome relief. Paradoxically, the existence of hierarchy in the party is regarded as an assurance that selfishness of egotism on the part of local cadre will not prevail over the common good.

On the other hand, local cadre seem to have great latitude in carrying out *ajusticiamientos* (settling of accounts), sometimes by execution, against those who are considered to be enemies, spies, or traitors to the movement, including men accused of rape. Many women, who perhaps have more accounts to settle than do men, do not seem to find this disturbing. In reaction to media reports about seemingly wanton violence committed by Senderistas, I have heard women find ways to justify the action, by declaring the reports to be false or expressing confidence that those who committed errors or excesses will be brought to judgment by the party. They know they will not be raped by a Shining Path soldier; they will not be humiliated and degraded for being poor, for being Indian, or for being female. Lack of formal education will not be held against them, and their interests will not be compromised for personal gain.

The latent political energies of Peru's poor Indian women have been tapped by a movement that supports them in their drive to recover land for community use and to reclaim unity between women and men in the rebuilding and development of their communities. There is no guarantee that these characteristics will continue to define the organization if it achieves state power. Women have always been active participants in revolutionary movements, especially peasant movements, but their power has always been undermined in the end. It is unlikely that Sendero's "New Democracy" will be democratic enough to permit independent grassroots movements to flourish (given the persistence of counter-revolution worldwide). So the women of Shining Path will have to make sure they don't relinquish their arms.

Lucía, the leader I met with on the day of the prison massacres, told me that "El Guía" asked revolutionary cadre to envision constantly the kind of society they would like to achieve, and to be ready to overcome every obstacle in the realization of that vision. Whatever the outcome of the present political crisis in Peru, Sendero Luminoso has presented an enormous challenge to its detractors. An understanding of the movement's social history and of its peculiar attraction for women is important in developing a critique of political forces at work in that country and in many other places where the impact of "development" on women is particularly severe.□

1. An early Sendero document is Antonio Díaz Martínez, *Ayacucho, Hambre y Esperanza* (Ayacucho: Ediciones Waman Puma, 1969). See also Colin Harding, "Antonio Díaz Martínez and

the Ideology of Sendero Luminoso," *Bulletin of Latin American Research,* Vol. 7, No. 1, 1988, pp. 65–73, and "Notes on Sendero Luminoso," *Communist Affairs,* Jan. 1984, pp. 45–61. For an interpretation of other early Shining Path documents, see Roger Mercado, *Los Partidos Políticos en el Perú: el APRA, el P.C.P., y Sendero Luminoso* (Lima: Ediciones Latinoamericanas, 1985). Recent study documents were published in *El Diario* (Lima) in January of 1988. The political program of Shining Path was distributed in pamphlet form after the Party Congress held in clandestinity and attended by some 2000 delegates in 1988. A lengthy interview with Abimael Guzmán was published in *El Diario* on July 31, 1988.

2. Magdelena León and Carmen Diana Deere, "The Latin American Agrarian Reform Experience," in *Rural Women and State Policy* (Boulder, Colorado: Westview Press, 1987).

3. See Ricardo Melgar Bao, "Las Guerrillas de Sendero y la Ilusión Andina del Poder," paper presented at the XII Congress of the Latin American Studies Association, Albuquerque, New Mexico, April 1985.

4. See Maria Rostorowski, *Estructuras Andinas del Poder: Ideología religiosa y política* (Lima: Instituto de Estudios Peruanos, 1983, 1986). It should be emphasized that not all the mythological images of women in Peru are those of aggressiveness in combat. Nevertheless, women's and men's roles throughout most of the history of the region are those of dual and complementary power in the governing of society and the conduct of ritual and of daily work.

5. *Cambio* (Lima), Oct. 18, 1985.

6. *Mujer y Sociedad* (Lima), July 1986.

7. *La Tortuga* (Lima), Dec. 1986. Sybila Arredondo was arrested for the third time in June 1990.

8

A Lingering Legacy

At the end of the twentieth century, poverty persists throughout Latin America. It remains a dominant economic reality despite a century-and-a-half of modernization schemes, foreign investments, burgeoning exports, and erratic, often impressive, economic growth. Not only do most of the people fail to benefit from the munificent and varied resources of Latin America but many indicators suggest a serious deterioration of their quality of life during the last quarter of the twentieth century. The ultimate condemnation of the present economic structure is the inability of Latin America to feed itself despite such promising potential.

Political institutions rest on weak economic foundations. Contractual government functions with difficulty under such conditions. Social unrest springs from the inability of citizens to identify with the institutions that govern them. Identification is difficult when institutions confer few benefits. Cycles of democracy and dictatorship historically reflect the economic cycles of growth and despair. The major challenge confronting Latin Americans on the eve of the twenty-first century is how to develop economically, to utilize the rich resources of the region for the benefit of the majority. To create viable nations, Latin Americans must reassess the institutions inherited from a colonial past. The words pronounced by Alberto Tôrres at the opening of the twentieth century seem just as valid—and their realization just as elusive—as the century ends: "A people cannot be free if they do not control their own sources of wealth, produce their own food, and direct their own industry and commerce."

Failure to Resolve the Agrarian Issue

Rational use of land marks the initial step toward development. First, nations must feed themselves and then they must produce for export in order to earn the hard currencies needed to purchase capital goods. Yet, Latin American governments hesitate to put unused or underused arable land to work by providing access to it for the dispossessed eager to cultivate it. The well-entrenched landed class regards such a change as a threat both to their own lands and to their control of labor.

In this essay Oscar Delgado emphasizes that with a few notable exceptions the Latin Americans entered the last half of the twentieth century abusing the land and thereby thwarting development. Delgado was pessimistic about the possibilities for rural change, and the succeeding decades seem to have confirmed that pessimism.

LATIN AMERICA had a population of 199 million in 1960, according to a United Nations estimate. Of this total, 108 million or 54 per cent live in rural areas, and of these 28½ million are economically active.

All rural dwellers who are economically active have family and social responsibilities, but almost all of them are underemployed and many are victims of seasonal unemployment. Their income is extremely low, and considerable numbers of them live only on the margin of money economy. Generally speaking, they work the soil in a primitive or almost primitive fashion. The average percentage of rural Latin America [illiteracy] is around 80; but vast areas have no schools at all and an illiteracy rate of 100 per cent.

Indians form some 15 per cent of Latin America's rural population. The majority of them speak only an Indian language, though some of them are bilingual. The Indian policy of Latin American governments generally aims to keep them isolated from the white peasantry of their countries. Moreover, Indian communities benefit very little from government aid or not at all, and it is an open secret that such programs have been a complete failure because of inadequate funds and lack of any real interest on the part of the governments concerned.

In spite of these obstacles, some Indians have established contact with the white peasants. These have adopted the cultural patterns of that peasantry. Wherever such cultural contacts take place, the Indians suffer from exploitation not only by the white bourgeoisie but also by the white and *ladino* (mestizo) peasants.

These 28½ million have to produce food not only for themselves but also directly for their 70½ million dependents and, more indirectly, for the 91 million urban dwellers. Moreover, in terms of the national economy, they have to produce a surplus for economic development. And yet, 63 per cent of them—18 million adult farmers—have no land at all. Some 5½ million have an insufficient amount of land; 1.9 million have enough land, and 100,000—mostly absentee landlords—have too much land.

Source: Oscar Delgado, "Revolution, Reform, Conservatism: Three Types of Agrarian Structure," *Dissent,* 9:4 (Autumn 1962), pp. 350–354, 358–359.

One out of every 185,000 Latin Americans—or one out of every 100,000 rural Latin Americans—owns over 1,000 hectares [a hectare equals 2½ acres]. For 107,955 landlords, or 1.5 per cent of all landholders, own 471 hectares, or 65 per cent of all land in private hands. Each of them owns an average of 4,300 hectares; but many have more than 10,000, and some have hundreds of thousands—even millions.

So much for individuals. But properties belonging to several members of a family can be registered under the name of its head. There are Latin American families who own more land than is occupied by a number of sovereign nations. In fact, there are families or groups of interrelated families in the Argentine, Brazil, Chile and Venezuela, of which each has more land than several countries put together. This is a situation with no parallel elsewhere. Statistically speaking, Latin America has the highest index of concentrated accumulation of rural property in the world.

Latin America is now beginning to develop, however slowly. Its indices of urbanization and industrialization are progressively rising. However, this progress is generally unnoticeable because the population rapidly increases at one of the highest rates of growth in the world. Internal migration to the cities is constant and growing, but it does not absorb the rural population explosion caused by the rising birth rate and the falling death rate. This migration, a product of urbanization and industrialization, makes the rural population decrease relatively, in proportion to urban population; but it does not decrease it absolutely.

It is estimated that the percentage of rural population will fall from 54 to 46 in 1970. However, the rural population as a whole and hence also the number of actual and potential agricultural workers, will actually rise by that date from 108 million to 133 million. . . . There can be no question that the rural—and agricultural—population of Latin America is increasing today in a geometrical progression. Every year, every month and every day there are new mouths to feed and new hands to be provided with work, land, tools, and money. Given an annual rate of increase of 3 per cent, this means about 6 million new mouths and new pairs of hands every year in all Latin America, and 3.8 milion in the rural sector.

How can this problem be solved? The answer is simple and can be reduced to four words: Economic and social development.

We can deal here only with one aspect of this urgent problem: The different agrarian policies which can become stimulants or obstacles to the improvement of agricultural production and productivity, and to the white, mestizo, and indigenous rural population which participates—or is unable to participate—in growing crops and raising cattle.

In three countries of Latin America, a political revolution produced an agrarian policy of redistributing the property and tenancy of land: Mexico (1915), Bolivia (1953), and Cuba (1959). In these countries, new ruling groups and new ideologies replaced the old and changed the traditional values. The old ruling groups had governed with the support of traditional ideas, and their rule was tolerated by the masses who lived in utmost ignorance, submission, and political apathy.

In two other countries, conservative governments, representing a bourgeois-landlord-military-clerical coalition have introduced a land reform: Venezuela (1959) and Colombia (1961). This reform has meant a "parcellation" of cultivated land or a "colonization" of virgin soil.

"Parcellation," as used in this article means:

a.   The acquisition by a government agency of land used for crops or cattle by purchase from its private owners paid in cash and at once and

b.   the subdivision of this land for resale as private property to landless or landpoor peasants by payment of an amount of money equal or similar to that laid out by the government agency on the installment system, with a fixed term and a low interest rate.

Similarly, "colonization" means here the opening or preparation of new agricultural, cattle-raising, or forest land owned by the government or of no definite ownership, and the settlement in it of rural population.

In all the remaining countries of Latin America, there has been no serious program of redistribution or parcellation. The countries which tried colonization in the course of the present century were successful only as regards a few fortunate individuals; for the rest, colonization completely failed to solve their agrarian problem.

Parcellation, as a method of land reform, leaves the large estates practically intact. The concentration of land in a few hands is not affected by it, and it leaves the problems of the rural population unsolved. This is why it is the favorite method of land reform in "rural conservative" countries.

This phrase also requires some explanation. At first sight it seems strange to apply the label of "rural conservative" to seventeen countries which differ so much economically, socially, and politically. They include two countries at the very extremes of economic and social development: Argentina and Haiti. This is also true of political development: They include, on the one hand, the Central American republics dominated by "strong executives" and custodians of foreign interests and, on the other, a country like Uruguay, with its markedly developed democracy. Nor is it easy to include in the same group countries which never had any significant colonization or foreign immigration with others which have intermittently tried out colonization ever since the beginning of the 19th century, though on a small scale in relation to their open spaces and settled population.

Still, it is convenient to group together the countries of recent parcellation (Venezuela and Colombia), those of colonization (Argentina, Brazil, Chile, and Uruguay), and those dominated by large estates (the rest of the seventeen). They have something in common—rural conservatism—which distinguishes them from the countries of revolutionary land reform, which we may call countries of "agricultural transformation."

A closer look at the three countries where a revolution occurred with a broad popular participation will reveal certain distinctions which will require separate categories.

In Cuba, the large estates and ranches were not divided by the Castro Revolution; they continue in operation by either a government agency or a peasant cooperative. Both in Mexico and in Bolivia, land reform marked a notable social progress, though it was limited to only a part of the rural population. The national economy of these two countries benefited somewhat from the land reform, but the benefits were limited by an excessive fragmentation of the estates which were distributed. Also, neither country made a sufficient effort to foster government, collective, or cooperative operation of agriculture and cattle-breeding.

We can now classify the Latin American countries as follows:

I. *Agricultural Transformation:*
   1. Agrarian revolution (Cuba)
   2. Land reform (Mexico and Bolivia)
II. *Rural Conservatism:*
   1. Parcellation (Venezuela and Colombia)
   2. Colonization (Argentina, Brazil, Chile, and Uruguay)
   3. Rural conservatism, in the narrower meaning of that phrase (the remaining countries).

The countries of agricultural transformation have a dynamic agrarian situation: Their agricultural population—or at least a large part of it—has a genuine opportunity to raise its standard of living. The countries of rural conservatism have a static agrarian situation; such an opportunity is limited or non-existent in them. . . .

The reason Cuba falls into a different category from Mexico and Bolivia is that the transformation happened there with surprising efficiency and speed. This is no longer land reform; it must be called an "agrarian revolution." In Mexico and Bolivia, the rhythm of change has been much slower than in Cuba, for all the positive achievements of their land policies. But it has been very fast by comparison with Venezuela and Colombia.

In Mexico today, 47 years after the Land Reform Law was signed, 106 million hectares remain in private hands, and 71 million (76%) belong to private individuals who own more than 1,000 hectares each. In Bolivia, land reform has moved at a faster pace than in Mexico; but even here, 9 years after the law was passed, 28.5 milion hectares—87 per cent of all utilized land—are still in the hands of landlords who own more than 1,000 hectares each.

The land reform laws of Cuba, Mexico, and Bolivia stipulate that the former owners of expropriated land be indemnified with long-term bonds. But, in actual practice, none of these countries has paid the compensation required by the law. The small payment was made in money, not in bonds. How else would it have been possible to redistribute 61 million hectares (52 in Mexico, 5 in Cuba, 4 in Bolivia)?

The laws of Venezuela and Colombia, on the other hand, authorize the expropriation of land, with payment partly in cash and partly in medium-term bonds. Both, however, have actually preferred parcellation.

The Venezuelan government has bought about half a million hectares, at market prices, from landlords who sold their land voluntarily. They actually received payment, almost full and immediate. This land has not been given to the peasants, as happened in Cuba, Mexico, and Bolivia. It was sold to them at cost price, which included the value of improvements and the wages of the officials in charge of the transactions. The peasants pay in annual installments for a medium-term period.

In Cuba, the large estates and ranches were taken from individual owners and national and foreign companies. They were not subdivided, but continue to be operated as wholes by the government or by peasant cooperatives.

In Mexico and Bolivia, on the contrary, they were subdivided into very small farms—an average of 4 hectares of unirrigated lands—and handed over to the peasants. But the beneficiaries of the land reform were, in both countries, abandoned to their fate. Because of financial stringency or for other reasons, they have received hardly any credit, technical assistance and other services needed for efficient farming.

Among the different types of rural conservatism, parcellation deserves special treatment. In most of the literature on the subject, "land reform" actually means parcellation. This is because, for many people, parcellation means an "agrarian transformation," and so they associate what is happening in Venezuela and Colombia with what happened in Mexico, Bolivia, and Cuba. . . .

Some of these oligarchies seem to have found a magic formula which would permit them to maintain the existing agricultural structure while proclaiming that they had transformed it. The formula is "parcellation," i.e., the subdivision of large properties and the fostering of homesteads. . . . What this formula means in practice, however, is the stimulation of the *minifundio* in a disguised and uneconomic form, within the framework of a subsistence rather than market-oriented agriculture. The rural population will remain poor, and the backward tenancy systems and the exploitation of agricultural labor will continue. The levels of rural income and buying power will not stimulate savings and consumption, so that they will not benefit industrialization. There will be, in fact, no social or political change.

As the president of the University of California, Clark Kerr, puts it: "The successful perpetuation of the family homestead. . . . serves to maintain contact with the old society."[1] In other words, the old elites will continue in power at the expense of representative democracy and the participation of the mass of the population in national life. Other investigators also point out this danger.

There exist alternative policies to parcellation, namely cooperative and/or communal exploitation of land. A number of Latin American experts favor cooperatism on a large scale while the American experts are divided. But the official U. S. policy, as embodied in the Alliance for Progress, does not take these alternatives into consideration.

Of the Latin American countries themselves, the laws of Venezuela and Colombia indulge in some rhetoric in favor of cooperatives, but the actual policies of these countries have restrained rather than favored the growth of different types of cooperatives. In Mexico and Bolivia, official support of cooperatives has considerably fallen off as their governments gradually veered away from revolutionary agrarianism. □

[1]Clark Kerr, "Changing Social Structures, pp. 348–59 in W. E. Moore and A. S. Feldman, eds., *Labor Commitment and Social Change in Developing Areas* (New York: Soical Science Research Council, 1960), p. 354.

The End to Food Self-Sufficiency
in Mexico

A diminishing per capita production of food accompanied by rising prices for basic products—rice, corn, and beans—occurred throughout much of Latin America by the late nineteenth century. Despite technological advances and a few attempts at land reform during the twentieth century, those trends accelerated. Using Mexico as an example, David Barkin, professor of economics at the Universidad Autónoma Metropolitana, Mexico City, suggests the economic costs and human tragedy that result. Malnourished or hungry people cannot promote development.

MEXICO HAS CEASED to be self-sufficient in food. Its tortillas are no longer made from locally grown raw materials; it cannot supply all of its demand for meat and dairy products, or even animal feed. This crisis had its origins in economic policies of the 1960s and was exacerbated by a great drought in 1979 and 1980. In 1981, the Aztec rain god Tlaloc cooperated; and the Sistema Alimentario Mexicano (Mexican Food System, or SAM), a presidential initiative to lead the country back to the road of food self-sufficiency, contributed to a temporary dramatic increase in agricultural production and nutritional standards by raising crop prices and subsidizing production costs. But money and rain were not enough to overcome the obstacles that provoked the crisis in agriculture, and the small landholders did not have the opportunity to rebuild their communities and productive organizations before government budgets were eroded by inflation and falling petroleum prices. Despite an unprecedented series of abundant rains since then (1982 and 1986 excepted), basic food production could not be sustained at its previous levels. The value of the country's food imports exceeded its agricultural exports from 1979 to 1985; even as the agricultural trade balance went into surplus in 1986, the volume of maize imports continued to be high.

This dependence on imports can no longer be considered the result of an unfortunate conjuncture. Mexico has required substantial maize imports for more than a decade despite the availability of the natural and human resources and technology needed to supply the country's own needs. In the midst of a profound economic crisis of international scope, the old debates about the advisability of self-sufficiency are no longer simply academic battlegrounds—the country is obliged to import billions of dollars of food products it can not afford, food that could be produced by small farmers on lands that presently stand idle. And yet the magnitude of the political and social changes required to reverse this deficit is sufficient to discourage even the most enthusiastic of political reformers.

The loss of food self-sufficiency, while a political and economic issue for policymakers and editorialists, poses a basic problem of survival for families and

Source: David Barkin, "The End of Food Self-Sufficiency in Mexico," *Latin American Perspectives*, Issue 54, 41:3 (Summer 1987), pp. 271–273, 291–293. With the permission of Sage Publications, Inc.

communities. Recognizing the high costs and physical difficulties of transport, together with the uncertainty that food would be available for purchase elsewhere, they have traditionally organized their own production of basic foodstuffs in a fundamental strategy for family and community security. The internationalization of agriculture makes pursuit of this strategy increasingly difficult.

Agricultural development proceeds through a complex interaction of market pressures and government policy. Through the price system, the market informs investors about the most profitable opportunities for new production. Economic policy rearranges priorities by modifying prices and profit rates in different activities: historically, governments have accorded priority to industrialization and export. In Mexico (as elsewhere) this bias precipitated the present problem of food dependency. . . .

The loss of food self-sufficiency is one particularly visible manifestation of the profound crisis now afflicting Mexico. The crisis is the outcome of the successful implantation of a model of economic growth that has been exported to many countries in Latin America. Years of rapid growth and transformation restructured space and production, generating jobs, and raising real living standards for virtually every segment of society. Although the benefits were inequitably distributed, the internationalization process effectively broke down local resistance and barriers to national integration. The outpouring of consumer goods went preferentially to an affluent upper third of the population, the real beneficiaries of that period. The unwillingness (or inability) to charge the high costs of economic growth to these local groups, who might have paid the costs of this development model, did not provoke a crisis because of a unique conjuncture: the emerging surfeit of liquidity in world capital markets that increased as growth in the United States slowed in the 1960s forced bankers to search for new places for their future expansion.

After being bribed to accept the growth model based on debt and oil revenues, broad segments of Mexican society are now being obliged to service the debt with personal austerity and national depression. They are told that there is no alternative. The model is consistent and all-embracing. Furthermore, with the formerly isolated groups now integrated into a national society, the crisis imposes an even heavier burden on these people: they have *less* freedom (ability) to defend themselves by retreating into their communities where self-sufficiency and mutual support were once the norm. They have nowhere to turn.

To confront this dilemma, the Mexican people must recognize that they are at war. The economic war pits the country against its bankers, its leaders, against its people. The war is more deadly than if it were fought with munitions. It is against forces—internal and external—that threaten its very integrity as a nation. The onslaught of recessionary policies is unraveling the social and economic fabric, while protectionist policies, international competition, and growing debt service burdens combine to make sound international economic management more difficult. To respond effectively to these conflicting pressures, Mexico must reorganize. Priorities must be reshaped to increase domestic production to satisfy internal needs and to generate exports to finance a realistic program of debt service. A modified war economy strategy requires new political alliances so that all available natural, produced, and human resources can be mobilized to resuscitate production and facilitate broad participation. Once the resources have been mustered, then productivity and efficiency can become important concerns. It is impossible as long as national priorities and policies are dictated by the international market.

The transition to a war economy strategy might be initiated by stimulating small-scale production for the satisfaction of basic needs that, in turn, would reinvigorate the entire national economy. This strategy involves the reincorporation of vast areas of farmland and large segments of the rural population who have been displaced by the transformation process that accompanied the integration of national economies into the global market. In Mexico, millions of tons of grains are imported, all of which could be produced locally. There are 10 million hectares of idle farmland in the hands of smallholders, much of which could be put back into production with appropriate incentives. In addition, there are more than 2 million hectares of irrigated farmland planted in grains that could be sown in dryland agriculture, thus freeing more land for export production and generating even more employment and internal demand. This massive insertion of lands and people into production with domestically available resources could be structured so as not to compete with existing production for export and other markets. The local production of basic consumption items (food, clothing, and shelter) and infrastructure must be accompanied by other elements of a policy for a war economy, including efficient rationing of available goods to ensure their equitable distribution among all social groups and limitations on the consumption of nonessential goods requiring imported inputs.

The modified war economy strategy will not be implemented by a government committed to financing its deficits with funds from abroad and exacting greater sacrifices from one or another of the sectors of the working population. It requires the construction of a broad based alliance among social groups that would create a new platform for a more equitable pattern of long-term economic growth in Mexico, as in most of Latin America. The country's basic consumption needs would be produced domestically and broadly distributed to permit a higher standard of living than is presently possible for most people. Exports would continue to be encouraged, but with policies that did not penalize domestic production of mass consumption items. With a more vigorous rate of domestic activity and a broader basis for participation in production, more resources would be available. In a relatively rich country such as Mexico, such a strategy would generate new savings for further growth based on a fuller use of present productive capacity. Private production could expand on a more solid footing, and the nation would have a structurally lower demand for foreign goods. Thus it could more easily meet its international financial obligations while also becoming a more prosperous and stable member of the international community.□

Hunger in Honduras

The Honduran government proudly boasts that its air force pilots fly the most modern jet fighter planes in Central America. It is less inclined to reveal that its population suffers some of the most acute hunger pangs in the hemisphere. The death rate among children under five, those who suffer most from malnourishment, soars like one of the jet fighters. Intertwined, militarism and hunger are Honduran legacies. They perpetuate underdevelopment.

E VERY MAY, as the rains come and the crops run out, doctors at the Honduran national children's hospital see the deaths climb. Every November, as the crops come in, they see the deaths fall.

In the past few months there has been no drop, and the doctors fear that the steady influx of underfed babies portends a swing from declining infant mortality back to the days when one Honduran child in three died of infection before reaching age five.

Experts say Honduras faces growing famine that stems from drought, population growth, and—some say—American farm and foreign policy.

The food shortage is worsening, economists say, because per capita production and food aid are down. They worry that nearly half the country's 4.5 million people are being malnourished.

One of them, Maria Lopez, has no time to worry about statistics. She holds Crecencia, 3 who whimpers as nurses at the hospital insert intravenous tubes to counter undernourishment and pneumonia.

Crecencia weights 11 pounds.

Doctors say she will likely die. They say child deaths have skyrocketed in the past two months due to calorie and protein deficiencies so severe that simple lung infections, diarrhea, or drops in body temperature killed them.

"The problem is a lack of food," says Dr. Jorge Humberto Melendez, director of children's health programs for the Ministry of Public Health. "All children get colds and diarrhea, but they don't die from them unless they're malnourished."

With help from the largest U.S.-financed child survival program in the Western Hemisphere—about $3 million annually—only one Honduran child in seven now dies. Infant mortality has fallen from 80 per 1,000 live births in 1983 to about 76 per 1,000. About 156,000 babies are born each year.

Like Crecencia, about half of Honduras' 662,000 children under five are chronically underfed, according to a 1987 nationwide nutritional survey by the Ministry of Public Health. Four percent are acutely malnourished; in Crecencia's area, about 10%.

"Those numbers are misleadingly optimistic," says Dina Eguiguire, a nutritionist with CARE. "Every family in the countryside has problems, sometimes pretty severe. Hunger wasn't that widespread a few years ago."

Nutrition is declining along with the harvest. Since 1976, annual corn production has fallen from 58 pounds per capita to 51 pounds, and of beans from six pounds to five. Poor rains last year cut harvests of basic grains by another 17%.

In part, the production decline stems from spiraling population growth— the annual 3.4% rate is the hemisphere's highest.

Source: Mary Coyle, "Hunger Comes to Honduras," *The Times of the Americas* (Washington, D.C.), February 21, 1990. With permission of Pacific News Service.

But grain production is also dwindling "because the U.S. government, which practically manages farm policy here, wants everyone to grow export crops instead," says Marcos A. Aguero, an economist with the United Nations-affiliated World Food Program. "They even send teams around to get the small farmers to move out of grains into fruits and vegetables."

U.S. officials say that, though their policies have cut grain production, Honduras desperately needs foreign exchange, and one of the few ways it can earn it is by selling farm products.

One potentially tragic area of shortfall is milk donations, virtually halted in 1988 when the United States, the major donor, stopped shipments due to squeezed U.S. dairy production. U.S. ranchers say that rebuilding herds big enough to resume donations to Honduras could take 10 years.

"This is the worst shortfall I have ever seen," says Aguero, who predicts that donations will bottom out in 1992.

The cutoff is critical because "milk is so important as a concentrated source of protein and calories that we won't run child-survival programs without it," says Aguero. A program serving 12,000 women and children in the extremely malnourished western region was suspended in late 1989 for lack of milk; at the earliest, it will resume late this year.

Aid and government officials say about 20% of food in Honduras is sold illegally by government officials or rots away in warehouses.

The rest is poorly distributed. Only one-third of the children who needed food supplements in Crecencia's town got them, according to the 1987 nutritional survey, although many well-fed children got extra food on the north coast, a wealthier region that strongly backs the government.

One of Maria Lopez's children died because of malnutrition, doctors say.

Another died of diarrhea, which accounts for one-third of Honduran children's deaths. A simple packet of salt and sugar, mixed with water, could have replenished the child's fluids, but such aid is usually only available in cities because the health ministry lacks rural transport.

The ministry is proud of its broad immunization program, which it says has provided about 75% coverage against whooping cough, tuberculosis, diphtheria polio, measles, and tetanus. Only 18 cases of polio were reported in 1988.

But doctors at the children's hospital say only about half of the parents are up-to-date on their shots.

Looking down at Crecencia, Maria Lopez recalls each child's death and worries that she will lose yet another—this time due to the sudden food shortage. □

The Burden of the Brazilian Child

In Latin America, fully 50 percent of the population is under eighteen years of age. The child symbolizes the future. If the condition and treatment of the child foretell society's future, the cause of development looks bleak in Latin America.

THERE IS LITTLE JOY to childhood in Brazil—little time for play, for study, for growing up. Childhood is a time for work.

From heavy industry to food production to prostitution, the Brazilian economy, the eighth-largest in the world, is built in large part on the labor of children.

For tens of millions of children in this country of 122 million people, the business of economic survival begins at age 5, sometimes younger.

Statistics, academic studies and experiences reported by children give strong support to the conclusion that life for most ordinary Brazilian children is one of work, exploitation, degradation and sometimes virtual slavery.

According to the government's 1980 census, children between the ages of 10 and 17 make up almost 13% of the total Brazilian labor force.

In the countryside, where farm work is still done largely by hand under harsh and primitive conditions, more than 8% of the rural labor force is between 10 and 14 years old, while those 15 to 17 make up an additional 17%.

The situation grows steadily more serious. A partial census conducted earlier this year reports that half of all Brazilian children over the age of 10 work.

These statistics are admittedly incomplete, however. Studies by various private universities, research institutions and the Roman Catholic Church indicate a situation far worse.

Rosa Maria Fischer Ferreira is a sociologist at the University of Sao Paulo and author of a 1979 book called "Meninos da Rua," or "Children of the Street."

She found that Brazil has an estimated 55 million "marginalized" children—that is, children living in substandard conditions, either alone or with families unable to properly feed, clothe or educate them. A large portion of Brazils' growing population is under the age of 15.

Of these 55 million, 80%—or about 44 million children—have gone into the streets to work by the time they are 5 years old, Fischer said.

"There is no youth for them," said Geraldo Miller, an agricultural economist with the Brazilian Center of Analysis and Planning, one of the country's leading private research centers. "They go from babies to workers," he said. "By the time they are 12, they are adults."

They are indeed adults. Children as young as 8 make bricks. There are 10-year-olds working in 110-degree heat blowing glass. Pre-teen-agers cut sugar cane in the fields. And, in some places, 12-year-olds work as prostitutes.

As in most developing countries, child labor is common and legal in Brazil, at least for those 14 and older. The law provides that workers, including the 14-year-olds, must register and are guaranteed a minimum monthly salary, health care and other benefits and a safe place to work.

Lia Junqueira, a lawyer and founder of the Sao Paulo Movement in Defense of Minors, said, "The code to protect minors is more rigorous than the law against criminals."

But, she added, "In reality, nothing is done." In the last year, Junqueira

Source: Kenneth Freed, "To Brazilian Child, Life Is a Burden," *Los Angeles Times,* December 20, 1982, pp. 1, 14–15.

said, "I have filed 189 complaints about employer abuses of working children. None succeeded."

If that sounds bad, the reality is far worse since only a small percentage of children actually register or are allowed to register.

Why do so many children work, particularly in a society that brags of its "economic miracle," of having turned a primitive, agriculture-based economy into a modern industrial power in less than 20 years?

One answer is found in the uneven distribution of wealth. Cheywa R. Spindel, an economist at the Pontifical Catholic University and a specialist in child labor, said 70% of Brazil's wealth is controlled by 10% of the population.

"Most families in the 'popular classes' are large, with irregular employment," said Fischer, the University of Sao Paulo sociologist, "and they have to have a child working."

The national minimum monthly wage is 23,000 cruzeiros, or about $95. Fischer, Spindel and others say a family of five needs three times that, a minimum of 69,000 cruzeiros, to survive.

In 1950, only one member of the average Brazilian family worked but now a family must have three people in the labor force to be able to eke out a subsistence existence.

Individual cases make clear what the child labor situation is in Brazil and what life is like for children here. Junqueira told of a 3-year-old girl who goes into the streets of Sao Paulo's flower-market district each night at 10 o'clock to sell flowers.

"Her mother sends her out there every night," Junqueira said, "because she has no other way to get the money for food. It is not uncommon."

The little girl makes about 100 cruzeiros a night, less than $3 a week.

Thirteen miles north of Sao Paulo lies the shabby city of Embu, a center of brick-making because there are large clay deposits nearby. It is the home of Agenor dos Santos Costa, his wife and 10 children.

One of those children is 8-year-old Anita. She gets out of bed at 3 a.m. with the rest of the family and starts making bricks.

While Santos Costa and his older children mix the clay with water, Anita fills the molds, cuts away the excess, knocks the bricks from the molds, puts them out to dry and then shoves them into the oven.

It is hot, heavy and hard work, not the ordinary task of a tiny 8-year-old. And it goes on, with a single break, until noon.

"It is necessary," the father said, "because we are paid by each 1,000 bricks we make. The whole family has to work—to live."

About an hour's drive west of Sao Paulo is Ferraz, a working-class city housing thousands of unemployed men and women whose children work in the many glass factories nearby.

During the noon lunch break at one of those factories, the 60 workers, who make cups and drinking glasses, sit outside for relief from the 110 degree-heat inside the windowless, cinder-block building.

It looks like a grade school playground during recess. Most of the workers are 15 or younger and some appeared to be no more than 10. Of Sao Paulo state's 23,000 glass workers, almost 9,000 are under 17.

A physician employed by the Sao Paulo glass workers' union said conditions inside the factories are so bad that "children shouldn't be working there at all. The young body can't adapt as well to the heat as an adult. The heat stunts their growth."

Most of the children working in the glass factories would not talk to a reporter for fear of losing their jobs. But union officials gave an account of what it is like inside.

"They work eight hours a day, six days a week," Carlos Ferreira, president of the union said. "The heat is unbearable and they breathe in pounds of silicon, particularly when they blow the glass into shapes."

The doctor said the incidence of silicosis for the children is 30% higher than that for adult workers.

They are paid 30,000 cruzeiros a month, about $125, if they are listed as fully experienced, full-time workers. But many are categorized by the bosses as apprentices, which means that they receive only half as much pay.

"However," Ferreira said, "they don't get the study time and training time an apprentice should get. They are treated like full-time production workers, but paid like apprentices."

Miller, the agricultural economist, said the children who serve as migrant laborers in the fields receive even worse treatment.

"They have no work cards, no job security," he said. "They cannot go to school and they don't develop their minds. These people are pushed to the side. They have no real part in the society."

A 1975 study by Maria Helena Rocha Antuniassi of the Center of Urban and Rural Studies in the state of Bahia showed that 5- and 6-year-olds work as a matter of course, harvesting tobacco, onions and sugar cane.

The same study found that "the children are an indispensable part of the labor force." Yet they were paid 30% less than adults doing the same work.

Then there are the children who work in supermarkets. Usually 12 or younger, they bag groceries, push shopping carts and make deliveries. According to Junqueira, the lawyer who defends children's rights, there are thousands of these chidlren, nearly all of them unregistered.

They work up to 12 hours a day, longer during the Christmas holiday season. But, according to Junqueira, the long hours are the least of the abuses they suffer.

"The supermarkets practically rent these children," she said of the system under which the stores get the benefit of having young workers at low wages without assuming any responsibility for them.

It works this way: A parent decides that his or her child has to work to help support the family. Because the child is below the legal age to work, the parent goes to one of several so-called "civic clubs," which advertise that they can provide education and training for young children.

The civic club then sends the child to a supermarket to work eight-hour days and six- or sometimes even seven-day weeks. The market pays the civic club an agreed-on sum, usually the minimum wage.

In turn, the civic club pays the child's parents, but usually only after deducting half of the salary for "service charges."

Because the law considers what the civic club pays the parents to be "an educational grant," the child is not considered employed and is therefore outside the protection of the law.

The supermarkets insist that the children do not work for them and are the responsibility of the civic clubs, which say they provide only a place for training and have nothing to do with working conditions. As a result, the family of a 12-year-old boy who was killed recently while delivering groceries for a supermarket was unable to obtain even burial benefits.

Earlier this year, the supermarket children went on strike for better pay, improved working conditions and benefits. The strike failed when all the children were fired.

Even if a supermarket is fined by the government for violating child labor laws, the fines are relatively small and apparently well worth the risk.

The El Dorado supermarket in Sao Paulo, which employs 180 to 200 children, has been fined twice this year for hiring unregistered minors. The fines totaled 100,000 cruzeiros, or $416.

Junqueira said that no more than 10 or 15 of the El Dorado child workers are legally registered, so the penalty is small compared to the savings the store makes in using children to do the work.

Probably the most difficult and sensitive aspect of Brazil's child labor situation concerns the country's thousands of child prostitutes.

In the Amazon delta city of Belem alone, there are more than 15,000 child prostitutes, according to municipal juvenile court estimates.

They can be found in posh brothels such as Veronica's, in one of the city's most fashionable neighborhoods, or in popular, middle-class bars like Tocaia Chendengo on Gaspar Viana Street in the center of town.

More often, however, the prostitutes, some of whom are only 10, work in the many shabby motels bordering the highways that cut through Belem.

It was near one of these roads that Simone (not her real name) was found walking not long ago, her clothes ripped and her face swollen and covered with blood. Simone is 12.

She said she had been beaten by the owner of the motel where she worked after she accused a regular customer of trying to leave without paying. Despite the pleas of friends, she returned to the motel that night because she said, there was no other choice.

She had been taken to the motel a year earlier by her mother and she will have to work there until her mother, who gets nearly all of her pay, says she can leave.

"It is virtual slavery," said a Sao Paulo juvenile court worker of the child prostitutes. "Once they start, they are caught," a judgment seconded by a veteran of the trade.

"That is what is so bad about these young girls," said Baiana, a veteran prostitute in Belem.

"All they know is smoke cigarettes, drink liquor, the four walls of the hotel room and the men they have sex with," Baiana said. "They wouldn't even know what the world is like outside. They can't even find their way around."

Baiana, world-weary and street-wise, is 19. She has been a prostitute for four years.

Father Bruno Sechi, 43, a Roman Catholic priest who works with child prostitutes, blames the problem on Brazil's rapid industrialization and the resulting migration of rural families into the cities.

"There was no housing and no work for the migrants," he said, adding that most of the migrants have no marketable skills and end up living in slums "with only one daily concern—how to survive."

One way for a family to survive is to put its young daughters to work as prostitutes among the large number of skilled workers brought in to build dams, roads and other products of industrialization.

"Increasing numbers of small girls find a way of getting the money to help the family make ends meet," the priest said. "Just as their brothers sell peanuts, they sell their bodies."

But prostitution is not the only plague on the lives of Brazilian children. Poor, often black, children from the countryside far too frequently are trapped into another system of exploitation that resembles slavery.

They are called *empregadas*—live-in maids who clean house, wash clothes, iron and baby-sit.

According to Junqueira, the lawyer who defends the rights of children, there are thousands upon thousands of such maids, living like captives, in Sao Paulo alone. On any given day, several girls, often only 11 or 12, find their way into Junqueira's office seeking help.

The root cause for all of these abuses is economic. The overwhelming majority of Brazilians, despite all of the country's real and potential wealth, are still very poor.

"Families simply cannot survive without their children working," said Ferreira, the glass workers' union president.

"The families take advantage of the situation because they have to," said Maria Carmen Nogueira Kotscho, a sociologist at the Foundation for the Welfare of Minors in Sao Paulo.

Even Junqueira, who otherwise professes "radical opposition to the concept of child labor," admits that most Brazilian families would collapse without their children at work. "The parents can't afford to oppose it," she said, "and the authorities don't care." □

"It Can Hurt Plenty"

Statistics concerning hunger in Latin America provide the clinical dimension of an unnecessary tragedy. The brilliant Brazilian writer Mário de Andrade (1893–1945) provides its emotional dimension in his pithy short story "It Can Hurt Plenty." Through the child Paulino, he conveys both the feeling of hunger and its ultimate consequence. Subtly and symbolically, he also suggests that "change" has not altered reality.

Andrade wrote this story in the early 1930s. One-half century later, of every thousand children born alive in Latin America, 82 died before reaching their first birthday because of malnourishment. Fully two-thirds of the 150 million Brazilians consumed less than the 2,480 daily calories that the United Nations Food and Agriculture Organization considers the minimum intake necessary for a normal life. Such realities prompted the Brazilian theologian Leonardo Boff to conclude, "The current structuring of society cannot please God, because most people are excluded; there is little participation and much oppression of the poor."

YOU REMEMBER TERESINHA whose husband went to jail for killing those two brothers, Aldo and Tino? In an indirect sort of way it was Teresinha who really killed them. And she suffered plenty, what with her two kids and no husband. But anyway, his sacrifice seemed to break the hex she put on people. Nobody committed any more crimes on account of her. Only, poor Alfredo was stuck in that retreat up the river, slowly chewing and swallowing the twenty years that his nemesis of a mate cooked up for him. Injustice, bitterness . . . things that are hard to digest. Result: Alfredo had such a stomachache that he became one of the most unwelcome guests in the penitentiary. Nobody liked him and he was always in some kind of trouble. I'm wasting too much time on him.

Teresinha suffered, poor thing! She was still half-goodlooking, with a nice shape. She could brag that lots of guys wanted to sleep with her and were even willing to pay for it. She refused. At first because she was thinking of Alfredo the beloved; then later because she was thinking of Alfredo the murderer. She was sometimes on the point of giving in, but then she pictured Alfredo coming out of the penitentiary with a new knife in his hand to disembowel her. So she stayed virtuous in a cold sweat. She got no pleasure out of life. She was angry at the whole situation and she didn't have any outlet, so she'd come home and take it out on whoever was weaker than she was. She'd see her mother, prematurely old and practically dying on her feet, take five minutes to lift a suit of long underwear out of the washtub. Right away she'd throw some more dirty wash at her.

"If you don't look out, you'll fall asleep with that stuff in your hands."

She was home. But could you really call it a home? It looked like one of those road huts where the mule drivers rest. Just about as dirty. Two things that looked vaguely like chairs. One table. One bed. On the floor there was a mattress where the cockroaches lived. At night they came out and danced on the old lady's face. After all, where do all the insects of this world perform their tribal dances? On somebody's face, right?

There was another room, where nobody slept. Small and stuffy. A tiny stove was there, but sometimes for two days in a row nobody lit a match because that would have implied food to cook and coal to burn, of each of which there was often none. But the stove was there, so in Teresinha's and her mother's dictionary it had the grand name of kitchen.

Source: William L. Grossman, translator, "It Can Hurt Plenty," *Modern Brazilian Short Stories* (Berkeley and Los Angeles: University of California Press, 1967), pp. 12–26. Copyright ©1967 The Regents of the University of California.

They lived in this hut with Teresinha's whelp, who was a sort of leftover—in every sense of the term. How could Teresinha spare any feeling for him? Good heavens, living with all kinds of injustice, wanting a man and not having any, thinking all the time about what Alfredo might do to her, and with the death of the two brothers on her conscience. . . . And all she had in her hands, dipped in the gentle water, was somebody's underwear and socks, hardened with seven days' sweat. Some of her customers owed her for two weeks, and she hated them. . . . So, you see, Teresinha was carrying quite a burden. And as if this wasn't enough to plug up the fountain of maternal love, she had to put up with her pest of a mother-in-law, a big mulatto woman, whom she despised but needed because of the ten milreis she left there every month. The *figlia dun cane* would strut up to the house, very superior because she had maybe thirty contos in the bank, and would find fault with everything.

How could Teresinha feel any love for the little guy? She was a grown woman who never had any real fun in her entire thirty years on earth. She had a warm, live body and a cold, dead soul. . . . Paulino was almost four, and not since the first eight months did he know what it was to feel the warmth of her breast with her arms hugging him and her mouth coming close to his face and saying *figlioulo mio* and then giving him a noisy little sucking kiss, a mother's kiss. . . .

Paulino was just a leftover in that house. And he was all the more so because his smart older brother, when he saw that everything was going to pot, had his guardian angel put a typhoid microbe on his tongue. The microbe went down to his little belly and started having children of its own, millions every hour, and within two nights they had paraded around there so much that they wore out the pavement. And off went the unbaptized soul to the limbo of innocent pagans. Paulino was left over.

Being a logical little fellow he never thought he was a leftover, because in that house he never saw anything left over. Paulino grew up on hunger, hunger was his daily bread. Sometimes, in the small hours of the night, he would wake up terrified. His angel was standing there. His guardian angel? Hell, no. His wicked angel, waking him up so he wouldn't die. The miserable kid would open his eyes in the foul-smelling dark and would half understand that he was eating himself up inside. The first few times he wept.

"*Stá zito guaglion!*"

What do you mean, *stá zito!* Did you ever feel real hunger gnawing at your entrails? . . . Paulino would sometimes stand up on his bowlegs and, with a sort of rocking gait, go over to his mother's bed. Bed, did I say? She hurt her foot and didn't have any money for the doctor who fixed it up. She had a choice: she could either get into the bed with the doctor or sell it to pay him. She sold it. Then she cut the mattress in two and put one half on top of three big boxes. That was the bed.

Teresinha woke up out of a sound sleep with her son's little hand patting her face. In a rage she struck out blindly, hitting him in the eyes and then in the pit of the stomach, wham! Paulino rolled on the floor. He wanted to scream, but his body reminded him of once when he cried too loud and got hit in the mouth

with the heel of his mother's wooded slipper, and so he lost his taste for scream-
ing. He just whimpered, so softly that it sort of lulled Teresinha back to sleep.
He was all curled up very small like a pill bug. His pain and anguish were so
intense that he paid no attention to the pinching of hunger. Finally he fell asleep.

In the cold early dawn his body woke up, and Paulino was surprised to find
himself sleeping on the floor, far away from his grandmother's mattress. He had
an ache in his shoulder, another in his knee, another in the part of his forehead
that had been against the floor. But he hardly noticed these aches because of the
immense pain of the cold. He crawled apprehensively, for the beginning of day
outside was throwing ghostly glimmers through the cracks in the wall. He scared
away the cockroaches and curled in the illusory warmth of his grandmother's
bones. He didn't fall asleep again.

Finally, about six o'clock, Paulino was brought back to a consciousness of
life in the world by the sound of the first people in the street: milkmen, baker's
men, and food vendors of all sorts. His body felt a vague warmth. The noises
outside woke Teresinha. She stretched and sat up, vibrating with that matutinal
sensuality that drives a person crazy with longing. She pressed her arms against
her well-developed breasts and against her belly and all, and pressed her thighs
together so hard it hurt around the kidneys. That restless, aimless hatred started
up again. It came from a chastity preserved at great cost, a chastity which she
herself knew must end sooner or later. She looked for her wooden slipper. Then
she screamed at her mother: what was she doing in bed at this hour, why hadn't
she put water in the tub, etcetera.

Before the women got up, Paulino had left the warmth of his place on the
mattress and was prowling about the kitchen, for the grandest thing that ever
happened to him was imminent: he was going to get something to eat, a piece of
bread. It was a glorious holiday for him when a customer paid, or his rich grandmother came, or anything like that, because then, in addition to the bread, they
had coffee with sugar! He always drank it too fast, that hot water flavored with
a pinch of coffee, burning his tongue and his pale little lips. And then he went
and ate his bread outside the house.

Not right in front of the house, for that's where the faucet, the tubs, and
the bleaching stone were. The two women would be doing the washing there and
fighting. Before long, they'd turn their wrath on him and, as a bonus, they'd
give him a knuckle rap on the top of his head. Don't kid yourself, a knuckle rap
can hurt; it can hurt plenty.

So he never ate there any more. He'd open the kitchen door—it never closed
all the way—and go down the step. Then he'd run off, laughing for joy at his
companion, the cold, and lose himself in the tall grass and the cocklebur thickets
behind the house. This was his forest. Here Paulino nursed his sorrows without
anyone seeing or scolding. He sat on the ground or stood with his heel on an ant
heap, and began to eat. Then all of a sudden, ouch! He almost fell as he raised
his little leg to kill the sauba ant that had its stingers embedded in his ankle. He
picked up his bread, now buttered with dirt, and went on with his breakfast,
enjoying the music of the grit as it crunched between his teeth. It sounded like a
maraca.

But he didn't forget about the ant. When he had finished his bread, the boy warrior in him took over and he didn't even notice that he was still hungry. He looked for a piece of wood suitable for the hunting of ants in the great forest—a stunted forest, alas, penetrated by even the weakest sun.

With stick in hand he set out in search of ants. Not ordinary little ants; he couldn't be bothered with them. Only sauba ants. When he found one, he followed it patiently, breaking through the branches of the shrubs when necessary. Often his hand or leg burned because he had brushed against the stinging hairs of a butterfly larva. When he finally got the sauba ant into the open, he spent hours playing with the little wretch, until it died.

Then he felt hungry again. The sun was high, but Paulino knew that only after the factory whistles blew would there be beans and rice when things were going well or another piece of bread when they weren't. He tried to distract himself by hunting for another sauba ant, but it didn't work. His daily suffering from hunger induced a mood of meditative melancholy. He would sit down, turn his head, and rest his cheek on his hand. Then one day, in the lacy shade of a bush, he learned how to forget his hunger for a while by falling asleep. He never dreamed in his sleep. The flies came and buzzed around his open mouth, attracted by the vestige of sweetness. Paulino stirred a little, pressed his tormented lips together, spread his legs a bit, and urinated.

Paulino woke up long before the time for the factories to whistle. He passed his tongue over his lips and chewed. There was the grit with its rhythmic scrunch—and something more, something small and sweetish, in his mouth. He took it out with his fingers to see what it was. It was two flies. Yes, flies. Didn't you know they tasted sort of sweet? He put them on his tongue, sucked their flavor, and swallowed them.

This was the beginning of a sustained effort to hide his hunger from himself by eating everything in the forest that could possibly be swallowed. Instead of wasting time hunting for sauba ants, he treated himself to little picnics of damp earth. Then he found something better. With tongue in readiness he would place his cheek on the ground next to an anthill. When an ant appeared he would shoot out his tongue, which soon became skilled in this maneuver. He would retract his tongue with the ant stuck to it and would press the infinitesimally small, round thing against the roof of his mouth. He'd place it between his teeth, crush it, and swallow his saliva—an illusion of eating. And what a bonanza if he came upon a whole line of ants! He'd get on his knees, with his backside to the clouds, and lick the ground like an anteater. In twenty seconds he could liquidate a procession a yard long.

Once, in this effort to kill his hunger, Paulino descended from the high epicurean level that I've been describing: he caught a cockroach, put it in his mouth, and chewed it as he walked away. Totally unaware that he was doing something disgusting. Of course, you must bear in mind that these things he ate provided almost no nourishment. The factory would whistle, and the prospect of rice and beans found Paulino sated, his belly filled with illusions. He grew weaker and weaker. He looked as bleak as a day in midwinter.

Teresinha never noticed. The rein of virtue was by then so spent that the mare would soon break free and run wild. As a warm-up, she clouted Paulino—blindly, at random, her blows landing on every part of his body.

Fernandez the carter generally walked her home these days. He was an erect young fellow, of decent family, no more than twenty-five years old, and somewhat slow in his mental processes but physically energetic. The rein broke. Teresinha let him carry her bundle of wash, he came into the house, and she offered him coffee and consent. The old lady dirtied her mouth with some filthy language that no one exactly understood, took her mattress and her utterly astounded grandson, and moved into the kitchen.

Anyway, the meals improved and the little belly learned the secret delights of baked macaroni. Only, he was afraid of the man. Fernandez had made a little fuss over him when he first came into the house. The next morning, when they were all having breakfast together, Paulino began to play with one of the man's long legs and got a shove that left him with his ears drooping.

Naturally, the mother-in-law learned what was going on and came over. Teresinha was embarrassed. She said good-morning and got barked at in reply. But Teresinha didn't need the mulatto woman's money any more and so she came back at her like a wildcat. A terrifying scene! Paulino wanted to run away, but he stood there fascinated because the mother-in-law kept pointing to him and saying "my grandson" every other second. She said Teresinha would have to get along without her help now, because she wasn't going to pay for any hankypanky of a cheap Italian girl with a Spaniard. Teresinha shouted that a Spaniard was a lot better than a Brazilian any day, you daughter of a Negro! Mother of a murderer! I don't need you, you understand? Mulatto! Mother of a murderer!

"You're the murderer, you pig! You made my son do it, you damned wop, you pig!"

"Get out of here, mother of a murderer! You never bothered with your grandson before, and now all of a sudden you're worried about him. Take him along with you if you want to."

"I'll take him all right! Poor innocent little thing, he doesn't know what kind of a mother he has. You pig! Pig!"

She picked up Paulino with one arm and adjusting her Sunday shawl, walked quickly away. A few women of the neighborhood looked with curiosity at her and the boy, who was kicking furiously. To show these onlookers that she was in the right, she turned around and shouted:

"Listen! I'm not going to pay your rent any more. I protected you because you were the wife of my unfortunate son, but I'm not going to support a loose woman, understand?"

Teresinha, mad with hate, was already looking around for a piece of wood with which to beat her mother-in-law to death. The older woman thought it prudent to quit while she was ahead and stalked off in triumph, clump, clump.

Paulino, jostled rhythmically against all that warm flesh, wept with fear. He was bewildered: a street he had never seen before, lots of people, this strange-acting woman, and he without mother, without bread, without his forest, without grandma. . . . What was happening to him? Terror crept through his little bluish body, but he was afraid to cry very loudly because he noticed that the old lady was wearing shoes with big heels, bigger even than the heels on wooden slippers. If she ever hit him in the mouth with one of those heels, it would tear his lips to pieces. . . . And Paulino, horror-stricken, forced his hands into his mouth, thus inventing a kind of mute.

"My poor grandson!"

With her big, warm hand she took his little head and placed it against her rubbery neck. It was sort of nice being carried in those strong arms, with the shawl providing extra warmth. . . . And the old woman looking at him with eyes of compassion and comfort. . . . My heavens, what is all this, that makes a fellow feel so good? Don't you know, Paulino? It's affection, that's what it is. It's tenderness. It's love. The old lady hugged him against her breast, placed his cheeck against hers, and then kissed him again and again. In short, she introduced the kid to the great mystery.

Paulino became calmer. For the first time in his life, his concept of the future extended all the way to the next day. He felt he was protected and that tomorrow he would certainly have coffee and sugar. For hadn't the old woman put her mouth to his face and given him those big, wonderfully noisy kisses? And so Paulino's thoughts extended to tomorrow, and he imagined a huge cup, as big as the old lady, filled to the brim with coffee and sugar. He smiled at the two tears running down her cheeks, but then he saw, in the middle of one of the tears, a shoe. . . . growing, growing, until its heel was as big as the old lady. Paulino began to cry softly again, as he did back home in the early morning when his crying served Teresinha as a lullaby. Until she woke up and screamed at him:

"For Christ's sake, that's enough! Get up now. Come on!"

The heel grew longer, enormously longer, and became the chimney of a building on the other side of the street. Paulino, choked with fear, stopped sobbing. They had arrived.

This was a real house. You went in by the garden, with flowers, and you wanted to pick all the roses. You went up a few stairs and there was a parlor with two big pictures on the wall—a man and a woman. The woman was the old lady. Plenty of chairs, and one big one on which lots of people could sit at the same time. On a small table in the middle of the room, there was a vase with a pink flower that never withered. And those little white doilies on the chairs and on the table, they could keep you amused just counting the round tassels. The rest of the house was just as amazing.

Afterwards, two very pretty girls appeared, wearing the navy-blue skirts and white blouses of normal-school students. They stared unpleasantly at him. Those four dark eyes came down like hard knuckles on the skull of Paulino's soul. He stood glued to the floor, motionless, dizzy.

Then there was a terrible row. The old lady made some remark and one of the girls replied crossly. The old lady raised her voice and spoke of "my grandson." The other girl shouted at her, and there came a tempest of "my grandson" and "your grandson," with lightning striking all around Paulino's head. It got worse and worse. When the three voices could rise no higher, the old lady slapped the girl nearer her and aimed a spoon at the head of the other one, but she ducked and ran out of the room.

Paulino's imagination couldn't have conjured up a more terrifying situation. And the funny thing is that, for the first time, terror awakened his intelligence. His prior concept of the next day disappeared, and Paulino saw that there would be nothing but anger and abuse tomorrow and tomorrow and more than three million years of tomorrows.

"Go pick up that spoon!"

His bowlegs moved, God knows how. He picked up the spoon and gave it to the old lady. She put it away and left the dining room. Everything was settled, the room was empty. The shadows of late afternoon came in quickly and hid the unknown objects. Only the table stood out clearly, especially the red and white stripes of the tablecloth. Paulino leaned against one of the table legs. He was trembling. A nice sizzling sound and a delicious smell came from inside, and a soothing ticktock seemed to be trying to calm him.

Paulino sat on the floor. A great peace settled on his exhausted mind: he had nothing to fear from the old lady's heel. She wasn't like his mother. When she got angry she didn't throw a shoe, she just threw a light little spoon, all gleaming and silver. Paulino curled up, his cheek against the floor. He was so sleepy after all he had been through. There was no more danger of a rap in the teeth with the heel of a wooden slipper; the old mulatto woman would only throw a silver spoon at him. And Paulino didn't know whether a silver spoon could hurt. He fell asleep.

"Get up off the floor! How this child must have suffered, Margot! See how skinny he is."

"No wonder! With his mother enjoying herself in orgies day and night, what would you expect!"

"Margot. . . . you know what 'whore' means, don't you? Well, I think Paulino is what the old writers used to call a whoreson."

They laughed.

"Margot!"

"Yes?"

"Send Paulino here so he can get something to eat."

"Go in there, boy."

The bandy legs rocked rapidly as Paulino went into the kitchen. He soon learned that in this room he must not move around or touch anything. The kind old lady pushed the door mat with her foot.

"Sit down there and eat everything, you hear?"

It was rice and beans. With longing eyes he watched the meat disappear through the door to the dining room. The old lady probably thought that a boy of four didn't need meat, especially in view of the financial burden of bringing up two daughters.

Paulino's life was still miserable, but the nature of the misery had changed. The food had improved and there was enough of it, yet Paulino was haunted by a longing for the things he used to eat in his little forest. The old mulatto woman never suffered any recurrence of tenderness. It must have been a sort of reflex associated with a sense of duty. Those kisses she gave him were sincere all right, but only within the framework of tragedy. When the tragedy, as she saw it, was ended, so was the tenderness. She left Paulino with a terrible yearning for kisses.

He wanted to be close to the two girls, but they were always annoyed with him and pinched him for no apparent reason. Nevertheless, the younger, Nininha, who had an immense curiosity and who never got grades as high as Margot's took it upon herself to give Paulino his bath. When Saturday came, she put him in the tub. He was amazed. He was also scared that he'd get pinched again. But instead he felt the caress of a face, hot and pretty, rubbing against his little body. The bath always ended with her angry at him and putting the nightshirt on him very fast, almost brutally. "Stand up straight, you pest!" she'd say, and she'd give him a twisting sort of pinch. It hurt, it hurt.

Paulino went down the kitchen steps and walked listlessly along the alleyway at the side of the house leading to the front garden. With considerable effort he pulled open the gate, which was always slightly ajar. He went out, sat down, rested his cheek on his hand with his head turned sideways, and watched the world go by.

And so, between pinches and hard words, most of which he did not understand, he too went by, like the world: sad, bewildered, afraid, tied to the earth, and progressively failing. But what could he do? He would drink his coffee and they would tell him to eat his bread in the yard or—pig!—he'd mess up the whole house. He went to the yard. The earth was so moist, it was a terrible temptation. Not that he thought of it as a temptation, for no one threatened him with a knuckle rap on the head if he ate earth. *Treck-trrleck,* he chewed a little piece, swallowed it, chewed another little piece, swallowed it. And then, around ten o'clock, he had to sit down on that doormat, with its fibers always pricking him, and had to swallow beans and rice, which he found nauseating.

"Good heavens, this boy doesn't eat! Just see how he looks at his food! Why do you get earth all over your face like a pig, eh?"

Paulino was afraid he'd get a rap with a spoon, and so he swallowed some beans, dry. Then the old lady's mind suddenly clicked.

"Is it possible!. . . . You've been eating earth, haven't you? Let me see."

She pulled Paulino to the door of the kitchen and, with those two enormous, hot hands:

"Open your mouth, boy!"

She drew back his lips. Earth between his teeth and on his gums.

"Open your mouth, I told you!"

And her fingers opened his little mouth wide. She looked at his tongue. It was the color of earth all the way back to the root. Paulino got hit so often he thought it would never end. First came a slap on the mouth, which was still open, making a funny sort of sound, pah! Then came an avalanche of slaps, wallops, twisting pinches, knuckle raps on the head. And nasty words, which for little kids are also slaps in the face, right?

Then began Paulino's greatest martyrdom. Nobody wanted him to be in the house, he practically had to live in the backyard. Along with his bread he always got a tongue lashing of threats that almost knocked him out, honest to God! Paulino went down the steps to the yard, munching his bread. He was dazed. He felt the whole world hitting him. And then? . . . The bread was gone, and the tasty earth was still there, calling to him, offering itself to him. But those three women, those pinchers, didn't want him to eat it. . . . Oh, what a temptation to our poor little Saint Anthony! He wanted to eat it but he couldn't. Well, he could, but then the old lady would come and stick her big fingers in his mouth. . . . To eat or not to eat? . . . He fled his temptation, climbed the steps, and sat down, looking at the wall of the house so that he could not see the good earth. But it was there, calling him, all his, just five small steps below. . . .

Luckily, he suffered this temptation only three days, for then he started to cough. It got worse and worse. The old lady was fit to be tied. Paulino heard her say it was one of those rasping coughs that are so annoying. Maybe he caught it from the boys across the street; he was playing with them in front of the gate. Let's give him the syrup that Dona Emilia taught us how to make. But Dona Emilia's syrup didn't help, nor did the five milreis spent for a patent medicine at the cut-rate drugstore. He just had to wait and hope that the cough would lose its voice and slink away by itself.

Paulino didn't like the scratchy feeling in his throat. He swallowed a lot to see if he could make it stop. When he got a coughing attack he went over to a wall and leaned against it. His eyes were running, his nose was running, and he was dribbling from the mouth, which he kept open all the time. The little guy sat down wherever he was, because otherwise he would have fallen. The chair was spinning, the table was spinning, even the smell in the kitchen was spinning. Paulino felt nauseous and his whole body hurt.

"Poor thing! Look, go cough outside, you're getting the floor all dirty. Go on!"

Fear gave Paulino the necessary strength, and he went out. He had another attack. He lay down, his mouth pressed against the earth, but with no desire to eat. For a long time he was stretched out on the ground without moving. His body didn't hurt any more. His head didn't think anymore. He just stayed there. The dampness of the ground would have made his cough worse and he might have died, but he finally got up. He wanted to go back into the house. But he might get it dirty and then they'd pinch him in the chest. And it wouldn't do any good anyway, because they'd just send him right out again. . . .

It was late afternoon. Street cars were going by, carrying the workers home. Paulino sat down at the front gate and watched them with his moist eyes. Night would fall soon, bringing new life. A light, dusty April wind touched his cheek. The sun, clutching in vain at the horizon, stained the tired air of day with red and green. The groups of workers walking past looked almost black against the sky. Everything was mysterious in contrasted light and shadow.

At that moment Teresinha came walking down the street. Stunningly dressed. To start from the bottom: her shoes were a dull yellow, her stockings gave a pink glow to her pretty legs, which were revealed up to the knee, and her dress was of a light blue lovelier than the April sky. And mama's face, how beautiful it was, with some of that dark hair done up in a lustrous topknot and some of it drawn from the center across her forehead, giving a glow of Neapolitan blue to the swarthy skin, which was illuminated also by the colors of French cosmetics.

With a confusion of joyous instincts in his body, and not exactly aware of what he was doing, Paulino got up.

"Mama!"

Teresinha turned. It was her *figlioulo*. I don't know just what happened in her mind, but she ran to him and kneeled down on the sidewalk in her silk stockings. She hugged Paulino against her ample breasts. It hurt, but deliciously. And Teresinha cried, because after all she was very unhappy too. Fernandez had walked out on her and, after some indecision, she had become a full-time prostitute. Now, seeing Paulino so dirty and sick-looking, she suddenly had an impulse to give up the life she was living. She cried in remorse and self-pity.

Only then did she feel bad about her son, so horribly thin and more fragile than virtue. He must have been suffering there in the mulatto woman's house. . . . For a moment she considered taking Paulino with her. But she quickly hid the thought from herself, for he would obviously be in the way whenever. . . . She looked at his clothes. They weren't of the very best material, but they were serviceable. She placated her conscience by pretending to think that her son was being treated well. She planted a kiss on the little mouth, moist with phlegm, and swallowed a tear. Then she hugged him and kissed him several times. She walked off, adjusting her clothes.

Paulino, not very firm on his feet, made no motion, no gesture. He watched the blue dress disappear in the distance. He turned away. A piece of greasy wrapping paper was rolling merrily on the ground. He would have to take three steps to catch it.. . . . It wasn't worth it. He sat on the step again. The colors of the evening were gently blending into a common gray. Paulino rested his cheek on the palm of his hand. In an indifference born of exhaustion, he half heard, half saw the world about him. His mouth was open; phlegm and saliva ran out onto his hand. From there it dripped on his shirt, which was dark so that it wouldn't show the dirt.□

"The Glass of Milk"

On the western side of the South American continent, far from the São Paulo of Mário de Andrade, the Chilean Manuel Rojas (1896–1973) took up the theme of hunger in this tale laced with ironies. His young protagonist also is hungry. The two people who offer him food are an English-speaking sailor and a blond woman with a Castilian accent, both foreigners. He finds a temporary job loading a ship with food for export, to foreigners. What larger meanings do these ironies suggest? Why does the youth feel the "shame of hunger" rather than a rage of hunger? The realities Rojas briefly describes require an explanation just as they beg a solution. Significantly, those are not realities of one moment in time or one place. At the end of the twentieth century, over half of the Latin Americans are malnourished.

P ROPPED ON THE STARBOARD RAIL, the sailor seemed to be waiting for someone. A bundle wrapped in white paper, grease-spotted, was in his left hand; his right tended his pipe.

Source: Manuel Rojas, "The Glass of Milk," in Arturo Torres-Rioseco (ed.), *Short Stories of Latin America* (New York: Las Americas Publishing Co., 1963), pp. 121–129.

From behind some freight-cars, a thin youth appeared; he paused a moment, looked out to sea, and then walked on along the edge of the wharf with his hands in his pockets, idling or thinking.

When he passed in front of the ship, the sailor called out to him in English: "I say, look here!"

The youth raised his head, and without stopping, answered in the same language:

"Hello! What?"

"Are you hungry?"

There was a brief silence during which the youth seemed to be thinking, and took one shorter step as if to stop, but then replied, smiling feebly at the sailor:

"No, I'm not hungry. Thanks, sailor."

"All right."

The sailor took his pipe out of his mouth, spat, and replacing it, looked away. The youth, ashamed that he had seemed to need charity, walked a little faster, as if afraid he might change his mind.

A moment later, a gaudy tramp with a long, blond beard and blue eyes, dressed in odd rags and oversized, torn shoes, passed before the sailor, who without greeting called to him:

"Are you hungry?"

He had not yet finished the phrase when the tramp looked with shining eyes at the package the sailor held in his hand and answered hurriedly:

"Yes, sir; I'm very much hungry!"

The sailor smiled. The package flew through the air and landed in the eager hands. The hungry fellow did not even say "thanks," but sat right down on the ground, opened the still-warm bundle, and happily rubbed his hands as he saw what it contained. A port loafer might not speak English well, but he would never forgive himself if he didn't know enough to ask food from someone who did speak it.

The youth who passed by first had stopped nearby, and had seen what happened.

He was hungry too. He had not eaten for exactly three days, three long days. And more from timidity and shame than from pride, he refused to wait by the gangways at mealtimes, hoping the generosity of the sailors would produce some package of left-overs and bits of meat. He could not do it, he would never be able to do it. And when, as just now, someone did offer him a handout, the boy refused it heroically, though he felt his hunger increase with the refusal.

He had been wandering for six days around the side streets and docks of that port. An English vessel had left him there after bringing him from Punta Arenas, where he had jumped a previous ship on which he had served as captain's mess boy. He had spent a month there helping an Austrian crabber and then had stowed away on the first ship bound north.

He was discovered the day after sailing, and put to work in the boiler room. At the first large port of call, he had been put off, and there he had remained, like a bale without a label, without an acquaintance, without a penny, and without a trade.

As long as the ship was in port, the boy managed to eat, but after that. . . . The great city that rose up beyond the back streets with their taverns and cheap inns did not attract him; it seemed a place of slavery: stale, dark, without the grand sweep of the sea; among its high walls and narrow streets people lived and died bewildered by agonizing drudgery.

The boy was gripped by that fascination of the sea which molds the most peaceful and orderly lives as a strong arm a thin rod. Although very young, he had already made several trips along the coast of South America on various ships, doing odd jobs and tasks, tasks and odd jobs which were almost useless on land.

After the ship left him, the boy walked and walked, hoping to chance upon something that would enable him to live somehow until he could get back to his home grounds; but he found nothing. The port was not very busy, and the few ships that had work would not take him on.

The docks were swarming with confirmed tramps: sailors on the beach, like himself, who had either jumped ship or were fleeing some crime; loafers given to idleness, who kept alive one knows not how, by begging or stealing, spending their days as if they were the beads of some grimy rosary, waiting for who knows what extraordinary events, or not expecting anything; people of the strangest and most exotic races and places, and even some in whose existence one doesn't believe until one sees a living example. . . .

The following day, convinced that he could not hold out much longer, the youth decided to resort to any means to get some food.

Walking along, he found himself in front of a ship that had docked the night before, and was loading wheat. A line of men, heavy sacks on their shoulders, shuttled from the freight-cars, across the gangplank to the hatchways of the ship's hold where the stevedores received the cargo.

He watched for a while, until he dared to speak to the foreman, offering his services. He was accepted, and enthusiastically he took his place in the long line of dock workers.

During the first period of the day he worked well; but later, he began to feel tired and dizzy; he swayed as he crossed the gangplank, the heavy load on his shoulder, on seeing at his feet the opening between the side of the ship and the thick wall of the wharf, at the bottom of which the sea, stained with oil and littered with garbage, lapped quietly.

There was a brief pause at lunch time, and while some of the men went off to the nearby eating places, and others ate what they had brought, the boy stretched out on the ground to rest, hiding his hunger.

He finished the day's work feeling completely exhausted, covered with sweat, at the end of his rope. While the laborers were leaving, the boy sat on some sacks, watching for the foreman, and when the last man had gone, approached him; confused and stuttering, he asked, without explaining what was happening to him, if he could be paid immediately, or if it were possible to get an advance on his earnings.

The foreman answered that it was customary to pay at the end of a job, and that it would still be necessary to work the following day in order to finish loading the ship. One more day! On the other hand, they never paid a cent in advance.

"But," he said, "if you need it, I could lend you about forty cents. . . . That's all I have."

The boy thanked him for his offer with an anguished smile, and left.

Then the boy was seized by acute despair. He was hungry, hungry, hungry! Hunger doubled him over, like a heavy, broad whiplash. He saw everything through a blue haze, and he staggered like a drunk when he walked. Nevertheless, he would not have been able to complain or to shout, for his suffering was deep and exhausting; it was not pain, but anguish, the end! It seemed to him that he was flattened out by a great weight.

Suddenly he felt his entrails on fire, and he stood still. He began to bend down, down, doubling over forcibly like a rod of steel, until he thought that he would drop. At that instant, as if a window opened before him, he saw his home, the view from it, the faces of his mother, brothers and sisters, all that he wanted and loved appeared and disappeared before his eyes shut by fatigue. . . . Then, little by little, the giddiness passed and he began to straighten up, while the burning subsided gradually. Finally, he straightened up, breathing deeply. One more hour and he would drop unconscious to the ground.

He quickened his step, as if fleeing another dizzy spell, and, as he walked, he made up his mind to eat anywhere, without paying, even if they shamed him, beat him, sent him to jail, anything; the main thing was to eat, eat, eat. A hundred times he mentally repeated the word: eat, eat, eat, until it lost its meaning, leaving his head feeling hot and empty.

He did not intend to run away; he would simply say to the owner, "Sir, I was hungry, hungry, hungry, and I can't pay. . . . Do what you want.". . .

He came to the outskirts of the city, and on one of the first streets he found a milk bar. It was a small, clean, and airy place, with little tables with marble tops. Behind the counter stood a blonde lady in a very white apron.

He chose that place. There were few passersby. He could have eaten at one of the cheap grills near the wharves but they were always full of people who gambled and drank.

There was only one customer in the milk bar. He was a little old man with glasses, who sat reading, his nose stuck between the pages of a newspaper, motionless, as if glued to his chair. On the little table there was a half-empty glass of milk.

While he waited for him to leave, the boy walked up and down the sidewalk; he felt the burning sensation in his stomach returning little by little; and he waited five, ten, up to fifteen minutes. He grew tired, and stood to one side of the door, from where he cast glances like stones at the old man.

What the devil could he be reading with such attention? The boy even imagined the old man was his enemy, who knew his intentions and had decided to frustrate them. He felt like entering and saying something insulting that would force the old man to leave, a rude word or phrase that would show him he had no right to sit there reading for an hour for so small a purchase.

Finally, the client finished what he was reading, or at least, interrupted it.

He downed the rest of the milk in one gulp, rose slowly, paid, and walked toward the door. He went out. He was a stoop-shouldered old man, probably a carpenter or varnisher.

Once in the street, the old man put on his glasses, stuck his nose in the newspaper again, and walked slowly away, stopping every ten steps to read more closely.

The youth waited until he was some distance away, and then entered. For a moment the boy stood by the entrance, undecided, not knowing where to sit. Finally, he chose a table and walked toward it, but halfway there he changed his mind, walked back, tripped over a chair, and finally installed himself in a corner.

The lady came, wiped the tabletop with a rag, and in a soft voice that had a trace of Castilian accent, asked him:

"What will you have?"

"A glass of milk."

"Large?"

"Yes, large."

"Is that all?"

"Are there any biscuits?"

"No. Vanilla wafers."

"Well, vanilla wafers."

When the lady had turned away, he wiped his hands on his knees, rejoicing, as if he were cold and were about to drink something hot.

The lady returned, and placed before him a large glass of milk, and a dish full of vanilla wafers; then she went back to her place behind the counter.

His first impulse was to drink the milk in one gulp and then eat the vanilla wafers; but he immediately changed his mind. He felt the woman's eyes watching him with curiosity and attention. He did not dare to look at her; he felt that if he did she would guess his situation and his shameful intentions, and he would have to get up and leave without touching what he had ordered.

Slowly, he took a vanilla wafer and moistening it in the milk, he took a bite; he took a sip of milk, and he felt the burning in his stomach diminishing, dying away. But he became aware of the reality of his desperate situation at once, and he felt something tight and hot well up inside, choking him. He realized that he was about to cry, to sob aloud, and although he knew that the lady was looking at him, he could neither hold back nor undo the burning knot of tears that grew tighter and tighter. He fought it, and as he fought he ate hurriedly, as if frightened, afraid that crying would keep him from eating. When he had finished the milk and the wafers, he eyes clouded and something hot rolled down his nose and into the glass. A terrible sob racked his whole body.

He held his head in his hands, and for a long time he cried, cried with rage, cried with shame, crying as he had never cried before. . . .

He was hunched over crying when he felt a hand caress his tired head, and heard a woman's voice with a sweet Castilian accent say to him:

"Cry, son, cry. . . ."

Again his eyes filled with tears and he cried as intensely as before, but this time, not with pain but with joy; he felt a great refreshing sensation spread inside him, extinguishing the hot something that had nearly strangled him. As he cried, it seemed to him that his life and feelings were cleansed like a glass under a stream of water, recovering the clearness and firmness of former days.

When the crying spell passed, he wiped his eyes and face with his handkerchief, feeling relieved. He raised his head and looked at the lady, but she was no longer looking at him, she was gazing out at the street, at a distant point in space, and her face seemed sad.

On the table before him there was another glass of milk and another dish heaped with vanilla wafers. He ate slowly, without thinking about anything, as if nothing had happened to him, as if he were at home and his mother were that woman who was standing behind the counter.

When he had finished, it had grown dark, and the place was lit by an electric light. He remained seated for a while, wondering what he would say to the lady when he left, without thinking of anything appropriate.

At last he got up and said simply.

"Thank you very much, ma'am; goodbye. . . ."

"Goodbye, son," she answered.

He went out. The wind blowing from the sea refreshed his face, still hot from crying. He walked about aimlessly for a while, then went down a street that led to the docks. It was a very beautiful night, and large stars gleamed in the summer sky.

He thought about the blonde lady who had treated him so generously, resolving to repay her, to reward her as she deserved, when he got some money. But these thoughts of gratitude vanished with the burning of his face, until not one remained, and the recent event receded and was lost in the recesses of his past life.

Suddenly, he surprised himself humming. He straightened up happily, strode on with assurance and determination. . . .

He came to the edge of the sea, and walked back and forth with a spring in his step; he felt like a new man, as if his inner forces, previously scattered, had reassembled and united solidly.

Then he sat down on a pile of burlap sacks; fatigue, like a tingling sensation, climbed up his legs. He looked at the sea. The lights of the wharf and ships spread over the water in a reddish-gold ripple, trembling softly. He stretched out on his back, looking up at the sky for a long time. He did not feel like thinking, or singing, or talking. He just felt alive, that was all. Then he fell asleep with his face toward the sea. □

A Major Transformation: Rural to Urban

Urban growth, a salient characteristic of Latin America in the twentieth century, both fulfilled promises and created problems. Clearly a major change occurred. A traditionally rural society urbanized at phenomenal rates. At the opening of the twentieth century less than a quarter of the population lived in towns and cities of more than 2,000 inhabitants; by mid-century the figure had risen to 50 percent; and by the end of the century it will surpass 75 percent. This trend ranks Latin America as one of the most urbanized regions of the globe, containing some of the world's largest cities. Rural institutions such as land ownership and use patterns, as well as successful industrialization, account for much of the growth. Desperate people migrate to the cities because they find no future in the countryside. Others, filled with hope, embrace the cities to renew their lives. For some time, Latin Americans believed urbanization—and the industrialization and modernization associated with it—might be the panacea for the problems delaying development. Alas, it may have created more than it resolved. Many planners conclude that the first step in meeting the challenges of urban growth is the resolution of the old problems of inequity and production in the countryside.

No WAR CLOUDS hang over the cities of Latin America and the Caribbean, as they did over Kuwait and Baghdad. Yet the governments of the American republics face an urban crisis every bit as daunting as the challenge to rebuild the war-torn cities of the Persian Gulf countries.

The Gulf cities have been bombed or torched into oblivion by a savage war. The newspapers and television tell us of the plight of thousands of Iraqis and Kuwaitis who are short of food, without running water or electricity, and are threatened by outbreaks of epidemic diseases.

Unfortunately, what is a crisis in the Gulf is commonplace in the giant slums that surround virtually every Latin American capital. Millions of slum dwellers are short of food, unemployed, have no access to running water or electricity and face the threat of endemic disease.

In Lima, Peru, for instance, an outbreak of cholera, spread by poor sanitation and bad water supplies, runs rampant today through the city's garbage-strewn hovels.

This is not meant to downplay the tragic conditions brought on by the Gulf war. There is, however, an important difference between the urban crisis in the Gulf and the one in Latin America. The Gulf states have lost in a few weeks an urban infrastructure painstakingly erected over the course of years.

The Latin American cities, by contrast, have never had the chance to build an infrastructure capable of adequately serving their rapidly expanding populations.

We may expect massive efforts to repair the war damage in the Gulf cities. In Latin America, though, governments will continue to struggle and continue to fall behind in the effort to make their cities more habitable.

War is the problem in the Persion Gulf, but in Latin America the culprit is growth, an incredible almost cancerous, swelling of urban population that has transformed once moderate-sized cities into huge unmanageable metropolises.

The rise of mega-cities has been the dominant demographic trend in Latin

Source: Richard C. Schroeder, "Urban Decay in Latin America," *The Times of the Americas* (Washington, D. C.), March 20, 1991, p. 5. With permission of the publisher.

America in the latter part of this century and will continue to be so well into the next. Rapid and widespread urbanization adds an ominous dimension to the world's already serious population problems. The issue is not merely one of numbers, but distribution. Excessive crowding into giant megalopolises brings a multitude of ills—air and water pollution, the accumulation of mountains of garbage, traffic jams, housing shortages, crime.

Perhaps worst of all is the apparent inability of governments to deal with such problems. Urbanization is more rapid in Latin America than anywhere else in the world. A new book published by the United Nations Economic Commission for Latin America and the Caribbean (ECLAC) observes that by the year 2000 the region will have "the largest human agglomerations in the world without having yet found an answer to the challenges presented by this situation."

According to ECLAC, in less than ten years, three quarters of all the people in Latin America will be living in urbanized areas, more than a third of them in cities of more than a million and a half inhabitants. All other developing regions, including the densely populated countries of Asia, will have fewer than one fifth of their populations concentrated in metropolises of that size.

In fact, virtually all population experts agree that by the end of the current decade the world's two largest cities will be located in Latin America: Mexico City with an expected 31 million people and Sao Paulo, Brazil, with 25.8 million.

Of the 35 largest cities in the world, six will be Latin American. Rio de Janeiro will rank seventh with 19 million people; Buenos Aires will be number 15 with 12.1 million, Bogota number 26 with 9.6 million and Lima/Callao, Peru, number 31 with 8.6 million.

Massive urbanization is a recent phenomenon in Latin America. Until the middle of this century the bulk of the region's population was rural. City living was a distant dream for millions of campesinos who grubbed a subsistence living from the land.

The dam broke in the 1950s ECLAC says. As nutrition and public health measures began to improve death rates, especially infant mortality rates, declined dramatically, fueling an explosion in Latin America's over-all-population growth rate.

In rural areas, as families grew, farmland was subdivided into plots too small to sustain all the family members. Overcropping and overgrazing, together with erosion added to the strains. Those able to do so fled the rural areas to the beckoning bright lights of the cities. The exodus was so massive in the sixties, seventies and eighties that the urban areas were overwhelmed.

Between 1960 and 1980 the metropolitan population of Latin America mushroomed from 31 million to 100 million, comprising nearly 30% of the region's total population. Even more alarming crowding lies ahead.

In the six cities mentioned above the total pupulation reached 59 million in 1980, and will climb to 109 million by the year 2000.

Latin America's cities have grown at a rate never before seen in human history, and the quality of life in the most impacted cities has declined as rapidly as populations have swelled.

The Washington, D.C.-based Population Crisis Committee says that 60%

of all the people in Bogota and 42% in Mexico City live in slums so bad that even minimal social services such as potable water, sewers, electricity and solid waste disposal are unavailable.

The slums are sometimes built on hills that are subject to mudslides or in depressions prone to flooding. They also proliferate around industrial zones where air and water pollution reach dangerous levels or where major accidents can put residential populations at risk.

In 1985, the year of its devastating earthquake, Mexico City gained the dubious honor of being the most heavily populated place on earth. The quality of life had been declining there for years under the crushing impact of the migration of compesinos. Each year the city adds 700,000 more people to its teeming masses.

Over two million residents of the city have no running water. Three million are without sewage facilities. Mexico City produces about 14,000 tons of garbage daily but is able to process only about 8,000 tons. The exhaust fumes of three million cars and 13,000 factories so foul the air that it is a rare day when the sun breaks through the smog.

High-tech warfare has wasted the cities of the Gulf. Their residents are victims of sudden explosions of international fury. Latin American city dwellers, on the other hand, are both the victims and the cause of urban crisis. Their sheer numbers defeat even the best-willed attempts to make the cities more habitable.

So, grieve for those Middle Easterners whose lives have been disrupted by war. But save some compassion for millions of hapless Latin Americans whose dream of the shining city has become a nightmare.□

The Challenge to Democracy

In a familiar historical cycle of authoritarian government and formalistic democracy, democracy prevailed as Latin America entered the final decade of the twentieth century. To succeed, democracy must promote impressive institutional changes and economic development. Otherwise, the lagacies of dictatorship, militarism, dependency, and underdevelopment threaten democratic experiments.

D EMOCRATIC NORMS now prevail throughout Latin America and the Caribbean. Yet the practice of democracy remains very uneven—vigorous in some nations, but floundering in many others.

The greatest threat to democratic progress comes from the gradual erosion of public confidence in elected governments that are unable to effectively address fundamental problems affecting national life: prolonged economic deterioration;

Source: "The Americas in a New World," the 1990 report of the Inter-American Dialogue of the Aspen Institute, co-chaired by Sol M. Linowitz, former U.S. ambassador to the Organization of American States, and Daniel Oduber, former president of Costa Rica. *Los Angeles Times,* December 7, 1990, p. E5. With the permission of the Inter-American Dialogue.

intense civil strife; enormous disparities in income and wealth; unresponsive public institutions; continuing military interference in political affairs and widespread crime and official corruption. These are the challenges that democratic leaders must confront if Latin America's political openings are to be sustained and deepened—and if democracy is truly to serve the people of the region.

In four countries—Colombia, Peru, Guatemala and El Salvador—protracted guerrila insurgencies have led to vicious circles of violence that undermine the institutions, procedures and values essential to democracy.

Even where guerrillas do not threaten, democratic rule is often challenged by armed forces that are not effectively subordinated to civilian control. Civil-military relations vary considerably from country to country, but they remain troublesome nearly everywhere in Latin America and are a source of serious tension on many nations.

Constitutional democracy requires that all military forces be subject to the effective direction of elected civilian authorities. Today, only a few countries in the region—Costa Rica, Mexico, Venezuela and the Commonwealth Caribbean nations—meet that basic condition.

Political violence and military incursion into politics are not the only dangers to democratic rule in Latin America. Stunted by prior coups and military governments, political and civic organizations remain weak in most countries. Yet effective democratic practice requires structured and dependable institutions, accepted rules of political conduct and established legal protections. In their absence, politics often become personalized and erratic.

Legislatures and judicial systems in much of Latin America lack the autonomy, stature and competence to carry out their constitutional functions. Presidents, frustrated by delay and indecision, often use exceptional procedures to bypass the legislative process. In doing so, they debase the formal institutions of government, compromise legal norms, and—in the end—undercut democratic legitimacy.

Political parties in many countries of Latin America and the Caribbean lack effective ties to regular constituencies and are often little more than vehicles for contesting elections and distributing patronage. They rarely offer coherent programs and are frequently manipulated to serve the personal ambitions of their leaders. The weakness of political party structures allowed independent candidates without national party affiliation to win presidential elections in both Brazil and Peru this year. It is difficult, however, for the new presidents to govern because they lack the organized support needed to forge legislative majorities and mobilize popular backing on crucial policy issues.

Democratic progress in Latin America is hampered by the lack of sustained citizen participation in political life. Few countries in the region boast a vigorous array of non-governmental institutions through which the demands of ordinary people can be expressed, mediated and brought to the attention of authorities. In much of the region, trade unions, business groups, professional organizations and civic associations are weak, fragmented and too narrowly based to play constructive political roles. Free and independent media are vital to democracy, and press freedoms have expanded markedly in Latin America. But in many countries, the print media still represent only a relatively narrow range of opinion; in some places, governments continue to monopolize ownership of the media or limit access through licensing or censorship.

Even in those nations with relatively strong political institutions, democratic governance is threatened when citizens fail to participate in political life because of disillusionment, apathy or a sense that they have been unfairly excluded or disadvantaged. Representative self-government depends on the active involvement of all citizens and on fundamental respect for political leadership. When these falter, democracy runs the risk of atrophy.

Throughout the hemisphere—the United States and Canada included—there is a growing distrust of politics. Abstention from elections and skepticism about their significance are rising at an alarming rate. That voters in many countries are casting their ballots for political newcomers reflects, in part, their low regard for established democratic leaders.

Three crucial lessons have emerged from Latin America's recent turn toward democracy:

–Elections do not necessarily lead to genuine democratic openings or to sustained democratic advance. Free and fair elections scheduled on a regular basis are a fundamental requirement for democracy, but other vital requirements must also be fulfilled. Most important is the development of strong representative institutions that maintain the rule of law and protect the right of all citizens, effectively respond to popular demands and give citizens a continuing voice in government policy decisions.

For such institutions to emerge and take root in Latin America, political violence has to be brought under control, armed forces must be fully subordinated to civilian authority, citizens from all social and ethnic groups must be politically engaged, and sharp inequalities of income and wealth need to be reduced.

–Democratic institutions cannot be expected to thrive under conditions of economic duress, when millions are without jobs, adequate shelter and nutrition, basic education, or hope for the the future.

All the countries of the Americas, individually and together, must establish and sustain economic programs that can renew investment, improve productivity and create new opportunities for vulnerable groups. The resumption of economic growth, combined with concrete measures to alleviate poverty and inequality, would do the most to restore confidence in democratic rule.

–Democracy is never fully achieved or secured. It is always on trial. Democratic institutions and procedures must be consistently respected, protected and strengthened. If they are not, they will remain at risk of corruption, of manipulation by those with special power or privilege, and of losing their vitality. Democracy can never be taken for granted. □

Misguided Development

For the Peruvian scholar Luís Guillermo Lumbreras, "misguided development" serves as a euphemism for underdevelopment. The type of modernization Peru pursued—and pursues—condemned the majority of its inhabitants to a deteriorating quality of life. If Peru is to develop, it must challenge the colonial legacy imposed by Spain and strengthened by subsequent foreign models and draw from its own experiences. Lumbreras's forthright nationalism echoes the ideas of José Martí, Alberto Tôrres, and José Carlos Mariátegui, demonstrating a remarkable continuity among Latin American thinkers.

FIVE HUNDRED YEARS AGO, through the mountains of what today are Argentina, Bolivia, Peru and Chile, merchant caravans with hundreds of llamas trooped along broad and well-tended roads.[1] From Atacama in northern Chile to the Bolivian altiplano around Lake Titicaca, they carried the precious chañar wood–soft when newly cut, hardening as it dries, making it perfect for fashioning dinnerware and adornments. From the desert, they carried copper and semiprecious stones; from the tropical forests, brilliantly colored feathers and hard woods; from the cold seas, salted fish. Charki (dehydrated llama or guanaco meat), chuño (dehydrated potatoes) and many varieties of corn were traded back and forth from west to east, north to south.[2]

At the time the Spaniards arrived, in Francisco Pizarro's fateful expedition of 1531, Andean society had reached a stage of development comparable to that of Europe in the times of classical Greece and Rome. Tawantinsuyu, the great Inka empire exending through the Andes from Colombia to Chile, was a sophisticated urban society.[3] On its edges were simpler societies of horticulturalists and hunters and gatherers—whom the Inkas considered "barbarians." But even these simpler societies were learning new tricks for survival in the rugged Anean conditions.

The victorious Spaniards introduced an alien technology, which had been developed through thousands of years of experimentation, from the Old World's Paleolithic Age to the Renaissance. It had served Europe well, but in a very different ecosystem. Convinced that the same techniques would work anywhere, the newcomers scorned those of native societies and set out to make the New World like the Old. Much of our continent's economic weakness and dependency can be traced to that fateful decision.

In the Andes, where the great Inka empire and its predecessors had achieved economic success on entirely different principles, the consequences were disastrous. Our fields became filled with new plants and animals, displacing those better adapted to the environment. New cities and a productive infrastructure were faithfully copied from Europe, at great expense: the same food, the same clothing, the same social and productive organization. We Andeans began to measure our success by an "index of modernity" which meant nothing other than how close our systems were to those of Europe. Aboriginal customs and people were segregated and marginalized, and anything "Indian" became stigmatized.

Human settlement began in all parts of the Andes at about the same time, more than twelve thousand years ago. These earliest Andeans all started out as hunters and gatherers. Over thousands of years, Andean societies became highly

Source: Luis G. Lumbreras, "Misguided Development." Reprinted from *NACLA Report on the Americas,* 24:5 (February 1991), pp. 18–22. With the permission of North American Congress on Latin America.

diversified, pursuing different ways of mastering their resources, each according to its circumstances.

Such unequal development has usually been interpreted linearly, as though everyone were traveling the same development path, on which the Europeans (as they saw it) had advanced the farthest. In reality, they were on separate paths, because they were confronting very different problems and had to invent very different types of solutions.

It is generally thought that agriculture in the Andes was discovered in the moist forests of northern and eastern Peru. If so, this was not the only place. Agriculture in the region goes back to the eighth or ninth millenium B.C., probably with such plants as yucca, sweet potato, and peanuts, which reproduce easily in the humid tropical climate and do not require complex methods of cultivation.

As long as cultivation was confined to a few gardens for minor consumption, people could take advantage of a few natural clearings. Once they began seeking larger harvests, however, they had to clear and prepare fields. Gradually, Andeans learned to rotate their crops, to program the productive cycles and to maintain quality. In the process, they discovered new plant species, increasing the food supply, and this in turn supported a population increase, as evidenced by the larger size of villages.

In those areas that were constantly inundated from heavy rains, the ancient Andeans learned to build elevated fields, now called "camellones," separated by deep furrows. Abandoned for nearly five centuries, their vestiges have been discovered in Colombia, Ecuador, Peru and Bolivia. They look like fields plowed by giants, with furrows one to four meters wide and deep separating broad flat lands. Recent experiments show that these lands, today barren and absolutely unusable in times of flooding, must at one time have been highly productive.[4]

Where agriculture was impossible, as in the Chocó region in western Colombia, hunters and gatherers perfected their techniques, for example by developing traps for burrowing animals.

In the puna, the high, barren plateau at the summit of the central and southern Andes, there were very successful societies of hunters of camelids—the camel-like llamas, vicuñas, and guanacos. Living from this meat, plus the tubers and wild grasses they gathered, these societies not only survived but grew. Thousands of years after their formation, descendants of these societies began to domesticate the animals and plants. Probably by selective breeding of llamas, they developed the wool-bearing subspecies, the alpaca. The plants they sowed included potato, olluco (with tuberous roots like a small new potato), quinoa ("pigweed," an annual plant, the seeds of which are ground as cereal and the leaves eaten like spinach), and caniwa or canahua (a food grass similar to millet).

During the second millenium B.C., people domesticated all the Andean species of plants and animals possible. This era is sometimes referred to as the Andes' "neolithic" age, comparable in its accomplishments to the neolithic age of the Old World (which began around 10,000 B.C. in the Mideast, later in other areas).

In Cuzco, the Inkas had established experimental agricultural centers, which still functioned when the Spaniards arrived in the 1500s. There they tested the adaptability of plants to different ecosystems and improved their qualities and their productivity. Naturally, they also called on the experience and knowledge of the "amautas," or wise elders. There must have been similar experimentation, at a much earlier time, that led to the production of the alpaca.

The domestication of plants and animals is only the first level in the advance of humans' transformation of their natural environment. The next step was to use this new knowledge in ways that furthered the reproduction and growth of the human species.

In this regard, the Andean "neolithic" period was successful in very diverse zones. In the forest areas, domestication soon led to the formation of villages that engaged in cultivation along with hunting, fishing and gathering. Their populations grew, even though they had to move from place to place in pursuit of the various sources of subsistence. In the western forests, near the rivers from Ecuador to Chile, material cultures became quite sophisticated. The Valdivia culture of central Chile flourished around 3000 B.C., and Chorrera on the coast of Ecuador around 1500 B.C. The first to make ceramics were on the Atlantic coast of Colombia, followed by those in the Guayas region in Ecuador. The copper alloy "tumbaga" was developed through a chemical process, using natural vegetable acids, which makes the copper look like gold. Communities in the tropical forest seem to have begun making cloth around 3000 B.C., as well as producing ceramics.

Thus, there was a nascent manufacturing in these areas, including pottery-making, basket-making, wood-working, and the use of animal parts and plants to make polychrome feathered cloths, headpieces, musical instruments, and so on.

In the coastal desert of Peru, plants were first domesticated around the sixth millennium B.C. Cotton, used mainly by fishermen for nets and cords, turned out to be a superior fiber to anything they had known previously for binding the gourds they used as floaters and as containers. But before plant cultivation could have the transforming effect it had had in other areas, coastal peoples had to conquer the desert. This led to another kind of technological breakthrough: the control of water.

In the desert, the rivers that come down from the mountains leave cones of deposits in the form of irregular deltas. Because of the steepness of the slopes, the waters are torrential and flow rapidly toward the sea, easily changing their course each summer when the rains fall in the highlands. In addition, some years the waters do not come down at all and the rivers dry up, and other years the waters pour forth in great quantities at any time of the summer. When there is water, it is distributed unevenly, moistening only those areas near the riverbed and leaving the edges extremely arid. This greatly accelerates desertification and sanding of the surrounding area. In those conditions, agriculture cannot develop without a very complex irrigation infrastructure.

The fishing societies' growing experience in weather prediction, and their increasing population—giving them more labor power—made it possible for them to develop irrigation to "domesticate" water via irrigation. They also undertook costly (in labor power) projects of clearing and leveling the lands. This in turn permitted a great expansion of the agriculture in the second millenium B.C. Although the coastal people continued fishing and shellfish gathering, agriculture soon became their main means of subsistence.

Causeways were built to channel water beyond the area of the alluvial deposits, forming artificial valleys. These channels also permitted the rationalization of water consumption and the drainage of excess. Pre-colonial canals extended kilometer after kilometer, to supply precisely measured levels and amounts of water. When they crossed the desert hills that surround these artificial valleys, water would seep from one canal into another, creating a moist interstice on the hillside where people grew crops. In the desert landscape these must have looked like hanging gardens twelve to fifteen meters long, amidst the hills. Today, uncultivated and barren, they look like a long necklace with rectangular pendants of varying widths and lengths, attached to a very straight line crossing the sand-covered hills.[5]

The coastal people were very careful not to destroy what they had so laboriously constructed, because agricultural land is very scarce in Peru. For that reason they never invaded the agricultural lands for urban projects. They used barren lands for their cities, some of which eventually grew to great size and complexity. Chan Chan in northern Peru, where the valleys of Moche and Chicama intersect at the edge of the cultivated fields and close to the sea, was six kilometers long in the fifteenth century. Sufficient water was carried to the city via canals, complemented by a system of wells—"huachaques"—that drew waters from the subsoil.

Today, the cities have invaded the valleys, so that the desert area has widened, cement being added to sand. River water carries off the urban waste which is deposited on the beaches, infecting marine flora and fauna in the proximity. The old canals are lost in the desert, and those parts that remain are taken as examples of the impenetrable mysticism of the Indians, with no thought about how they might be used. The new hydraulic projects, designed with dams built according to the Western tradition, bring water to the valleys but remove the natural nutrients that come down with the annual turbulences, and in their course impoverish the fauna and flora of the coast.

In the heights of Arequipa, beyond Pocsi, there are hundreds of hectares of lands prepared by building stone-walled terraces known as "andenes." Though abandoned, they, and the canals that brought them water, are still part of the desert landscape. Below them, in a little valley, lie exquisite gardens of fruits, pastures for thoroughbred European cattle and crops that have enough water to thrive. The terraces had doubled the cultivable area of the little valley. But they were not practical for pasture for Arequipa's dairy industry, and so were left to die.

The "andenes" represented a productive strategy for maximum utilization of the scarce water resources of the central Andes. They made it possible to prepare lands on the slopes for sowing without serious dangers of erosion. When the Spaniards arrived, evidence shows, they were under construction in many parts of Tawantinsuyu.

In the Andes such terracing was a momemtous discovery, which our West-

ern mentality has yet to appreciate. As with the "camellones" to counter flooding, or the great canals of the desert, the West did not know what to do with the
terraces and classified them as "primitive." We froze them, turning those that
existed into ruins and curiosities and taking no heed of any possibility of turning
to them and using them creatively.[6]

The West became our paradigm; no time or resources would be invested in
developing or reproducing the methods of the indigenous world, considered the
antithesis of development and modernization. The pursuit of such "modernity"
came at a high cost, because our tropical and mountainous lands were not necessarily suited for the procedures of the prairies and cold forests. Very early on,
colonial societies had to rely on the importation of capital and consumer goods
to satisfy the Old World paradigm. "High technology" industry would arrive in
our lands as long as we had the means to pay; when we fell behind in our payments the technology grew ever more difficult and costly to acquire, and our
status as poor "Westerners" grew worse, distancing us ever more from the
model-countries.

A thousand rich Indians paid tribute to Spain with products of their stock-
raising in Chucuito in the sixteenth century. They were truly rich, all of them
owners of thousands of head of camelids. These were only one thousand among
many thousands of indigenous taxpayers who maintained, even in the early colonial period, a stock of native animals which today we cannot even imagine. From
the south of Colombia to the beginnings of the Chilean archipelago in Chiloé,
livestock was used for transport, meat, wool and hides. Today the native livestock is unknown in all the north—except for certain limited areas—and in the
south is important only in traditional Andean communities. In Lima the sale of
llama or guanaco meat is punished the same as the selling of the meat of dogs.
Few people living have had the opportunity to eat roast alpaca or llama "charki."
Instead, the West has brought sheep and beef, devastating existing pastures and
demanding preparation of special lands for them. This sacrificed the cultivation
of foodstuffs, but bestowed the seal of modernity.

The great projects of Andean antiquity were abandoned because of Western
arrogance and the limitations of Western experience, which did not include having to produce food in the desert. The "neolithic" age of the Europeans had
provided them with plants suitable for well-watered lands; their "metal" age had
given them access to instruments for plowing lands hardened by the winter cold
and for cutting down the trees of the cold forests. None of this knowledge was
of use here in the desert. Sowing of plants of European origin in many cases was
done at the cost of abandoning immense areas of native cultivation, given the
demand for water that agriculture for Western taste required.

In the 500 years since the arrival of the Europeans, nothing new has been
done in the direction of developing our own unique ecological resources. The
ancestral experiments remain frozen. The forests are used only for the exploitation of their wood, frequently causing irreversible devastation. Having in their
culture no procedures for dealing with the humid evergreen forests of America,
the Europeans and their imitators have applied methods suitable for the cold
leaf-shedding forests of Europe, with disastrous results.

We are still blind to the misdirection of our development. The Andean world remains impoverished because we are unable to see except through colonial lenses. As the pre-European technical development of the Andes demonstrates, our impoverishment is not explained by race or geography, as has often been assumed—that is, it is not due to any technical incapacity of our Indian and mestizo people, nor to the special difficulties of our terrain. Rather, it is a question of recovering the knowledge of our ancestors, and of sovereignty—the capacity to make use of that knowledge. It is not we who have failed; our underdevelopment is the product of a historic failure of the West, whose own patrimony prevented it from perceiving the limits of its power.□

1. John Hyslop, *The Inka Road System* (New York: Academic Press, 1984). The spelling "Inka" is preferred (over the older "Inca") by modern anthropologists to distinguish a "k" sound in Quechua which is distinct from the Spanish or English hard "c."
2. Lautaro A. Núñez and Tom Dillehay, *Movilidad giratoria, harmonía social y desarrollo en los Andes meridionales: patrones de tráfico e interacción económica* (Antofagasta, Chile: Universidad del Norte, 1978).
3. Frank Salomon, *Los señores étnicos de Quito en la época de los Incas* (Cambridge University Press).
4. Marc J. Dourojeanni, *Amazonía: ¿Qué hacer?* (Iquitos, Peru: Estudios Teológicos de la Amazonía, 1990).
5. Paul Kosok, *Life, Land and Water in Ancient Peru* (New York: Long Island University Press, 1965).
6. John Murra, *The Economic Organization of the Inca State* (Greenwich, CT, JAI Press: 1980); García Diez de San Miguel, *Visita hecha a la provincia de Chucuito por García Diez de San Miguel en el año 1567* (Lima: La Casa de la Cultura del Peru, 1964).

Making Our Own History

A resident of one of the *favelas* (slums) of Rio de Janeiro, Benedita da Silva summarized her political and social observations in the following essay, written in the mid-1980s. At that time, amid high hopes and expectations, Brazil returned to democratic forms of governance after two decades of brutal military dictatorship. While the burdens of and challenges to Benedita da Silva were many, she maintained the conviction—perhaps it was part of the great hope all felt at that historical moment—that she could bring about change, indeed, could transform society. Maybe she possessed that ability. Certainly she was unique, the first *favela* resident, male or female, elected to the Brazilian congress. The election instilled confidence that ordinary people could "forge" their own history. Benedita da Silva articulated well her desire, and those of her constituents, to take positive action, However, the barriers between desire and action remain formidable. Why?

W HAT IS THE DAY-TO-DAY LIFE of a *favela* woman?
　　　　She wakes up early in the morning. She has to see to her children, to leave some baby bottles ready. She goes off to work. She leaves her three, four

Source: Frances O'Gorman and Women from Rocinha and Santa Marta, *Hillside Woman* (Rio de Janeiro: Ecumenical Center for Action and Reflection, 1985), pp. 152–156.

or five-year old at home for an eight-year old to look after. She rushes to serve breakfast to the master's children, to take them to school, to hurry back to the house and prepare the master's lunch. Then she runs out to pick up the children from school. She gives them their lunch, sees to it that they take a rest. Meanwhile she goes to the tub to wash clothes. She cleans one thing, then another. She takes the children out for a walk. All this the *favela* woman does to supply the daily bread because what her husband earns is not enough.

Imagine how this woman must feel, seeing these healthy, well-nourished children, surrounded by loving care and support. Their parents have the means to be able to pay for someone to take care of them while they work or enjoy their free time. We all dream of that for our own children. And we keep on worrying: "I wonder if gas is leaking from the stove . . . and that knife? . . . I wonder if they went to look for something to eat . . . did they light the stove?"

We clean these swanky apartments, then go home to our tin-roofed shacks. Often at the end of the day's work, the mistress has forgotten to go to the bank. The children are waiting at home, perhaps the husband is unemployed, and we get home empty-handed. The electricity has been cut off because we didn't have enough money to pay the bill.

We get home dead tired, worried about the children. It's far. There's no water. Often our companion, already knowing what's awaiting him, lingers at the bar along the *favela* pathway drowning his bitterness, his pain, his poverty. It was an exhausting day's work, and in his lunch pail there was only a bit of rice and an egg, or perhaps nothing at all.

A factory overseer once told me that she noticed that all the workers placed their lunches to heat on a certain stove. One day she decided to look into the lunch containers, one by one. She discovered that some lunch containers were completely empty. Empty! This hurts deep down in the heart of the working person.

Later on this workman wants to make love to his wife. But I ask you— what happens to the sexuality of the *favela* woman, if, in order to survive, she is reduced to the condition of a knob on the kitchen stove, whether in her own house or in someone else's? How can she ever be in a state of mind to think of herself, to feel pleasure?

This woman's life becomes totally taken up with earning her daily bread. The system in which we live has forced women to be more man than woman. Why? Because from the moment we have to compete in the labor market, given the disadvantaged conditions in which we *favela* women live, it becomes very difficult to be aware of what it means to be a woman and to fight for emancipation.

What do the communication media say to us *favela* women?

A woman, with the sweat of her brow, manages to bring a television set into her house, the sole distraction. In the soap operas we see daily a well-spread table (which is not Brazilian reality), a well-dressed executive (when the workman is starving to death in the *favela*), a pretty woman, that is, a well-mannered white woman who has an elitist education, a woman who has rejected the cultural values of the *favela* woman, of the black woman. In the soap operas we find the poor, old, fat, black woman in subservient roles. And this woman's family never appears in the story.

Where are our forefathers? Where are our roots? On top of it all, they want to divide our Negro race. They've added another stereotype—the *mulatas*—for export. Just what do these women represent? We are reduced to mere objects for use in the kitchen and in bed. They even say that if Brazil wanted to export *mulatas* it could pay off its foreign debt.

We see an alienating, discriminating education. Through this education they can enforce all kinds of authoritarianisms and arbitrariness. The teachers are mere headstuffers, each day manufacturing more alienated persons. The *favela* student cannot find himself in the textbook.

There is a school near our *favela*. The teacher assigned a composition on the theme "My house." Half of the children didn't do it. The teacher asked:

"Why didn't you write the composition?"

"Teacher, I don't have a house. I have a shanty."

This is very serious. The child does not have a house . . . can't write about it. To feel strong and capable, to have hope in the struggle and in life itself, a person has to feel as "someone." The house represents this "someone's" place. The child was "no one" at that moment. He wasn't able to write because he didn't live in a house. And textbooks only show houses.

We mothers suffer when we see wealthy people go in their cars up the hill and give our children money to buy their drugs. Tomorrow we're going to find these children hooked, because "What is this thing that gives such a profit, that they pay me so well for." And they'll go around snatching people's purses on the street because they don't have the means. Or they'll get into drug peddling. But tomorrow they'll be arrested. They'll go to jail. They'll be called criminals. "They have deviated from society's standards." No one asks how they became criminals.

What's more, according to the machismo of our society, it seems that everyone is child of a mother, but not of a father. It's the mother who has to bring up the children. We take all this in. We end up in this process of submission which reduces women to a stove-side position. They have passed on to our companions this terrible machismo of an alienating system which has its roots in our history. We *favela* women suffer so much with this sexual differentiation which has been totally transformed into inequality.

For example, what is happening to women in family planning? What is being done *to* women? The low-income woman, the *favela* woman, doesn't want to have a flock of children. But at same time, we cannot accept that, in the name of the International Monetary Fund, which lays down the rules (and as politician from the *favela* I can affirm this) we are going to carry out family planning in the very womb which bore the cheap labor force which produced the wealth of this country. And when it comes to dividing this wealth, this womb is violated. All of a sudden they blame us for the poverty of this country. Family planning is imposed on women who are starving, offering contraceptives which no other countries use. They make us into their guinea pigs. We have to denounce these things.

We have no voice in determining what we should do with our bodies. We can't even discuss anything that is related to our bodies. It's the men who discuss these things. They do the deciding. If these discussions at least involved our companions, who are with us in our daily struggle, then the issue might be of interest. But just who are these men who are discussing family planning? And where are they taking us?

We belong to different sexes. However, we don't want inequalities. As soon as we women have the wherewithall, we will bring about a transformation. Men and women with their differences, but with the same rights.

In the greater Rio de Janeiro ciy alone we have four hundred and thirty seven *favelas* with more than two million persons. Yet it's the first time in the history of Brazil that a black, *favelada* woman has had a parliamentary role. How come such a victory? It came about because of women. They competed with men for this space. I only felt capable because they told me, "Go ahead. We want you! We're with you". It was our victory. But the news media ignored it. It could have been any one of us—Benedita, Joana, Maria. It was a political victory which we *favela* women gained.

I'm an Evangelical woman. My philosophy is based on the Bible, from Genesis to Apocalipse. I learned that Jesus Christ, as the silent lamb, was led to slaughter but never opened his mouth. It was because that silence called for an immediate response. He didn't open his mouth because he had already said what he had to say. But that response must be given today.

He said, "Father, I ask you not to take them out of the world, but to keep them." And after his death he enabled us to be strong and to have hope in transforming this society, and in giving witness to a new world, a world without this social injustice, a world where men and women, although different, might have the same rights.

We want to forge our own history—with grit, with strength, with audacity, with certainty in the conviction that it shall be forged by us. □

New Leadership: Fear and Hope

Haiti ranks as the poorest nation in the Western Hemisphere—indeed, as one of the twenty-five most impoverished in the world. Yet, during the eighteenth century, it glistened as a bright jewel in France's colonial crown, providing lucrative harvests of sugar for the European markets. Independence in 1804 bestowed manumission and nominal liberties, but the ordinary people of Haiti continued to suffer, seldom more so than under the brutal and corrupt Duvalier family dictatorships and military regimes from the mid-1950s until 1990.

On December 16, 1990, in what international observers described as Haiti's first free and fair election, two-thirds of the electorate voted for a young, populist, Roman Catholic priest, Jean-Bertrand Aristide, for president. With no links to established political parties, Aristide knew firsthand the festering slums of Port-au-Prince. His inauguration on February 7, 1991, opened the doors of political power to an entirely new group, the people of Haiti. The following two selections reflect the fear and hope accompanying such changes throughout Latin America.

Haiti: Turning into Another Cuba?

The old ruling elite and the generals feared President Aristide as a threat to their traditional power and privileges. Likewise, some foreign observers expressed an uneasiness with this new popular force. Michael G. Wilson, a policy analyst for Latin America and Caribbean affairs with the Heritage Foundation in Washington, D.C., summarized their fears and concerns.

HAITI'S NASCENT DEMOCRATIC experiment could be short lived. The new government in Port-au-Prince may be steering Haiti toward a communist dictatorship, hostile to the United States.

A leftist dictatorship by Jean-Bertrand Aristide on the Cuban model would harm greatly U.S. interests in the Caribbean Basin. Increased political and economic chaos in Haiti could become infectious, destabilizing the region at a time when democracy and free-market economies are taking hold in such neighboring countries as the Dominican Republic and Jamaica.

Moreover, strategically located only 750 miles southeast of Miami and just 100 miles east of Cuba, Haiti has been a target of subversion by Cuban dictator Fidel Castro for three decades. As early as August 1959, just months after Castro seized power, a small force of Cuban revolutionaries tried to invade Haiti. Based in Cuba are several military camps which train leftists from all over the world. Haitians are believed to be training at camps in Pinar del Rio Province and Guanabo, according to U.S. intelligence sources.

Just as troubling, Haiti is attractive to the Colombian narcotics cartels as a transshipment point for cocaine flowing to the United States. Cocaine seizures in Haiti increased from 667 kilos (1,467 lbs) in 1987 to 1.80 metric tons last year.

Finally, Aristide is a lifelong leftist, a fervent nationalist, and a strong advocate of liberation theology—which promotes the ideals of communism thinly veiled with religion. In fact, Aristide, who is a Roman Catholic priest, was ousted from the Salesian Order of the Roman Catholic Church in 1988 because it considered him a revolutionary.

The president's platform calls for the destruction of all remnants of the nearly three-decade-long Duvalier family dictatorship and emphasizes the redistribution of wealth from the rich to the poor. Much of Aristide's campaign rhetoric blames the United States for Haiti's economic and political troubles. He has often been quoted as saying, for example, that the United States is "responsible for the worst abuses of the Duvalierists."

Yet, despite Aristide's record, the United States was quick to offer support to the president-elect. Assistant Secretary of State for Inter-American Affairs Bernard Aronson said on Dec. 18 that relations with Aristide "got off to a good

Source: "Haiti: Turning into Another Cuba?" *The Times of the Americas* (Washington, D.C.), February 20, 1991. With permission of the Heritage Foundation.

start.'' After meeting Aristide in Port-au-Prince, Aronson stressed that the United States ''looked forward to working with him.'' U.S. officials are now discussing the possibility of increasing Haiti's economic assistance.

However, economic support for Aristide under the present circumstances would be unwise. While the United States should welcome and applaud Haiti's democratic elections, it should take a wait-and-see approach before considering any assistance to the new government.

So far, the signals coming from Port-au-Prince are discouraging. Aristide's campaign platform gives improving relations with Washington a low priority. In fact, Aristide has stated that his government might be unwilling to accept assistance from the United States, claiming that U.S. aid has only produced misery in Haiti.

Even former President Jimmy Carter and former Secretary of Defense Robert S. McNamara, who met with Aristide following his election, said in a joint statement on Dec. 18 that ''he was violently anti-U.S. and hostile.''

There are troubling signs that the Aristide government could degenerate into a left-wing dictatorship. Aristide invited the Castro government to send a delegation to attend his Feb. 7 inauguration. Despite the fact that Haiti and Cuba have never had diplomatic relations, it appears that such relations will be forged in the coming months. Aristide's party is sending ''young volunteers'' to Cuba for training as ''political party operatives'' and creating neighborhood militia called ''vigilance committees'' to mobilize against Haiti's political opposition.

Government-sponsored street violence is growing in Haiti. A demonstration sponsored by Aristide's party was held in Port-au-Prince on Jan. 26, threatening the life of U.S. Ambassador Alvin Adams and calling for the burning of the U.S. embassy.

While the United States alone cannot save Haiti, the Bush admnistration should withhold its financial support until Aristide has proven that he will not erect an anti-American leftist dictatorship. Washington must make sure it does not repeat the mistakes it made in 1959 with Castro and in 1979 with communist Sandinistas in Nicaragua by providing assistance to an anti-democratic and anti-U.S. regime.

If the Aristide government in fact does follow Castro's path, the Bush administration should:

*Temporarily freeze all economic and security aid for Haiti.

*Impose a trade embargo on Haiti.

*Encourage Venezuela and other Caribbean Basin and European countries like France to isolate Aristide and promote a return to democracy in Haiti by temporarily suspending trade with and financial assistance to Port-au-Prince.

*Work with Caribbean Basin democracies and European countries to assist financially such moderate Haitian pro-democratic parties as the National Alliance for Democracy and Progress.

The Bush administration should tell Aristide that a return to dictatorship, reprisals against political opponents and closer ties to Castro will jeopardize

U.S.-Haitian relations. Aristide is not yet a lost cause for the United States. If he understands clearly that the United States has no intention of supporting his attempts to erect a leftist dictatorship, he may desist from his anti-American policies and put Haiti on the path toward real democracy and economic prosperity. □

Haiti: A Plea for Grassroots Development

Haitian President Jean-Bertrand Aristide promised no miracles. He advocated no elaborate modernization schemes and glamorous development projects. He quoted no economic experts and hardly mentioned foreign economic aid. He did not take the customary trip to Washington, D.C., to beg alms. Rather, he spoke of plans, unorthodox in Latin American capitals, of ordinary people improving their own quality of life, a kind of grassroots economic development. Humbly, President Aristide offered hope that local people could resolve their own problems, a simple yet novel idea in Latin America at the end of the twentieth century. While his simplicity amused economic experts, his infectious optimism inspired ordinary Haitians.

Still, the haunting question remained: Would hope and optimism suffice?

OPEN YOUR EYES WITH ME, sisters and brothers. It is morning. The night has been a long one, very long. Now, the dawn seems to be climbing up slowly from beneath the horizon. Wisps of smoke are rising up from the little houses of the village, and you can smell good cornmeal cereal cooking. The sky grows pink. An hour later, the children in their tidy, well-fitting uniforms run off to school, clutching new books in their arms. Women wearing shoes head off to market, some on horseback and donkey, others on motorcycle and bicycle. They all take the new paved road, down which buses take other women and men to market for the day. If you listen closely, you can hear the sound of running water, of faucets being turned on in houses. Then the men emerge, carrying shiny new tools, laughing together, their bodies strong and well fed. They head off for the fields. A new irrigation project has been installed and the crops are growing where before there was almost a desert. Throughout the village, you can hear laughter and the sound of jokes being told and listened to.

This is the village I call Esperancia. The day is coming when this village will exist, though now it is called Despair and its residents wear rags and never laugh. Yet when we look around this village I call Esperancia, we can see that not very much has changed since it was called Despair. This is what has changed: Everyone now eats a decent poor man's breakfast. There is a new road. The children now have books. The women have shoes. There is water, and running water. There is an irrigation project.

This is not very much to change. Yet just those few changes can turn Despair into Hope, and all it takes to change them is organization. In a year, the village of Esperancia could exist in any of our lands. Esperancia, El Salvador;

Source: Jean-Bertrand Aristide, *In the Parish of the Poor: Writings from Haiti* (Maryknoll, N.Y.: Orbis Books, 1991), pp. 69–70. With permission of Orbis Books.

Esperancia, Honduras; Esperancia, Guatemala. It is an honorable address in the parishes of the poor.

Let us leave our old homes of cardboard and mud floors. Let us make a plan to douse them with gasoline, and burn them to the ground. Let us turn our backs on that great fire and on that way of life, and hand in hand, calmly, intelligently, walk forward into the darkness toward the sunrise of Hope. Let us trust one another, keep faith with one another, and never falter.

Take my hand. If you see me stumble, hold me up. If I feel you weaken, I will support you. You, brother, hold up the lamp of solidarity before us. Sister, you carry the supplies. Yes, the road is long. I fear there are criminals on either side of us, waiting to attack. Do you hear them in the bushes, brothers and sisters? Hush! Yes, I can hear them loading their guns. Let us ignore their threats. Let us be fearless.

Let them come. They do not know it, but though they kill us, though they shoot and cut down every last one of us, there is another battalion about a mile back, coming and coming down this long path toward sunrise. And behind that battalion, another and another and another. God is for the big battalions, and the big battalions are the people. Let us keep the lamp of solidarity lit, and move forward.

Amen.□

A Postscript

The hope and optimism of the majority did not suffice in Haiti. On September 30, 1991, the military, encouraged by the old ruling elite, businessmen, and puppet politicians of the past, overthrew President Jean-Bertrand Aristide, sending him into exile after only eight months in office. Haiti returned to minority, authoritarian rule. Terrorism and violence again engulfed the nation. Although a single political incident in a small Caribbean nation, the brutal military coup d'etat vividly illustrates the difficulty of introducing even modest change into the hoary institutions that shape Latin America. Much conflict remains. A Latin America characterized by social, economic, and political justice has yet to be created.